Biblical Citations from A Course in Miracles

Full Version
Second Edition

Compiled by
Emmanuel M. Viriña

Copyright 2023 Emmanuel M Viriña

IngramSpark Print Edition

ISBN-13: 978-0-9945849-3-9

This book is also available in Kindle and e-Pub formats from major online retailers.

CONTENTS

I. Introduction   1
     Acknowledgment   2
     Notes on Referential Notation   3
II. Biblical References and Citations from A Course in Miracles   5
     A. Genesis   5
     B. Exodus   42
     C. Leviticus   52
     D. Numbers   54
     E. Deuteronomy   55
     F. Joshua   58
     G. 1 Kings   59
     H. Job   61
     I. Psalms   63
     J. Proverbs   81
     K. Ecclesiastes   83
     L. Isaiah   84
     M. Jeremiah   93
     N. Ezekiel   94
     O. Hosea   97
     P. Matthew   99
     Q. Mark   262
     R. Luke   266
     S. John   327
     T. Acts   411
     U. Romans   423
     V. 1 Corinthians   431

W. 2 Corinthians	441
X. Galatians	447
Y. Ephesians	449
Z. Philippians	457
AA. Colossians	460
BB. 1 Thessalonians	462
CC. 1 Timothy	465
DD. Hebrews	467
EE. 1 Peter	471
FF. 1 John	472
GG. Revelation	486
III. Epilogue	501
Footnotes	503
Index of Biblical References	504
About the Author	508

I. Introduction

A citation can be a word, phrase, clause or sentence or more taken from the Bible in the course of discussions from A Course in Miracles. Or it could be an idea that can be deduced or implied from passages in the Bible and cited in the Course. A Course in Miracle or ACIM or the "Course" as shortly referred here is a book written by Drs Helen Schucman and William Thetford, former Professors of Medical Psychology at Columbia University's College of Physicians and Surgeons in New York City through a process called "inner dictation"[1] from the "Voice" Dr Schucman believed to be that of Jesus Christ[2]. The materials were received by Dr Schucman and then typed by Dr Thetford as they are read to him the following day. The process is a collaborated effort on the two since Dr Schucman, the receiver of or the medium through whom the materials were given was an ambivalent participant who needed continuing encouragement and support from her colleague. It took them seven years to complete the book. The whole process especially the "Source" of the materials may sound incredible to many but the two Scribes "believed the material must stand on its own, regardless of its alleged authorship."[3] To the readers though with open minds, the saying "the proof of the pudding is in the eating" may apply; thus read the Course and decide for yourself.

The Course is not an easy reading though. The third edition is composed of four volumes and two supplements of reading materials totalling 1,367 pages. The volumes are made of the Text, the theoretical foundation, the Workbook which is the practical application of the Course in a form of daily lessons and exercises, the Manual for Teachers, and the Clarification of Terms. The supplements are the Psychotherapy: Purpose, Process and Practice, and the Song of Prayer. By its mere size alone reading thus is a bit intimidating.

Dr Kenneth Wapnick in his book Love Does Not Condemn said that the contextual framework of the Course "... is Christian, with its language and terminology coming from the Judaeo-Christian world of the Bible."[4] Thus, it is just natural that Bible verses and references are used in its discussions. This book (Biblical Citations from A Course in Miracles) is a compilation of those Bible verses and references and is one way of introducing you to the topics and teachings discussed in the Course with said Bible verses and references as the starting points. Some of the discussions may relate to the context of the Bible verses but most of them were cited in another context or were cited as part of the Author's terminology to emphasise other ideas or thoughts.

The citations are arranged in the order of the books or chapters of the Bible. In this second edition of the this book unlike in the first, the verses within the particular book or chapter of the Bible are arranged in their sequential order so they are easy to find and also ensure the contextual continuity of the verses being quoted. The compilation starts with the particular quotation from the Bible followed by the quotation or quotations from the Course. Quotations from the Course are mostly in paragraphs so the reader would know the context of the discussions. The first person references in the Course ("I", "me", "my", etc.) refers to the Jesus Christ, the Voice behind the dictated Course except in the Workbook lessons and exercises where the references at times are intended for us individually doing the practising. In some cases I have inserted clarifying terms in solid brackets like [Holy Spirit], [Christ], [A Course in Miracles], [Workbook Lesson Title], etc. to clarify the nouns or subject matters in the quoted materials.

Acknowledgment

Most of the Biblical references used in the previous edition of this book were taken from the book of Dr Kenneth Wapnick, <u>Glossary-Index for a Course in Miracles</u> in its third edition. In this second edition I have updated these references using the sixth edition of Dr Wapnick's Glossary Index book. The Biblical references are not part of the printed book but come as a separate pamphlet. The Foundation for A Course in Miracles provided me their electronic copy of the pamphlet for free.

I did not include all references from the pamphlet because some were cited for different or conflicting context. I also excluded those with lengthy Biblical or Course references like the whole section of the Bible or the Course. I have added my own Biblical references though with the corresponding references from the Course.

The Biblical quotations used in this compilation were taken from the King James Version as published by the BibleGateway website. The King James Version is the version used in the Course.

All quotes from *A Course in Miracles*© were taken from the on-line version made available by the Miracle Distribution Center from its website (www.miraclecenter.org/a-course-in-miracles/) and more recently since 8April 2021 from the Web Edition of the same Course as published by the Foundation for Inner Peace (https://www.acim.org/acim/en/). All such quotes are from its 3rd Edition, 2007 and are used with written permission from the Foundation for Inner Peace, publisher and copyright holder, 448 Ignacio Blvd., #306, Novato, CA 94949, www.acim.org and info@acim.org.

I would like to thank my wife, Michaela, for the support she has given me in publishing this book. She helped me resolve a few problems I have encountered along the way. She also edited the editable sections (like the Introduction, Epilogue, About the Author, and the narrative at the back cover) of this book.

Notes on Referential Notation

I have used the accepted referential notation for the Course as outlined in the Annotation page, under the Online Learning Aids section of the Foundation for A Course in Miracles webpage (http://www.facim.org/online-learning-aids/annotation/). The Annotation specifies the letters and abbreviations to be used in the notation. The first capital letter of the notation refers to the source of the material. This can be "T" which stands for the Text volume of the Course; "W" for the Workbook; "M" for the Manual for Teachers; "C" for Clarification of Terms; "P" for Psychotherapy: Purpose, Process and Practice; and "S" for Song of Prayer. The letter is then followed by the chapter number, section, paragraph, and sentence numbers. The Workbook is divided into two parts so this is specified as "pI" or "pII" in place of the chapter number. This is then followed by the Lesson Number. The Manual for Teachers and Clarification of Terms have a shorter composition because they do not have chapters in them. The separator between the letter source and the chapter or section is denoted by a hyphen (-). The separator between the chapter, section, and paragraph is denoted by a period (.) The separator between paragraph and sentence is denoted by a colon (:). Examples of such notations are as follows:

>T-24.VI.2:3, P-2.VI.5:1, S-2.II.7:7,
>W-pI.182.4:1,
>M-13.3:2 and C-6.4:6.

I added two other abbreviations to the Annotation. The first one are the letters "ti" which stand for the title. I usually used this in the Workbook to start the annotation with the title of the lesson followed by the corresponding paragraph. For example the notation "W-pI.91.ti-2" stands for Workbook Part I, lesson 91 starting from the title of the lesson to paragraph 2. The second abbreviation are the letters "pr" which stand for the Preface. For example "T-pr.HIC.1:8-13" stands for the preface in the Text volume followed by the first letters of the section (How It Came), then the paragraph number and finally the sentence numbers.

I also did a minor revision to the Annotation to correct the way computers sort data. I have used a database software to store all my compilation using the notations as the key. For instance, without the change W-pI.158.10 will be listed first in my database before W-pI.158.5. This means that paragraph 10 of Lesson 158 will come ahead of paragraph 5. To remedy the situation I have inserted a nought or zero ("0") to the paragraph number of the latter to become W-pl.158.05 so it will appear in its proper logical sequence. I have applied this change on the chapter, section, paragraph and sentence numbering selectively using it only when there is a need to sequence the citations properly.

II. Biblical References and Citations from A Course in Miracles

A. Genesis

The following are the references from the above Biblical book cited in the Course:

[1:1], [1:3], [1:26], [1:28], [1:31], [2:7], [2:15-17], [2:21], [3:1-7], [3:8-9], [3:23-24], [4:9], [7:9], [19:23-26], [25:31-33], and [28:16-17].

Bible Reference - Text

Genesis 1:1 - In the beginning God created the heaven and the earth.

Course Ref/s - Citation/s

W-pI.145.7 - Under all the senseless thoughts and mad ideas with which you have cluttered up your mind are the thoughts that you thought with God <u>in the beginning</u>. They are there in your mind now, completely unchanged. They will always be in your mind, exactly as they always were. Everything you have thought since then will change, but the Foundation on which it rests is wholly changeless.

Bible Reference - Text

Genesis 1:3 - And God said, Let there be light: and there was light.

Course Ref/s - Citation/s

T-09.V.6:2-6 - When God said, "<u>Let there be light</u>," there was light. Can you find light by analyzing darkness, as the psychotherapist does, or like the theologian, by acknowledging darkness in yourself and looking for a distant light to remove it, while emphasizing the distance? Healing is not mysterious. Nothing will change unless it is understood, since light is understanding. A "miserable sinner" cannot be healed without magic, nor can an "unimportant mind" esteem itself without magic.

T-13.V.8 - Vision depends on light. You cannot see in darkness. Yet in darkness, in the private world of sleep, you see in dreams although your eyes are closed. And it is here that what you see you made. But let the darkness go and all you made you will no longer see, for sight of it depends upon denying vision. Yet from denying vision it does not follow you cannot see. But this is what denial does, for by it you accept insanity, believing you can make a private world and rule your own perception. Yet for this, light must be excluded. Dreams disappear when light has come and you can see.

T-13.VI.11 - There is a light that this world cannot give. Yet you can give it, as it was given you. And as you give it, it shines forth to call you from the world and follow it. For this light will attract you as nothing in this world can do. And you will lay aside the world and find another. This other world is bright with love which you have given it. And here will everything remind you of your Father and His holy Son. Light is unlimited, and spreads across this world in quiet joy. All those you brought with you will shine on you, and you will shine on them in gratitude because they brought you here. Your light will join with theirs in power so compelling, that it will draw the others out of darkness as you look on them.

W-pI.73.10:2-3 - I will there be light. Let me behold the light that reflects God's Will and mine.

W-pI.73.11:3-4 - I will there be light. Darkness is not my will. I will there be light. Darkness is not my will.

W-pI.87.1 - I will there be light. I will use the power of my will today. It is not my will to grope about in darkness, fearful of shadows and afraid of things unseen and unreal. Light shall be my guide today. I will follow it where it leads me, and I will look only on what it shows me. This day I will experience the peace of true perception.

W-pI.91.ti-2 - Miracles are seen in light.

It is important to remember that miracles and vision necessarily go together. This needs repeating, and frequent repeating. It is a central idea in your new thought system, and the perception that it produces. The miracle is always there. Its presence is not caused by your vision; its absence is not the result of your failure to see. It is only your awareness of miracles that is affected. You will see them in the light; you will not see them in the dark.

To you, then, light is crucial. While you remain in darkness, the miracle remains unseen. Thus you are convinced it is not there. This follows from the premises from which the darkness comes. Denial of light leads to failure to perceive it. Failure to perceive light is to perceive darkness. <u>The light</u> is useless to you then, even though it <u>is there</u>. You cannot use it because its presence is unknown to you. And the seeming reality of the darkness makes the idea of light meaningless.

Bible Reference - Text

Genesis 1:3 - And God said, Let there be light: and there was light. (Continued)

Course Ref/s - Citation/s

W-pI.92.3-4 - It is God's strength in you that is the light in which you see, as it is His Mind with which you think. His strength denies your weakness. It is your weakness that sees through the body's eyes, peering about in darkness to behold the likeness of itself; the small, the weak, the sickly and the dying, those in need, the helpless and afraid, the sad, the poor, the starving and the joyless. These are seen through eyes that cannot see and cannot bless.

Strength overlooks these things by seeing past appearances. It keeps its steady gaze upon the light that lies beyond them. It unites with light, of which it is a part. It sees itself. It brings the light in which your Self appears. In darkness you perceive a self that is not there. Strength is the truth about you; weakness is an idol falsely worshipped and adored that strength may be dispelled, and darkness rule where God appointed that <u>there should be light</u>.

W-pI.99.7:3-8:4 - Your Father loves you. All the world of pain is not His Will. Forgive yourself the thought He wanted this for you. Then let the Thought with which He has replaced all your mistakes enter the darkened places of your mind that thought the thoughts that never were His Will.

This part belongs to God, as does the rest. It does not think its solitary thoughts, and make them real by hiding them from Him. <u>Let in the light</u>, and you will look upon no obstacle to what He wills for you. Open your secrets to His kindly light, and see how bright this light still shines in you.

A. Genesis

Bible Reference - Text

Genesis 1:26 - And God said, Let us make man in our image, after our likeness: and let them have dominion over the fish of the sea, and over the fowl of the air, and over the cattle, and over all the earth, and over every creeping thing that creepeth upon the earth.

Course Ref/s - Citation/s

T-01.I.24 - Miracles enable you to heal the sick and raise the dead because you made sickness and death yourself, and can therefore abolish both. You are a miracle, capable of creating <u>in the likeness of your Creator</u>. Everything else is your own nightmare, and does not exist. Only the creations of light are real.

T-02.I.1-2 - To extend is a fundamental aspect of God which He gave to His Son. In the creation, God extended Himself to His creations and imbued them with the same loving Will to create. You have not only been fully created, but have also been created perfect. There is no emptiness in you. Because of your <u>likeness to your Creator</u> you are creative. No child of God can lose this ability because it is inherent in what he is, but he can use it inappropriately by projecting. The inappropriate use of extension, or projection, occurs when you believe that some emptiness or lack exists in you, and that you can fill it with your own ideas instead of truth. This process involves the following steps:

> First, you believe that what God created can be changed by your own mind.
> Second, you believe that what is perfect can be rendered imperfect or lacking.
> Third, you believe that you can distort the creations of God, including yourself.
> Fourth, you believe that you can create yourself, and that the direction of your own creation is up to you.

These related distortions represent a picture of what actually occurred in the separation, or the "detour into fear." None of this existed before the separation, nor does it actually exist now. Everything God created is like Him. Extension, as undertaken by God, is similar to the inner radiance that the children of the Father inherit from Him. Its real source is internal. This is as true of the Son as of the Father. In this sense the creation includes both the creation of the Son by God, and the Son's creations when his mind is healed. This requires God's endowment of the Son with free will, because all loving creation is freely given in one continuous line, in which all aspects are of the same order.

T-03.II.4 - You are afraid of God's Will because you have used your own mind, which He created <u>in the likeness of His Own</u>, to miscreate. The mind can miscreate only when it believes it is not free. An "imprisoned" mind is not free because it is possessed, or held back, by itself. It is therefore limited, and the will is not free to assert itself. To be one is to be of one

mind or will. When the Will of the Sonship and the Father are one, their perfect accord is Heaven.

T-03.V.7:1-4 - The statement "<u>God created man in his own image and likeness</u>" needs reinterpretation. "Image" can be understood as "thought," and "likeness" as "of a like quality." God did create spirit in His Own Thought and of a quality like to His Own. There is nothing else.

T-08.V.2 - The undivided will of the Sonship is the perfect creator, being wholly <u>in the likeness of God</u>, Whose Will it is. You cannot be exempt from it if you are to understand what it is and what you are. By the belief that your will is separate from mine [Jesus'], you are exempting yourself from the Will of God which is yourself. Yet to heal is still to make whole. Therefore, to heal is to unite with those who are like you, because perceiving this likeness is to recognize the Father. If your perfection is in Him and only in Him, how can you know it without recognizing Him? The recognition of God is the recognition of yourself. There is no separation of God and His creation. You will realize this when you understand that there is no separation between your will and mine. Let the Love of God shine upon you by your acceptance of me. My reality is yours and His. By joining your mind with mine you are signifying your awareness that the Will of God is One.

T-11.III.7 - Only God's Comforter can comfort you. In the quiet of His temple, He waits to give you the peace that is yours. Give His peace, that you may enter the temple and find it waiting for you. But be holy in the Presence of God, or you will not know that you are there. For <u>what is unlike God</u> cannot enter His Mind, because it was not His Thought and therefore does not belong to Him. And your mind must be as pure as His, if you would know what belongs to you. Guard carefully His temple, for He Himself dwells there and abides in peace. You cannot enter God's Presence with the dark companions beside you, but you also cannot enter alone. All your brothers must enter with you, for until you have accepted them you cannot enter. For you cannot understand wholeness unless you are whole, and no part of the Son can be excluded if he would know the Wholeness of his Father.

Bible Reference - Text

Genesis 1:26 - And God said, Let us make man in our image.... (Continued) - (To read the full text of the above go to page 8.)

Course Ref/s - Citation/s

T-14.XI.11 - God's Son will always be indivisible. As we are held as one in God, so do we learn as one in Him. God's Teacher is <u>as like to His Creator</u> as is His Son, and through His Teacher does God proclaim His Oneness and His Son's. Listen in silence, and do not raise your voice against Him. For He teaches the miracle of oneness, and before His lesson division disappears. Teach like Him here, and you will remember that you have always created like your Father. The miracle of creation has never ceased, having the holy stamp of immortality upon it. This is the Will of God for all creation, and all creation joins in willing this.

T-31.VIII.12 - And now we say "Amen." For Christ has come to dwell in the abode You set for Him before time was, in calm eternity. The journey closes, ending at the place where it began. No trace of it remains. Not one illusion is accorded faith, and not one spot of darkness still remains to hide the face of Christ from anyone. Thy Will is done, complete and perfectly, and all creation recognizes You, and knows You as the only Source it has. Clear <u>in Your likeness</u> does the light shine forth from everything that lives and moves in You. For we have reached where all of us are one, and we are home, where You would have us be.

W-pI.16.1 - The idea for today is a beginning step in dispelling the belief that your thoughts have no effect. Everything you see is the result of your thoughts. There is no exception to this fact. Thoughts are not big or little; powerful or weak. They are merely true or false. Those that are true <u>create their own likeness</u>. Those that are false make theirs.

A. Genesis

W-pI.68.1 - You who were <u>created by love like itself</u> can hold no grievances and know your Self. To hold a grievance is to forget who you are. To hold a grievance is to see yourself as a body. To hold a grievance is to let the ego rule your mind and to condemn the body to death. Perhaps you do not yet fully realize just what holding grievances does to your mind. It seems to split you off from your Source and make you unlike Him. It makes you believe that He is like what you think you have become, for no one can conceive of his Creator as unlike himself.

W-pI.68.3 - It is as sure that those who hold grievances will redefine God in their own image, as it is certain that <u>God created them like Himself</u>, and defined them as part of Him. It is as sure that those who hold grievances will suffer guilt, as it is certain that those who forgive will find peace. It is as sure that those who hold grievances will forget who they are, as it is certain that those who forgive will remember.

W-pI.84.1 - Love created me like itself. I am <u>in the likeness of my Creator</u>. I cannot suffer, I cannot experience loss and I cannot die. I am not a body. I would recognize my reality today. I will worship no idols, nor raise my own self-concept to replace my Self. I am in the likeness of my Creator. Love created me like itself.

W-pI.156.5 - The light in you is what the universe longs to behold. All living things are still before you, for they recognize Who walks with you. The light you carry is their own. And thus they see in you their holiness, saluting you as savior and as God. Accept their reverence, for it is due to Holiness Itself, which walks with you, transforming in Its gentle light all things unto <u>Its likeness</u> and Its purity.

W-pI.158.11 - It matters not when revelation comes, for that is not of time. Yet time has still one gift to give, in which true knowledge is reflected in a way so accurate <u>its image</u> shares its unseen holiness;<u> its likeness</u> shines with its immortal lov<u>e</u>. We practice seeing with the eyes of Christ today. And by the holy gifts we give, Christ's vision looks upon ourselves as well.

W-pI.160.4 - Who is the stranger? Is it fear or you that is unsuited to the home which God provided for His Son? Is fear His Own, created <u>in His likeness</u>? Is it fear that love completes, and is completed by? There is no home can shelter love and fear. They cannot coexist. If you are real, then fear must be illusion. And if fear is real, then you do not exist at all.

Bible Reference - Text

A. Genesis

Genesis 1:26 - And God said, Let us make man in our image....
(Continued) - (To read the full text of the above go to page 8.)

Course Ref/s - Citation/s

W-pII.322.1 - I sacrifice illusions; nothing more. And as illusions go I find the gifts illusions tried to hide, awaiting me in shining welcome, and in

readiness to give God's ancient messages to me. His memory abides in every gift that I receive of Him. And every dream serves only to conceal the Self which is God's only Son, <u>the likeness of Himself</u>, the Holy One Who still abides in Him forever, as He still abides in me.

C-6.1 - Jesus is the manifestation of the Holy Spirit, Whom he called down upon the earth after he ascended into Heaven, or became completely identified with the Christ, the Son of God as He created Him. The Holy Spirit, being a creation of the one Creator, creating with Him and <u>in His likeness</u> or spirit, is eternal and has never changed. He was "called down upon the earth" in the sense that it was now possible to accept Him and to hear His Voice. His is the Voice for God, and has therefore taken form. This form is not His reality, which God alone knows along with Christ, His real Son, Who is part of Him.

S-3.IV.2 - As witness to forgiveness, aid to prayer, and the effect of mercy truly taught, healing is blessing. And the world responds in quickened chorus through the voice of prayer. Forgiveness shines its merciful reprieve upon each blade of grass and feathered wing and all the living things upon the earth. Fear has no haven here, for love has come in all its holy oneness. Time remains only to let the last embrace of prayer rest on the earth an instant, as the world is shined away. This instant is the goal of all true healers, whom the Christ has taught to see <u>His likeness</u> and to teach like Him.

Bible Reference - Text

Genesis 1:28 - And God blessed them, and God said unto them, Be fruitful, and multiply, and replenish the earth, and subdue it: and have dominion over the fish of the sea, and over the fowl of the air, and over every living thing that moveth upon the earth.

Course Ref/s - Citation/s

T-19.IV.A.12 - Relationships in this world are the result of how the world is seen. And this depends on which emotion was called on to send its messengers to look upon it, and return with word of what they saw. Fear's messengers are trained through terror, and they tremble when their master calls on them to serve him. For fear is merciless even to its friends. Its messengers steal guiltily away in hungry search of guilt, for they are kept cold and starving and made very vicious by their master, who allows them to feast only upon what they return to him. No little shred of guilt escapes their hungry eyes. And in their savage search for sin they pounce on <u>any living thing</u> they see, and carry it screaming to their master, to be devoured.

T-19.IV.C.1 - To you and your brother, in whose special relationship the Holy Spirit entered, it is given to release and be released from the dedication to death. For it was offered you, and you accepted. Yet you must learn still more about this strange devotion, for it contains the third obstacle that peace must flow across. No one can die unless he chooses death. What seems to be the fear of death is really its attraction. Guilt, too, is feared and fearful. Yet it could have no hold at all except on those who are attracted to it and seek it out. And so it is with death. Made by the ego, its dark shadow falls across <u>all living things</u>, because the ego is the "enemy" of life.

T-19.IV.D.15 - This is your brother, crucified by sin and waiting for release from pain. Would you not offer him forgiveness, when only he can offer it to you? For his redemption he will give you yours, as surely as God created <u>every living thing</u> and loves it. And he will give it truly, for it will be both offered and received. There is no grace of Heaven that you cannot offer to your brother, and receive from your most holy Friend. Let him withhold it not, for by receiving it you offer it to him. And he will receive of you what you received of him. Redemption has been given you to give your brother, and thus receive it. Whom you forgive is free, and what you give you share. Forgive the sins your brother thinks he has committed, and all the guilt you think you see in him.

T-22.II.4 - Reason will tell you that the only way to escape from misery is to recognize it and go the other way. Truth is the same and misery the same, but they are different from each other in every way, in every instance and without exception. To believe that one exception can exist is to confuse what is the same with what is different. One illusion cherished and

A. Genesis

defended against the truth makes all truth meaningless, and all illusions real. Such is the power of belief. It cannot compromise. And faith in innocence is faith in sin, if the belief excludes <u>one living thing</u> and holds it out, apart from its forgiveness.

Bible Reference - Text

Genesis 1:28 - And God blessed them, and God said unto them.... (Continued) - (To read the full text of the above go to page 12.)

Course Ref/s - Citation/s

T-24.V.6-7 - The Christ in you is very still. He knows where you are going, and He leads you there in gentleness and blessing all the way. His Love for God replaces all the fear you thought you saw within yourself. His holiness shows you Himself in him whose hand you hold, and whom you lead to Him. And what you see is like yourself. For what but Christ is there to see and hear and love and follow home? He looked upon you first, but recognized that you were not complete. And so He sought for your completion in <u>each living thing</u> that He beholds and loves. And seeks it still, that each might offer you the Love of God.

Yet is He quiet, for He knows that love is in you now, and safely held in you by that same hand that holds your brother's in your own. Christ's hand holds all His brothers in Himself. He gives them vision for their sightless eyes, and sings to them of Heaven, that their ears may hear no more the sound of battle and of death. He reaches through them, holding out His hand, that everyone may bless <u>all living things</u>, and see their holiness. And He rejoices that these sights are yours, to look upon with Him and share His joy. His perfect lack of specialness He offers you, that you may save, all living things from death, receiving from each one the gift of life that your forgiveness offers to your Self. The sight of Christ is all there is to see. The song of Christ is all there is to hear. The hand of Christ is all there is to hold. There is no journey but to walk with Him.

T-26.IX.4 - What is a hundred or a thousand years to Them [holy Brothers], or tens of thousands? When They come, time's purpose is fulfilled. What never was passes to nothingness when They have come. What hatred claimed is given up to love, and freedom lights up <u>every living thing</u> and lifts it into Heaven, where the lights grow ever brighter as each one comes home. The incomplete is made complete again, and Heaven's joy has been increased because what is its own has been restored to it. The bloodied earth is cleansed, and the insane have shed their garments of insanity to join Them on the ground whereon you stand.

T-26.X.2 - What does it mean if you perceive attack in certain forms to be unfair to you? It means that there must be some forms in which you think it fair. For otherwise, how could some be evaluated as unfair? Some, then, are given meaning and perceived as sensible. And only some are seen as meaningless. And this denies the fact that all are senseless, equally without a cause or consequence, and cannot have effects of any kind. Their Presence [God the Father and the Son] is obscured by any veil that stands between Their shining innocence, and your awareness that it is your own and equally belongs to <u>every living thing</u> along with you. God limits not. And what is limited cannot be Heaven. So it must be hell.

T-26.X.5 - You think your brother is unfair to you because you think that one must be unfair to make the other innocent. And in this game do you perceive one purpose for your whole relationship. And this you seek to add unto the purpose given it. The Holy Spirit's purpose is to let the Presence of your holy Guests [God the Father and the Son] be known to you. And to this purpose nothing can be added, for the world is purposeless except for this. To add or take away from this one goal is but to take away all purpose from the world and from yourself. And each unfairness that the world appears to lay upon you, you have laid on it by rendering it purposeless, without the function that the Holy Spirit sees. And simple justice has been thus denied to <u>every living thing upon the earth</u>.

T-27.II.3 - To witness sin and yet forgive it is a paradox that reason cannot see. For it maintains what has been done to you deserves no pardon. And by giving it, you grant your brother mercy but retain the proof he is not really innocent. The sick remain accusers. They cannot forgive their brothers and themselves as well. For no one in whom true forgiveness rests can suffer. He holds not the proof of sin before his brother's eyes. And thus he must have overlooked it and removed it from his own. Forgiveness cannot be for one and not the other. Who forgives is healed. And in his healing lies the proof that he has truly pardoned, and retains no trace of condemnation that he still would hold against himself or <u>any living thing</u>.

Bible Reference - Text

Genesis 1:28 - And God blessed them, and God said unto them....
(Continued) - (To read the full text of the above go to page 12.)

Course Ref/s - Citation/s

T-29.II.5-6:1 - You do not see how much you now can give, because of everything you have received. Yet He Who entered in but waits for you to come where you invited Him to be. There is no other place where He can find His host, nor where His host can meet with Him. And nowhere else His gifts of peace and joy, and all the happiness His Presence brings, can be obtained. For they are where He is Who brought them with Him, that they might be yours. You cannot see your Guest, but you can see the gifts He brought. And when you look on them, you will believe His Presence must be there. For what you now can do could not be done without the love and grace His Presence holds.

Such is the promise of the living God; His Son have life and <u>every living thing</u> be part of him, and nothing else have life.

T-29.III.2 - Think you the Father lost Himself when He created you? Was He made weak because He shared His Love? Was He made incomplete by your perfection? Or are you the proof that He is perfect and complete? Deny Him not His witness in the dream His Son prefers to his reality. He must be savior from the dream he made, that he be free of it. He must see someone else as not a body, one with him without the wall the world has built to keep apart <u>all living things</u> who know not that they live.

T-29.VIII.6 - An idol is established by belief, and when it is withdrawn the idol "dies." This is the anti-Christ; the strange idea there is a power past omnipotence, a place beyond the infinite, a time transcending the eternal. Here the world of idols has been set by the idea this power and place and time are given form, and shape the world where the impossible has happened. Here the deathless come to die, the all-encompassing to suffer loss, the timeless to be made the slaves of time. Here does the changeless change; the peace of God, forever given to <u>all living things</u>, give way to chaos. And the Son of God, as perfect, sinless and as loving as his Father, come to hate a little while; to suffer pain and finally to die.

T-29.VIII.9 - God has not many Sons, but only One. Who can have more, and who be given less? In Heaven would the Son of God but laugh, if idols could intrude upon his peace. It is for him the Holy Spirit speaks, and tells you idols have no purpose here. For more than Heaven can you never have.

If Heaven is within, why would you seek for idols that would make of Heaven less, to give you more than God bestowed upon your brother and on you, as one with Him? God gave you all there is. And to be sure you could not lose it, did He also give the same to every living thing as well. And thus is every living thing a part of you, as of Himself. No idol can establish you as more than God. But you will never be content with being less.

T-31.I.9 - There is no living thing that does not share the universal Will that it be whole, and that you do not leave its call unheard. Without your answer is it left to die, as it is saved from death when you have heard its calling as the ancient call to life, and understood that it is but your own. The Christ in you remembers God with all the certainty with which He knows His Love. But only if His Son is innocent can He be Love. For God were fear indeed if he whom He created innocent could be a slave to guilt. God's perfect Son remembers his creation. But in guilt he has forgotten what he really is.

T-31.VIII.6 - You are as God created you, and so is every living thing you look upon, regardless of the images you see. What you behold as sickness and as pain, as weakness and as suffering and loss, is but temptation to perceive yourself defenseless and in hell. Yield not to this, and you will see all pain, in every form, wherever it occurs, but disappear as mists before the sun. A miracle has come to heal God's Son, and close the door upon his dreams of weakness, opening the way to his salvation and release. Choose once again what you would have him be, remembering that every choice you make establishes your own identity as you will see it and believe it is.

W-pI.038.5:3-5 - There is nothing my holiness cannot do because the power of God lies in it.

Introduce whatever variations appeal to you, but keep the exercises focused on the theme, "There is nothing my holiness cannot do." The purpose of today's exercises is to begin to instill in you a sense that you have dominion over all things because of what you are.

W-pI.097.4 - You are the spirit in whose mind abides the miracle in which all time stands still; the miracle in which a minute spent in using these ideas becomes a time that has no limit and that has no end. Give, then, these minutes willingly, and count on Him Who promised to lay timelessness beside them. He will offer all His strength to every little effort that you make. Give Him the minutes which He needs today, to help you understand with Him you are the spirit that abides in Him, and that calls through His Voice to <u>every living thing</u>; offers His sight to everyone who asks; replaces error with the simple truth.

Bible Reference - Text

Genesis 1:28 - And God blessed them, and God said unto them.... (Continued) - (To read the full text of the above go to page 12.)

Course Ref/s - Citation/s

W-pI.132.14 - Today our purpose is to free the world from all the idle thoughts we ever held about it, and about <u>all living things</u> we see upon it. They can not be there. No more can we. For we are in the home our Father set for us, along with them. And we who are as He created us would loose the world this day from every one of our illusions, that we may be free.

W-pI.139.1-2 - Here is the end of choice. For here we come to a decision to accept ourselves as God created us. And what is choice except uncertainty of what we are? There is no doubt that is not rooted here. There is no question but reflects this one. There is no conflict that does not entail the single, simple question, "What am I?"

Yet who could ask this question except one who has refused to recognize himself? Only refusal to accept yourself could make the question seem to be sincere. The only thing that can be surely known by <u>any living thing</u> is what it is. From this one point of certainty, it looks on other things as certain as itself.

W-pI.156.5 - The light in you is what the universe longs to behold. <u>All living things</u> are still before you, for they recognize Who walks with you. The light you carry is their own. And thus they see in you their holiness, saluting you as savior and as God. Accept their reverence, for it is due to Holiness Itself, which walks with you, transforming in Its gentle light all things unto Its likeness and Its purity.

W-pI.158.1 - What has been given you? The knowledge that you are a mind, in Mind and purely mind, sinless forever, wholly unafraid, because you were created out of love. Nor have you left your Source, remaining as you were created. This was given you as knowledge which you cannot lose. It was given as well to <u>every living thing</u>, for by that knowledge only does it live.

W-pI.163.1-2 - Death is a thought that takes on many forms, often unrecognized. It may appear as sadness, fear, anxiety or doubt; as anger, faithlessness and lack of trust; concern for bodies, envy, and all forms in which the wish to be as you are not may come to tempt you. All such thoughts are but reflections of the worshipping of death as savior and as giver of release.

Embodiment of fear, the host of sin, god of the guilty and the lord of all illusions and deceptions, does the thought of death seem mighty. For it seems to hold <u>all living things</u> within its withered hand; all hopes and wishes in its blighting grasp; all goals perceived but in its sightless eyes. The frail, the helpless and the sick bow down before its image, thinking it alone is real, inevitable, worthy of their trust. For it alone will surely come.

W-pI.163.9 - Our Father, bless our eyes today. We are Your messengers, and we would look upon the glorious reflection of Your Love which shines in everything. We live and move in You alone. We are not separate from Your eternal life. There is no death, for death is not Your Will. And we abide where You have placed us, in the life we share with You and with <u>all living things</u>, to be like You and part of You forever. We accept Your Thoughts as ours, and our will is one with Yours eternally. Amen.

W-pI.184.15 - Father, our Name is Yours. In It we are united with <u>all living things</u>, and You Who are their one Creator. What we made and call by many different names is but a shadow we have tried to cast across Your Own reality. And we are glad and thankful we were wrong. All our mistakes we give to You, that we may be absolved from all effects our errors seemed to have. And we accept the truth You give, in place of every one of them. Your Name is our salvation and escape from what we made. Your Name unites us in the oneness which is our inheritance and peace. Amen.

W-pI.188.3 - The peace of God is shining in you now, and from your heart extends around the world. It pauses to caress <u>each living thing</u>, and leaves a blessing with it that remains forever and forever. What it gives must be eternal. It removes all thoughts of the ephemeral and valueless. It brings renewal to all tired hearts, and lights all vision as it passes by. All of its gifts are given everyone, and everyone unites in giving thanks to you who give, and you who have received.

Bible Reference - Text

A. Genesis

Genesis 1:28 - And God blessed them, and God said unto them....
(Continued) - (To read the full text of the above go to page 12.)

Course Ref/s - Citation/s

W-pI.188.5 - The peace of God can never be contained. Who recognizes it within himself must give it. And the means for giving it are in his understanding. He forgives because he recognized the truth in him. The peace of God is shining in you now, and in <u>all living things</u>. In quietness is it acknowledged universally. For what your inward vision looks upon is your perception of the universe.

W-pI.188.9-10 - We practice coming nearer to the light in us today. We take our wandering thoughts, and gently bring them back to where they fall in line with all the thoughts we share with God. We will not let them stray. We let the light within our minds direct them to come home. We have betrayed them, ordering that they depart from us. But now we call them back, and wash them clean of strange desires and disordered wishes. We restore to them the holiness of their inheritance.

Thus are our minds restored with them, and we acknowledge that the peace of God still shines in us, and from us to <u>all living things</u> that share our life. We will forgive them all, absolving all the world from what we thought it did to us. For it is we who make the world as we would have it. Now we choose that it be innocent, devoid of sin and open to salvation. And we lay our saving blessing on it, as we say:

The peace of God is shining in me now.

Let all things shine upon me in that peace,

And let me bless them with the light in me.

W-pI.190.6 - My holy brother, think of this awhile: The world you see does nothing. It has no effects at all. It merely represents your thoughts. And it will change entirely as you elect to change your mind, and choose the joy of God as what you really want. Your Self is radiant in this holy joy, unchanged, unchanging and unchangeable, forever and forever. And would you deny a little corner of your mind its own inheritance, and keep it as a hospital for pain; a sickly place where <u>living things</u> must come at last to die?

W-pI.195.6 - We thank our Father for one thing alone; that we are separate from no living thing, and therefore one with Him. And we rejoice that no exceptions ever can be made which would reduce our wholeness, nor impair or change our function to complete the One Who is Himself completion. We give thanks for <u>every living thing</u>, for otherwise we offer thanks for nothing, and we fail to recognize the gifts of God to us.

W-pI.rI.57.5 - As I share the peace of the world with my brothers, I begin to understand that this peace comes from deep within myself. The world I look upon has taken on the light of my forgiveness, and shines forgiveness back at me. In this light I begin to see what my illusions about myself kept hidden. I begin to understand the holiness of <u>all living things</u>, including myself, and their oneness with me.

W-pII.9.2 - It is the all-inclusive nature of Christ's Second Coming that permits it to embrace the world and hold you safe within its gentle advent, which encompasses <u>all living things</u> with you. There is no end to the release the Second Coming brings, as God's creation must be limitless. Forgiveness lights the Second Coming's way, because it shines on everything as one. And thus is oneness recognized at last.

M-23.2 - We have repeatedly said that one who has perfectly accepted the Atonement for himself can heal the world. Indeed, he has already done so. Temptation may recur to others, but never to this One. He has become the risen Son of God. He has overcome death because he has accepted life. He has recognized himself as God created him, and in so doing he has

recognized <u>all living things</u> as part of him. There is now no limit on his power, because it is the Power of God. So has his name become the Name of God, for he no longer sees himself as separate from Him.

M-28.2 - The resurrection is the denial of death, being the assertion of life. Thus is all the thinking of the world reversed entirely. Life is now recognized as salvation, and pain and misery of any kind perceived as hell. Love is no longer feared, but gladly welcomed. Idols have disappeared, and the remembrance of God shines unimpeded across the world. Christ's face is seen in <u>every living thing</u>, and nothing is held in darkness, apart from the light of forgiveness. There is no sorrow still upon the earth. The joy of Heaven has come upon it.

S-3.IV.2 - As witness to forgiveness, aid to prayer, and the effect of mercy truly taught, healing is blessing. And the world responds in quickened chorus through the voice of prayer. Forgiveness shines its merciful reprieve upon each blade of grass and feathered wing and <u>all the living things upon the earth</u>. Fear has no haven here, for love has come in all its holy oneness. Time remains only to let the last embrace of prayer rest on the earth an instant, as the world is shined away. This instant is the goal of all true healers, whom the Christ has taught to see His likeness and to teach like Him.

Bible Reference - Text

Genesis 1:31 - And God saw every thing that he had made, and, behold, it was very good. And the evening and the morning were the sixth day.

Course Ref/s - Citation/s

P-3.II.4 - <u>God is said to have looked on all He created and pronounced it good.</u> No, He declared it perfect, and so it was. And since His creations do not change and last forever, so it is now. Yet neither a perfect therapist nor a perfect patient can possibly exist. Both must have denied their perfection, for their very need for each other implies a sense of lack. A one-to- one relationship is not One Relationship. Yet it is the means of return; the way God chose for the return of His Son. In that strange dream a strange correction must enter, for only that is the call to awake. And what else should therapy be? Awake and be glad, for all your sins have been forgiven you. This is the only message that any two should ever give each other.

T-02.VIII.4 - The first step toward freedom involves a sorting out of the false from the true. This is a process of separation in the constructive sense, and reflects the true meaning of the Apocalypse. Everyone will ultimately look upon his own creations and choose to preserve only what is good, just as <u>God Himself looked upon what He had created and knew that it was good</u>. At this point, the mind can begin to look with love on its own creations because of their worthiness. At the same time the mind will inevitably disown its miscreations which, without belief, will no longer exist.

Bible Reference - Text

Genesis 2:7 - And the Lord God formed man of the dust of the ground, and breathed into his nostrils the breath of life; and man became a living soul.

Course Ref/s - Citation/s

T-13.IV.1 - And now the reason why you are afraid of this course [A Course in Miracles] should be apparent. For this is a course on love, because it is about you. You have been told that your function in this world is healing, and your function in Heaven is creating. The ego teaches that your function on earth is destruction, and you have no function at all in Heaven. It would thus destroy you here and bury you here, leaving you no inheritance except <u>the dust out of which it thinks you were made</u>. As long as it is reasonably satisfied with you, as its reasoning goes, it offers you oblivion. When it becomes overtly savage, it offers you hell.

W-pI.135.5-6 - Yet it is not the body that can fear, nor be a thing of fear. It has no needs but those which you assign to it. It needs no complicated structures of defense, no health-inducing medicine, no care and no concern at all. Defend its life, or give it gifts to make it beautiful or walls to make it safe, and you but say your home is open to the thief of time, corruptible and crumbling, so unsafe it must be guarded with your very life.

Is not this picture fearful? Can you be at peace with such a concept of your home? Yet what endowed the body with the right to serve you thus except your own belief? It is your mind which gave the body all the functions that you see in it, and set its value far beyond <u>a little pile of dust</u> and water. Who would make defense of something that he recognized as this?

W-pI.136.8-10 - How do you think that sickness can succeed in shielding you from truth? Because it proves the body is not separate from you, and so you must be separate from the truth. You suffer pain because the body does, and in this pain are you made one with it. Thus is your "true" identity preserved, and the strange, haunting thought that you might be something beyond this <u>little pile of dust</u> silenced and stilled. For see, this dust can make you suffer, twist your limbs and stop your heart, commanding you to die and cease to be.

Thus is the body stronger than the truth, which asks you live, but cannot overcome your choice to die. And so the body is more powerful than everlasting life, Heaven more frail than hell, and God's design for the salvation of His Son opposed by a decision stronger than His Will. His Son is dust, the Father incomplete, and chaos sits in triumph on His throne.

Such is your planning for your own defense. And you believe that Heaven quails before such mad attacks as these, with God made blind by your illusions, truth turned into lies, and all the universe made slave to laws which your defenses would impose on it. Yet who believes illusions but the one who made them up? Who else can see them and react to them as if they were the truth?

S-3.I.1 - Do not mistake effect for cause, nor think that sickness is apart and separate from what its cause must be. It is a sign, a shadow of an evil thought that seems to have reality and to be just, according to the usage of the world. It is external proof of inner "sins," and witnesses to unforgiving thoughts that injure and would hurt the Son of God. Healing the body is impossible, and this is shown by the brief nature of the " cure." The body yet must die, and so its healing but delays its turning back to <u>dust, where it was born</u> and will return.

Bible Reference - Text

Genesis 2:15-17 - And the Lord God took the man, and put him into the garden of Eden to dress it and to keep it. And the Lord God commanded the man, saying, Of every tree of the garden thou mayest freely eat: But of the tree of the knowledge of good and evil, thou shalt not eat of it: for in the day that thou eatest thereof thou shalt surely die.

Course Ref/s - Citation/s

T-02.I.3:1-5 - The <u>Garden of Eden</u>, or the pre-separation condition, was a state of mind in which nothing was needed. When Adam listened to the "lies of the serpent," all he heard was untruth. You do not have to continue to believe what is not true unless you choose to do so. All that can literally disappear in the twinkling of an eye because it is merely a misperception. What is seen in dreams seems to be very real.

T-03.VII.3 - We have discussed the fall or separation before, but its meaning must be clearly understood. The separation is a system of thought real enough in time, though not in eternity. All beliefs are real to the believer. The fruit of only one tree was "forbidden" in the symbolic garden. But God could not have forbidden it, or it could not have been eaten.
If God knows His children, and I assure you that He does, would He have put them in a position where their own destruction was possible?
The "forbidden tree" was named the "<u>tree of knowledge</u>." Yet God created knowledge and gave it freely to His creations. The symbolism here has been given many interpretations, but you may be sure that any

interpretation that sees either God or His creations as capable of destroying Their Own purpose is in error.

T-03.VII.4 - <u>Eating of the fruit of the tree of knowledge</u> is a symbolic expression for usurping the ability for self-creating. This is the only sense in which God and His creations are not co-creators. The belief that they are is implicit in the "self- concept," or the tendency of the self to make an image of itself. Images are perceived, not known. Knowledge cannot deceive, but perception can. You can perceive yourself as self-creating, but you cannot do more than believe it. You cannot make it true. And, as I said before, when you finally perceive correctly you can only be glad that you cannot. Until then, however, the belief that you can is the foundation stone in your thought system, and all your defenses are used to attack ideas that might bring it to light. You still believe you are an image of your own making. Your mind is split with the Holy Spirit on this point, and there is no resolution while you believe the one thing that is literally inconceivable. That is why you cannot create and are filled with fear about what you make.

Bible Reference - Text

Genesis 2:21 - And the Lord God caused a deep sleep to fall upon Adam, and he slept: and he took one of his ribs, and closed up the flesh instead thereof;

Course Ref/s - Citation/s

T-02.I.3 - The Garden of Eden, or the pre-separation condition, was a state of mind in which nothing was needed. When Adam listened to the "lies of the serpent," all he heard was untruth. You do not have to continue to believe what is not true unless you choose to do so. All that can literally disappear in the twinkling of an eye because it is merely a misperception. What is seen in dreams seems to be very real. Yet the Bible says that a <u>deep sleep fell upon Adam,</u> and nowhere is there reference to his waking up. The world has not yet experienced any comprehensive reawakening or rebirth. Such a rebirth is impossible as long as you continue to project or miscreate. It still remains within you, however, to extend as God extended His Spirit to you. In reality this is your only choice, because your free will was given you for your joy in creating the perfect.

T-02.I.4 - All fear is ultimately reducible to the basic misperception that you have the ability to usurp the power of God. Of course, you neither can nor have been able to do this. Here is the real basis for your escape from fear. The escape is brought about by your acceptance of the Atonement, which enables you to realize that your errors never really occurred. Only after the <u>deep sleep fell upon Adam</u> could he experience nightmares. If a light is suddenly turned on while someone is dreaming a fearful dream, he may initially interpret the light itself as part of his dream and be afraid of it. However, when he awakens, the light is correctly perceived as the release from the dream, which is then no longer accorded reality. This release does not depend on illusions. The knowledge that illuminates not only sets you free, but also shows you clearly that you *are* free.

T-12.VI.4 - Correction is for all who cannot see. To open the eyes of the blind is the Holy Spirit's mission, for He knows that they have not lost their vision, but merely <u>sleep</u>. He would awaken them from the sleep of forgetting to the remembering of God. Christ's eyes are open, and He will look upon whatever you see with love if you accept His vision as yours. The Holy Spirit keeps the vision of Christ for every Son of God who sleeps. In His sight the Son of God is perfect, and He longs to share His vision with you. He will show you the real world because God gave you Heaven. Through Him your Father calls His Son to remember.
The awakening of His Son begins with his investment in the real world, and by this he will learn to re-invest in himself. For reality is one with the Father and the Son, and the Holy Spirit blesses the real world in Their Name.

T-13.V.8 - Vision depends on light. You cannot see in darkness. Yet in darkness, in the private world of <u>sleep</u>, you see in dreams although your eyes are closed. And it is here that what you see you made. But let the darkness go and all you made you will no longer see, for sight of it depends upon denying vision. Yet from denying vision it does not follow you cannot see. But this is what denial does, for by it you accept insanity, believing you can make a private world and rule your own perception. Yet for this, light must be excluded. Dreams disappear when light has come and you can see.

T-13.VI.12 - Awaking unto Christ is following the laws of love of your free will, and out of quiet recognition of the truth in them. The attraction of light must draw you willingly, and willingness is signified by giving. Those who accept love of you become your willing witnesses to the love you gave them, and it is they who hold it out to you. In <u>sleep</u> you are alone, and your awareness is narrowed to yourself. And that is why the nightmares come. You dream of isolation because your eyes are closed. You do not see your brothers, and in the darkness you cannot look upon the light you gave to them.

T-13.VI.13 - And yet the laws of love are not suspended because you sleep. And you have followed them through all your nightmares, and have been faithful in your giving, for you were not alone. Even in sleep has Christ protected you, ensuring the real world for you when you awake. In your name He has given for you, and given you the gifts He gave. God's Son is still as loving as his Father. Continuous with his Father, he has no past apart from Him. So he has never ceased to be his Father's witness and his own. Although he slept, Christ's vision did not leave him. And so it is that he can call unto himself the witnesses that teach him that he never slept.

Bible Reference - Text

Genesis 3:1-7 - Now the serpent was more subtle than any of the beasts of the earth which the Lord God had made. And he said to the woman: Why hath God commanded you, that you should not eat of every tree of paradise?

And the woman answered him, saying: Of the fruit of the trees that are in paradise we do eat: But of the fruit of the tree which is in the midst of paradise, God hath commanded us that we should not eat; and that we should not touch it, lest perhaps we die.

And the serpent said to the woman: No, you shall not die the death. For God doth know that in what day soever you shall eat thereof, your eyes shall be opened: and you shall be as Gods, knowing good and evil.

And the woman saw that the tree was good to eat, and fair to the eyes, and delightful to behold: and she took of the fruit thereof, and did eat, and gave to her husband who did eat. And the eyes of them both were opened: and when they perceived themselves to be naked, they sewed together fig leaves, and made themselves aprons.

Course Ref/s - Citation/s

A. Genesis

T-01.VI.1 - You who want peace can find it only by complete forgiveness. No learning is acquired by anyone unless he wants to learn it and believes in some way that he needs it. While lack does not exist in the creation of God, it is very apparent in what you have made. It is, in fact, the essential difference between them. Lack implies that you would be better off in a state somehow different from the one you are in. Until the "separation," which is the meaning of the "fall," nothing was lacking. There were no needs at all. Needs arise only when you deprive yourself. You act according to the particular order of needs you establish. This, in turn, depends on your perception of what you are.

T-17.IV.4 - In a sense, the special relationship was the ego's answer to the creation of the Holy Spirit, who was God's Answer to the separation. For although the ego did not understand what had been created, it was aware of threat. The whole defense system the ego evolved to protect the separation from the Holy Spirit was in response to the gift with which God blessed it, and by His blessing enabled it to be healed. This blessing holds within itself the truth about everything. And the truth is that the Holy Spirit is in close relationship with you, because in Him is your relationship with God restored to you. The relationship with Him has never been broken, because the Holy Spirit has not been separate from anyone since the separation. And through Him have all your holy relationships been carefully preserved, to serve God's purpose for you.

P-2.IV.9-10 - A madman will defend his own illusions because in them he sees his own salvation. Thus, he will attack the one who tries to save him from them, believing that he is attacking him. This curious circle of attack-defense is one of the most difficult problems with which the psychotherapist must deal. In fact, this is his central task; the core of psychotherapy. The therapist is seen as one who is attacking the patient's most cherished possession; his picture of himself. And since this picture has become the patient's security as he perceives it, the therapist cannot but be seen as a real source of danger, to be attacked and even killed.

The psychotherapist, then, has a tremendous responsibility. He must meet attack without attack, and therefore without defense. It is his task to demonstrate that defenses are not necessary, and that defenselessness is strength. This must be his teaching, if his lesson is to be that sanity is safe. It cannot be too strongly emphasized that the insane believe that sanity is threat. This is the corollary of the "original sin"; the belief that guilt is real and fully justified. It is therefore the psychotherapist's function to teach that guilt, being unreal, cannot be justified. But neither is it safe. And thus it must remain unwanted as well as unreal.

Bible Reference - Text

Genesis 3:8-9 - And they heard the voice of the Lord God walking in the garden in the cool of the day: and Adam and his wife hid themselves from the presence of the Lord God amongst the trees of the garden. And the Lord God called unto Adam, and said unto him, Where art thou?

Course Ref/s - Citation/s

T-11.III.5 - God hides nothing from His Son, even though His Son would hide himself. Yet the Son of God cannot hide his glory, for God wills him to be glorious, and gave him the light that shines in him. You will never lose your way, for God leads you. When you wander, you but undertake a journey that is not real. The dark companions, the dark way, are all illusions. Turn toward the light, for the little spark in you is part of a Light so great that it can sweep you out of all darkness forever. For your Father is your Creator, and you are like Him.

W-pI.168.1 - God speaks to us. Shall we not speak to Him? He is not distant. He makes no attempt to hide from us. We try to hide from Him, and suffer from deception. He remains entirely accessible. He loves His Son. There is no certainty but this, yet this suffices. He will love His Son forever. When his mind remains asleep, He loves him still. And when his mind awakes, He loves him with a never-changing Love.

Bible Reference - Text

Genesis 3:23-24 - Therefore the Lord God sent him forth from the garden of Eden, to till the ground from whence he was taken. So he drove out the man; and he placed at the east of the garden of Eden Cherubims, and a flaming sword which turned every way, to keep the way of the tree of life.

Course Ref/s - Citation/s

T-03.I.3 - The statement "Vengeance is mine, sayeth the Lord" is a misperception by which one assigns his own "evil" past to God. The "evil" past has nothing to do with God. He did not create it and He does not maintain it. God does not believe in retribution. His Mind does not create that way. He does not hold your "evil" deeds against you. Is it likely that He would hold them against me [Jesus]? Be very sure that you recognize how utterly impossible this assumption is, and how entirely it arises from projection. This kind of error is responsible for a host of related errors, including the belief that <u>God rejected Adam and forced him out of the Garden of Eden</u>. It is also why you may believe from time to time that I am misdirecting you. I have made every effort to use words that are almost impossible to distort, but it is always possible to twist symbols around if you wish.

T-13.In.2-3 - The acceptance of guilt into the mind of God's Son was the beginning of the separation, as the acceptance of the Atonement is its end. The world you see is the delusional system of those made mad by guilt. Look carefully at this world, and you will realize that this is so. For this world is the symbol of punishment, and all the laws that seem to govern it are the laws of death. Children are born into it through pain and in pain. Their growth is attended by suffering, and they learn of sorrow and separation and death. Their minds seem to be trapped in their brain, and its powers to decline if their bodies are hurt. They seem to love, yet they desert and are deserted. They appear to lose what they love, perhaps the most insane belief of all. And their bodies wither and gasp and are laid in the ground, and are no more. Not one of them but has thought that God is cruel.

If this were the real world, God would be cruel. For no Father could subject His children to this as the price of salvation and be loving. Love does not kill to save. If it did, attack would be salvation, and this is the ego's interpretation, not God's. Only the world of guilt could demand this, for only the guilty could conceive of it. Adam's "sin" could have touched no one, had he not believed it was <u>the Father Who drove him out of paradise</u>. For in that belief the knowledge of the Father was lost, since only those who do not understand Him could believe it.

T-24.III.3-4 - It is not you who are so vulnerable and open to attack that just a word, a little whisper that you do not like, a circumstance that suits you not, or an event that you did not anticipate upsets your world, and hurls it into chaos. Truth is not frail. Illusions leave it perfectly unmoved and undisturbed. But specialness is not the truth in you. It can be thrown off balance by anything. What rests on nothing never can be stable. However large and overblown it seems to be, it still must rock and turn and whirl about with every breeze.

Without foundation nothing is secure. Would God have left His Son in such a state, where safety has no meaning? No, His Son is safe, resting on Him. It is your specialness that is attacked by everything that walks and breathes, or creeps or crawls, or even lives at all. Nothing is safe from its attack, and it is safe from nothing. It will forevermore be unforgiving, for that is what it is; a secret vow that what God wants for you will never be, and that you will oppose His Will forever. Nor is it possible the two can ever be the same, while specialness stands like a flaming sword of death between them, and makes them enemies.

Bible Reference - Text

Genesis 4:9 - And the Lord said unto Cain, Where is Abel thy brother? And he said, I know not: Am I my brother's keeper?

Course Ref/s - Citation/s

T-24.II.11 - You are your brother's; part of love was not denied to him. But can it be that you have lost because he is complete? What has been given him makes you complete, as it does him. God's Love gave you to him and him to you because He gave Himself. What is the same as God is one with Him. And only specialness could make the truth of God and you as one seem anything but Heaven, with the hope of peace at last in sight.

Bible Reference - Text

Genesis 7:9 - There went in two and two unto Noah into the ark, the male and the female, as God had commanded Noah.

Course Ref/s - Citation/s

T-20.IV.6 - The plan is not of you, nor need you be concerned with anything except the part that has been given you to learn. For He Who

A. Genesis

knows the rest will see to it without your help. But think not that He does not need your part to help Him with the rest. For in your part lies all of it, without which is no part complete, nor is the whole completed without your part. The ark of peace is entered two by two, yet the beginning of another world goes with them. Each holy relationship must enter here, to learn its special function in the Holy Spirit's plan, now that it shares His purpose. And as this purpose is fulfilled, a new world rises in which sin can enter not, and where the Son of God can enter without fear and where he rests a while, to forget imprisonment and to remember freedom.
How can he enter, to rest and to remember, without you? Except you be there, he is not complete. And it is his completion that he remembers there.

T-28.VII.7 - Your home is built upon your brother's health, upon his happiness, his sinlessness, and everything his Father promised him.
No secret promise you have made instead has shaken the Foundation of his home. The winds will blow upon it and the rain will beat against it, but with no effect. The world will wash away and yet this house will stand forever, for its strength lies not within itself alone. It is an ark of safety, resting on God's promise that His Son is safe forever in Himself. What gap can interpose itself between the safety of this shelter and its Source? From here the body can be seen as what it is, and neither less nor more in worth than the extent to which it can be used to liberate God's Son unto his home. And with this holy purpose is it made a home of holiness a little while, because it shares your Father's Will with you.

Bible Reference - Text

Genesis 19:23-26 - The sun was risen upon the earth when Lot entered into Zoar. Then the Lord rained upon Sodom and upon Gomorrah brimstone and fire from the Lord out of heaven; And he overthrew those cities, and all the plain, and all the inhabitants of the cities, and that which grew upon the ground. But his wife looked back from behind him, and she became a pillar of salt.

Course Ref/s - Citation/s

T-14.II.6 - If you would be a happy learner, you must give everything you have learned to the Holy Spirit, to be unlearned for you. And then begin to learn the joyous lessons that come quickly on the firm foundation that truth is true. For what is builded there is true, and built on truth. The universe of learning will open up before you in all its gracious simplicity. With truth before you, you will not look back.

T-20.VI.9 - Idols must disappear, and leave no trace behind their going. The unholy instant of their seeming power is frail as is a snowflake, but without its loveliness. Is this the substitute you want for the eternal blessing of the holy instant and its unlimited beneficence? Is the malevolence of the unholy relationship, so seeming powerful and so bitterly misunderstood and so invested in a false attraction your preference to the holy instant, which offers you peace and understanding? Then lay aside the body and quietly transcend it, rising to welcome what you really want. And from His holy temple, look you not back on what you have awakened from. For no illusions can attract the mind that has transcended them, and left them far behind.

T-30.V.07 - When brothers join in purpose in the world of fear, they stand already at the edge of the real world. Perhaps they still look back, and think they see an idol that they want. Yet has their path been surely set away from idols toward reality. For when they joined their hands it was Christ's hand they took, and they will look on Him Whose hand they hold. The face of Christ is looked upon before the Father is remembered. For He must be unremembered till His Son has reached beyond forgiveness to the Love of God. Yet is the Love of Christ accepted first. And then will come the knowledge They are one.

T-30.V.9-10 - An ancient hate is passing from the world. And with it goes all hatred and all fear. Look back no longer, for what lies ahead is all you ever wanted in your heart. Give up the world! But not to sacrifice. You never wanted it. What happiness have you sought here that did not bring you pain? What moment of content has not been bought at fearful price in coins of suffering? Joy has no cost. It is your sacred right, and what you pay for is not happiness. Be speeded on your way by honesty, and let not your experiences here deceive in retrospect. They were not free from bitter cost and joyless consequence.

Do not look back except in honesty. And when an idol tempts you, think of this: There never was a time an idol brought you anything except the "gift" of guilt. Not one was bought except at cost of pain, nor was it ever paid by you alone. Be merciful unto your brother, then. And do not choose an idol thoughtlessly, remembering that he will pay the cost as well as you. For he will be delayed when you look back, and you will not perceive Whose loving hand you hold. Look forward, then; in confidence walk with a happy heart that beats in hope and does not pound in fear.

W-pII.In.6 - I am so close to you we cannot fail. Father, we give these holy times to You, in gratitude to Him Who taught us how to leave the world of sorrow in exchange for its replacement, given us by You. We <u>look</u> not <u>back</u>ward now. We look ahead, and fix our eyes upon the journey's end. Accept these little gifts of thanks from us, as through Christ's vision we behold a world beyond the one we made, and take that world to be the full replacement of our own.

Bible Reference - Text

Genesis 25:31-33 - And Jacob said, Sell me this day thy birthright. And Esau said, Behold, I am at the point to die: and what profit shall this birthright do to me? And Jacob said, Swear to me this day; and he sware unto him: and he sold his birthright unto Jacob.

Course Ref/s - Citation/s

T-12.IV.6 - Behold the Guide your Father gave you, that you might learn you have eternal life. For death is not your Father's Will nor yours, and whatever is true is the Will of the Father. You pay no price for life for that was given you, but you do pay a price for death, and a very heavy one. If death is your treasure, you will sell everything else to purchase it. And you will believe that you have purchased it, because you have sold everything else. Yet you cannot sell the Kingdom of Heaven. <u>Your inheritance can neither be bought nor sold</u>. There can be no disinherited parts of the Sonship, for God is whole and all His extensions are like Him.

T-12.IV.7 - The Atonement is not the price of your wholeness, but it is the price of your awareness of your wholeness. For what you chose to "sell" had to be kept for you, since you could not "buy" it back. Yet you must invest in it, not with money but with spirit. For spirit is will, and will is the "price" of the Kingdom. Your <u>inheritance</u> awaits only the recognition that you have been redeemed. The Holy Spirit guides you into life eternal, but you must relinquish your investment in death, or you will not see life though it is all around you.

T-24.III.2 - Whatever form of specialness you cherish, you have made sin. Inviolate it stands, strongly defended with all your puny might against the Will of God. And thus it stands against yourself; your enemy, not God's. So does it seem to split you off from God, and make you separate from Him as its defender. You would protect what God created not. And yet, this idol that seems to give you power has taken it away. For you have given your brother's birthright to it, leaving him alone and unforgiven, and yourself in sin beside him, both in misery, before the idol that can save you not.

Bible Reference - Text

Genesis 28:16-17 - And Jacob awaked out of his sleep, and he said, Surely the Lord is in this place; and I knew it not. And he was afraid, and said, How dreadful is this place! This is none other but the house of God, and this is the gate of heaven.

Course Ref/s - Citation/s

T-13.VIII.10 - Yet in this world your perfection is un- witnessed. God knows it, but you do not, and so you do not share His witness to it. Nor do you witness unto Him, for reality is witnessed to as one. God waits your witness to His Son and to Himself. The miracles you do on earth are lifted up to Heaven and to Him. They witness to what you do not know, and as they reach the gates of Heaven, God will open them. For never would He leave His Own beloved Son outside them, and beyond Himself.

T-13.X.14 - Praise be to you who make the Father one with His Own Son. Alone we are all lowly, but together we shine with brightness so intense that none of us alone can even think of it. Before the glorious radiance of the Kingdom guilt melts away, and transformed into kindness will never more be what it was. Every reaction you experience will be so purified that it is fitting as a hymn of praise unto your Father. See only praise of Him in what He has created, for He will never cease His praise of you. United in this praise we stand before the gates of Heaven where we will surely enter in our sinlessness. God loves you. Could I [Jesus], then, lack faith in you and love Him perfectly?

T-26.III.2-3 - There is a borderland of thought that stands between this world and Heaven. It is not a place, and when you reach it is apart from time. Here is the meeting place where thoughts are brought together; where conflicting values meet and all illusions are laid down beside the truth, where they are judged to be untrue. This borderland is just beyond <u>the gate of Heaven</u>. Here is every thought made pure and wholly simple. Here is sin denied, and everything that is received instead.

This is the journey's end. We have referred to it as the real world. And yet there is a contradiction here, in that the words imply a limited reality, a partial truth, a segment of the universe made true. This is because knowledge makes no attack upon perception. They are brought together, and only one continues past the gate where Oneness is. Salvation is a borderland where place and time and choice have meaning still, and yet it can be seen that they are temporary, out of place, and every choice has been already made.

T-26.IV.1 - Forgiveness is this world's equivalent of Heaven's justice. It translates the world of sin into a simple world, where justice can be reflected from beyond the gate behind which total lack of limits lies. Nothing in boundless love could need forgiveness. And what is charity within the world gives way to simple justice past <u>the gate that opens into Heaven</u>. No one forgives unless he has believed in sin, and still believes that he has much to be forgiven. Forgiveness thus becomes the means by which he learns he has done nothing to forgive. Forgiveness always rests upon the one who offers it, until he sees himself as needing it no more. And thus is he returned to his real function of creating, which his forgiveness offers him again.

T-26.IV.4-6 - Forgiveness brings no little miracles to lay before <u>the gate of Heaven</u>. Here the Son of God Himself comes to receive each gift that brings him nearer to his home. Not one is lost, and none is cherished more than any other. Each reminds him of his Father's Love as surely as the rest. And each one teaches him that what he feared he loves the most. What but a miracle could change his mind, so that he understands that love cannot be feared? What other miracle is there but this? And what else need there be to make the space between you disappear?

Where sin once was perceived will rise a world that will become an altar to the truth, and you will join the lights of Heaven there, and sing their song of gratitude and praise. And as they come to you to be complete, so will you go with them. For no one hears the song of Heaven and remains without a voice that adds its power to the song, and makes it sweeter still. And each one joins the singing at the altar that was raised within the tiny spot that sin proclaimed to be its own. And what was tiny then has soared into a magnitude of song in which the universe has joined with but a single voice.

This tiny spot of sin that stands between you and your brother still is holding back the happy opening of Heaven's gate. How little is the hindrance that withholds the wealth of Heaven from you. And how great will be the joy in Heaven when you join the mighty chorus to the Love of God!

Bible Reference - Text

Genesis 28:16-17 - And Jacob awaked out of his sleep, and he said.... (Continued) - (To read the full text of the above go to page 35.)

Course Ref/s - Citation/s

T-26.V.1-2 - A little hindrance can seem large indeed to those who do not understand that miracles are all the same. Yet teaching that is what this course is for. This is its only purpose, for only that is all there is to learn. And you can learn it in many different ways. All learning is a help or hindrance to the gate of Heaven. Nothing in between is possible. There are two teachers only, who point in different ways. And you will go along the way your chosen teacher leads. There are but two directions you can take, while time remains and choice is meaningful. For never will another road be made except the way to Heaven. You but choose whether to go toward Heaven, or away to nowhere. There is nothing else to choose.

Nothing is ever lost but time, which in the end is meaningless. For it is but a little hindrance to eternity, quite meaningless to the real Teacher of the world. Yet since you do believe in it, why should you waste it going nowhere, when it can be used to reach a goal as high as learning can achieve? Think not the way to Heaven's gate is difficult at all. Nothing you undertake with certain purpose and high resolve and happy confidence, holding your brother's hand and keeping step to Heaven's song, is difficult to do. But it is hard indeed to wander off, alone and miserable, down a road that leads to nothing and that has no purpose.

T-26.V.14 - Forgive the past and let it go, for it is gone. You stand no longer on the ground that lies between the worlds. You have gone on, and reached the world that lies at Heaven's gate. There is no hindrance to the

Will of God, nor any need that you repeat again a journey that was over long ago. Look gently on your brother, and behold the world in which perception of your hate has been transformed into a world of love.

T-30.V.8 - How light and easy is the step across the narrow boundaries of the world of fear when you have recognized Whose hand you hold! Within your hand is everything you need to walk with perfect confidence away from fear forever, and to go straight on, and quickly reach <u>the gate of Heaven</u> itself. For He Whose hand you hold was waiting but for you to join Him. Now that you have come, would He delay in showing you the way that He must walk with you? His blessing lies on you as surely as His Father's Love rests upon Him. His gratitude to you is past your understanding, for you have enabled Him to rise from chains and go with you, together, to His Father's house.

W-pI.133.13-14 - Heaven itself is reached with empty hands and open minds, which come with nothing to find everything and claim it as their own. We will attempt to reach this state today, with self-deception laid aside, and with an honest willingness to value but the truly valuable and the real. Our two extended practice periods of fifteen minutes each begin with this:

I will not value what is valueless, and only what has value do I seek, for only that do I desire to find.

And then receive what waits for everyone who reaches, unencumbered, to <u>the gate of Heaven</u>, which swings open as he comes. Should you begin to let yourself collect some needless burdens, or believe you see some difficult decisions facing you, be quick to answer with this simple thought:

I will not value what is valueless, for what is valuable belongs to me.

W-pI.134.9-10 - There is a simple way to find the door to true forgiveness, and perceive that it is open wide in welcome. When you feel that you are tempted to accuse someone of sin in any form, do not allow your mind to dwell on what you think he did, for that is self-deception. Ask instead, "Would I accuse myself of doing this"?

Thus will you see alternatives for choice in terms that render choosing meaningful, and keep your mind as free of guilt and pain as God Himself intended it to be, and as it is in truth. It is but lies that would condemn. In truth is innocence the only thing there is. Forgiveness stands between illusions and the truth; between the world you see and that which lies beyond; between the hell of guilt and <u>Heaven's gate</u>.

Bible Reference - Text

Genesis 28:16-17 - And Jacob awaked out of his sleep, and he said.... (Continued) - (To read the full text of the above go to page 35.)

Course Ref/s - Citation/s

W-pI.193.13 - This is the lesson God would have you learn: There is a way to look on everything that lets it be to you another step to Him, and to salvation of the world. To all that speaks of terror, answer thus:

I will forgive, and this will disappear.

To every apprehension, every care and every form of suffering, repeat these selfsame words. And then you hold the key that opens Heaven's gate, and brings the Love of God the Father down to earth at last, to raise it up to Heaven. God will take this final step Himself. Do not deny the little steps He asks you take to Him.

W-pI.194.ti-1 - I place the future in the Hands of God.

Today's idea takes another step toward quick salvation, and a giant stride it is indeed! So great the distance is that it encompasses, it sets you down just short of Heaven, with the goal in sight and obstacles behind. Your foot has reached the lawns that welcome you to Heaven's gate; the quiet place of peace, where you await with certainty the final step of God. How far are we progressing now from earth! How close are we approaching to our goal! How short the journey still to be pursued!

W-pI.200.7-8 - There is no peace except the peace of God, because He has one Son who cannot make a world in opposition to God's Will and to his own, which is the same as His. What could he hope to find in such a world? It cannot have reality, because it never was created. Is it here that he would seek for peace? Or must he see that, as he looks on it, the world can but deceive? Yet can he learn to look on it another way, and find the peace of God.

Peace is the bridge that everyone will cross, to leave this world behind. But peace begins within the world perceived as different, and leading from this fresh perception to the gate of Heaven and the way beyond. Peace is the answer to conflicting goals, to senseless journeys, frantic, vain pursuits, and meaningless endeavors. Now the way is easy, sloping gently toward the bridge where freedom lies within the peace of God.

W-pII.14.3 - We are the bringers of salvation. We accept our part as saviors of the world, which through our joint forgiveness is redeemed. And this, our gift, is therefore given us. We look on everyone as brother, and perceive all things as kindly and as good. We do not seek a function that is past the gate of Heaven. Knowledge will return when we have done our part. We are concerned only with giving welcome to the truth.

W-pII.14.5 - We are the holy messengers of God who speak for Him, and carrying His Word to everyone whom He has sent to us, we learn that it is written on our hearts. And thus our minds are changed about the aim for which we came, and which we seek to serve. We bring glad tidings to the Son of God, who thought he suffered. Now is he redeemed. And as he sees the gate of Heaven stand open before him, he will enter in and disappear into the Heart of God.

W-pII.342.ti-2 - I let forgiveness rest upon all things, For thus forgiveness will be given me.

I thank You, Father, for Your plan to save me from the hell I made. It is not real. And You have given me the means to prove its unreality to me. The key is in my hand, and I have reached the door beyond which lies the end of dreams. I stand before the gate of Heaven, wondering if I should enter in and be at home. Let me not wait again today. Let me forgive all things, and let creation be as You would have it be and as it is. Let me remember that I am Your Son, and opening the door at last, forget illusions in the blazing light of truth, as memory of You returns to me.

Brother, forgive me now. I come to you to take you home with me. And as we go, the world goes with us on our way to God.

M-16.10-11 - There is no substitute for the Will of God. In simple statement, it is to this fact that the teacher of God devotes his day. Each substitute he may accept as real can but deceive him. But he is safe from all deception if he so decides. Perhaps he needs to remember, "God is with me. I cannot be deceived." Perhaps he prefers other words, or only one, or none at all. Yet each temptation to accept magic as true must be abandoned through his recognition, not that it is fearful, not that it is sinful, not that it is dangerous, but merely that it is meaningless. Rooted in sacrifice and separation, two aspects of one error and no more, he merely chooses to give up all that he never had. And for this "sacrifice" is Heaven restored to his awareness.

Is not this an exchange that you would want? The world would gladly make it, if it knew it could be made. It is God's teachers who must teach it that it can. And so it is their function to make sure that they have learned it. No risk is possible throughout the day except to put your trust in magic, for it is only this that leads to pain. "There is no will but God's." His teachers know that this is so, and have learned that everything but this is magic. All belief in magic is maintained by just one simple-minded illusion;-that it works. All through his training, every day and every hour, and even every minute and second, must God's teachers learn to recognize the forms of magic and perceive their meaninglessness. Fear is withdrawn from them, and so they go. And thus the gate of Heaven is reopened, and its light can shine again on an untroubled mind.

Bible Reference - Text

Genesis 28:16-17 - And Jacob awaked out of his sleep, and he said…. (Continued) - (To read the full text of the above go to page 35.)

Course Ref/s - Citation/s

C-3.4 - The face of Christ has to be seen before the memory of God can return. The reason is obvious. Seeing the face of Christ involves perception. No one can look on knowledge. But the face of Christ is the great symbol of forgiveness. It is salvation. It is the symbol of the real world. Whoever looks on this no longer sees the world. He is as near to Heaven as is possible outside the gate. Yet from this gate it is no more than just a step inside. It is the final step. And this we leave to God.

B. Exodus

The following verses from the above book are cited in the Course:

[3:5], [3:13-14], [20:3], [20:4-5], [20:16] and [26:33].

Bible Reference - Text

Exodus 3:5 - And he said, Draw not nigh hither: put off thy shoes from off thy feet, for the place whereon thou standest is holy ground.

Course Ref/s - Citation/s

T-14.V.9 - Blessed are you who teach with me. Our power comes not of us, but of our Father. In guiltlessness we know Him, as He knows us guiltless. I stand within the circle, calling you to peace. Teach peace with me, and <u>stand with me on holy ground</u>. Remember for everyone your Father's power that He has given him. Believe not that you cannot teach His perfect peace. Stand not outside, but join with me within. Fail not the only purpose to which my teaching calls you. Restore to God His Son as He created him, by teaching him his innocence.

T-18.I.09 - In your relationship with your brother, where He [the Holy Spirit] has taken charge of everything at your request, He has set the course inward to the truth you share. In the mad world outside you nothing can be shared but only substituted, and sharing and substituting have nothing in common in reality. Within yourself you love your brother with a perfect love. Here is <u>holy ground,</u> in which no substitution can enter, and where only the truth in your brother can abide. Here you are joined in God, as much together as you are with Him. The original error has not entered here, nor ever will. Here is the radiant truth, to which the Holy Spirit has committed your relationship. Let Him bring it here, where you would have it be. Give Him but a little faith in your brother, to help Him show you that no substitute you made for Heaven can keep you from it.

T-18.I.10 - In you there is no separation, and no substitute can keep you from your brother. Your reality was God's creation, and has no substitute. You are so firmly joined in truth that only God is there. And He would never accept something else instead of you. He loves you both, equally and as one. And as He loves you, so you are. You are not joined together in illusions, but in the Thought so holy and so perfect that illusions cannot remain to darken <u>the holy place in which you stand</u> together. God is with you, my brother. Let us join in Him in peace and gratitude, and accept His gift as our most holy and perfect reality, which we share in Him.

T-26.IV.3 - <u>The holy place on which you stand</u> is but the space that sin has left. And here you see the face of Christ, arising in its place. Who could behold the face of Christ and not recall His Father as He really is? Who could fear love, and stand upon the ground where sin has left a place for Heaven's altar to rise and tower far above the world, and reach beyond the universe to touch the Heart of all creation? What is Heaven but a song of gratitude and love and praise by everything created to the Source of its creation? The holiest of altars is set where once sin was believed to be. And here does every light of Heaven come, to be rekindled and increased in joy. For here is what was lost restored to them, and all their radiance made whole again.

T-26.IX.2-3 - Is it too much to ask a little trust for him who carries Christ to you, that you may be forgiven all your sins, and left without a single one you cherish still? Forget not that a shadow held between your brother and yourself obscures the face of Christ and memory of God. And would you trade Them for an ancient hate? <u>The ground whereon you stand is holy ground</u> because of Them Who, standing there with you, have blessed it with Their innocence and peace.

The blood of hatred fades to let the grass grow green again, and let the flowers be all white and sparkling in the summer sun. What was a place of death has now become a living temple in a world of light. Because of Them. It is Their Presence which has lifted holiness again to take its ancient place upon an ancient throne. Because of Them have miracles sprung up as grass and flowers on the barren ground that hate had scorched and rendered desolate. What hate has wrought have They undone. And now you stand on ground so holy Heaven leans to join with it, and make it like itself. The shadow of an ancient hate has gone, and all the blight and withering have passed forever from the land where They have come.

T-29.II.4 - Your Guest [Christ] has come. You asked Him, and He came. You did not hear Him enter, for you did not wholly welcome Him. And yet His gifts came with Him. He has laid them at your feet, and asks you now that you will look on them and take them for your own. He needs your help in giving them to all who walk apart, believing they are separate and alone. They will be healed when you accept your gifts, because your Guest will welcome everyone whose feet have touched <u>the holy ground whereon you stand</u>, and where His gifts for them are laid.

B. Exodus

W-pI.159.8 - Christ's vision is the <u>holy ground</u> in which the lilies of forgiveness set their roots. This is their home. They can be brought from here back to the world, but they can never grow in its unnourishing and shallow soil. They need the light and warmth and kindly care Christ's charity provides. They need the love with which He looks on them. And they become His messengers, who give as they received.

W-pI.182.4 - Perhaps you think it is your childhood home that you would find again. The childhood of your body, and its place of shelter, are a memory now so distorted that you merely hold a picture of a past that never happened. Yet there is a Child in you Who seeks His Father's house, and knows that He is alien here. This childhood is eternal, with an innocence that will endure forever. Where this Child shall go is <u>holy ground</u>. It is His Holiness that lights up Heaven, and that brings to earth the pure reflection of the light above, wherein are earth and Heaven joined as one.

Bible Reference - Text

Exodus 3:13-14 - And Moses said unto God, Behold, when I come unto the children of Israel, and shall say unto them, The God of your fathers hath sent me unto you; and they shall say to me, What is his name? what shall I say unto them? And God said unto Moses, I Am That I Am: and he said, Thus shalt thou say unto the children of Israel, I Am hath sent me unto you.

Course Ref/s - Citation/s

W-pI.184.12 - <u>God has no name</u>. And yet His Name becomes the final lesson that all things are one, and at this lesson does all learning end. All names are unified; all space is filled with truth's reflection. Every gap is closed, and separation healed. The Name of God is the inheritance He gave to those who chose the teaching of the world to take the place of Heaven. In our practicing, our purpose is to let our minds accept what God has given as the answer to the pitiful inheritance you made as fitting tribute to the Son He loves.

W-pI.184.13 - No one can fail who seeks the meaning of the <u>Name of God</u>. Experience must come to supplement the Word. But first you must accept the Name for all reality, and realize the many names you gave its aspects have distorted what you see, but have not interfered with truth at all. One Name we bring into our practicing. One Name we use to unify our sight.

W-pI.184.14 - And though we use a different name for each awareness of an aspect of God's Son, we understand that they have but one Name, which He has given them. It is this Name we use in practicing. And through Its use, all foolish separations disappear which kept us blind. And we are given strength to see beyond them. Now our sight is blessed with blessings we can give as we receive.

W-pI.184.15 - Father, our Name is Yours. In It we are united with all living things, and You Who are their one Creator. What we made and call by many different names is but a shadow we have tried to cast across Your Own reality. And we are glad and thankful we were wrong. All our mistakes we give to You, that we may be absolved from all effects our errors seemed to have. And we accept the truth You give, in place of every one of them. Your Name is our salvation and escape from what we made. Your Name unites us in the oneness which is our inheritance and peace. Amen.

Bible Reference - Text

Exodus 20:3 - Thou shalt have no other gods before me.

Course Ref/s - Citation/s

T-04.III.6 - No force except your own will is strong enough or worthy enough to guide you. In this you are as free as God, and must remain so forever. Let us ask the Father in my name to keep you mindful of His Love for you and yours for Him. He has never failed to answer this request, because it asks only for what He has already willed. Those who call truly are always answered. Thou shalt have no other gods before Him because there are none.

T-10.III.08 - I do not bring God's message with deception, and you will learn this as you learn that you always receive as much as you accept. You could accept peace now for everyone, and offer them perfect freedom from all illusions because you heard His Voice. But have no other gods before Him or you will not hear. God is not jealous of the gods you make, but you are. You would save them and serve them, because you believe that they made you. You think they are your father, because you are projecting onto them the fearful fact that you made them to replace God. Yet when they seem to speak to you, remember that nothing can replace God, and whatever replacements you have attempted are nothing.

T-10.III.10 - If God has but one Son, there is but one God. You share reality with Him, because reality is not divided. To accept <u>other gods before Him</u> is to place other images before yourself. You do not realize how much you listen to your gods, and how vigilant you are on their behalf. Yet they exist only because you honor them. Place honor where it is due, and peace will be yours. It is your inheritance from your real Father. You cannot make your Father, and the father you made did not make you. Honor is not due to illusions, for to honor them is to honor nothing. Yet fear is not due them either, for nothing cannot be fearful. You have chosen to fear love because of its perfect harmlessness, and because of this fear you have been willing to give up your own perfect helpfulness and your own perfect Help.

T-10.III.11 - Only at the altar of God will you find peace. And this altar is in you because God put it there. His Voice still calls you to return, and He will be heard when you place <u>no other gods before Him</u>. You can give up the god of sickness for your brothers; in fact, you would have to do so if you give him up for yourself. For if you see the god of sickness anywhere, you have accepted him. And if you accept him you will bow down and worship him, because he was made as God's replacement. He is the belief that you can choose which god is real. Although it is clear this has nothing to do with reality, it is equally clear that it has everything to do with reality as you perceive it.

T-10.IV.1 - All magic is an attempt at reconciling the irreconcilable. All religion is the recognition that the irreconcilable cannot be reconciled. Sickness and perfection are irreconcilable. If God created you perfect, you are perfect. If you believe you can be sick, you have placed <u>other gods before Him</u>. God is not at war with the god of sickness you made, but you are. He is the symbol of deciding against God, and you are afraid of him because he cannot be reconciled with God's Will. If you attack him, you will make him real to you. But if you refuse to worship him in whatever form he may appear to you, and wherever you think you see him, he will disappear into the nothingness out of which he was made.

Bible Reference - Text

Exodus 20:3 - Thou shalt have no other gods before me. (Continued)

Course Ref/s - Citation/s

T-10.IV.3 - The Sonship cannot be perceived as partly sick, because to perceive it that way is not to perceive it at all. If the Sonship is one, it is one in all respects. Oneness cannot be divided. If you perceive <u>other gods</u> your mind is split, and you will not be able to limit the split, because it is the sign that you have removed part of your mind from God's Will. This means it is out of control. To be out of control is to be out of reason, and then the mind does become unreasonable. By defining the mind wrongly, you perceive it as functioning wrongly.

T-11.III.6 - The children of light cannot abide in darkness, for darkness is not in them. Do not be deceived by the dark comforters, and never let them enter the mind of God's Son, for they have no place in His temple. When you are tempted to deny Him remember that there are <u>no other gods to place before Him</u>, and accept His Will for you in peace. For you cannot accept it otherwise.

T-16.V.13 - See in the special relationship nothing more than a meaningless attempt to raise <u>other gods before Him</u>, and by worshipping them to obscure their tininess and His greatness. In the name of your completion you do not want this. For every idol that you raise to place before Him stands before you, in place of what you are.

W-pI.53.5:2-7 - Whatever I see reflects my thoughts. It is my thoughts that tell me where I am and what I am. The fact that I see a world in which there is suffering and loss and death shows me that I am seeing only the representation of my insane thoughts, and am not allowing my real thoughts to cast their beneficent light on what I see. Yet God's way is sure. The images I have made cannot prevail against Him because it is not my will that they do so. My will is His, and I will place <u>no other gods before Him</u>.

S-1.I.4 - The secret of true prayer is to forget the things you think you need. To ask for the specific is much the same as to look on sin and then forgive it. Also in the same way, in prayer you overlook your specific needs as you see them, and let them go into God's Hands. There they become your gifts to Him, for they tell Him that you would have <u>no gods</u>

before Him; no Love but His. What could His answer be but your remembrance of Him? Can this be traded for a bit of trifling advice about a problem of an instant's duration? God answers only for eternity. But still all little answers are contained in this.

Bible Reference - Text

Exodus 20:4-5 - Thou shalt not make unto thee any graven image, or any likeness of any thing that is in heaven above, or that is in the earth beneath, or that is in the water under the earth. Thou shalt not bow down thyself to them, nor serve them: for I the Lord thy God am a jealous God, visiting the iniquity of the fathers upon the children unto the third and fourth generation of them that hate me;

Course Ref/s - Citation/s

T-05.VI.8 - "I will visit the sins of the fathers unto the third and fourth generation," as interpreted by the ego, is particularly vicious. It becomes merely an attempt to guarantee the ego's own survival. To the Holy Spirit, the statement means that in later generations He can still reinterpret what former generations had misunderstood, and thus release the thoughts from the ability to produce fear.

T-10.III.8 - I do not bring God's message with deception, and you will learn this as you learn that you always receive as much as you accept. You could accept peace now for everyone, and offer them perfect freedom from all illusions because you heard His Voice. But have no other gods before Him or you will not hear. God is not jealous of the gods you make, but you are. You would save them and serve them, because you believe that they made you. You think they are your father, because you are projecting onto them the fearful fact that you made them to replace God. Yet when they seem to speak to you, remember that nothing can replace God, and whatever replacements you have attempted are nothing.

T-30.VI.9-10 - God's Son is perfect, or he cannot be God's Son. Nor will you know him, if you think he does not merit the escape from guilt in all its consequences and its forms. There is no way to think of him but this, if you would know the truth about yourself.

> I thank You, Father, for Your perfect Son,
> and in his glory will I see my own.

Here is the joyful statement that there are no forms of evil that can overcome the Will of God; the glad acknowledgement that guilt has not succeeded by your wish to make illusions real. And what is this except a simple statement of the truth?

Look on your brother with this hope in you, and you will understand he could not make an error that could change the truth in him. It is not difficult to overlook mistakes that have been given no effects. But what you see as having power to make an idol of the Son of God you will not pardon. For he has become to you <u>a graven image</u> and a sign of death. Is this your savior? Is his Father wrong about His Son? Or have you been deceived in him who has been given you to heal, for your salvation and deliverance?

W-pI.110.09 - You are as God created you. Today honor your Self. Let <u>graven images</u> you made to be the Son of God instead of what he is be worshipped not today. Deep in your mind the holy Christ in you is waiting your acknowledgment as you. And you are lost and do not know yourself while He is unacknowledged and unknown.

Bible Reference - Text

Exodus 20:16 - Thou shalt not bear false witness against thy neighbour.

Course Ref/s - Citation/s

T-05.VI.10 - You need not fear the Higher Court [the Holy Spirit] will condemn you. It will merely dismiss the case against you. There can be no case against a child of God, and every witness to guilt in God's creations is <u>bearing false witness</u> to God Himself. Appeal everything you believe gladly to God's Own Higher Court, because it speaks for Him and therefore speaks truly. It will dismiss the case against you, however carefully you have built it up. The case may be fool-proof, but it is not God-proof. The Holy Spirit will not hear it, because He can only witness truly. His verdict will always be "thine is the Kingdom," because He was given to you to remind you of what you are.

T-11.V.18 - Every brother you meet becomes a witness for Christ or for the ego, depending on what you perceive in him. Everyone convinces you of what you want to perceive, and of the reality of the kingdom you have chosen for your vigilance. Everything you perceive is a witness to the thought system you want to be true. Every brother has the power to release you, if you choose to be free. You cannot accept false witness of him unless you have evoked <u>false witnesses against him</u>. If he speaks not of Christ to you, you spoke not of Christ to him. You hear but your own voice, and if Christ speaks through you, you will hear Him.

W-pI.151.6-7 - Hear not its [ego's] voice. The witnesses it sends to prove to you its evil is your own are false, and speak with certainty of what they do not know. Your faith in them is blind because you would not share the doubts their lord can not completely vanquish. You believe to doubt his vassals is to doubt yourself.

Yet you must learn to doubt their evidence will clear the way to recognize yourself, and let the Voice for God alone be Judge of what is worthy of your own belief. He will not tell you that your brother should be judged by what your eyes behold in him, nor what his body's mouth says to your ears, nor what your fingers' touch reports of him. He passes by such idle witnesses, which merely <u>bear false witness</u> to God's Son. He recognizes only what God loves, and in the holy light of what He sees do all the ego's dreams of what you are vanish before the splendor He beholds.

Bible Reference - Text

Exodus 26:33 - And thou shalt hang up the vail under the taches, that thou mayest bring in thither within the vail the ark of the testimony: and the vail shall divide unto you between the holy place and the most holy.

Course Ref/s - Citation/s

W-pI.151.11-12 - He [the Holy Spirit] will select the elements in Them which represent the truth, and disregard Those aspects which reflect but idle dreams. And He will reinterpret all you see, and all occurrences, each circumstance, and every happening that seems to touch on you in any way from His one frame of reference, wholly unified and sure. And you will see the love beyond the hate, the constancy in change, the pure in sin, and only Heaven's blessing on the world.

Such is your resurrection, for your life is not a part of anything you see. It stands beyond the body and the world, past every witness for unholiness, within the Holy, holy as Itself. In everyone and everything His Voice would speak to you of nothing but your Self and your Creator, Who is one with Him. So will you see the holy face of Christ in everything, and hear in everything no sound except the echo of God's Voice.

C-ep.1 - Forget not once this journey is begun the end is certain. Doubt along the way will come and go and go to come again. Yet is the ending sure. No one can fail to do what God appointed him to do. When you forget, remember that you walk with Him and with His Word upon your heart. Who could despair when hope like this is his? Illusions of despair may seem to come, but learn how not to be deceived by them. Behind each one there is reality and there is God. Why would you wait for this and trade it for illusions, when His Love is but an instant farther on the road where all illusions end? The end is sure and guaranteed by God. Who stands before a lifeless image when a step away the Holy of the Holies opens up an ancient door that leads beyond the world?

C. Leviticus

Verse [19:18] from Leviticus is the only reference cited in the Course.

Bible Reference - Text

Leviticus 19:18 - Thou shalt not avenge, nor bear any grudge against the children of thy people, but thou shalt love thy neighbour as thyself: I am the Lord.

Course Ref/s - Citation/s

T-01.I.18 - A miracle is a service. It is the maximal service you can render to another. It is a way of <u>loving your neighbor as yourself</u>. You recognize your own and your neighbor's worth simultaneously.

T-05.In.3 - You are being blessed by every beneficent thought of any of your brothers anywhere. You should want to bless them in return, out of gratitude. You need not know them individually, or they you. The light is so strong that it radiates throughout the Sonship and returns thanks to the Father for radiating His joy upon it. Only God's holy children are worthy channels of His beautiful joy, because only they are beautiful enough to hold it by sharing it. It is impossible for a child of God to <u>love his neighbor except as himself</u>. That is why the healer's prayer is: Let me know this brother as I know myself.

T-05.IV.8 - How can you who are so holy suffer? All your past except its beauty is gone, and nothing is left but a blessing. I [Jesus Christ] have saved all your kindnesses and every loving thought you ever had. I have purified them of the errors that hid their light, and kept them for you in their own perfect radiance. They are beyond destruction and beyond guilt. They came from the Holy Spirit within you, and we know what God creates is eternal. You can indeed depart in peace because <u>I have loved you as I loved myself</u>. You go with my blessing and for my blessing. Hold it and share it, that it may always be ours. I place the peace of God in your heart and in your hands, to hold and share. The heart is pure to hold it, and the hands are strong to give it. We cannot lose. My judgment is as strong as the wisdom of God, in Whose Heart and Hands we have our being. His quiet children are His blessed Sons. The Thoughts of God are with you.

T-18.V.5 - It is no dream to <u>love your brother as yourself</u>. Nor is your holy relationship a dream. All that remains of dreams within it is that it is still a special relationship. Yet it is very useful to the Holy Spirit, Who has a special function here. It will become the happy dream through which He can spread joy to thousands on thousands who believe that love is fear, not happiness. Let Him fulfil the function that He gave to your relationship by accepting it for you, and nothing will be wanting that would make of it what He would have it be.

C-ep.2 - You are a stranger here. But you belong to <u>Him Who loves you as He loves Himself</u>. Ask but my help to roll the stone away, and it is done according to His Will. We have begun the journey. Long ago the end was written in the stars and set into the Heavens with a shining Ray that held it safe within eternity and through all time as well. And holds it still; unchanged, unchanging and unchangeable.

D. Numbers

Verses [6:25-26] from Leviticus are the only reference cited in the Course.

Bible Reference - Text

Numbers 25:25-26 - The Lord make his face shine upon thee, and be gracious unto thee: The Lord lift up his countenance upon thee, and give thee peace.

Course Ref/s - Citation/s

T-04.IV.9 - You are a mirror of truth, in which God Himself shines in perfect light. To the ego's dark glass you need but say, "I will not look there because I know these images are not true." Then let the Holy One shine on you in peace, knowing that this and only this must be. His Mind shone on you in your creation and brought your mind into being. His Mind still shines on you and must shine through you. Your ego cannot prevent Him from shining on you, but it can prevent you from letting Him shine through you.

T-14.II.4 - Like you, the Holy Spirit did not make truth. Like God, He knows it to be true. He brings the light of truth into the darkness, and lets it shine on you. And as it shines your brothers see it, and realizing that this light is not what you have made, they see in you more than you see. They will be happy learners of the lesson this light brings to them, because it teaches them release from nothing and from all the works of nothing. The heavy chains that seem to bind them to despair they do not see as nothing, until you bring the light to them. And then they see the chains have disappeared, and so they must have been nothing. And you will see it with them. Because you taught them gladness and release, they will become your teachers in release and gladness.

E. Deuteronomy

There are three references from Deuteronomy cited in the Course. They are:

[5:26], [**31:6**] and [**33:27**].

Bible Reference - Text

Deuteronomy 5:26 - For who is there of all flesh, that hath heard the voice of the living God speaking out of the midst of the fire, as we have, and lived?

Course Ref/s - Citation/s

T-04.IV.11 - I do not attack your ego. I do work with your higher mind, the home of the Holy Spirit, whether you are asleep or awake, just as your ego does with your lower mind, which is its home. I am your vigilance in this, because you are too confused to recognize your own hope. I am not mistaken. Your mind will elect to join with mine, and together we are invincible. You and your brother will yet come together in my name, and your sanity will be restored. I raised the dead by knowing that life is an eternal attribute of everything that the living God created. Why do you believe it is harder for me to inspire the dis-spirited or to stabilize the unstable? I do not believe that there is an order of difficulty in miracles; you do. I have called and you will answer. I understand that miracles are natural, because they are expressions of love. My calling you is as natural as your answer, and as inevitable.

T-07.VII.5 - The gift of life is yours to give, because it was given you. You are unaware of your gift because you do not give it. You cannot make nothing live, since nothing cannot be enlivened. Therefore, you are not extending the gift you both have and are, and so you do not know your being. All confusion comes from not extending life, because that is not the Will of your Creator. You can do nothing apart from Him, and you do do nothing apart from Him. Keep His way to remember yourself, and teach His way lest you forget yourself. Give only honor to the Sons of the living God, and count yourself among them gladly.

T-18.I.8 - When you seem to see some twisted form of the original error rising to frighten you, say only, "God is not fear, but Love," and it will disappear. The truth will save you. It has not left you, to go out into the mad world and so depart from you. Inward is sanity; insanity is outside you. You but believe it is the other way; that truth is outside, and error and guilt within. Your little, senseless substitutions, touched with insanity and swirling lightly off on a mad course like feathers dancing insanely in the wind, have no substance. They fuse and merge and separate, in shifting and totally meaningless patterns that need not be judged at all. To judge them individually is pointless. Their tiny differences in form are no real differences at all. None of them matters. That they have in common and nothing else. Yet what else is necessary to make them all the same? Let them all go, dancing in the wind, dipping and turning till they disappear from sight, far, far outside of you. And turn you to the stately calm within, where in holy stillness dwells the living God you never left, and Who never left you. The Holy Spirit takes you gently by the hand, and retraces with you your mad journey outside yourself, leading you gently back to the truth and safety within. He brings all your insane projections and the wild substitutions that you have placed outside you to the truth. Thus He reverses the course of insanity and restores you to reason.

T-26.IX.8 - Now is the temple of the living God rebuilt as host again to Him by Whom it was created. Where He dwells, His Son dwells with Him, never separate. And They give thanks that They are welcome made at last. Where stood a cross stands now the risen Christ, and ancient scars are healed within His sight. An ancient miracle has come to bless and to replace an ancient enmity that came to kill. In gentle gratitude do God the Father and the Son return to what is Theirs, and will forever be. Now is the Holy Spirit's purpose done. For They have come! For They have come at last!

T-29.II.6 - Such is the promise of the living God; His Son have life and every living thing be part of him, and nothing else have life. What you have given "life" is not alive, and symbolizes but your wish to be alive apart from life, alive in death, with death perceived as life, and living, death. Confusion follows on confusion here, for on confusion has this world been based, and there is nothing else it rests upon. Its basis does not change, although it seems to be in constant change. Yet what is that except the state confusion really means? Stability to those who are confused is meaningless, and shift and change become the law on which they predicate their lives.

Bible Reference - Text

Deuteronomy 31:6 - Be strong and of a good courage, fear not, nor be afraid of them: for the Lord thy God, he it is that doth go with thee; he will not fail thee, nor forsake thee.

Course Ref/s - Citation/s

T-24.In.1 - Forget not that the motivation for this course [A Course in Miracles] is the attainment and the keeping of the state of peace. Given this state the mind is quiet, and the condition in which God is remembered is attained. It is not necessary to tell Him what to do. <u>He will not fail</u>. Where He can enter, there He is already. And can it be He cannot enter where He wills to be? Peace will be yours because it is His Will. Can you believe a shadow can hold back the Will that holds the universe secure? God does not wait upon illusions to let Him be Himself. No more His Son. They are. And what illusion that idly seems to drift between them has the power to defeat what is Their Will?

Bible Reference - Text

Deuteronomy 33:27 - The eternal God is thy refuge, and underneath are the everlasting arms: and he shall thrust out the enemy from before thee; and shall say, Destroy them.

Course Ref/s - Citation/s

T-20.VI.10 - The holy relationship reflects the true relationship the Son of God has with his Father in reality. The Holy Spirit rests within it in the certainty it will endure forever. Its firm foundation is eternally upheld by truth, and love shines on it with the gentle smile and tender blessing it offers to its own. Here the unholy instant is exchanged in gladness for the holy one of safe return. Here is the way to true relationships held gently open, through which you and your brother walk together, leaving the body thankfully behind and resting in the <u>Everlasting Arms</u>. Love's Arms are open to receive you, and give you peace forever.

F. Joshua

There is only one reference from Joshua cited in the Course. It is verse [6:20].

Bible Reference - Text

Joshua 6:20 - So the people shouted when the priests blew with the trumpets: and it came to pass, when the people heard the sound of the trumpet, and the people shouted with a great shout, that the wall fell down flat, so that the people went up into the city, every man straight before him, and they took the city.

Course Ref/s - Citation/s

M-25.2 - Certainly there are many "psychic" powers that are clearly in line with this course. Communication is not limited to the small range of channels the world recognizes. If it were, there would be little point in trying to teach salvation. It would be impossible to do so. The limits the world places on communication are the chief barriers to direct experience of the Holy Spirit, Whose Presence is always there and Whose Voice is available but for the hearing. These limits are placed out of fear, for without them <u>the walls that surround all the separate places of the world would fall</u> at the holy sound of His Voice. Who transcends these limits in any way is merely becoming more natural. He is doing nothing special, and there is no magic in his accomplishments.

G. 1 Kings

There is only one reference from 1 Kings cited in the Course. It is verse [19:12-13].

Bible Reference - Text

1 Kings 19:12-13 - And after the earthquake a fire; but the Lord was not in the fire: and after the fire a still small voice. And it was so, when Elijah heard it, that he wrapped his face in his mantle, and went out, and stood in the entering in of the cave. And, behold, there came a voice unto him, and said, What doest thou here, Elijah?

Course Ref/s - Citation/s

T-21.V.1 - Perception selects, and makes the world you see. It literally picks it out as the mind directs. The laws of size and shape and brightness would hold, perhaps, if other things were equal. They are not equal. For what you look for you are far more likely to discover than what you would prefer to overlook. The still, small Voice for God is not drowned out by all the ego's raucous screams and senseless ravings to those who want to hear It. Perception is a choice and not a fact. But on this choice depends far more than you may realize as yet. For on the voice you choose to hear, and on the sights you choose to see, depends entirely your whole belief in what you are. Perception is a witness but to this, and never to reality. Yet it can show you the conditions in which awareness of reality is possible, or those where it could never be.

T-31.I.5-6 - Learning is an ability you made and gave yourself. It was not made to do the Will of God, but to uphold a wish that it could be opposed, and that a will apart from it was yet more real than it. And this has learning sought to demonstrate, and you have learned what it was made to teach. Now does your ancient over-learning stand implacable before the Voice of truth, and teach you that Its lessons are not true; too hard to learn, too difficult to see, and too opposed to what is really true. Yet you will learn them, for their learning is the only purpose for your learning skill the Holy Spirit sees in all the world. His simple lessons in forgiveness have a power mightier than yours, because they call from God and from your Self to you.

Is this <u>a little Voice, so small and still</u> It cannot rise above the senseless noise of sounds that have no meaning? God willed not His Son forget Him. And the power of His Will is in the Voice that speaks for Him. Which lesson will you learn? What outcome is inevitable, sure as God, and far beyond all doubt and question? Can it be your little learning, strange in outcome and incredible in difficulty will withstand the simple lessons being taught to you in every moment of each day, since time began and learning had been made?

H. Job

There are two references cited in the Course from the Book of Job. They are:

> [**2:9**] and [**19:25**].

Bible Reference - Text

Job 2:9 - Then said his wife unto him, Dost thou still retain thine integrity? curse God, and die.

Course Ref/s - Citation/s

T-24.III.7 - The special ones are all asleep, surrounded by a world of loveliness they do not see. Freedom and peace and joy stand there, beside the bier on which they sleep, and call them to come forth and waken from their dream of death. Yet they hear nothing. They are lost in dreams of specialness. They hate the call that would awaken them, and they curse God because He did not make their dream reality. Curse God and die, but not by Him Who made not death; but only in the dream. Open your eyes a little; see the savior God gave to you that you might look on him, and give him back his birthright. It is yours.

Bible Reference - Text

Job 19:5 - For I know that my redeemer liveth, and that he shall stand at the latter day upon the earth:

Course Ref/s - Citation/s

T-11.VI.9 - You will awaken to your own call, for the Call to awake is within you. If I live in you, you are awake. Yet you must see the works I do through you, or you will not perceive that I have done them unto you. Do not set limits on what you believe I can do through you, or you will not accept what I can do for you. Yet it is done already, and unless you give all that you have received you will not know that your Redeemer liveth, and that you have awakened with him. Redemption is recognized only by sharing it.

T-12.II.9- You who have tried to banish love have not succeeded, but you who choose to banish fear must succeed. The Lord is with you, but you know it not. Yet your <u>Redeemer liveth,</u> and abideth in you in the peace out of which He was created. Would you not exchange this awareness for the awareness of fear? When we have overcome fear—not by hiding it, not by minimizing it, and not by denying its full import in any way—this is what you will really see. You cannot lay aside the obstacles to real vision without looking upon them, for to lay aside means to judge against. If you will look, the Holy Spirit will judge, and He will judge truly. Yet He cannot shine away what you keep hidden, for you have not offered it to Him and He cannot take it from you.

I. Psalms

The following are the references from the Book of Psalms which are cited in the Course:

[8:4], [16:10], [23:1-3], [23:4], [23:6], [37:20], [40:8], [46:1], [46:7], [46:10], [62:1-2], [89:46], [121:1], [139:5], [149:6] and [150:1-6].

Bible Reference - Text

Psalms 8:4 - What is man, that thou art mindful of him? and the son of man, that thou visitest him?

Course Ref/s - Citation/s

T-20.V.8 - Be comforted, and feel the Holy Spirit watching over you in love and perfect confidence in what He sees. He knows the Son of God, and shares his Father's certainty the universe rests in his gentle hands in safety and in peace. Let us consider now what he must learn, to share his Father's confidence in him. <u>What is he</u>, that the Creator of the universe should offer it to him and know it rests in safety? He looks upon himself not as his Father knows him. And yet it is impossible the confidence of God should be misplaced.

Bible Reference - Text

Psalms 16:10 - For thou wilt not leave my soul in hell; neither wilt thou suffer thine Holy One to see corruption.

Course Ref/s - Citation/s

T-04.III.7 - It has never really entered your mind to give up every idea you ever had that opposes knowledge. You retain thousands of little scraps of fear that prevent the <u>Holy One</u> from entering. Light cannot penetrate through the walls you make to block it, and it is forever unwilling to destroy what you have made. No one can see through a wall, but I [Jesus] can step around it. Watch your mind for the scraps of fear, or you will be unable to ask me to do so. I can help you only as our Father created us. I will love you and honor you and maintain complete respect for what you have made, but I will not uphold it unless it is true. I will never forsake you any more than God will, but I must wait as long as you choose to forsake yourself. Because I wait in love and not in impatience, you will surely ask me truly. I will come in response to a single unequivocal call.

T-04.III.8 - Watch carefully and see what it is you are really asking for. Be very honest with yourself in this, for we must hide nothing from each other. If you will really try to do this, you have taken the first step toward preparing your mind for the Holy One to enter. We will prepare for this together, for once He has come, you will be ready to help me to make other minds ready for Him. How long will you deny Him His Kingdom?

T-04.IV.9 - You are a mirror of truth, in which God Himself shines in perfect light. To the ego's dark glass you need but say, "I will not look there because I know these images are not true." Then let the Holy One shine on you in peace, knowing that this and only this must be. His Mind shone on you in your creation and brought your mind into being. His Mind still shines on you and must shine through you. Your ego cannot prevent Him from shining on you, but it can prevent you from letting Him shine through you.

T-04.VI.6 - My [Jesus'] trust in you is greater than yours in me at the moment, but it will not always be that way. Your mission is very simple. You are asked to live so as to demonstrate that you are not an ego, and I do not choose God's channels wrongly. The Holy One shares my trust, and accepts my Atonement decisions because my will is never out of accord with His. I have said before that I am in charge of the Atonement. This is only because I completed my part in it as a man, and can now complete it through others. My chosen channels cannot fail, because I will lend them my strength as long as theirs is wanting.

T-04.VI.7 - I will go with you to the Holy One, and through my perception He can bridge the little gap. Your gratitude to your brother is the only gift I want. I will bring it to God for you, knowing that to know your brother is to know God. If you are grateful to your brother, you are grateful to God for what He created. Through your gratitude you come to know your brother, and one moment of real recognition makes everyone your brother because each of them is of your Father. Love does not conquer all things, but it does set all things right. Because you are the Kingdom of God I can lead you back to your own creations. You do not recognize them now, but what has been dissociated is still there.

Bible Reference - Text

Psalms 16:10 - For thou wilt not leave my soul in hell; neither wilt thou suffer thine Holy One to see corruption. (Continued)

Course Ref/s - Citation/s

T-23.I.11 - How can the resting place of God turn on itself, and seek to overcome the One Who dwells there? And think what happens when the house of God perceives itself divided. The altar disappears, the light grows dim, the temple of the Holy One becomes a house of sin. And nothing is remembered except illusions. Illusions can conflict, because their forms are different. And they do battle only to establish which form is true.

T-24.III.6 - Forgive the great Creator of the universe, the Source of life, of love and holiness, the perfect Father of a perfect Son, for your illusions of your specialness. Here is the hell you chose to be your home. He chose not this for you. Ask not He enter this. The way is barred to love and to salvation. Yet if you would release your brother from the depths of hell, you have forgiven Him Whose Will it is you rest forever in the arms of peace, in perfect safety, and without the heat and malice of one thought of specialness to mar your rest. Forgive the Holy One the specialness He could not give, and that you made instead.

W-pI.157.8-9 - Today we will embark upon a course [A Course in Miracles] you have not dreamed of. But the Holy One, the Giver of the happy dreams of life, Translator of perception into truth, the holy Guide to Heaven given you, has dreamed for you this journey which you make and start today, with the experience this day holds out to you to be your own.

Into Christ's Presence will we enter now, serenely unaware of everything except His shining face and perfect Love. The vision of His face will stay with you, but there will be an instant which transcends all vision, even this, the holiest. This you will never teach, for you attained it not through learning. Yet the vision speaks of your remembrance of what you knew that instant, and will surely know again.

W-pII.322.1 - I sacrifice illusions; nothing more. And as illusions go I find the gifts illusions tried to hide, awaiting me in shining welcome, and in readiness to give God's ancient messages to me. His memory abides in every gift that I receive of Him. And every dream serves only to conceal the Self which is God's only Son, the likeness of Himself, the Holy One Who still abides in Him forever, as He still abides in me.

Bible Reference - Text

Psalms 23:1-3 - The Lord is my shepherd; I shall not want. He maketh me to lie down in green pastures: he leadeth me beside the still waters. He restoreth my soul: he leadeth me in the paths of righteousness for his name's sake.

Course Ref/s - Citation/s

T-14.III.19 - Whenever you are in doubt what you should do, think of His Presence [the Holy Spirit] in you, and tell yourself this, and only this: He leadeth me and knows the way, which I know not. Yet He will never keep from me what He would have me learn. And so I trust Him to communicate to me all that He knows for me. Then let Him teach you quietly how to perceive your guiltlessness, which is already there.

T-19.IV.D.17 - Give faith to your brother, for faith and hope and mercy are yours to give. Into the hands that give, the gift is given. Look on your brother, and see in him the gift of God you would receive. It is almost Easter, the time of resurrection. Let us give redemption to each other and share in it, that we may rise as one in resurrection, not separate in death. Behold the gift of freedom that I gave the Holy Spirit for you. And be you and your brother free together, as you offer to the Holy Spirit this same gift. And giving it, receive it of Him in return for what you gave. He leadeth you and me together, that we might meet here in this holy place, and make the same decision.

Bible Reference - Text

Psalms 23:4 - Yea, though I walk through the valley of the shadow of death, I will fear no evil: for thou art with me; thy rod and thy staff they comfort me.

Course Ref/s - Citation/s

T-23.In.3 - Walk you in glory, with your head held high, and <u>fear no evil</u>. The innocent are safe because they share their innocence. Nothing they see is harmful, for their awareness of the truth releases everything from the illusion of harmfulness. And what seemed harmful now stands shining in their innocence, released from sin and fear and happily returned to love. They share the strength of love because they looked on innocence.
And every error disappeared because they saw it not. Who looks for glory finds it where it is. Where could it be but in the innocent?

T-27.I.1 - The wish to be unfairly treated is a compromise attempt that would combine attack and innocence. Who can combine the wholly incompatible, and make a unity of what can never join? Walk you the gentle way, and you <u>will fear no evil</u> and no shadows in the night.
But place no terror symbols on your path, or you will weave a crown of thorns from which your brother and yourself will not escape. You cannot crucify yourself alone. And if you are unfairly treated, he must suffer the unfairness that you see. You cannot sacrifice yourself alone. For sacrifice is total. If it could occur at all it would entail the whole of God's creation, and the Father with the sacrifice of His beloved Son.

Bible Reference - Text

Psalms 23:6 - Surely goodness and mercy shall follow me all the days of my life: and I will dwell in the house of the Lord for ever.

Course Ref/s - Citation/s

T-13.I.6 - When you have accepted the Atonement for yourself, you will realize there is no guilt in God's Son. And only as you look upon him as guiltless can you understand his oneness. For the idea of guilt brings a belief in condemnation of one by another, projecting separation in place of unity. You can condemn only yourself, and by so doing you cannot know that you are God's Son. You have denied the condition of his being, which is his perfect blamelessness. Out of love he was created, and in love he abides. <u>Goodness and mercy have always followed</u> him, for he has always extended the Love of his Father.

Bible Reference - Text

Psalms 37:20 - But the wicked shall perish, and the enemies of the Lord shall be as the fat of lambs: they shall consume; into smoke shall they consume away.

Course Ref/s - Citation/s

T-05.VI.9 - "<u>The wicked shall perish</u>" becomes a statement of Atonement, if the word "perish" is understood as "be undone." Every loveless thought must be undone, a word the ego cannot even understand. To the ego, to be undone means to be destroyed. The ego will not be destroyed because it is part of your thought, but because it is uncreative and therefore unsharing, it will be reinterpreted to release you from fear. The part of your mind that you have given to the ego will merely return to the Kingdom, where your whole mind belongs. You can delay the completion of the Kingdom, but you cannot introduce the concept of fear into it.

Bible Reference - Text

Psalms 40:8 - I delight to do thy will, O my God: yea, thy law is within my heart.

Course Ref/s - Citation/s

T-1.VII.1 - Your distorted perceptions produce a dense cover over miracle impulses, making it hard for them to reach your own awareness. The confusion of miracle impulses with physical impulses is a major perceptual distortion. Physical impulses are misdirected miracle impulses. All real pleasure comes from <u>doing God's Will</u>. This is because not doing it is a denial of Self. Denial of Self results in illusions, while correction of the error brings release from it. Do not deceive yourself into believing that you can relate in peace to God or to your brothers with anything external.

Bible Reference - Text

Psalms 46:1 - God is our refuge and strength, a very present help in trouble.

Course Ref/s - Citation/s

W-pII.261.1 - I will identify with what I think is refuge and security. I will behold myself where I perceive my strength, and think I live within the citadel where I am safe and cannot be attacked. Let me today seek not security in danger, nor attempt to find my peace in murderous attack. I live in God. In Him I find <u>my refuge and my strength</u>. In Him is my Identity. In Him is everlasting peace. And only there will I remember Who I really am.

Bible Reference - Text

Psalms 46:7 - The Lord of hosts is with us; the God of Jacob is our refuge. Selah.

Course Ref/s - Citation/s

W-pI.rIV.5:2-6:4 - Open your mind, and clear it of all thoughts that would deceive, and let this thought alone engage it fully, and remove the rest:

> My mind holds only what I think with God.

Five minutes with this thought will be enough to set the day along the lines which God appointed, and to place His Mind in charge of all the thoughts you will receive that day.

They will not come from you alone, for they will all be shared with Him. And so each one will bring the message of His Love to you, returning messages of yours to Him. So will communion with <u>the Lord of Hosts</u> be yours, as He Himself has willed it be. And as His Own completion joins with Him, so will He join with you who are complete as you unite with Him, and He with you.

Bible Reference - Text

Psalms 46:10 - Be still, and know that I am God: I will be exalted among the heathen, I will be exalted in the earth.

Course Ref/s - Citation/s

T-04.I.8 - The ego tries to exploit all situations into forms of praise for itself in order to overcome its doubts. It will remain doubtful as long as you believe in its existence. You who made it cannot trust it, because in your right mind you realize it is not real. The only sane solution is not to try to change reality, which is indeed a fearful attempt, but to accept it as it is. You are part of reality, which stands unchanged beyond the reach of your ego but within easy reach of spirit. When you are afraid, <u>be still and know that God</u> is real, and you are His beloved Son in whom He is well pleased. Do not let your ego dispute this, because the ego cannot know what is as far beyond its reach as you are.

T-04.In.2 - You can speak from the spirit or from the ego, as you choose. If you speak from spirit you have chosen to "<u>Be still and know that I am God</u>." These words are inspired because they reflect knowledge. If you speak from the ego you are disclaiming knowledge instead of affirming it, and are thus dis-spiriting yourself. Do not embark on useless journeys, because they are indeed in vain. The ego may desire them, but spirit cannot embark on them because it is forever unwilling to depart from its Foundation.

T-13.X.11 - You cannot enter into real relationships with any of God's Sons unless you love them all and equally. Love is not special. If you single out part of the Sonship for your love, you are imposing guilt on all your relationships and making them unreal. You can love only as God loves. Seek not to love unlike Him, for there is no love apart from His. Until you recognize that this is true, you will have no idea what love is like. No one who condemns a brother can see himself as guiltless and in the peace of God. If he is guiltless and in peace and sees it not, he is delusional, and has not looked upon himself. To him I say,

Behold the Son of God, and look upon his purity and <u>be still</u>. In quiet look upon his holiness, and offer thanks unto his Father that no guilt has ever touched him.

T-29.V.3-4 - Here is the role the Holy Spirit gives to you who wait upon the Son of God, and would behold him waken and be glad. He is a part of you and you of him, because he is his Father's Son, and not for any purpose you may see in him. Nothing is asked of you but to accept the changeless and eternal that abide in him, for your Identity is there. The peace in you can but be found in him. And every thought of love you offer him but brings you nearer to your wakening to peace eternal and to endless joy.

This sacred Son of God is like yourself; the mirror of his Father's Love for you, the soft reminder of his Father's Love by which he was created and which still abides in him as it abides in you. <u>Be very still</u> and hear God's Voice in him, and let It tell you what his function is. He was created that you might be whole, for only the complete can be a part of God's completion, which created you.

T-31.I.12 - Let us <u>be still</u> an instant, and forget all things we ever learned, all thoughts we had, and every preconception that we hold of what things mean and what their purpose is. Let us remember not our own ideas of what the world is for. We do not know. Let every image held of everyone be loosened from our minds and swept away.

T-31.II.6:2-7:6 - The answer that I give my brother is what I am asking for. And what I learn of him is what I learn about myself.

Then let us wait an instant and <u>be still</u>, forgetting everything we thought we heard; remembering how much we do not know. This brother neither leads nor follows us, but walks beside us on the selfsame road. He is like us, as near or far away from what we want as we will let him be. We make no gains he does not make with us, and we fall back if he does not advance. Take not his hand in anger but in love, for in his progress do you count your own. And we go separately along the way unless you keep him safely by your side.

Because he is your equal in God's Love, you will be saved from all appearances and answer to the Christ Who calls to you. Be still and listen. Think not ancient thoughts. Forget the dismal lessons that you learned about this Son of God who calls to you. Christ calls to all with equal tenderness, seeing no leaders and no followers, and hearing but one answer to them all. Because He hears one Voice, he cannot hear a different answer from the one He gave when God appointed Him His only Son.

T-31.II.8 - <u>Be very still</u> an instant. Come without all thought of what you ever learned before, and put aside all images you made. The old will fall away before the new without your opposition or intent. There will be no attack upon the things you thought were precious and in need of care. There will be no assault upon your wish to hear a call that never has been made. Nothing will hurt you in this holy place, to which you come to listen silently and learn the truth of what you really want. No more than this will you be asked to learn. But as you hear it, you will understand you need but come away without the thoughts you did not want, and that were never true.

Bible Reference - Text

Psalms 46:10 - Be still, and know that I am God: I will be exalted among the heathen, I will be exalted in the earth. (Continued)

Course Ref/s - Citation/s

W-pI.049.4 - Listen in deep silence. <u>Be very still</u> and open your mind. Go past all the raucous shrieks and sick imaginings that cover your real thoughts and obscure your eternal link with God. Sink deep into the peace that waits for you beyond the frantic, riotous thoughts and sights and sounds of this insane world. You do not live here. We are trying to reach your real home. We are trying to reach the place where you are truly welcome. We are trying to reach God.

W-pI.081.1 - I am the light of the world.
How holy am I, who have been given the function of lighting up the world! Let me <u>be still</u> before my holiness. In its calm light let all my conflicts disappear. In its peace let me remember who I am.

W-pI.106.2 - Listen, and hear your Father speak to you through His appointed Voice, which silences the thunder of the meaningless, and shows the way to peace to those who cannot see. <u>Be still</u> today and listen to the truth. Be not deceived by voices of the dead, which tell you they have found the source of life and offer it to you for your belief. Attend them not, but listen to the truth.

W-pI.106.3 - Be not afraid to circumvent the voices of the world. Walk lightly past their meaningless persuasion. Hear them not. <u>Be still</u> today and listen to the truth. Go past all things which do not speak of Him Who holds your happiness within His Hand, held out to you in welcome and in love. Hear only Him today, and do not wait to reach Him longer. Hear one Voice today.

W-pI.106.7 - Thus does salvation start and thus it ends; when everything is yours and everything is given away, it will remain with you forever. And the lesson has been learned. Today we practice giving, not the way you understand it now, but as it is. Each hour's exercises should begin with this request for your enlightenment:
I will <u>be still</u> and listen to the truth.
What does it mean to give and to receive?

W-pI.106.9-10 - <u>Be still</u> and listen to the truth today. For each five minutes spent in listening, a thousand minds are opened to the truth and they will hear the holy Word you hear. And when the hour is past, you will again release a thousand more who pause to ask that truth be given them, along with you.
Today the holy Word of God is kept through your receiving it to give away, so you can teach the world what giving means by listening and learning it of Him. Do not forget today to reinforce your choice to hear and to receive the Word by this reminder, given to yourself as often as is possible today:
Let me be still and listen to the truth.
I am the messenger of God today,
My voice is His, to give what I receive.

W-pI.109.5 - In Him you have no cares and no concerns, no burdens, no anxiety, no pain, no fear of future and no past regrets. In timelessness you rest, while time goes by without its touch upon you, for your rest can never change in any way at all. You rest today. And as you close your eyes, sink into stillness. Let these periods of rest and respite reassure your mind that all its frantic fantasies were but the dreams of fever that has passed away. Let it <u>be still</u> and thankfully accept its healing. No more fearful dreams will come, now that you rest in God. Take time today to slip away from dreams and into peace.

W-pI.118.2 - Let me <u>be still</u> and listen to the truth.
Let my own feeble voice be still, and let me hear the mighty Voice for Truth Itself assure me that I am God's perfect Son.

W-pI.125.9 - Only be quiet. You will need no rule but this, to let your practicing today lift you above the thinking of the world, and free your vision from the body's eyes. Only <u>be still</u> and listen. You will hear the word in which the Will of God the Son joins in his Father's Will, at one with it, with no illusions interposed between the wholly indivisible and true. As every hour passes by today, be still a moment and remind yourself you have a special purpose for this day; in quiet to receive the Word of God.

Bible Reference - Text

Psalms 46:10 - Be still, and know that I am God: I will be exalted among the heathen, I will be exalted in the earth. (Continued)

Course Ref/s - Citation/s

W-pI.128.6-7 - Pause and <u>be still</u> a little while, and see how far you rise above the world, when you release your mind from chains and let it seek the level where it finds itself at home. It will be grateful to be free a while. It knows where it belongs. But free its wings, and it will fly in sureness and in joy to join its holy purpose. Let it rest in its Creator, there to be restored to sanity, to freedom and to love.
Give it ten minutes rest three times today. And when your eyes are opened afterwards, you will not value anything you see as much as when you looked at it before. Your whole perspective on the world will shift by just a little, every time you let your mind escape its chains. The world is not where it belongs. And you belong where it would be, and where it goes to rest when you release it from the world. Your Guide is sure. Open your mind to Him. Be still and rest.

W-pI.140.10 - So do we lay aside our amulets, our charms and medicines, our chants and bits of magic in whatever form they take. We will <u>be still</u> and listen for the Voice of healing, which will cure all ills as one, restoring saneness to the Son of God. No voice but this can cure. Today we hear a single Voice which speaks to us of truth, where all illusions end, and peace returns to the eternal, quiet home of God.

W-pI.153.10 - <u>Be still</u> a moment, and in silence think how holy is your purpose, how secure you rest, untouchable within its light. God's ministers have chosen that the truth be with them. Who is holier than they? Who could be surer that his happiness is fully guaranteed? And who could be more mightily protected? What defense could possibly be needed by the ones who are among the chosen ones of God, by His election and their own as well?

W-pI.182.ti-1 - I will <u>be still</u> an instant and go home.

This world you seem to live in is not home to you. And somewhere in your mind you know that this is true. A memory of home keeps haunting you, as if there were a place that called you to return, although you do not recognize the voice, nor what it is the voice reminds you of. Yet still you feel an alien here, from somewhere all unknown. Nothing so definite that you could say with certainty you are an exile here. Just a persistent feeling, sometimes not more than a tiny throb, at other times hardly remembered, actively dismissed, but surely to return to mind again.

W-pI.182.12 - You have not lost your innocence. It is for this you yearn. This is your heart's desire. This is the voice you hear, and this the call which cannot be denied. The holy Child remains with you. His home is yours. Today He gives you His defenselessness, and you accept it in exchange for all the toys of battle you have made. And now the way is open, and the journey has an end in sight at last. <u>Be still</u> an instant and go home with Him, and be at peace a while.

W-pI.183.8 - Repeat God's Name, and you acknowledge Him as sole Creator of reality. And you acknowledge also that His Son is part of Him, creating in His Name. Sit silently, and let His Name become the all-encompassing idea that holds your mind completely. Let all thoughts <u>be still</u> except this one. And to all other thoughts respond with this, and see God's Name replace the thousand little names you gave your thoughts, not realizing that there is one Name for all there is, and all that there will be.

W-pI.189.7 - Simply do this: <u>Be still</u>, and lay aside all thoughts of what you are and what God is; all concepts you have learned about the world; all images you hold about yourself. Empty your mind of everything it thinks is either true or false, or good or bad, of every thought it judges worthy, and all the ideas of which it is ashamed. Hold onto nothing. Do not bring with you one thought the past has taught, nor one belief you ever learned before from anything. Forget this world, forget this course, and come with wholly empty hands unto your God.

W-pI.202.1 - I will <u>be still</u> an instant and go home.
Why would I choose to stay an instant more where I do not belong, when God Himself has given me His Voice to call me home?

W-pI.208.1 - The peace of God is shining in me now.
I will <u>be still</u>, and let the earth be still along with me. And in that stillness we will find the peace of God. It is within my heart, which witnesses to God Himself.

Bible Reference - Text

Psalms 46:10 - Be still, and know that I am God: I will be exalted among the heathen, I will be exalted in the earth. (Continued)

Course Ref/s - Citation/s

W-pI.219.1 - I am not a body. I am free.
I am God's Son. Be still, my mind, and think a moment upon this. And then return to earth, without confusion as to what my Father loves forever as His Son.

W-pI.rV.In.2 - Steady our feet, our Father. Let our doubts be quiet and our holy minds be still, and speak to us. We have no words to give to You. We would but listen to Your Word, and make it ours. Lead our practicing as does a father lead a little child along a way he does not understand. Yet does he follow, sure that he is safe because his father leads the way for him.

W-pII.221.2 - Now do we wait in quiet. God is here, because we wait together. I [Jesus] am sure that He will speak to you, and you will hear. Accept my confidence, for it is yours. Our minds are joined. We wait with one intent; to hear our Father's answer to our call, to let our thoughts be still and find His peace, to hear Him speak to us of what we are, and to reveal Himself unto His Son.

W-pII.254.ti-1 - Let every voice but God's be still in me.
Father, today I would but hear Your Voice. In deepest silence I would come to You, to hear Your Voice and to receive Your Word. I have no prayer but this: I come to You to ask You for the truth. And truth is but Your Will, which I would share with You today.

W-pII.337.2 - Listen today. Be very still, and hear the gentle Voice for God assuring you that He has judged you as the Son He loves.

W-pII.358.1 - You Who remember what I really am alone remember what I really want. You speak for God, and so You speak for me. And what You give me comes from God Himself. Your Voice, my Father, then is mine as well, and all I want is what You offer me, in just the form You choose that it be mine. Let me remember all I do not know, and let my voice be still, remembering. But let me not forget Your Love and care, keeping Your promise to Your Son in my awareness always. Let me not forget myself is nothing, but my Self is all.

W-pII.In.10 - Now is the need for practice almost done. For in this final section, we will come to understand that we need only call to God, and all temptations disappear. Instead of words, we need but feel His Love. Instead of prayers, we need but call His Name. Instead of judging, we need but <u>be still</u> and let all things be healed. We will accept the way God's plan will end, as we received the way it started. Now it is complete. This year has brought us to eternity.

P-2.II.9 - Communion is impossible alone. No one who stands apart can receive Christ's vision. It is held out to him, but he cannot hold out his hand to receive it. Let him <u>be still</u> and recognize his brother's need is his own. And let him then meet his brother's need as his and see that they are met as one, for such they are. What is religion but an aid in helping him to see that this is so? And what is psychotherapy except a help in just this same direction? It is the goal that makes these processes the same, for they are one in purpose and must thus be one in means.

S-3.IV.7 - He [Christ] comes for Me [Jesus] and speaks My Word to you. I would recall My weary Son to Me from dreams of malice to the sweet embrace of everlasting Love and perfect peace. My Arms are open to the Son I love, who does not understand that he is healed, and that his prayers have never ceased to sing his joyful thanks in unison with all creation, in the holiness of Love. <u>Be still</u> an instant. ⁵Underneath the sounds of harsh and bitter striving and defeat there is a Voice that speaks to you of Me. Hear this an instant and you will be healed. Hear this an instant and you have been saved.

Bible Reference - Text

Psalms 62:1-2 - Truly my soul waiteth upon God: from him cometh my salvation. He only is my rock and my salvation; he is my defence; I shall not be greatly moved.

Course Ref/s - Citation/s

W-pI.71.6:4-7:4 - <u>Only God's plan for salvation</u> will work. There can be no real conflict about this, because there is no possible alternative to God's plan that will save you. His is the only plan that is certain in its outcome. His is the only plan that must succeed.

Let us practice recognizing this certainty today. And let us rejoice that there is an answer to what seems to be a conflict with no resolution possible. All things are possible to God. Salvation must be yours because of His plan, which cannot fail.

Bible Reference - Text

Psalms 89:46 - How long, Lord? wilt thou hide thyself for ever? shall thy wrath burn like fire?

Course Ref/s - Citation/s

W-pII.4.5 - How long, O Son of God, will you maintain the game of sin? Shall we not put away these sharp-edged children's toys? How soon will you be ready to come home? Perhaps today? There is no sin. Creation is unchanged. Would you still hold return to Heaven back? How long, O holy Son of God, how long?

Bible Reference - Text

Psalms 121:1 - I will lift up mine eyes unto the hills, from whence cometh my help.

Course Ref/s - Citation/s

T-20.II.8 - Your chosen home is on the other side, beyond the veil. It has been carefully prepared for you, and it is ready to receive you now.
You will not see it with the body's eyes. Yet all you need you have. Your home has called to you since time began, nor have you ever failed entirely to hear. You heard, but knew not how to look, nor where. And now you know. In you the knowledge lies, ready to be unveiled and freed from all the terror that kept it hidden. There is no fear in love. The song of Easter is the glad refrain the Son of God was never crucified. Let us lift up our eyes together, not in fear but faith. And there will be no fear in us, for in our

vision will be no illusions; only a pathway to the open door of Heaven, the home we share in quietness and where we live in gentleness and peace, as one together.

Bible Reference - Text

Psalms 139:5 - Thou hast beset me behind and before, and laid thine hand upon me.

Course Ref/s - Citation/s

W-pII.264.ti-1 - I am surrounded by the Love of God.

Father, You stand <u>before me and behind</u>, beside me, in the place I see myself, and everywhere I go. You are in all the things I look upon, the sounds I hear, and every hand that reaches for my own. In You time disappears, and place becomes a meaningless belief. For what surrounds Your Son and keeps him safe is Love itself. There is no Source but this, and nothing is that does not share its holiness; that stands beyond Your one creation, or without the Love which holds all things within itself. Father, Your Son is like Yourself. We come to You in Your Own Name today, to be at peace within Your everlasting Love.

Bible Reference - Text

Psalms 149:6 - Let the high praises of God be in their mouth, and a two-edged sword in their hand;

Course Ref/s - Citation/s

T-2.II.4.8 - The Atonement is the only defense that cannot be used destructively because it is not a device you made. The Atonement principle was in effect long before the Atonement began. The principle was love and the Atonement was an act of love. Acts were not necessary before the separation, because belief in space and time did not exist. It was only after the separation that the Atonement and the conditions necessary for its fulfillment were planned. Then a defense so splendid was needed that it

I. Psalms

could not be misused, although it could be refused. Refusal could not, however, turn it into a weapon of attack, which is the inherent characteristic of other defenses. The Atonement thus becomes the only defense that is not <u>a two-edged sword</u>. It can only heal.

Bible Reference - Text

Psalms 150:1-6 - Praise ye the Lord. Praise God in his sanctuary: praise him in the firmament of his power. Praise him for his mighty acts: praise him according to his excellent greatness. Praise him with the sound of the trumpet: praise him with the psaltery and harp. Praise him with the timbrel and dance: praise him with stringed instruments and organs. Praise him upon the loud cymbals: praise him upon the high sounding cymbals. Let every thing that hath breath praise the Lord. Praise ye the Lord.

Course Ref/s - Citation/s

T-04.VII.6 - <u>The Bible repeatedly states that you should praise God</u>. This hardly means that you should tell Him how wonderful He is. He has no ego with which to accept such praise, and no perception with which to judge it. But unless you take your part in the creation, His joy is not complete because yours is incomplete. And this He does know. He knows it in His Own Being and its experience of His Son's experience. The constant going out of His Love is blocked when His channels are closed, and He is lonely when the minds He created do not communicate fully with Him.

T-13.X.14 - Praise be to you who make the Father one with His Own Son. Alone we are all lowly, but together we shine with brightness so intense that none of us alone can even think of it. Before the glorious radiance of the Kingdom guilt melts away, and transformed into kindness will never more be what it was. Every reaction you experience will be so purified that it is fitting as a hymn of <u>praise unto your Father</u>. See only praise of Him in what He has created, for He will never cease His praise of you. United in this praise we stand before the gates of Heaven where we will surely enter in our sinlessness. God loves you. Could I [Jesus], then, lack faith in you and love Him perfectly?

J. Proverbs

There are two references from the book of Proverbs cited in the Course; they are verses [10:2] and [**23:7**].

Bible Reference - Text

Proverbs 10:2 - Treasures of wickedness profit nothing: but righteousness delivereth from death.

Course Ref/s - Citation/s

T-12.VI.1 - The ego is trying to teach you how to gain the whole world and lose your own soul. The Holy Spirit teaches that you cannot lose your soul and there is no gain in the world, for of itself it <u>profits nothing</u>. To invest without profit is surely to impoverish yourself, and the overhead is high. Not only is there no profit in the investment, but the cost to you is enormous. For this investment costs you the world's reality by denying yours, and gives you nothing in return. You cannot sell your soul, but you can sell your awareness of it. You cannot perceive your soul, but you will not know it while you perceive something else as more valuable.

W-pI.182.11 - Take time today to lay aside your shield which <u>profits nothing</u>, and lay down the spear and sword you raised against an enemy without existence. Christ has called you friend and brother. He has even come to ask your help in letting Him go home today, completed and completely. He has come as does a little child, who must beseech his father for protection and for love. He rules the universe, and yet He asks unceasingly that you return with Him, and take illusions as your gods no more.

Bible Reference - Text

Proverbs 23:7 - For as he thinketh in his heart, so is he: Eat and drink, saith he to thee; but his heart is not with thee.

Course Ref/s - Citation/s

T-1.III.2 - "Heaven and earth shall pass away" means that they will not continue to exist as separate states. My word, which is the resurrection and the life, shall not pass away because life is eternal. You are the work of God, and His work is wholly loveable and wholly loving. <u>This is how a man must think of himself in his heart, because this is what he is.</u>

T-21.In.1 - Projection makes perception. The world you see is what you gave it, nothing more than that. But though it is no more than that, it is not less. Therefore, to you it is important. It is the witness to your state of mind, the outside picture of an inward condition. <u>As a man thinketh, so does he perceive.</u> Therefore, seek not to change the world, but choose to change your mind about the world. Perception is a result and not a cause. And that is why order of difficulty in miracles is meaningless. Everything looked upon with vision is healed and holy. Nothing perceived without it means anything. And where there is no meaning, there is chaos.

K. Ecclesiastes

There is also one reference cited from the Biblical Book Ecclesiastes that is cited in the Course. It is verse [23:13].

Bible Reference - Text

Ecclesiastes 12:13 - Let us hear the conclusion of the whole matter: Fear God, and keep his commandments: for this is the whole duty of man.

Course Ref/s - Citation/s

T-03.III.6 - Right perception is necessary before God can communicate directly to His altars, which He established in His Sons. There He can communicate His certainty, and His knowledge will bring peace without question. God is not a stranger to His Sons, and His Sons are not strangers to each other. Knowledge preceded both perception and time, and will ultimately replace them. That is the real meaning of "Alpha and Omega, the beginning and the end" and "Before Abraham was I am." Perception can and must be stabilised, but knowledge is stable. "<u>Fear God and keep His commandments</u>" becomes "Know God and accept His certainty."

L. Isaiah

The following are the references from the Book of Isaiah that are cited in the Course:

> [1:18], [9:6], [11:6], [25:8], [26:19], [37:10],
> [40:3], [45:21], [51:3], [60:1-2] and [64:4].

Bible Reference - Text

Isaiah 1:18 - Come now, and let us reason together, saith the Lord: though your sins be as scarlet, they shall be as white as snow; though they be red like crimson, they shall be as wool.

Course Ref/s - Citation/s

W-pI.134.3-4 - The major difficulty that you find in genuine forgiveness on your part is that you still believe you must forgive the truth, and not illusions. You conceive of pardon as a vain attempt to look past what is there; to overlook the truth, in an unfounded effort to deceive yourself by making an illusion true. This twisted viewpoint but reflects the hold that the idea of sin retains as yet upon your mind, as you regard yourself.

Because you think your sins are real, you look on pardon as deception. For it is impossible to think of sin as true and not believe forgiveness is a lie. Thus is forgiveness really but a sin, like all the rest. It says the truth is false, and smiles on the corrupt as if they were as blameless as the grass; <u>as white as snow</u>. It is delusional in what it thinks it can accomplish. It would see as right the plainly wrong; the loathsome as the good.

Bible Reference - Text

Isaiah 9:6 - For unto us a child is born, unto us a son is given: and the government shall be upon his shoulder: and his name shall be called Wonderful, Counsellor, The mighty God, The everlasting Father, The Prince of Peace.

Course Ref/s - Citation/s

T-15.III.8 - Is it a sacrifice to leave littleness behind, and wander not in vain? It is not sacrifice to wake to glory. But it is sacrifice to accept anything less than glory. Learn that you must be worthy of the Prince of Peace, born in you in honor of Him Whose host you are. You know not what love means because you have sought to purchase it with little gifts, thus valuing it too little to understand its magnitude. Love is not little and love dwells in you, for you are host to Him. Before the greatness that lives in you, your poor appreciation of yourself and all the little offerings you give slip into nothingness.

T-15.XI.7 - In the holy instant the condition of love is met, for minds are joined without the body's interference, and where there is communication there is peace. The Prince of Peace was born to re-establish the condition of love by teaching that communication remains unbroken even if the body is destroyed, provided that you see not the body as the necessary means of communication. And if you understand this lesson, you will realize that to sacrifice the body is to sacrifice nothing, and communication, which must be of the mind, cannot be sacrificed. Where, then, is sacrifice? The lesson I was born to teach, and still would teach to all my brothers, is that sacrifice is nowhere and love is everywhere. For communication embraces everything, and in the peace it re-establishes, love comes of itself.

T-22.VI.6 - Child of peace, the light has come to you. The light you bring you do not recognize, and yet you will remember. Who can deny himself the vision that he brings to others? And who would fail to recognize a gift he let be laid in Heaven through himself? The gentle service that you give the Holy Spirit is service to yourself. You who are now His means must love all that He loves. And what you bring is your remembrance of everything that is eternal. No trace of anything in time can long remain in a mind that serves the timeless. And no illusion can disturb the peace of a relationship that has become the means of peace.

Bible Reference - Text

Isaiah 11:6 - The wolf also shall dwell with the lamb, and the leopard shall lie down with the kid; and the calf and the young lion and the fatling together; and a little child shall lead them.

Course Ref/s - Citation/s

L. Isaiah

T-03.I.5 - I have been correctly referred to as "the lamb of God who taketh away the sins of the world," but those who represent the lamb as blood-stained do not understand the meaning of the symbol. Correctly understood, it is a very simple symbol that speaks of my innocence. The lion and the lamb lying down together symbolize that strength and innocence are not in conflict, but naturally live in peace. "Blessed are the pure in heart for they shall see God" is another way of saying the same thing. A pure mind knows the truth and this is its strength. It does not confuse destruction with innocence because it associates innocence with strength, not with weakness.

Bible Reference - Text

Isaiah 25:8 - He will swallow up death in victory; and the Lord God will wipe away tears from off all faces; and the rebuke of his people shall he take away from off all the earth: for the Lord hath spoken it.

Course Ref/s - Citation/s

T-27.I.5 - Now in the hands made gentle by His touch, the Holy Spirit lays a picture of a different you. It is a picture of a body still, for what you really are cannot be seen nor pictured. Yet this one has not been used for purpose of attack, and therefore never suffered pain at all. It witnesses to the eternal truth that you cannot be hurt, and points beyond itself to both your innocence and his. Show this unto your brother, who will see that every scar is healed, and every tear is wiped away in laughter and in love. And he will look on his forgiveness there, and with healed eyes will look beyond it to the innocence that he beholds in you. Here is the proof that he has never sinned; that nothing which his madness bid him do was ever done, or ever had effects of any kind. That no reproach he laid upon his heart was ever justified, and no attack can ever touch him with the poisoned and relentless sting of fear.

W-pI.193.9 - All things are lessons God would have you learn. He would not leave an unforgiving thought without correction, nor one thorn or nail to hurt His holy Son in any way. He would ensure his holy rest remain untroubled and serene, without a care, in an eternal home which cares for him. And He would have all tears be wiped away, with none remaining yet unshed, and none but waiting their appointed time to fall. For God has willed that laughter should replace each one, and that His Son be free again.

W-pII.10.4 - God's Final Judgment is as merciful as every step in His appointed plan to bless His Son, and call him to return to the eternal peace He shares with him. Be not afraid of love. For it alone can heal all sorrow, wipe away all tears, and gently waken from his dream of pain the Son whom God acknowledges as His. Be not afraid of this. Salvation asks you give it welcome. And the world awaits your glad acceptance, which will set it free.

W-pII.301.ti-2 - And God Himself shall wipe away all tears.

Father, unless I judge I cannot weep. Nor can I suffer pain, or feel I am abandoned or unneeded in the world. This is my home because I judge it not, and therefore is it only what You will. Let me today behold it uncondemned, through happy eyes forgiveness has released from all distortion. Let me see Your world instead of mine. And all the tears I shed will be forgotten, for their source is gone. Father, I will not judge Your world today.

God's world is happy. Those who look on it can only add their joy to it, and bless it as a cause of further joy in them. We wept because we did not understand. But we have learned the world we saw was false, and we will look upon God's world today.

Bible Reference - Text

Isaiah 26:19 - Thy dead men shall live, together with my dead body shall they arise. Awake and sing, ye that dwell in dust: for thy dew is as the dew of herbs, and the earth shall cast out the dead.

Course Ref/s - Citation/s

T-27.VI.5 - The miracle makes no distinctions in the names by which sin's witnesses are called. It merely proves that what they represent has no effects. And this it proves because its own effects have come to take their place. It matters not the name by which you called your suffering. It is no longer there. The One Who brings the miracle perceives them all as one, and called by name of fear. As fear is witness unto death, so is the miracle the witness unto life. It is a witness no one can deny, for it is the effects of life it brings. <u>The dying live, the dead arise</u>, and pain has vanished. Yet a miracle speaks not but for itself, but what it represents.

W-pI.132.8:2-4 - Today's idea [I loose the world from all I thought it was.] is true because the world does not exist. And if it is indeed your own imagining, then you can loose it from all things you ever thought it was by merely changing all the thoughts that gave it these appearances. The sick are healed as you let go all thoughts of sickness, and the <u>dead arise</u> when you let thoughts of life replace all thoughts you ever held of death.

Bible Reference - Text

Isaiah 37:10 - Thus shall ye speak to Hezekiah king of Judah, saying, Let not thy God, in whom thou trustest, deceive thee, saying, Jerusalem shall not be given into the hand of the king of Assyria.

Course Ref/s - Citation/s

M-15.3 - You who are sometimes sad and sometimes angry; who sometimes feel your just due is not given you, and your efforts meet with lack of appreciation and even contempt; give up these foolish thoughts! They are too small and meaningless to occupy your holy mind an instant longer. God's Judgment waits for you to set you free. What can the world hold out to you, regardless of your judgments on its gifts, that you would rather have? You will be judged, and judged in fairness and in honesty. <u>There is no deceit in God</u>. His promises are sure. Only remember that. His promises have guaranteed His Judgment, and His alone, will be accepted in the end. It is your function to make that end be soon. It is your, function to hold it to your heart, and offer it to all the world to keep it safe.

M-16.10 - There is no substitute for the Will of God. In simple statement, it is to this fact that the teacher of God devotes his day. Each substitute he may accept as real can but deceive him. But he is safe from all deception if he so decides. Perhaps he needs to remember, "<u>God is with me. I cannot be deceived.</u>" Perhaps he prefers other words, or only one, or none at all. Yet each temptation to accept magic as true must be abandoned through his recognition, not that it is fearful, not that it is sinful, not that it is dangerous, but merely that it is meaningless. Rooted in sacrifice and separation, two aspects of one error and no more, he merely chooses to give up all that he never had. And for this "sacrifice" is Heaven restored to his awareness.

Bible Reference - Text

Isaiah 40:3 - The voice of him that crieth in the wilderness, Prepare ye the way of the Lord, make straight in the desert a highway for our God.

Course Ref/s - Citation/s

T-20.IV.8 - You may wonder how you can be at peace when, while you are in time, there is so much that must be done before the way to peace is open. Perhaps this seems impossible to you. But ask yourself if it is possible that God would have a plan for your salvation that does not work. Once you accept His plan as the one function that you would fulfil, there will be nothing else the Holy Spirit will not arrange for you without your effort. He will go before you making straight your path, and leaving in your way no stones to trip on, and no obstacles to bar your way. Nothing you need will be denied you. Not one seeming difficulty but will melt away before you reach it. You need take thought for nothing, careless of everything except the only purpose that you would fulfil. As that was given you, so will its fulfilment be. God's guarantee will hold against all obstacles, for it rests on certainty and not contingency. It rests on you. And what can be more certain than a Son of God?

W-pI.200.9 - Let us not lose our way again today. We go to Heaven, and the path is straight. Only if we attempt to wander can there be delay, and needless wasted time on thorny byways. God alone is sure, and He will guide our footsteps. He will not desert His Son in need, nor let him stray forever from his home. The Father calls; the Son will hear. And that is all there is to what appears to be a world apart from God, where bodies have reality.

Bible Reference - Text

Isaiah 45:21 - Tell ye, and bring them near; yea, let them take counsel together: who hath declared this from ancient time? who hath told it from that time? have not I the Lord? and there is no God else beside me; a just God and a Saviour; there is none beside me.

Course Ref/s - Citation/s

T-30.VI.3:5-4:9 - Unjustified forgiveness is attack. And this is all the world can ever give. It pardons "sinners" sometimes, but remains aware that they have sinned. And so they do not merit the forgiveness that it gives.

This is the false forgiveness which the world employs to keep the sense of sin alive. And recognizing God is just, it seems impossible His pardon could be real. Thus is the fear of God the sure result of seeing pardon as unmerited. No one who sees himself as guilty can avoid the fear of God. But he is saved from this dilemma if he can forgive. The mind must think of its Creator as it looks upon itself. If you can see your brother merits pardon, you have learned forgiveness is your right as much as his. Nor will you think that God intends for you a fearful judgment that your brother does not merit. For it is the truth that you can merit neither more nor less than he.

Bible Reference - Text

Isaiah 51:3 - For the Lord shall comfort Zion: he will comfort all her waste places; and he will make her wilderness like Eden, and her desert like the garden of the Lord; joy and gladness shall be found therein, thanksgiving, and the voice of melody.

Course Ref/s - Citation/s

T-18.VIII.9 - The Thought of God surrounds your little kingdom, waiting at the barrier you built to come inside and shine upon the barren ground. See how life springs up everywhere! The desert becomes a garden, green and deep and quiet, offering rest to those who lost their way and wander in the dust. Give them a place of refuge, prepared by love for them where once a desert was. And everyone you welcome will bring love with him from Heaven for you. They enter one by one into this holy place, but they will not depart as they had come, alone. The love they brought with them will stay with them, as it will stay with you. And under its beneficence your little garden will expand, and reach out to everyone who thirsts for living water, but has grown too weary to go on alone.

Bible Reference - Text

Isaiah 60:1-2 - Arise, shine; for thy light is come, and the glory of the Lord is risen upon thee. For, behold, the darkness shall cover the earth, and gross darkness the people: but the Lord shall arise upon thee, and his glory shall be seen upon thee.

Course Ref/s - Citation/s

W-pII.237.ti-1 - Now would I be as God created me.

Today I will accept the truth about myself. I will arise in glory, and allow the light in me to shine upon the world throughout the day. I bring the world the tidings of salvation which I hear as God my Father speaks to me. And I behold the world that Christ would have me see, aware it ends the bitter dream of death; aware it is my Father's Call to me.

Bible Reference - Text

Isaiah 64:4 - For since the beginning of the world men have not heard, nor perceived by the ear, neither hath the eye seen, O God, beside thee, what he hath prepared for him that waiteth for him.

Course Ref/s - Citation/s

T-27.III.6:9-7:9 - And what will ultimately take the place of every learning aid will merely be.

Forgiveness vanishes and symbols fade, and nothing that the eyes have ever seen or ears have heard remains to be perceived. A power wholly limitless has come, not to destroy, but to receive its own. There is no choice of function anywhere. The choice you fear to lose you never had. Yet only this appears to interfere with power unlimited and single thoughts, complete and happy, without opposite. You do not know the peace of power that opposes nothing. Yet no other kind can be at all. Give welcome to the power beyond forgiveness, and beyond the world of symbols and of limitations. He would merely be, and so He merely is.

M. Jeremiah

The only reference from Jeremiah that is cited in the Course is verse [31:3].

Bible Reference - Text

Jeremiah 31:3 - The Lord hath appeared of old unto me, saying, Yea, I have loved thee with an everlasting love: therefore with lovingkindness have I drawn thee.

Course Ref/s - Citation/s

T-25.I.1 - It cannot be that it is hard to do the task that Christ appointed you to do, since it is He Who does it. And in the doing of it will you learn the body merely seems to be the means to do it. For the Mind is His. And so it must be yours. His Holiness directs the body through the mind at one with Him. And you are manifest unto your holy brother, as he to you. Here is the meeting of the holy Christ unto Himself; nor any differences perceived to stand between the aspects of His Holiness, which meet and join and raise Him to His Father, whole and pure and worthy of <u>His everlasting Love</u>.

W-pI.168.1 - God speaks to us. Shall we not speak to Him? He is not distant. He makes no attempt to hide from us. We try to hide from Him, and suffer from deception. He remains entirely accessible. He loves His Son. There is no certainty but this, yet this suffices. <u>He will love His Son forever</u>. When his mind remains asleep, He loves him still. And when his mind awakes, He loves him with a never-changing Love.

W-pII.4.4 - A madman's dreams are frightening, and sin appears indeed to terrify. And yet what sin perceives is but a childish game. The Son of God may play he has become a body, prey to evil and to guilt, with but a little life that ends in death. But all the while his Father shines on him, and <u>loves him with an everlasting Love</u> which his pretenses cannot change at all.

N. Ezekiel

There is also one reference from Ezekiel that is cited in the Course. It is verse [6:6].

Bible Reference - Text

Ezekiel 2:1 - And he said unto me, Son of man, stand upon thy feet, and I will speak unto thee.

Course Ref/s - Citation/s

T-13.II.9 -   Little child, this is not so. Your "guilty secret" is nothing, and if you will but bring it to the light, the light will dispel it. And then no dark cloud will remain between you and the remembrance of your Father, for you will remember His guiltless Son, who did not die because he is immortal. And you will see that you were redeemed with him, and have never been separated from him. In this understanding lies your remembering, for it is the recognition of love without fear. There will be great joy in Heaven on your homecoming, and the joy will be yours. For the redeemed son of man is the guiltless Son of God, and to recognize him is your redemption.

T-24.VII.9-11 - Look at yourself, and you will see a body. Look at this body in a different light and it looks different. And without a light it seems that it is gone. Yet you are reassured that it is there because you still can feel it with your hands and hear it move. Here is an image that you want to be yourself. It is the means to make your wish come true. It gives the eyes with which you look on it, the hands that feel it, and the ears with which you listen to the sounds it makes. It proves its own reality to you.

Thus is the body made a theory of yourself, with no provisions made for evidence beyond itself, and no escape within its sight. Its course is sure, when seen through its own eyes. It grows and withers, flourishes and dies. And you cannot conceive of you apart from it. You brand it sinful and you hate its acts, judging it evil. Yet your specialness whispers, "Here is my own beloved son, in whom I am well pleased." Thus does the "son" become the means to serve his "father's" purpose. Not identical, not even like, but still a means to offer to the "father" what he wants. Such is the travesty on God's creation. For as His Son's creation gave Him joy and witness to His Love and shared His purpose, so does the body testify to the idea that made it, and speak for its reality and truth.

And thus are two sons made, and both appear to walk this earth without a meeting place and no encounter. One do you perceive outside yourself, your own beloved son. The other rests within, his Father's Son, within your brother as he is in you. Their difference does not lie in how they look, nor where they go, nor even what they do. They have a different purpose. It is this that joins them to their like, and separates each from all aspects with a different purpose. The Son of God retains His Father's Will. The son of man perceives an alien will and wishes it were so. And thus does his perception serve his wish by giving it appearances of truth. Yet can perception serve another goal. It is not bound to specialness but by your choice. And it is given you to make a different choice, and use perception for a different purpose. And what you see will serve that purpose well, and prove its own reality to you.

T-25.In.2 - No one who carries Christ in him can fail to recognize Him everywhere. Except in bodies. And as long as he believes he is in a body, where he thinks he is He cannot be. And so he carries Him unknowingly, and does not make Him manifest. And thus he does not recognize Him where He is. The son of man is not the risen Christ. Yet does the Son of God abide exactly where he is, and walks with him within his holiness, as plain to see as is his specialness set forth within his body.

M-12.ti-2 - HOW MANY TEACHERS OF GOD ARE NEEDED TO SAVE THE WORLD?
1 The answer to this question is-one. One wholly perfect teacher, whose learning is complete, suffices. This one, sanctified and redeemed, becomes the Self Who is the Son of God. He who was always wholly spirit now no longer sees himself as a body, or even as in a body. Therefore he is limitless. And being limitless, his thoughts are joined with God's forever and ever. His perception of himself is based upon God's judgment, not his own. Thus does he share God's Will, and bring His Thoughts to still deluded minds. He is forever one, because he is as God created him. He has accepted Christ; and he is saved.
2 Thus does the son of man become the Son of God. It is not really a change; it is a change of mind. Nothing external alters, but everything internal now reflects only the Love of God. God can no longer be feared, for the mind sees no cause for punishment. God's teachers appear to be many, for that is what is the world's need. Yet being joined in one purpose, and one they share with God, how could they be separate from each other?

What does it matter if they then appear in many forms? Their minds are one; their joining is complete. And God works through them now as one, for that is what they are.

O. Hosea

There is also one reference from Hosea that is cited in the Course. It is verse [6:6].

Bible Reference - Text

Hosea 6:6 - For I desired mercy, and not sacrifice; and the knowledge of God more than burnt offerings.

Course Ref/s - Citation/s

T-03.I.8 - The innocence of God is the true state of the mind of His Son. In this state your mind knows God, for God is not symbolic; He is Fact. Knowing His Son as he is, you realize that the Atonement not sacrifice, is the only appropriate gift for God's altar, where nothing except perfection belongs. The understanding of the innocent is truth. That is why their altars are truly radiant.

T-15.X.5 - It is not necessary to follow fear through all the circuitous routes by which it burrows underground and hides in darkness, to emerge in forms quite different from what it is. Yet it is necessary to examine each one as long as you would retain the principle that governs all of them. When you are willing to regard them, not as separate, but as different manifestations of the same idea, and one you do not want, they go together. The idea is simply this: you believe it is possible to be host to the ego or hostage to God. This is the choice you think you have, and the decision you believe that you must make. You see no other alternatives, for you cannot accept the fact that sacrifice gets nothing. Sacrifice is so essential to your thought system that salvation apart from sacrifice means nothing to you. Your confusion of sacrifice and love is so profound that you cannot conceive of love without sacrifice. And it is this that you must look upon; sacrifice is attack, not love. If you would accept but this one idea, your fear of love would vanish. Guilt cannot last when the idea of sacrifice has been removed. For if there is sacrifice, someone must pay and someone must get. And the only question that remains is how much is the price, and for getting what.

T-31.III.7 - The innocent release in gratitude for their release. And what they see upholds their freedom from imprisonment and death. Open your mind to change, and there will be no ancient penalty exacted from your brother or yourself. For God has said there is no sacrifice that can be asked; there is no sacrifice that can be made.

P. Matthew

There are 84 references from the Gospel of Matthew which are cited in the Course. They are as follows:

[1:23], [2:1-2], [3:16-17], [4:1-11], [4:18-19],
[5:3-11], [5:5], [5:8], [5:12], [5:14],
[5:16], [5:17], [5:29], [5:39], [5:41],
[5:43-45, [5:48], [6:7-8], [6:9-13], [6:14-15],
[6:19-21], [6:24], [6:25], [6:31-32], [6:33],

[7:1-2], [7:3-5], [7:7-8], [7:9-11], [7:12],
[7:15-16], [7:21], [7:24-27], [8:21-22], [8:26],
[9:2], [9:6], [9:20-22], [10:8], [10:19-20],
[10:34], [11:3-5], [11:15], [11:21-22], [11:25],
[11:27], [11:28], [11:29], [11:30], [12:24-25],

[12:30], [13:12], [13:44-46], [16:18], [16:19],
[16:26], [16:27], [17:1-2], [17:20], [18:3],
[18:11], [18:19-20], [19:6], [19:14], [19:18-21],
[19:24-26], [20:16], [20:18-19], [20:28], [21:22],
[22:19-21], [22:29], [24:35], [25:35], [25:40],

[25:44-45], [26:14-15], [26:24], [26:26-29], [26:63-65],
[27:29], [28:2], [28:18] and [28:19-20].

Bible Reference - Text

Matthew 1:23 - Behold, a virgin shall be with child, and shall bring forth a son, and they shall call his name Emmanuel, which being interpreted is, God with us.

Course Ref/s - Citation/s

T-18.I.10 - In you there is no separation, and no substitute can keep you from your brother. Your reality was God's creation, and has no substitute. You are so firmly joined in truth that only God is there. And He would never accept something else instead of you. He loves you both, equally and as one. And as He loves you, so you are. You are not joined together in illusions, but in the Thought so holy and so perfect that illusions cannot remain to darken the holy place in which you stand together. <u>God is with you</u>, my brother. Let us join in Him in peace and gratitude, and accept His gift as our most holy and perfect reality, which we share in Him.

T-25.In.1 - The Christ in you inhabits not a body. Yet He is in you. And thus it must be that you are not within a body. What is within you cannot be outside. And it is certain that you cannot be apart from what is at the very center of your life. What gives you life cannot be housed in death. No more can you. <u>Christ is within a frame of Holiness</u> whose only purpose is that He may be made manifest to those who know Him not, that He may call to them to come to Him and see Him where they thought their bodies were. Then will their bodies melt away, that they may frame His Holiness in them.

T-25.In.2 - No one who carries Christ in him can fail to recognize Him everywhere. Except in bodies. And as long as he believes he is in a body, where he thinks he is He cannot be. And so he carries Him unknowingly, and does not make Him manifest. And thus he does not recognize Him where He is. The son of man is not the risen Christ. Yet does the <u>Son of God</u> abide exactly where he is, and <u>walks with him within his holiness</u>, as plain to see as is his specialness set forth within his body.

P-3.III.8 - Physician, healer, therapist, teacher, heal thyself. Many will come to you carrying the gift of healing, if you so elect. The Holy Spirit never refuses an invitation to enter and abide with you. He will give you endless opportunities to open the door to your salvation, for such is His function. He will also tell you exactly what your function is in every circumstance and at all times. Whoever He sends you will reach you, holding out his hand to his Friend. Let the <u>Christ in you</u> bid him welcome, for that same <u>Christ is in him</u> as well. Deny him entrance, and you have denied the Christ in you. Remember the sorrowful story of the world, and the glad tidings of salvation. Remember the plan of God for the restoration of joy and peace. And do not forget how very simple are the ways of God: You were lost in the darkness of the world until you asked for light. And then God sent His Son to give it to you.

Bible Reference - Text

Matthew 2:1-2 - Now when Jesus was born in Bethlehem of Judaea in the days of Herod the king, behold, there came wise men from the east to Jerusalem, Saying, Where is he that is born King of the Jews? For we have seen his star in the east, and are come to worship him.

Course Ref/s - Citation/s

T-15.XI.2 - The sign of Christmas is a star, a light in darkness. See it not outside yourself, but shining in the Heaven within, and accept it as the sign the time of Christ has come. He comes demanding nothing. No sacrifice of any kind, of anyone, is asked by Him. In His Presence the whole idea of sacrifice loses all meaning. For He is Host to God. And you need but invite Him in Who is there already, by recognizing that His Host is One, and no thought alien to His Oneness can abide with Him there. Love must be total to give Him welcome, for the Presence of Holiness creates the holiness that surrounds it. No fear can touch the Host Who cradles God in the time of Christ, for the Host is as holy as the perfect Innocence which He protects, and Whose power protects Him.

Bible Reference - Text

Matthew 3:16-17 - And Jesus, when he was baptized, went up straightway out of the water: and, lo, the heavens were opened unto him, and he saw the Spirit of God descending like a dove, and lighting upon him: And lo a voice from heaven, saying, This is my beloved Son, in whom I am well pleased.

Course Ref/s - Citation/s

T-04.I.8 - The ego tries to exploit all situations into forms of praise for itself in order to overcome its doubts. It will remain doubtful as long as you believe in its existence. You who made it cannot trust it, because in your right mind you realize it is not real. The only sane solution is not to try to change reality, which is indeed a fearful attempt, but to accept it as it is. You are part of reality, which stands unchanged beyond the reach of your ego but within easy reach of spirit. When you are afraid, be still and know that God is real, and you are <u>His beloved Son in whom He is well pleased</u>. Do not let your ego dispute this, because the ego cannot know what is as far beyond its reach as you are.

T-07.VII.06 - Only honor is a fitting gift for those whom God Himself created worthy of honor, and whom He honors. Give them the appreciation God accords them always, because they are <u>His beloved Sons in whom He is well pleased</u>. You cannot be apart from them because you are not apart from Him. Rest in His Love and protect your rest by loving. But love everything He created, of which you are a part, or you cannot learn of His peace and accept His gift for yourself and as yourself. You cannot know your own perfection until you have honored all those who were created like you.

T-07.VII.11 - Perceive any part of the ego's thought system as wholly insane, wholly delusional and wholly undesirable, and you have correctly evaluated all of it. This correction enables you to perceive any part of creation as wholly real, wholly perfect and wholly desirable. Wanting this only you will have this only, and giving this only you will be only this. The gifts you offer to the ego are always experienced as sacrifices, but the gifts you offer to the Kingdom are gifts to you. They will always be treasured by God because they belong to <u>His beloved Sons</u>, who belong to Him. All power and glory are yours because the Kingdom is His.

T-24.VII.9-10 - Look at yourself, and you will see a body. Look at this body in a different light and it looks different. And without a light it seems that it is gone. Yet you are reassured that it is there because you still can feel it with your hands and hear it move. Here is an image that you want to be yourself. It is the means to make your wish come true. It gives the eyes with which you look on it, the hands that feel it, and the ears with which you listen to the sounds it makes. It proves its own reality to you.

Thus is the body made a theory of yourself, with no provisions made for evidence beyond itself, and no escape within its sight. Its course is sure, when seen through its own eyes. It grows and withers, flourishes and dies. And you cannot conceive of you apart from it. You brand it sinful and you hate its acts, judging it evil. Yet your specialness whispers, "<u>Here is my own beloved son, in whom I am well pleased.</u>" Thus does the "son" become the means to serve his "father's" purpose. Not identical, not even like, but still a means to offer to the "father" what he wants. Such is the travesty on God's creation. For as His Son's creation gave Him joy and witness to His Love and shared His purpose, so does the body testify to the idea that made it, and speak for its reality and truth.

Bible Reference - Text

Matthew 3:16-17 - And Jesus, when he was baptized, went up.... (Continued) - (To read the full text of the above go to page 101.)

Course Ref/s - Citation/s

T-25.VII.4 - To justify one value that the world upholds is to deny your Father's sanity and yours. For <u>God and His beloved Son</u> do not think differently. And it is the agreement of their thought that makes the Son a co-creator with the Mind Whose Thought created him. So if he chooses to believe one thought opposed to truth, he has decided he is not his Father's Son because the Son is mad, and sanity must lie apart from both the Father and the Son. This you believe. Think not that this belief depends upon the form it takes. Who thinks the world is sane in any way, is justified in anything it thinks, or is maintained by any form of reason, believes this to be true. Sin is not real because the Father and the Son are not insane. This world is meaningless because it rests on sin. Who could create the changeless if it does not rest on truth?

T-27.I.1 - The wish to be unfairly treated is a compromise attempt that would combine attack and innocence. Who can combine the wholly incompatible, and make a unity of what can never join? Walk you the gentle way, and you will fear no evil and no shadows in the night. But place no terror symbols on your path, or you will weave a crown of thorns from which your brother and yourself will not escape. You cannot crucify yourself alone. And if you are unfairly treated, he must suffer the unfairness that you see. You cannot sacrifice yourself alone. For sacrifice is total. If it could occur at all it would entail the whole of God's creation, and the Father with the sacrifice of <u>His beloved Son</u>.

T-28.VI.6 - Let this be your agreement with each one; that you be one with him and not apart. And he will keep the promise that you make with him, because it is the one that he has made to God, as God has made to him. God keeps His promises; His Son keeps his. In his creation did his Father say, "You are beloved of Me and I of you forever. Be you perfect as Myself, for you can never be apart from Me." His Son remembers not that he replied "I will," though in that promise he was born. Yet God reminds him of it every time he does not share a promise to be sick, but lets his mind be healed and unified. His secret vows are powerless before the Will of God, Whose promises he shares. And what he substitutes is not his will, who has made promise of himself to God.

W-pII.294.ti-2 - My body is a wholly neutral thing.

I am a Son of God. And can I be another thing as well? Did God create the mortal and corruptible? What use has God's beloved Son for what must die? And yet a neutral thing does not see death, for thoughts of fear are not invested there, nor is a mockery of love bestowed upon it. Its neutrality protects it while it has a use. And afterwards, without a purpose, it is laid aside. It is not sick nor old nor hurt. It is but functionless, unneeded and cast off. Let me not see it more than this today; of service for a while and fit to serve, to keep its usefulness while it can serve, and then to be replaced for greater good.

My body, Father, cannot be Your Son. And what is not created cannot be sinful nor sinless; neither good nor bad. Let me, then, use this dream to help Your plan that we awaken from all dreams we made.

W-pII.323.ti-1 - I gladly make the "sacrifice" of fear.

Here is the only "sacrifice" You ask of Your beloved Son; You ask him to give up all suffering, all sense of loss and sadness, all anxiety and doubt, and freely let Your Love come streaming in to his awareness, healing him of pain, and giving him Your Own eternal joy. Such is the "sacrifice" You ask of me, and one I gladly make; the only "cost" of restoration of Your memory to me, for the salvation of the world.

W-pII.338.ti-1 - I am affected only by my thoughts.

It needs but this to let salvation come to all the world. For in this single thought is everyone released at last from fear. Now has he learned that no one frightens him, and nothing can endanger him. He has no enemies, and he is safe from all external things. His thoughts can frighten him, but since these thoughts belong to him alone, he has the power to change them and exchange each fear thought for a happy thought of love. He crucified himself. Yet God has planned that His beloved Son will be redeemed.

Bible Reference - Text

Matthew 3:16-17 - And Jesus, when he was baptized, went up.... (Continued) - (To read the full text of the above go to page 101.)

Course Ref/s - Citation/s

M-22.7 - Who can limit the power of God Himself? Who, then, can say which one can be healed of what, and what must remain beyond God's power to forgive? This is insanity indeed. It is not up to God's teachers to set limits upon Him, because it is not up to them to judge His Son. And to judge His Son is to limit his Father. Both are equally meaningless. Yet this will not be understood until God's teacher recognizes that they are the same mistake. Herein does he receive Atonement, for he withdraws his judgment from the Son of God, accepting him as God created him. No longer does he stand apart from God, determining where healing should be given and where it should be withheld. Now can he say with God, "This is my beloved Son, created perfect and forever so."

Bible Reference - Text

Matthew 4:1-11 - Then was Jesus led up of the Spirit into the wilderness to be tempted of the devil. And when he had fasted forty days and forty nights, he was afterward an hungred. And when the tempter came to him, he said, If thou be the Son of God, command that these stones be made bread.

But he answered and said, It is written, Man shall not live by bread alone, but by every word that proceedeth out of the mouth of God.

Then the devil taketh him up into the holy city, and setteth him on a pinnacle of the temple, And saith unto him, If thou be the Son of God, cast thyself down: for it is written,

He shall give his angels charge concerning thee: and in their hands they shall bear thee up, lest at any time thou dash thy foot against a stone.

Jesus said unto him, It is written again, Thou shalt not tempt the Lord thy God.

Again, the devil taketh him up into an exceeding high mountain, and sheweth him all the kingdoms of the world, and the glory of them; And saith unto him, All these things will I give thee, if thou wilt fall down and worship me.

Then saith Jesus unto him, Get thee hence, Satan: for it is written, Thou shalt worship the Lord thy God, and him only shalt thou serve.

Then the devil leaveth him, and, behold, angels came and ministered unto him.

Course Ref/s - Citation/s

T-04.I.13 - I will substitute for your ego if you wish, but never for your spirit. A father can safely leave a child with an elder brother who has shown himself responsible, but this involves no confusion about the child's origin. The brother can protect the child's body and his ego, but he does not confuse himself with the father because he does this. I can be entrusted with your body and your ego only because this enables you not to be concerned with them, and lets me teach you their unimportance. I could not understand their importance to you if I had not once been tempted to believe in them myself. Let us undertake to learn this lesson together so we can be free of them together. I need devoted teachers who share my aim of healing the mind. Spirit is far beyond the need of your protection or mine. Remember this: In this world you need not have tribulation because I have overcome the world. That is why you should be of good cheer.

Bible Reference - Text

Matthew 4:18-19 - And Jesus, walking by the sea of Galilee, saw two brethren, Simon called Peter, and Andrew his brother, casting a net into the sea: for they were fishers. And he saith unto them, Follow me, and I will make you fishers of men.

Course Ref/s - Citation/s

T-01.V.6:1-2 - The miracle is a sign that the mind has chosen to be led by me in Christ's service. The abundance of Christ is the natural result of choosing to <u>follow Him</u>.

T-08.IV.4 - Do you not think the world needs peace as much as you do? Do you not want to give it to the world as much as you want to receive it? For unless you do, you will not receive it. If you want to have it of me, you must give it. Healing does not come from anyone else. You must accept guidance from within. The guidance must be what you want, or it will be meaningless to you. That is why healing is a collaborative venture. I can tell you what to do, but you must collaborate by believing that I know what you should do. Only then will your mind choose to <u>follow me</u>. Without this choice you could not be healed because you would have decided against healing, and this rejection of my decision for you makes healing impossible.

Bible Reference - Text

Matthew 5:3-11 - Blessed are the poor in spirit: for theirs is the kingdom of heaven. Blessed are they that mourn: for they shall be comforted. Blessed are the meek: for they shall inherit the earth. Blessed are they which do hunger and thirst after righteousness: for they shall be filled. Blessed are the merciful: for they shall obtain mercy. Blessed are the pure in heart: for they shall see God. Blessed are the peacemakers: for they shall be called the children of God. Blessed are they which are persecuted for righteousness' sake: for theirs is the kingdom of heaven. Blessed are ye, when men shall revile you, and persecute you, and shall say all manner of evil against you falsely, for my sake.

Course Ref/s - Citation/s

T-11.I.11 - You are asked to trust the Holy Spirit only because He speaks for you. He is the Voice for God, but never forget that God did not will to be alone. He shares His Will with you; He does not thrust it upon you. Always remember that what He gives He keeps, so that nothing He gives can contradict Him. You who share His life must share it to know it, for sharing is knowing. <u>Blessed are you</u> who learn that to hear the Will of your Father is to know your own. For it is your will to be like Him, Whose Will it is that it be so. God's Will is that His Son be one, and united with Him in

His Oneness. That is why healing is the beginning of the recognition that your will is His.

T-11.VIII.7 - Little child of God, you do not understand your Father. You believe in a world that takes, because you believe that you can get by taking. And by that perception you have lost sight of the real world. You are afraid of the world as you see it, but the real world is still yours for the asking. Do not deny it to yourself, for it can only free you. Nothing of God will enslave His Son whom He created free and whose freedom is protected by His Being. <u>Blessed are you</u> who are willing to ask the truth of God without fear, for only thus can you learn that His answer is the release from fear.

T-14.I.1 - If <u>you are blessed</u> and do not know it, you need to learn it must be so. The knowledge is not taught, but its conditions must be acquired for it is they that have been thrown away. You can learn to bless, and cannot give what you have not. If, then, you offer blessing, it must have come first to yourself. And you must also have accepted it as yours, for how else could you give it away? That is why miracles offer you the testimony that you are blessed. If what you offer is complete forgiveness you must have let guilt go, accepting the Atonement for yourself and learning you are guiltless. How could you learn what has been done for you, unknown to you, unless you do what you would have to do if it had been done for you?

T-14.In.1 - Yes, <u>you are blessed</u> indeed. Yet in this world you do not know it. But you have the means for learning it and seeing it quite clearly. The Holy Spirit uses logic as easily and as well as does the ego, except that His conclusions are not insane. They take a direction exactly opposite, pointing as clearly to Heaven as the ego points to darkness and to death. We have followed much of the ego's logic, and have seen its logical conclusions. And having seen them, we have realized that they cannot be seen except in illusions, for there alone their seeming clearness seems to be clearly seen. Let us now turn away from them, and follow the simple logic by which the Holy Spirit teaches the simple conclusions that speak for truth, and only truth.

T-14.V.9 - <u>Blessed are you</u> who teach with me. Our power comes not of us, but of our Father. In guiltlessness we know Him, as He knows us guiltless. I stand within the circle, calling you to peace. Teach peace with me, and stand with me on holy ground. Remember for everyone your Father's power that He has given him. Believe not that you cannot teach His perfect peace. Stand not outside, but join with me within. Fail not the only purpose to which my teaching calls you. Restore to God His Son as He created him, by teaching him his innocence.

T-29.V.6 - If you but knew the glorious goal that lies beyond forgiveness, you would not keep hold on any thought, however light the touch of evil on it may appear to be. For you would understand how great the cost of holding anything God did not give in minds that can direct the hand to bless, and lead God's Son unto his Father's house. Would you not want to be a friend to him, created by his Father as His home? If God esteems him worthy of Himself, would you attack him with the hands of hate? Who would lay bloody hands on Heaven itself, and hope to find its peace? Your brother thinks he holds the hand of death. Believe him not. But learn, instead, how <u>blessed are you</u> who can release him, just by offering him yours.

W-pI.63.1 - How holy are you who have the power to bring peace to every mind? How <u>blessed are you</u> who can learn to recognize the means for letting this be done through you! What purpose could you have that would bring you greater happiness?

M-4.X.3 - You may have noticed that the list of attributes of God's teachers [Trust, Honesty, Tolerance, Gentleness, Joy, Defenselessness, Generosity, Patience, Faithfulness and Open-Mindedness] does not include things that are the Son of God's inheritance. Terms like love, sinlessness, perfection, knowledge and eternal truth do not appear in this context. They would be most inappropriate here. What God has given is so far beyond our curriculum that learning but disappears in its presence. Yet while its presence is obscured, the focus properly belongs on the curriculum. It is the function of God's teachers to bring true learning to the world. Properly speaking it is unlearning that they bring, for that is "true learning" in the world. It is given to the teachers of God to bring the glad tidings of complete forgiveness to the world. <u>Blessed indeed are they</u>, for they are the bringers of salvation.

Bible Reference - Text

Matthew 5:5 - Blessed are the meek: for they shall inherit the earth.

Course Ref/s - Citation/s

T-02.II.7 - The Atonement is a total commitment. You may still think this is associated with loss, a mistake all the separated Sons of God make in one way or another. It is hard to believe a defense that cannot attack is the best defense. This is what is meant by "<u>the meek shall inherit the earth</u>." They will literally take it over because of their strength. A two-way defense is inherently weak precisely because it has two edges, and can be turned against you very unexpectedly. This possibility cannot be controlled except by miracles. The miracle turns the defense of Atonement to your real protection, and as you become more and more secure you assume your natural talent of protecting others, knowing yourself as both a brother and a Son.

T-04.I.12:2-6 - Humility is a lesson for the ego, not for the spirit. Spirit is beyond humility, because it recognizes its radiance and gladly sheds its light everywhere. <u>The meek shall inherit the earth</u> because their egos are humble, and this gives them truer perception. The Kingdom of Heaven is the spirit's right, whose beauty and dignity are far beyond doubt, beyond perception, and stand forever as the mark of the Love of God for His creations, who are wholly worthy of Him and only of Him. Nothing else is sufficiently worthy to be a gift for a creation of God Himself.

Bible Reference - Text

Matthew 5:8 - Blessed are the pure in heart: for they shall see God.

Course Ref/s - Citation/s

T-03.I.5 - I have been correctly referred to as "the lamb of God who taketh away the sins of the world," but those who represent the lamb as blood-stained do not understand the meaning of the symbol. Correctly understood, it is a very simple symbol that speaks of my innocence. The lion and the lamb lying down together symbolize that strength and innocence are not in conflict, but naturally live in peace. "<u>Blessed are the pure in heart for they shall see God</u>" is another way of saying the same thing. A pure mind knows the truth and this is its strength. It does not confuse destruction with innocence because it associates innocence with strength, not with weakness.

T-03.II.5 - Nothing can prevail against a Son of God who commends his Spirit into the Hands of his Father. By doing this the mind awakens from its sleep and remembers its Creator. All sense of separation disappears. The Son of God is part of the Holy Trinity, but the Trinity Itself is one. There is no confusion within Its Levels, because They are of one Mind and one Will. This single purpose creates perfect integration and establishes the peace of God. Yet this vision can be perceived only by the truly innocent. Because their <u>hearts are pure</u>, the innocent defend true perception instead of defending themselves against it. Understanding the lesson of the Atonement they are without the wish to attack, and therefore they see truly. This is what the Bible means when it says, "When he shall appear (or be perceived) we shall be like him, for we shall see him as he is."

T-20.III.11 - Your gift unto your brother has given me the certainty our union will be soon. Share, then, this faith with me, and know that it is justified. There is no fear in perfect love because it knows no sin, and it must look on others as on itself. Looking with charity within, what can it fear without? The innocent see safety, and <u>the pure in heart see God</u> within His Son, and look unto the Son to lead them to the Father. And where else would they go but where they will to be? You and your brother now will lead the other to the Father as surely as God created His Son holy, and kept him so. In your brother is the light of God's eternal promise of your immortality. See him as sinless, and there can *be* no fear in you.

Bible Reference - Text

Matthew 5:12 - Rejoice, and be exceeding glad: for great is your reward in heaven: for so persecuted they the prophets which were before you.

Course Ref/s - Citation/s

W-pI.20.2 - This is our first attempt to introduce structure. Do not misconstrue it as an effort to exert force or pressure. You want salvation. You want to be happy. You want peace. You do not have them now, because your mind is totally undisciplined, and you cannot distinguish between joy and sorrow, pleasure and pain, love and fear. You are now learning how to tell them apart. And <u>great indeed will be your reward</u>.

Bible Reference - Text

Matthew 5:14 - Ye are the light of the world. A city that is set on an hill cannot be hid.

Course Ref/s - Citation/s

T-05.II.10 - I have assured you that the Mind that decided for me is also in you, and that you can let it change you just as it changed me. This Mind is unequivocal, because it hears only one Voice and answers in only one way. You are the light of the world with me. Rest does not come from sleeping but from waking. The Holy Spirit is the Call to awaken and be glad.
The world is very tired, because it is the idea of weariness. Our task is the joyous one of waking it to the Call for God. Everyone will answer the Call of the Holy Spirit, or the Sonship cannot be as one. What better vocation could there be for any part of the Kingdom than to restore it to the perfect integration that can make it whole? Hear only this through the Holy Spirit within you, and teach your brothers to listen as I am teaching you.

T-06.II.13 - The Holy Spirit was given you with perfect impartiality, and only by recognizing Him impartially can you recognize Him at all. The ego is legion, but the Holy Spirit is one. No darkness abides anywhere in the Kingdom, but your part is only to allow no darkness to abide in your own mind. This alignment with light is unlimited, because it is in alignment with the light of the world. Each of us is the light of the world, and by joining our minds in this light we proclaim the Kingdom of God together and as one.

T-08.III.1 - Glory to God in the highest, and to you because He has so willed it. Ask and it shall be given you, because it has already been given. Ask for light and learn that you are light. If you want understanding and enlightenment you will learn it, because your decision to learn it is the decision to listen to the Teacher Who knows of light, and can therefore teach it to you. There is no limit on your learning because there is no limit on your mind. There is no limit on His teaching because He was created to teach. Understanding His function perfectly He fulfils it perfectly, because that is His joy and yours.

T-13.IX.8 - Do not be afraid to look within. The ego tells you all is black with guilt within you, and bids you not to look. Instead, it bids you look upon your brothers, and see the guilt in them. Yet this you cannot do without remaining blind. For those who see their brothers in the dark, and guilty in the dark in which they shroud them, are too afraid to look upon the light within. Within you is not what you believe is there, and what you put your faith in. Within you is the holy sign of perfect faith your Father has in you. He does not value you as you do. He knows Himself, and knows the truth in you. He knows there is no difference, for He knows not of differences. Can you see guilt where God knows there is perfect innocence? You can deny His knowledge, but you cannot change it. Look, then, upon <u>the light He placed within you</u>, and learn that what you feared was there has been replaced with love.

T-13.VI.08 - Now is the time of salvation, for now is the release from time. Reach out to all your brothers, and touch them with the touch of Christ. In timeless union with them is your continuity, unbroken because it is wholly shared. <u>God's guiltless Son is only light</u>. There is no darkness in him anywhere, for he is whole. Call all your brothers to witness to his wholeness, as I am calling you to join with me. Each voice has a part in the song of redemption, the hymn of gladness and thanksgiving for the light to the Creator of light. The holy light that shines forth from God's Son is the witness that his light is of his Father.

T-13.VI.10 - Child of Light, you know not that <u>the light is in you</u>. Yet you will find it through its witnesses, for having given light to them they will return it. Each one you see in light brings your light closer to your awareness. Love always leads to love. The sick, who ask for love, are grateful for it, and in their joy they shine with holy thanks. And this they offer you who gave them joy. They are your guides to joy, for having received it of you they would keep it. You have established them as guides to peace, for you have made it manifest in them. And seeing it, its beauty calls you home.

T-13.VI.11 - There is a light that this world cannot give. Yet you can give it, as it was given you. And as you give it, it shines forth to call you from the world and follow it. For this light will attract you as nothing in this world can do. And you will lay aside the world and find another. This other world is bright with love which you have given it. And here will everything remind you of your Father and His holy Son. <u>Light is unlimited, and spreads across this world</u> in quiet joy. All those you brought with you will shine on you, and you will shine on them in gratitude because they brought you here. Your light will join with theirs in power so compelling, that it will draw the others out of darkness as you look on them.

T-13.VIII.8 - When you have seen your brothers as yourself you will be released to knowledge, having learned to free yourself through Him Who knows of freedom. Unite with me under the holy banner of His teaching, and as we grow in strength the power of God's Son will move in us, and we will leave no one untouched and no one left alone. And suddenly time will be over, and we will all unite in the eternity of God the Father. The holy light you saw outside yourself, in every miracle you offered to your brothers, will be returned to you. And knowing that <u>the light is in you</u>, your creations will be there with you, as you are in your Father.

Bible Reference - Text

Matthew 5:14 - Ye are the light of the world. A city that is set on an hill cannot be hid. (Continued)

Course Ref/s - Citation/s

T-14.II.8 - Behold your brothers in their freedom, and learn of them how to be free of darkness. <u>The light in you</u> will waken them, and they will not leave you asleep. The vision of Christ is given the very instant that it is perceived. Where everything is clear, it is all holy. The quietness of its simplicity is so compelling that you will realize it is impossible to deny the simple truth. For there is nothing else. God is everywhere, and His Son is in Him with everything. Can he sing the dirge of sorrow when this is true?

T-18.III.8 - <u>Not one light in Heaven but goes with you</u>. Not one Ray that shines forever in the Mind of God but shines on you. Heaven is joined with you in your advance to Heaven. When such great lights have joined with you to give the little spark of your desire the power of God Himself, can you remain in darkness? You and your brother are coming home together, after a long and meaningless journey that you undertook apart, and that led nowhere. You have found your brother, and you will light each other's way. And from this light will the Great Rays extend back into darkness and forward unto God, to shine away the past and so make room for His eternal Presence, in which everything is radiant in the light.

W-pI.061.1-2 - Who is <u>the light of the world</u> except God's Son? This, then, is merely a statement of the truth about yourself. It is the opposite of a statement of pride, of arrogance, or of self-deception. It does not describe the self concept you have made. It does not refer to any of the characteristics with which you have endowed your idols. It refers to you as you were created by God. It simply states the truth.

To the ego, today's idea is the epitome of self-glorification. But the ego does not understand humility, mistaking it for self-debasement. Humility consists of accepting your role in salvation and in taking no other. It is not humility to insist you cannot be <u>the light of the world</u> if that is the function God assigned to you. It is only arrogance that would assert this function cannot be for you, and arrogance is always of the ego.

W-pI.061.5 - As many practice periods as possible should be undertaken today, although each one need not exceed a minute or two. They should begin with telling yourself:
<u>I am the light of the world</u>. That is my only function. That is why I am here.
Then think about these statements for a short while, preferably with your eyes closed if the situation permits. Let a few related thoughts come to you, and repeat the idea to yourself if your mind wanders away from the central thought.

W-pI.061.7 - Today's idea [I am the light of the world.] goes far beyond the ego's petty views of what you are and what your purpose is. As a bringer of salvation, this is obviously necessary. This is the first of a number of giant steps we will take in the next few weeks. Try today to begin to build a firm foundation for these advances. <u>You are the light of the world</u>. God has built His plan for the salvation of His Son on you.

W-pI.062.1 - It is your forgiveness that will bring the world of darkness to the light. It is your forgiveness that lets you recognize the light in which you see. Forgiveness is the demonstration that <u>you are the light of the world</u>. Through your forgiveness does the truth about yourself return to your memory. Therefore, in your forgiveness lies your salvation.

W-pI.062.5 - As often as you can, closing your eyes if possible, say to yourself today:

Forgiveness is my function as <u>the light of the world</u>.

I would fulfill my function that I may be happy.

Then devote a minute or two to considering your function and the happiness and release it will bring you. Let related thoughts come freely, for your heart will recognize these words, and in your mind is the awareness they are true. Should your attention wander, repeat the idea and add:

I would remember this because I want to be happy.

Bible Reference - Text

Matthew 5:14 - Ye are the light of the world. A city that is set on an hill cannot be hid. (Continued)

Course Ref/s - Citation/s

W-pI.063.ti-3 - The light of the world brings peace to every mind through my forgiveness.
1 How holy are you who have the power to bring peace to every mind? How blessed are you who can learn to recognize the means for letting this be done through you! What purpose could you have that would bring you greater happiness?
2 You are indeed the light of the world with such a function. The Son of God looks to you for his redemption. It is yours to give him, for it belongs to you. Accept no trivial purpose or meaningless desire in its place, or you will forget your function and leave the Son of God in hell. This is no idle request that is being asked of you. You are being asked to accept salvation that it may be yours to give.
3 Recognizing the importance of this function, we will be happy to remember it very often today. We will begin the day by acknowledging it, and close the day with the thought of it in our awareness. And throughout the day we will repeat this as often as we can:
The light of the world brings peace to every mind through my forgiveness. I am the means God has appointed for the salvation of the world.

W-pI.064.3 - To review our last few lessons, your function here is to be the light of the world, a function given you by God. It is only the arrogance of the ego that leads you to question this, and only the fear of the ego that induces you to regard yourself as unworthy of the task assigned to you by God Himself. The world's salvation awaits your forgiveness, because through it does the Son of God escape from all illusions, and thus from all temptation. The Son of God is you.

W-pI.067.1 - Today's idea [Love created me like itself.] is a complete and accurate statement of what you are. This is why you are the light of the world. This is why God appointed you as the world's savior. This is why the Son of God looks to you for his salvation. He is saved by what you are. We will make every effort today to reach this truth about you, and to realize fully, if only for a moment, that it is the truth.

W-pI.069.ti-3 - My grievances hide the light of the world in me.

1 No one can look upon what your grievances conceal. Because your grievances are hiding the light of the world in you, everyone stands in darkness, and you beside him. But as the veil of your grievances is lifted, you are released with him. Share your salvation now with him who stood beside you when you were in hell. He is your brother in the light of the world that saves you both.

2 Today let us make another real attempt to reach the light in you. Before we undertake this in our more extended practice period, let us devote several minutes to thinking about what we are trying to do. We are literally attempting to get in touch with the salvation of the world. We are trying to see past the veil of darkness that keeps it concealed. We are trying to let the veil be lifted, and to see the tears of God's Son disappear in the sunlight.

3 Let us begin our longer practice period today with the full realization that this is so, and with real determination to reach what is dearer to us than all else. Salvation is our only need. There is no other purpose here, and no other function to fulfill. Learning salvation is our only goal. Let us end the ancient search today by finding the light in us, and holding it up for everyone who searches with us to look upon and rejoice.

W-pI.069.9 - In the shorter practice periods, which you will want to do as often as possible in view of the importance of today's idea to you and your happiness, remind yourself that your grievances are hiding the light of the world from your awareness. Remind yourself also that you are not searching for it alone, and that you do know where to look for it. Say, then:

My grievances hide the light of the world in me. I cannot see what I have hidden. Yet I want to let it be revealed to me, for my salvation and the salvation of the world.

Also, be sure to tell yourself:

If I hold this grievance the light of the world will be hidden from me,

if you are tempted to hold anything against anyone today

W-pI.081.1-2 - I am the light of the world.
How holy am I, who have been given the function of lighting up the world! Let me be still before my holiness. In its calm light let all my conflicts disappear. In its peace let me remember who I am.

Some specific forms for applying this idea when special difficulties seem to arise might be:
Let me not obscure the light of the world in me.
Let the light of the world shine through this appearance.
This shadow will vanish before the light.

Bible Reference - Text

Matthew 5:14 - Ye are the light of the world. A city that is set on an hill cannot be hid. (Continued)

Course Ref/s - Citation/s

W-pI.081.3 - Forgiveness is my function as the light of the world.
It is through accepting my function that I will see the light in me. And in this light will my function stand clear and perfectly unambiguous before my sight. My acceptance does not depend on my recognizing what my function is, for I do not yet understand forgiveness. Yet I will trust that, in the light, I will see it as it is.

W-pI.082.1-2 - The light of the world brings peace to every mind through my forgiveness.
1 My forgiveness is the means by which the light of the world finds expression through me. My forgiveness is the means by which I become aware of the light of the world in me. My forgiveness is the means by which the world is healed, together with myself. Let me, then, forgive the world, that it may be healed along with me.
2 Suggestions for specific forms for applying this idea are:
Let peace extend from my mind to yours, [name].
I share the light of the world with you, [name].
Through my forgiveness I can see this as it is.

W-pI.085.1-2 - My grievances hide the light of the world in me.
1 My grievances show me what is not there, and hide from me what I would see. Recognizing this, what do I want my grievances for? They keep me in darkness and hide the light. Grievances and light cannot go together, but light and vision must be joined for me to see. To see, I must lay grievances aside. I want to see, and this will be the means by which I will succeed.
2 Specific applications of this idea might be made in these forms:

Let me not use this as a block to sight.
The light of the world will shine all this away.
I have no need for this. I want to see.

W-pI.188.1 - Why wait for Heaven? Those who seek the light are merely covering their eyes. The light is in them now. Enlightenment is but a recognition, not a change at all. Light is not of the world, yet you who bear the light in you are alien here as well. The light came with you from your native home, and stayed with you because it is your own. It is the only thing you bring with you from Him Who is your Source. It shines in you because it lights your home, and leads you back to where it came from and you are at home.

W-pI.188.6 - Sit quietly and close your eyes. The light within you is sufficient. It alone has power to give the gift of sight to you. Exclude the outer world, and let your thoughts fly to the peace within. They know the way. For honest thoughts, untainted by the dream of worldly things outside yourself, become the holy messengers of God Himself.

W-pI.189.1 - There is a light in you the world can not perceive. And with its eyes you will not see this light, for you are blinded by the world. Yet you have eyes to see it. It is there for you to look upon. It was not placed in you to be kept hidden from your sight. This light is a reflection of the thought [I feel the Love of God within me now.] we practice now. To feel the Love of God within you is to see the world anew, shining in innocence, alive with hope, and blessed with perfect charity and love.

Bible Reference - Text

Matthew 5:16 - Let your light so shine before men, that they may see your good works, and glorify your Father which is in heaven.

Course Ref/s - Citation/s

T-09.II.5 - The message your brother gives you is up to you. What does he say to you? What would you have him say? Your decision about him determines the message you receive. Remember that the Holy Spirit is in him, and His Voice speaks to you through him. What can so holy a brother tell you except truth? But are you listening to it? Your brother may not know who he is, but there is a light in his mind that does know. This light can shine into yours, giving truth to his words and making you able to hear them. His words are the Holy Spirit's answer to you. Is your faith in him strong enough to let you hear?

Bible Reference - Text

Matthew 5:17 - Think not that I am come to destroy the law, or the prophets: I am not come to destroy, but to fulfil.

Course Ref/s - Citation/s

T-01.IV.3-4 - Darkness is lack of light as sin is lack of love. It has no unique properties of its own. It is an example of the "scarcity" belief, from which only error can proceed. Truth is always abundant. Those who perceive and acknowledge that they have everything have no needs of any kind. The purpose of the Atonement is to restore everything to you; or rather, to restore it to your awareness. You were given everything when you were created, just as everyone was.

The emptiness engendered by fear must be replaced by forgiveness. That is what the Bible means by "There is no death," and why I could demonstrate that death does not exist. I came to fulfil the law by reinterpreting it. The law itself, if properly understood, offers only protection. It is those who have not yet changed their minds who brought the "hell-fire" concept into it. I assure you that I will witness for anyone who lets me, and to whatever extent he permits it. Your witnessing demonstrates your belief, and thus strengthens it. Those who witness for me are expressing, through their miracles, that they have abandoned the belief in deprivation in favor of the abundance they have learned belongs to them.

Bible Reference - Text

Matthew 5:29 - And if thy right eye offend thee, pluck it out, and cast it from thee: for it is profitable for thee that one of thy members should perish, and not that thy whole body should be cast into hell.

Course Ref/s - Citation/s

T-11.VIII.12 - If you perceive offense in a brother <u>pluck the offense</u> from your mind, for you are offended by Christ and are deceived in Him. Heal in Christ and be not offended by Him, for there is no offense in Him. If what you perceive offends you, you are offended in yourself and are condemning God's Son whom God condemneth not. Let the Holy Spirit remove all offenses of God's Son against himself and perceive no one but through His guidance, for He would save you from all condemnation. Accept His healing power and use it for all He sends you, for He wills to heal the Son of God, in whom He is not deceived.

Bible Reference - Text

Matthew 5:39 - But I say unto you, That ye resist not evil: but whosoever shall smite thee on thy right cheek, turn to him the other also.

Course Ref/s - Citation/s

T-05.IV.4 - I heard one Voice because I understood that I could not atone for myself alone. Listening to one Voice implies the decision to share It in order to hear It yourself. The Mind that was in me is still irresistibly drawn to every mind created by God, because God's Wholeness is the Wholeness of His Son. You cannot be hurt, and do not want to show your brother anything except your wholeness. Show him that he cannot hurt you and hold nothing against him, or you hold it against yourself. This is the meaning of "<u>turning the other cheek</u>."

T-09.VII.4 - You, then, have two conflicting evaluations of yourself in your mind, and they cannot both be true. You do not yet realize how completely different these evaluations are, because you do not understand how lofty the Holy Spirit's perception of you really is. He is not deceived by anything you do, because He never forgets what you are. The ego is deceived by everything you do, especially when you respond to the Holy Spirit, because at such times its confusion increases. The ego is, therefore, particularly likely to attack you when you react lovingly, because it has evaluated you as unloving and you are going against its judgment. The ego will attack your motives as soon as they become clearly out of accord with its perception of you. This is when it will shift abruptly from suspiciousness to viciousness, since its uncertainty is increased. Yet <u>it is</u>

surely pointless to attack in return. What can this mean except that you are agreeing with the ego's evaluation of what you are?

T-12.III.3 - Whenever you become angry with a brother, for whatever reason, you are believing that the ego is to be saved, and to be saved by attack. If he attacks, you are agreeing with this belief; and if you attack, you are reinforcing it. Remember that those who attack are poor. Their poverty asks for gifts, not for further impoverishment. You who could help them are surely acting destructively if you accept their poverty as yours. If you had not invested as they had, it would never occur to you to overlook their need.

Bible Reference - Text

Matthew 5:41 - And whosoever shall compel thee to go a mile, go with him twain.

Course Ref/s - Citation/s

T-04.In.1 - The Bible says that you should go with a brother twice as far as he asks. It certainly does not suggest that you set him back on his journey. Devotion to a brother cannot set you back either. It can lead only to mutual progress. The result of genuine devotion is inspiration, a word which properly understood is the opposite of fatigue. To be fatigued is to be dis-spirited, but to be inspired is to be in the spirit. To be egocentric is to be dis-spirited, but to be Self-centered in the right sense is to be inspired or in spirit. The truly inspired are enlightened and cannot abide in darkness.

T-12.III.2:1-5 - Suppose a brother insists on having you do something you think you do not want to do. His very insistence should tell you that he believes salvation lies in it. If you insist on refusing and experience a quick response of opposition, you are believing that your salvation lies in not doing it. You, then, are making the same mistake he is, and are making his error real to both of you. Insistence means investment, and what you invest in is always related to your notion of salvation.

T-12.III.4 - Recognize what does not matter, and if your brothers ask you for something "outrageous," do it because it does not matter. Refuse, and your opposition establishes that it does matter to you. It is only you, therefore, who have made the request outrageous, and every request of a brother is for you. Why would you insist in denying him? For to do so is to deny yourself and impoverish both. He is asking for salvation, as you are. Poverty is of the ego, and never of God. No "outrageous" requests can be made of one who recognizes what is valuable and wants to accept nothing else.

T-16.I.6 - The meaning of love is lost in any relationship that looks to weakness, and hopes to find love there. The power of love, which is its meaning, lies in the strength of God that hovers over it and blesses it silently by enveloping it in healing wings. Let this be, and do not try to substitute your "miracle" for this. <u>I have said that if a brother asks a foolish thing of you to do it</u>. But be certain that this does not mean to do a foolish thing that would hurt either him or you, for what would hurt one will hurt the other. Foolish requests are foolish merely because they conflict, since they always contain some element of specialness. Only the Holy Spirit recognizes foolish needs as well as real ones. And He will teach you how to meet both without losing either.

Bible Reference - Text

Matthew 5:43-45 - Ye have heard that it hath been said, Thou shalt love thy neighbour, and hate thine enemy. But I say unto you, Love your enemies, bless them that curse you, do good to them that hate you, and pray for them which despitefully use you, and persecute you; That ye may be the children of your Father which is in heaven: for he maketh his sun to rise on the evil and on the good, and sendeth rain on the just and on the unjust.

Course Ref/s - Citation/s

T-13.X.11 - <u>You cannot enter into real relationships with any of God's Sons unless you love them all and equally</u>. Love is not special. If you single out part of the Sonship for your love, you are imposing guilt on all your relationships and making them unreal. You can love only as God loves. Seek not to love unlike Him, for there is no love apart from His. Until you recognize that this is true, you will have no idea what love is like. No one who condemns a brother can see himself as guiltless and in the peace of God. If he is guiltless and in peace and sees it not, he is delusional, and has not looked upon himself. To him I say, Behold the Son of God, and look upon his purity and be still. In quiet look upon his holiness, and offer thanks unto his Father that no guilt has ever touched him.

T-27.II.2 - The unhealed cannot pardon. For they are the witnesses that pardon is unfair. They would retain the consequences of the guilt they overlook. Yet no one can forgive a sin that he believes is real. And what has consequences must be real, because what it has done is there to see. Forgiveness is not pity, which but seeks to pardon what it thinks to be the truth. <u>Good cannot be returned for evil,</u> for forgiveness does not first establish sin and then forgive it. Who can say and mean, "My brother, you have injured me, and yet, because I am the better of the two, I pardon you my hurt." His pardon and your hurt cannot exist together. One denies the other and must make it false.

S-1.II.6 - Let it never be forgotten that prayer at any level is always for yourself. If you unite with anyone in prayer, you make him part of you. The enemy is you, as is the Christ. Before it can become holy, then, prayer becomes a choice. You do not choose for another. You can but choose for yourself. <u>Pray truly for your enemies,</u> for herein lies your own salvation. Forgive them for your sins, and you will be forgiven indeed.

Bible Reference - Text

Matthew 5:48 - Be ye therefore perfect, even as your Father which is in heaven is perfect.

Course Ref/s - Citation/s

T-08.IX.7 - <u>The Bible enjoins you to be perfect</u>, to heal all errors, to take no thought of the body as separate and to accomplish all things in my name. This is not my name alone, for ours is a shared identification. The Name of God's Son is one, and you are enjoined to do the works of love because we share this Oneness. Our minds are whole because they are one. If you are sick you are withdrawing from me. Yet you cannot withdraw from me alone. You can only withdraw from yourself and me.

T-10.IV.1 - All magic is an attempt at reconciling the irreconcilable. All religion is the recognition that the irreconcilable cannot be reconciled. Sickness and perfection are irreconcilable. <u>If God created you perfect, you</u>

are perfect. If you believe you can be sick, you have placed other gods before Him. God is not at war with the god of sickness you made, but you are. He is the symbol of deciding against God, and you are afraid of him because he cannot be reconciled with God's Will. If you attack him, you will make him real to you. But if you refuse to worship him in whatever form he may appear to you, and wherever you think you see him, he will disappear into the nothingness out of which he was made.

T-10.V.12 - If God knows His children as wholly sinless, it is blasphemous to perceive them as guilty. If God knows His children as wholly without pain, it is blasphemous to perceive suffering anywhere. If God knows His children to be wholly joyous, it is blasphemous to feel depressed. All of these illusions, and the many other forms that blasphemy may take, are refusals to accept creation as it is. If God created His Son perfect, that is how you must learn to see him to learn of his reality. And as part of the Sonship, that is how you must see yourself to learn of yours.

T-13.X.14 - Praise be to you who make the Father one with His Own Son. Alone we are all lowly, but together we shine with brightness so intense that none of us alone can even think of it. Before the glorious radiance of the Kingdom guilt melts away, and transformed into kindness will never more be what it was. Every reaction you experience will be so purified that it is fitting as a hymn of praise unto your Father. See only praise of Him in what He has created, for He will never cease His praise of you. United in this praise we stand before the gates of Heaven where we will surely enter in our sinlessness. God loves you. Could I, then, lack faith in you and love Him perfectly?

T-28.VI.6 - Let this be your agreement with each one; that you be one with him and not apart. And he will keep the promise that you make with him, because it is the one that he has made to God, as God has made to him. God keeps His promises; His Son keeps his. In his creation did his Father say, "You are beloved of Me and I of you forever. Be you perfect as Myself, for you can never be apart from Me." His Son remembers not that he replied "I will," though in that promise he was born. Yet God reminds him of it every time he does not share a promise to be sick, but lets his mind be healed and unified. His secret vows are powerless before the Will of God, Whose promises he shares. And what he substitutes is not his will, who has made promise of himself to God.

Bible Reference - Text

Matthew 6:7-8 - But when ye pray, use not vain repetitions, as the heathen do: for they think that they shall be heard for their much speaking. Be not ye therefore like unto them: for your Father knoweth what things ye have need of, before ye ask him.

Course Ref/s - Citation/s

T-13.VII.10 - Praise, then, the Father for the perfect sanity of His most holy Son. <u>Your Father knoweth that you have need</u> of nothing. In Heaven this is so, for what could you need in eternity? In your world you do need things. It is a world of scarcity in which you find yourself because you are lacking. Yet can you find yourself in such a world? Without the Holy Spirit the answer would be no. Yet because of Him the answer is a joyous yes! As Mediator between the two worlds, He knows what you have need of and what will not hurt you. Ownership is a dangerous concept if it is left to you. The ego wants to have things for salvation, for possession is its law. Possession for its own sake is the ego's fundamental creed, a basic cornerstone in the churches it builds to itself. And at its altar it demands you lay all of the things it bids you get, leaving you no joy in them.

T-14.XI.7 - You cannot be your guide to miracles, for it is you who made them necessary. And because you did, the means on which you can depend for miracles has been provided for you. <u>God's Son can make no needs His Father will not meet</u>, if he but turn to Him ever so little. Yet He cannot compel His Son to turn to Him and remain Himself. It is impossible that God lose His Identity, for if He did, you would lose yours. And being yours He cannot change Himself, for your Identity is changeless. The miracle acknowledges His changelessness by seeing His Son as he always was, and not as he would make himself. The miracle brings the effects that only guiltlessness can bring, and thus establishes the fact that guiltlessness must be.

W-pII.349.2 - <u>Our Father knows our needs.</u> He gives us grace to meet them all. And so we trust in Him to send us miracles to bless the world, and heal our minds as we return to Him.

C-3.2-3 - Forgiveness might be called a kind of happy fiction; a way in which the unknowing can bridge the gap between their perception and the truth. They cannot go directly from perception to knowledge because they do not think it is their will to do so. This makes God appear to be an enemy instead of what He really is. And it is just this insane perception that makes them unwilling merely to rise up and to return to Him in peace.

And so they need an illusion of help because they are helpless; a Thought of peace because they are in conflict. <u>God knows what His Son needs before he asks</u>. He is not at all concerned with form, but having given the content it is His Will that it be understood. And that suffices. The form adapts itself to need; the content is unchanging, as eternal as its Creator.

Bible Reference - Text

Matthew 6:9-13 - After this manner therefore pray ye: Our Father which art in heaven, Hallowed be thy name. Thy kingdom come, Thy will be done in earth, as it is in heaven. Give us this day our daily bread. And forgive us our debts, as we forgive our debtors. And lead us not into temptation, but deliver us from evil: For thine is the kingdom, and the power, and the glory, for ever. Amen.

Course Ref/s - Citation/s

T-01.III.4 - I [Jesus] am the only one who can perform miracles indiscriminately, because I am the Atonement. You have a role in the Atonement which I will dictate to you. Ask me which miracles you should perform. This spares you needless effort, because you will be acting under direct communication. The impersonal nature of the miracle is an essential ingredient, because it enables me to direct its application, and under my guidance miracles lead to the highly personal experience of revelation. A guide does not control but he does direct, leaving it up to you to follow. "<u>Lead us not into temptation</u>" means "Recognize your errors and choose to abandon them by following my guidance."

T-02.III.5 - The children of God are entitled to the perfect comfort that comes from perfect trust. Until they achieve this, they waste themselves and their true creative powers on useless attempts to make themselves more comfortable by inappropriate means. But the real means are already provided, and do not involve any effort at all on their part. The Atonement is the only gift that is worthy of being offered at the altar of God, because of the value of the altar itself. It was created perfect and is entirely worthy of receiving perfection. God and His creations are completely dependent on Each Other. He depends on them because He created them perfect. He gave them His peace so they could not be shaken and could not be deceived. Whenever you are afraid you are deceived, and your mind cannot serve the Holy Spirit. This starves you by denying you <u>your daily bread</u>. God is lonely without His Sons, and they are lonely without Him. They must learn to look upon the world as a means of healing the separation. The Atonement is the guarantee that they will ultimately succeed.

T-05.II.8 - The Holy Spirit is your Guide in choosing. He is in the part of your mind that always speaks for the right choice, because He speaks for God. He is your remaining communication with God, which you can interrupt but cannot destroy. The Holy Spirit is the way in which <u>God's Will is done on earth as it is in Heaven</u>. Both Heaven and earth are in you, because the call of both is in your mind. The Voice for God comes from your own altars to Him. These altars are not things; they are devotions. Yet you have other devotions now. Your divided devotion has given you the two voices, and you must choose at which altar you want to serve. The call you answer now is an evaluation because it is a decision. The decision is very simple. It is made on the basis of which call is worth more to you.

T-05.VI.10 - You need not fear the Higher Court will condemn you. It will merely dismiss the case against you. There can be no case against a child of God, and every witness to guilt in God's creations is bearing false witness to God Himself. Appeal everything you believe gladly to God's Own Higher Court, because it speaks for Him and therefore speaks truly. It will dismiss the case against you, however carefully you have built it up. The case may be fool-proof, but it is not God-proof. The Holy Spirit will not hear it, because He can only witness truly. His verdict will always be "<u>thine is the Kingdom</u>," because He was given to you to remind you of what you are.

T-07.VII.11 - Perceive any part of the ego's thought system as wholly insane, wholly delusional and wholly undesirable, and you have correctly evaluated all of it. This correction enables you to perceive any part of creation as wholly real, wholly perfect and wholly desirable. Wanting this only you will have this only, and giving this only you will be only this. The gifts you offer to the ego are always experienced as sacrifices, but the gifts you offer to the Kingdom are gifts to you. They will always be treasured by God because they belong to His beloved Sons, who belong to Him. <u>All power and glory are yours because the Kingdom is His.</u>

Bible Reference - Text

Matthew 6:9-13 - After this manner therefore pray ye: Our Father ....
(Continued) - (To read the full text of the above go to page 127.)

Course Ref/s - Citation/s

T-08.II.7-8 – 7 When I said, "All power and glory are yours because the Kingdom is His," this is what I meant. The Will of God is without limit, and all power and glory lie within it. It is boundless in strength and in love and in peace. It has no boundaries because its extension is unlimited, and it encompasses all things because it created all things. By creating all things, it made them part of itself. You are the Will of God because that is how you were created. Because your Creator creates only like Himself, you are like Him. You are part of Him Who is all power and glory, and are therefore as unlimited as He is.
8 To what else except all power and glory can the Holy Spirit appeal to restore God's Kingdom? His appeal, then, is merely to what the Kingdom is, and for its own acknowledgement of what it is. When you acknowledge this you bring the acknowledgement automatically to everyone, because you have acknowledged everyone. By your recognition you awaken theirs, and through theirs yours is extended. Awakening runs easily and gladly through the Kingdom, in answer to the Call for God. This is the natural response of every Son of God to the Voice for his Creator, because It is the Voice for his creations and for his own extension.

T-08.III.2 - To fulfill the Will of God perfectly is the only joy and peace that can be fully known, because it is the only function that can be fully experienced. When this is accomplished, then, there is no other experience. Yet the wish for other experience will block its accomplishment, because God's Will cannot be forced upon you, being an experience of total willingness. The Holy Spirit understands how to teach this, but you do not. That is why you need Him, and why God gave Him to you. Only His teaching will release your will to God's, uniting it with His power and glory and establishing them as yours. You share them as God shares them, because this is the natural outcome of their being.

T-15.III.6 - The Holy Spirit can hold your magnitude, clean of all littleness, clearly and in perfect safety in your mind, untouched by every little gift the world of littleness would offer you. But for this, you cannot side against Him in what He wills for you. Decide for God through Him. For littleness, and the belief that you can be content with littleness, are decisions you make about yourself. <u>The power and the glory</u> that lie in you from God are for all who, like you, perceive themselves as little, and believe that littleness can be blown up into a sense of magnitude that can content them. Neither give littleness, nor accept it. All honor is due the host of God. Your littleness deceives you, but your magnitude is of Him Who dwells in you, and in Whom you dwell. Touch no one, then, with littleness in the Name of Christ, eternal Host unto His Father.

T-16.VII.12 - <u>Forgive us</u> our illusions, Father, and help us to accept our true relationship with You, in which there are no illusions, and where none can ever enter. Our holiness is Yours. What can there be in us that needs forgiveness when Yours is perfect? The sleep of forgetfulness is only the unwillingness to remember Your forgiveness and Your Love. Let us not wander into temptation, for the temptation of the Son of God is not Your Will. And let us receive only what You have given, and accept but this into the minds which You created and which You love. Amen.

T-17.IV.15 - As God ascends into His rightful place and you to yours, you will experience again the meaning of relationship and know it to be true. Let us ascend in peace together to the Father, by giving Him ascendance in our minds. We will gain everything by giving Him <u>the power and the glory</u>, and keeping no illusions of where they are. They are in us, through His ascendance. What He has given is His. It shines in every part of Him, as in the whole. The whole reality of your relationship with Him lies in our relationship to one another. The holy instant shines alike on all relationships, for in it they are one. For here is only healing, already complete and perfect. For here is God, and where He is only the perfect and complete can be.

T-18.V.4 - Happy dreams come true, not because they are dreams, but only because they are happy. And so they must be loving. Their message is, "<u>Thy Will be done</u>," and not, "I want it otherwise." The alignment of means and purpose is an undertaking impossible for you to understand. You do not even realize you have accepted the Holy Spirit's purpose as your own, and you would merely bring unholy means to its accomplishment. The little faith it needed to change the purpose is all that is required to receive the means and use them.

Bible Reference - Text

Matthew 6:9-13 - After this manner therefore pray ye: Our Father ....
(Continued) - (To read the full text of the above go to page 127.)

Course Ref/s - Citation/s

T-20.I.3 - A week is short, and yet this holy week is the symbol of the whole journey the Son of God has undertaken. He started with the sign of victory, the promise of the resurrection, already given him. <u>Let him not wander into the temptation</u> of crucifixion, and delay him there. Help him to go in peace beyond it, with the light of his own innocence lighting his way to his redemption and release. Hold him not back with thorns and nails when his redemption is so near. But let the whiteness of your shining gift of lilies speed him on his way to resurrection.

T-23.In.4-5 – 4 Let not the little interferers pull you to littleness. There can be no attraction of guilt in innocence. Think what a happy world you walk, with truth beside you! Do not give up this world of freedom for a little sigh of seeming sin, nor for a tiny stirring of guilt's attraction. Would you, for all these meaningless distractions, lay Heaven aside? Your destiny and purpose are far beyond them, in the clean place where littleness does not exist. Your purpose is at variance with littleness of any kind. And so it is at variance with sin.
5 Let us not let littleness <u>lead God's Son into temptation</u>. His glory is beyond it, measureless and timeless as eternity. Do not let time intrude upon your sight of him. Leave him not frightened and alone in his temptation, but help him rise above it and perceive the light of which he is a part. Your innocence will light the way to his, and so is yours protected and kept in your awareness. For who can know his glory, and perceive the little and the weak about him? Who can walk trembling in a fearful world, and realize that Heaven's glory shines on him?

T-24.III.5 - God asks for your forgiveness. He would have no separation, like an alien will, rise between what He wills for you and what you will. They are the same, for neither One wills specialness. How could They will the death of love itself? Yet They are powerless to make attack upon illusions. They are not bodies; as one Mind They wait for all illusions to be brought to Them, and left behind. Salvation challenges not even death.

And God Himself, Who knows that death is not your will, must say, "Thy will be done" because you think it is.

T-24.III.8 - The slaves of specialness will yet be free. Such is the Will of God and of His Son. Would God condemn Himself to hell and to damnation? And do you will that this be done unto your savior? God calls to you from him to join His Will to save you both from hell. Look on the print of nails upon his hands that he holds out for your forgiveness. God asks your mercy on His Son and on Himself. Deny Them not. They ask of you but that your will be done. They seek your love that you may love yourself. Love not your specialness instead of Them. The print of nails is on your hands as well. Forgive your Father it was not His Will that you be crucified.

T-25.V.6 - Against the hatred that the Son of God may cherish toward himself, is God believed to be without the power to save what He created from the pain of hell. But in the love he shows himself is God made free to let His Will be done. In your brother you see the picture of your own belief in what the Will of God must be for you. In your forgiveness will you understand His Love for you; through your attack believe He hates you, thinking Heaven must be hell. Look once again upon your brother, not without the understanding that he is the way to Heaven or to hell, as you perceive him. But forget not this; the role you give to him is given you, and you will walk the way you pointed out to him because it is your judgment on yourself.

T-26.VII.17 - In crucifixion is redemption laid, for healing is not needed where there is no pain or suffering. Forgiveness is the answer to attack of any kind. So is attack deprived of its effects, and hate is answered in the name of love. To you to whom it has been given to save the Son of God from crucifixion and from hell and death, all glory be forever. For you have power to save the Son of God because his Father willed that it be so. And in your hands does all salvation lie, to be both offered and received as one.

T-27.II.1-3 – 1 Is healing frightening? To many, yes. For accusation is a bar to love, and damaged bodies are accusers. They stand firmly in the way of trust and peace, proclaiming that the frail can have no trust and that the damaged have no grounds for peace. Who has been injured by his brother, and could love and trust him still? He has attacked and will attack again. Protect him not, because your damaged body shows that you must be

protected from him. To forgive may be an act of charity, but not his due. He may be pitied for his guilt, but not exonerated. And if you <u>forgive him his transgressions</u>, you but add to all the guilt that he has really earned.
2 The unhealed cannot pardon. For they are the witnesses that pardon is unfair. They would retain the consequences of the guilt they overlook. Yet no one can <u>forgive a sin</u> that he believes is real. And what has consequences must be real, because what it has done is there to see. Forgiveness is not pity, which but seeks to pardon what it thinks to be the truth. Good cannot be returned for evil, for forgiveness does not first establish sin and then forgive it. Who can say and mean, "My brother, you have injured me, and yet, because I am the better of the two, I pardon you my hurt." His pardon and your hurt cannot exist together. One denies the other and must make it false.
3 To witness <u>sin and yet forgive it</u> is a paradox that reason cannot see. For it maintains what has been done to you deserves no pardon. And by giving it, you grant your brother mercy but retain the proof he is not really innocent. The sick remain accusers. They cannot forgive their brothers and themselves as well. For no one in whom true forgiveness rests can suffer. He holds not the proof of sin before his brother's eyes. And thus he must have overlooked it and removed it from his own. Forgiveness cannot be for one and not the other. Who forgives is healed. And in his healing lies the proof that he has truly pardoned, and retains no trace of condemnation that he still would hold against himself or any living thing.

Bible Reference - Text

Matthew 6:9-13 - After this manner therefore pray ye: Our Father ....

(Continued) - (To read the full text of the above go to page 127.)

Course Ref/s - Citation/s

T-30.IV.7 - Salvation is a paradox indeed! What could it be except a happy dream? It asks you but that you forgive all things that no one ever did; to overlook what is not there, and not to look upon the unreal as reality. You are but asked to let <u>your will be done,</u> and seek no longer for the things you do not want. And you are asked to let yourself be free of all the dreams of what you never were, and seek no more to substitute the strength of idle wishes for the Will of God.

T-31.VI.4 - Only in arrogance could you conceive that you must make the way to Heaven plain. The means are given you by which to see the world that will replace the one you made. <u>Your will be done! In Heaven as on earth</u> this is forever true. It matters not where you believe you are, nor what you think the truth about yourself must really be. It makes no difference what you look upon, nor what you choose to feel or think or wish. For God Himself has said, "Your will be done." And it is done to you accordingly.

T-31.VI.6 - Are you invulnerable? Then the world is harmless in your sight. Do you forgive? Then is the world forgiving, for you <u>have forgiven it its trespasses,</u> and so it looks on you with eyes that see as yours. Are you a body? So is all the world perceived as treacherous, and out to kill. Are you a spirit, deathless, and without the promise of corruption and the stain of sin upon you? So the world is seen as stable, fully worthy of your trust; a happy place to rest in for a while, where nothing need be feared, but only loved. Who is unwelcome to the kind in heart? And what could hurt the truly innocent?

T-31.VI.7 - <u>Your will be done</u>, you holy child of God. It does not matter if you think you are in earth or Heaven. What your Father wills of you can never change. The truth in you remains as radiant as a star, as pure as light, as innocent as love itself. And you are worthy that your will be done!

T-31.VIII.12 - And now we say "Amen." For Christ has come to dwell in the abode You set for Him before time was, in calm eternity. The journey closes, ending at the place where it began. No trace of it remains. Not one illusion is accorded faith, and not one spot of darkness still remains to hide the face of Christ from anyone. <u>Thy Will is done</u>, complete and perfectly, and all creation recognizes You, and knows You as the only Source it has. Clear in Your likeness does the light shine forth from everything that lives and moves in You. For we have reached where all of us are one, and we are home, where You would have us be.

W-pI.020.3 - Your decision to see is all that vision requires. What you want is yours. Do not mistake the little effort that is asked of you for an indication that our goal is of little worth. Can the salvation of the world be a trivial purpose? And can the world be saved if you are not? God has one Son, and he is the resurrection and the life. <u>His will is done because all power is given him in Heaven and on earth.</u> In your determination to see is vision given you.

Bible Reference - Text

Matthew 6:9-13 - After this manner therefore pray ye: Our Father ....
(Continued) - (To read the full text of the above go to page 127.)

Course Ref/s - Citation/s

W-pI.064.1 - Today's idea is merely another way of saying "<u>Let me not wander into temptation.</u>" The purpose of the world you see is to obscure your function of forgiveness, and provide you with a justification for forgetting it. It is the temptation to abandon God and His Son by taking on a physical appearance. It is this the body's eyes look upon.

W-pI.069.8 - Have confidence in your Father today, and be certain that He has heard you and answered you. You may not recognize His answer yet, but you can indeed be sure that it is given you and you will yet receive it. Try, as you attempt to go through the clouds to the light, to hold this confidence in your mind. Try to remember that you are at last joining your will to God's. Try to keep the thought clearly in mind that what you undertake with God must succeed. Then let the power of God work in you and through you, that <u>His Will and yours be done</u>.

W-pI.073.8 - Therefore, we undertake the exercises for today in happy confidence, certain that we will find what it is your will to find, and remember what it is your will to remember. No idle wishes can detain us, nor deceive us with an illusion of strength. Today <u>let your will be done</u>, and end forever the insane belief that it is hell in place of Heaven that you choose.

W-pI.077.4-5 – 4 Begin the longer practice periods by telling yourself quite confidently that you are entitled to miracles. Closing your eyes, remind yourself that you are asking only for what is rightfully yours. Remind yourself also that miracles are never taken from one and given to another, and that in asking for your rights, you are upholding the rights of everyone. Miracles do not obey the laws of this world. They merely follow from the laws of God.
5 After this brief introductory phase, wait quietly for the assurance that your request is granted. You have asked for the salvation of the world, and

for your own. You have requested that you be given the means by which this is accomplished. You cannot fail to be assured in this. You are but asking that <u>the Will of God be done</u>.

W-pI.098.7:6 - 9:6 I will accept my part in God's plan for salvation.

In each five minutes that you spend with Him, He will accept your words and give them back to you all bright with faith and confidence so strong and steady they will light the world with hope and gladness. Do not lose one chance to be the glad receiver of His gifts, that you may give them to the world today.

Give Him the words, and He will do the rest. He will enable you to understand your special function. He will open up the way to happiness, and peace and trust will be His gifts; His answer to your words. He will respond with all His faith and joy and certainty that what you say is true. And you will have conviction then of Him Who knows the function that you have <u>on earth as well as Heaven</u>. He will be with you each practice period you share with Him, exchanging every instant of the time you offer Him for timelessness and peace.

W-pI.104.5 - So do we clear the way for Him today by simply recognizing that <u>His Will is done</u> already, and that joy and peace belong to us as His eternal gifts. We will not let ourselves lose sight of them between the times we come to seek for them where He has laid them. This reminder will we bring to mind as often as we can:
I seek but what belongs to me in truth.
God's gifts of joy and peace are all I want.

W-pI.159.4 - Christ's vision is the miracle in which all miracles are born. It is their source, remaining with each miracle you give, and yet remaining yours. It is the bond by which the giver and receiver are united in extension here <u>on earth, as they are one in Heaven</u>. Christ beholds no sin in anyone. And in His sight the sinless are as one. Their holiness was given by His Father and Himself.

W-pI.186.ti-1 - Salvation of the world depends on me.
1 Here is the statement that will one day take all arrogance away from every mind. Here is the thought of true humility, which holds no function

as your own but that which has been given you. It offers your acceptance of a part assigned to you, without insisting on another role. It does not judge your proper role. It but acknowledges the Will of God is done on earth as well as Heaven. It unites all wills on earth in Heaven's plan to save the world, restoring it to Heaven's peace.

Bible Reference - Text

Matthew 6:9-13 - After this manner therefore pray ye: Our Father ....

(Continued) - (To read the full text of the above go to page 127.)

Course Ref/s - Citation/s

W-pI.189.10 - Father, we do not know the way to You. But we have called, and You have answered us. We will not interfere. Salvation's ways are not our own, for they belong to You. And it is unto You we look for them. Our hands are open to receive Your gifts. We have no thoughts we think apart from You, and cherish no beliefs of what we are, or Who created us. Yours is the way that we would find and follow. And we ask but that Your Will, which is our own as well, be done in us and in the world, that it become a part of Heaven now. Amen.

W-pI.193.1 - God does not know of learning. Yet His Will extends to what He does not understand, in that He wills the happiness His Son inherited of Him be undisturbed; eternal and forever gaining scope, eternally expanding in the joy of full creation, and eternally open and wholly limitless in Him. That is His Will. And thus His Will provides the means to guarantee that it is done.

W-pI.198.10 - Accept the one illusion which proclaims there is no condemnation in God's Son, and Heaven is remembered instantly; the world forgotten, all its weird beliefs forgotten with it, as the face of Christ appears unveiled at last in this one dream. This is the gift the Holy Spirit holds for you from God your Father. Let today be celebrated both on earth and in your holy home as well. Be kind to both, as you forgive the trespasses you thought them guilty of, and see your innocence shining upon you from the face of Christ.

W-pI.rV.10 - Let this review become a time in which we share a new experience for you, yet one as old as time and older still. <u>Hallowed your Name</u>. Your glory undefiled forever. And your wholeness now complete, as God established it. You are His Son, completing His extension in your own. We practice but an ancient truth we knew before illusion seemed to claim the world. And we remind the world that it is free of all illusions every time we say: God is but Love, and therefore so am I.

W-pII.11.4 - We are creation; we the Sons of God. We seem to be discrete, and unaware of our eternal unity with Him. Yet back of all our doubts, past all our fears, there still is certainty. For love remains with all its Thoughts, its sureness being theirs. God's memory is in our holy minds, which know their oneness and their unity with their Creator. Let our function be only to let this memory return, only to let <u>God's Will be done on earth</u>, only to be restored to sanity, and to be but as God created us.

W-pII.292.1 - God's promises make no exceptions. And He guarantees that only joy can be the final outcome found for everything. Yet it is up to us when this is reached; how long we let an alien will appear to be opposing His. And while we think this will is real, we will not find the end He has appointed as the outcome of all problems we perceive, all trials we see, and every situation that we meet. Yet is the ending certain. For <u>God's Will is done in earth and Heaven</u>. We will seek and we will find according to His Will, which guarantees that our will is done.

W-pII.326.1 - Father, I was created in Your Mind, a holy Thought that never left its home. I am forever Your Effect, and You forever and forever are my Cause. As You created me I have remained. Where You established me I still abide. And all Your attributes abide in me, because it is Your Will to have a Son so like his Cause that Cause and Its Effect are indistinguishable. Let me know that I am an Effect of God, and so I have <u>the power to create like You. And as it is in Heaven</u>, so on earth. Your plan I follow here, and at the end I know that You will gather Your effects into the tranquil Heaven of Your Love, where earth will vanish, and all separate thoughts unite in glory as the Son of God.

M-14.5 - The world will end in joy, because it is a place of sorrow. When joy has come, the purpose of the world has gone. The world will end in peace, because it is a place of war. When peace has come, what is the purpose of the world? The world will end in laughter, because it is a place of tears. Where there is laughter, who can longer weep? And only complete forgiveness brings all this to bless the world. In blessing it departs, for it will not end as it began. To turn hell into Heaven is the function of God's teachers, for what they teach are lessons in which Heaven is reflected. And now sit down in true humility, and realize that all God would have you do you can do. Do not be arrogant and say you cannot learn His Own curriculum. His Word says otherwise. <u>His Will be done.</u> It cannot be otherwise. And be you thankful it is so.

Bible Reference - Text

Matthew 6:9-13 - After this manner therefore pray ye: Our Father ....

(Continued) - (To read the full text of the above go to page 127.)

Course Ref/s - Citation/s

C-4.8 - O my brothers, if you only knew the peace that will envelop you and hold you safe and pure and lovely in the Mind of God, you could but rush to meet Him where His altar is. <u>Hallowed your Name and His,</u> for they are joined here in this holy place. Here He leans down to lift you up to Him, out of illusions into holiness; out of the world and to eternity; out of all fear and given back to love.

P-2.V.7 - Somewhere all gifts of God must be received. In time no effort can be made in vain. It is not our perfection that is asked in our attempts to heal. We are deceived already, if we think there is a need of healing. And the truth will come to us only through one who seems to share our dream of sickness. Let us help him to <u>forgive himself for all the trespasses</u> with which he would condemn himself without a cause. His healing is our own. And as we see the sinlessness in him come shining through the veil of guilt that shrouds the Son of God, we will behold in him the face of Christ, and understand that it s but our own.

Bible Reference - Text

Matthew 6:14-15 - For if ye forgive men their trespasses, your heavenly Father will also forgive you: But if ye forgive not men their trespasses, neither will your Father forgive your trespasses.

P. Matthew

Course Ref/s - Citation/s

T-27.II.3 - <u>To witness sin and yet forgive it</u> is a paradox that reason cannot see. For it maintains what has been done to you deserves no pardon.
And by giving it, you grant your brother mercy but retain the proof he is not really innocent. The sick remain accusers. They cannot forgive their brothers and themselves as well. For no one in whom true forgiveness rests can suffer. He holds not the proof of sin before his brother's eyes. And thus he must have overlooked it and removed it from his own. Forgiveness cannot be for one and not the other. Who forgives is healed. And in his healing lies the proof that he has truly pardoned, and retains no trace of condemnation that he still would hold against himself or any living thing.

T-31.VI.6 - Are you invulnerable? Then the world is harmless in your sight. <u>Do you forgive? Then is the world forgiving, for you have forgiven it its trespasses,</u> and so it looks on you with eyes that see as yours. Are you a body? So is all the world perceived as treacherous, and out to kill.
Are you a spirit, deathless, and without the promise of corruption and the stain of sin upon you? So the world is seen as stable, fully worthy of your trust; a happy place to rest in for a while, where nothing need be feared, but only loved. Who is unwelcome to the kind in heart? And what could hurt the truly innocent?

W-pI.198.9-10 - Today we practice letting freedom come to make its home with you. The truth bestows these words upon your mind, that you may find the key to light and let the darkness end:

> Only my condemnation injures me.
> <u>Only my own forgiveness sets me free.</u>

Do not forget today that there can be no form of suffering that fails to hide an unforgiving thought. Nor can there be a form of pain forgiveness cannot heal.

Accept the one illusion which proclaims there is no condemnation in God's Son, and Heaven is remembered instantly; the world forgotten, all its weird beliefs forgotten with it, as the face of Christ appears unveiled at last in this one dream. This is the gift the Holy Spirit holds for you from God your Father. Let today be celebrated both on earth and in your holy home as well. Be kind to both, as you <u>forgive the trespasses</u> you thought them guilty of, and see your innocence shining upon you from the face of Christ.

Bible Reference - Text

Matthew 6:19-21 - Lay not up for yourselves treasures upon earth, where moth and rust doth corrupt, and where thieves break through and steal: But lay up for yourselves treasures in heaven, where neither moth nor rust doth corrupt, and where thieves do not break through nor steal: For where your treasure is, there will your heart be also.

Course Ref/s - Citation/s

T-02.II.1:5-14 - Remember that <u>where your heart is, there is your treasure also</u>. You believe in what you value. If you are afraid, you will inevitably value wrongly, and by endowing all thoughts with equal power will inevitably destroy peace. That is why the Bible speaks of "the peace of God which passeth understanding." This peace is totally incapable of being shaken by errors of any kind. It denies the ability of anything not of God to affect you. This is the proper use of denial. It is not used to hide anything, but to correct error. It brings all error into the light, and since error and darkness are the same, it corrects error automatically.

T-08.VI.10 - What God has willed for you is yours. He has given His Will to His treasure, whose treasure it is. <u>Your heart lies where your treasure is</u>, as His does. You who are beloved of God are wholly blessed. Learn this of me, and free the holy will of all those who are as blessed as you are.

T-13.IX.2 - Release from guilt is the ego's whole undoing. Make no one fearful, for his guilt is yours, and by obeying the ego's harsh commandments you bring its condemnation on yourself, and you will not escape the punishment it offers those who obey it. The ego rewards fidelity to it with pain, for faith in it is pain. And faith can be rewarded only in terms of the belief in which the faith was placed. Faith makes the power of belief, and where it is invested determines its reward. For faith is always given what is treasured, and <u>what is treasured is returned to you</u>.

T-13.X.13 - Like you, my faith and my belief are centered on <u>what I treasure</u>. The difference is that I love only what God loves with me, and because of this I treasure you beyond the value that you set on yourself, even unto the worth that God has placed upon you. I love all that He created, and all my faith and my belief I offer unto it. My faith in you is as strong as all the love I give my Father. My trust in you is without limit, and without the fear that you will hear me not. I thank the Father for your loveliness, and for the many gifts that you will let me offer to the Kingdom in honor of its wholeness that is of God.

T-14.II.1 - The Holy Spirit needs a happy learner, in whom His mission can be happily accomplished. You who are steadfastly devoted to misery must first recognize that you are miserable and not happy. The Holy Spirit cannot teach without this contrast, for you believe that misery is happiness. This has so confused you that you have undertaken to learn to do what you can never do, believing that unless you learn it you will not be happy.
You do not realize that the foundation on which this most peculiar learning goal depends means absolutely nothing. Yet it may still make sense to you. Have faith in nothing and you will find the "treasure" that you seek.
Yet you will add another burden to your already burdened mind. You will believe that nothing is of value, and will value it. A little piece of glass, a speck of dust, a body or a war are one to you. For if you value one thing made of nothing, you have believed that nothing can be precious, and that you can learn how to make the untrue true.

T-24.IV.3 - You can but hurt yourself. This has been oft repeated, but is difficult to grasp as yet. To minds intent on specialness it is impossible. Yet to those who wish to heal and not attack, it is quite obvious.
The purpose of attack is in the mind, and its effects are felt but where it is. Nor is the mind limited; so must it be that harmful purpose hurts the mind as one. Nothing could make less sense to specialness. Nothing could make more sense to miracles. For miracles are merely change of purpose from hurt to healing. This shift in purpose does "endanger" specialness, but only in the sense that all illusions are "threatened" by the truth. They will not stand before it. Yet what comfort has ever been in them, that you would keep the gift your Father asks from Him, and give it there instead? Given to Him, the universe is yours. Offered to them, no gifts can be returned. What you have given specialness has left you bankrupt and your treasure house barren and empty, with an open door inviting everything that would disturb your peace to enter and destroy.

T-25.IX.2 - To give reluctantly is not to gain the gift, because you are reluctant to accept it. It is saved for you until reluctance to receive it disappears, and you are willing it be given you. God's justice warrants gratitude, not fear. Nothing you give is lost to you or anyone, but cherished and preserved in Heaven, where all of the treasures given to God's Son are kept for him, and offered anyone who but holds out his hand in willingness they be received. Nor is the treasure less as it is given out. Each gift but adds to the supply. For God is fair. He does not fight against His Son's reluctance to perceive salvation as a gift from Him. Yet would His justice not be satisfied until it is received by everyone.

Bible Reference - Text

Matthew 6:19-21 - Lay not up for yourselves treasures....
(Continued) - (To read the full text of the above go to page 141.)

Course Ref/s - Citation/s

T-28.III.7 - Count, then, the silver miracles and golden dreams of happiness as all the treasures you would keep within the storehouse of the world. The door is open, not to thieves, but to your starving brothers, who mistook for gold the shining of a pebble, and who stored a heap of snow that shone like silver. They have nothing left behind the open door. What is the world except a little gap perceived to tear eternity apart, and break it into days and months and years? And what are you who live within the world except a picture of the Son of God in broken pieces, each concealed within a separate and uncertain bit of clay?

W-pII.316.ti-1 - All gifts I give my brothers are my own.

As every gift my brothers give is mine, so every gift I give belongs to me. Each one allows a past mistake to go, and leave no shadow on the holy mind my Father loves. His grace is given me in every gift a brother has received throughout all time, and past all time as well. My treasure house is full, and angels watch its open doors that not one gift is lost, and only more are added. Let me come to where my treasures are, and enter in where I am truly welcome and at home, among the gifts that God has given me.

W-pII.334.ti-2 - Today I claim the gifts forgiveness gives.

I will not wait another day to find the treasures that my Father offers me. Illusions are all vain, and dreams are gone even while they are woven out of thoughts that rest on false perceptions. Let me not accept such meager gifts again today. God's Voice is offering the peace of God to all who hear and choose to follow Him. This is my choice today. And so I go to find the treasures God has given me.

I seek but the eternal. For Your Son can be content with nothing less than this. What, then, can be his solace but what You are offering to his bewildered mind and frightened heart, to give him certainty and bring him peace? Today I would behold my brother sinless. This Your Will for me, for so will I behold my sinlessness.

W-pII.344.ti-1 - Today I learn the law of love; that what I give my brother is my gift to me.
This is Your law, my Father, not my own. I have not understood what giving means, and thought to save what I desired for myself alone. And as I looked upon the treasure that I thought I had, I found an empty place where nothing ever was or is or will be. Who can share a dream? And what can an illusion offer me? Yet he whom I forgive will give me gifts beyond the worth of anything on earth. Let my forgiven brothers fill my store with Heaven's treasures, which alone are real. Thus is the law of love fulfilled. And thus Your Son arises and returns to You.

Bible Reference - Text

Matthew 6:24 - No man can serve two masters: for either he will hate the one, and love the other; or else he will hold to the one, and despise the other. Ye cannot serve God and mammon.

Course Ref/s - Citation/s

T-01.V.5 - Whatever is true is eternal, and cannot change or be changed. Spirit is therefore unalterable because it is already perfect, but the mind can elect what it chooses to serve. The only limit put on its choice is that it cannot serve two masters. If it elects to do so, the mind can become the medium by which spirit creates along the line of its own creation. If it does not freely elect to do so, it retains its creative potential but places itself under tyrannous rather than Authoritative control. As a result it imprisons, because such are the dictates of tyrants. To change your mind means to place it at the disposal of true Authority.

T-17.I.1:8-2:6 - Fantasies change reality. That is their purpose. They cannot do so in reality, but they can do so in the mind that would have reality be different.

It is, then, only your wish to change reality that is fearful, because by your wish you think you have accomplished what you wish. This strange position, in a sense, acknowledges your power. Yet by distorting it and devoting it to "evil," it also makes it unreal. <u>You cannot be faithful to two masters</u> who ask conflicting things of you. What you use in fantasy you deny to truth. Yet what you give to truth to use for you is safe from fantasy.

T-19.IV.A.11 - Love's messengers are gently sent, and return with messages of love and gentleness. The messengers of fear are harshly ordered to seek out guilt, and cherish every scrap of evil and of sin that they can find, losing none of them on pain of death, and laying them respectfully before their lord and master. Perception <u>cannot obey two masters,</u> each asking for messages of different things in different languages. What fear would feed upon, love overlooks. What fear demands, love cannot even see. The fierce attraction that guilt holds for fear is wholly absent from love's gentle perception. What love would look upon is meaningless to fear, and quite invisible.

Bible Reference - Text

Matthew 6:25 - Therefore I say unto you, Take no thought for your life, what ye shall eat, or what ye shall drink; nor yet for your body, what ye shall put on. Is not the life more than meat, and the body than raiment?

Course Ref/s - Citation/s

T-14.X.10 - It is impossible to remember God in secret and alone. For remembering Him means you are not alone, and are willing to remember it. <u>Take no thought for yourself,</u> for no thought you hold is for yourself. If you would remember your Father, let the Holy Spirit order your thoughts and give only the answer with which He answers you. Everyone seeks for love as you do, but knows it not unless he joins with you in seeking it. If you undertake the search together, you bring with you a light so powerful that what you see is given meaning. The lonely journey fails because it has excluded what it would find.

Bible Reference - Text

Matthew 6:31-32 - Therefore take no thought, saying, What shall we eat? Or, What shall we drink? Or, Wherewithal shall we be clothed? (For after all these things do the Gentiles seek:) for your heavenly Father knoweth that ye have need of all these things.

Course Ref/s - Citation/s

T-13.VII.10 - Praise, then, the Father for the perfect sanity of His most holy Son. <u>Your Father knoweth that you have need</u> of nothing. In Heaven this is so, for what could you need in eternity? In your world you do need things. It is a world of scarcity in which you find yourself because you are lacking. Yet can you find yourself in such a world? Without the Holy Spirit the answer would be no. Yet because of Him the answer is a joyous yes! As Mediator between the two worlds, He knows what you have need of and what will not hurt you. Ownership is a dangerous concept if it is left to you. The ego wants to have things for salvation, for possession is its law. Possession for its own sake is the ego's fundamental creed, a basic cornerstone in the churches it builds to itself. And at its altar it demands you lay all of the things it bids you get, leaving you no joy in them.

T-14.XI.7 - You cannot be your guide to miracles, for it is you who made them necessary. And because you did, the means on which you can depend for miracles has been provided for you. <u>God's Son can make no needs His Father will not meet,</u> if he but turn to Him ever so little. Yet He cannot compel His Son to turn to Him and remain Himself. It is impossible that God lose His Identity, for if He did, you would lose yours. And being yours He cannot change Himself, for your Identity is changeless.
The miracle acknowledges His changelessness by seeing His Son as he always was, and not as he would make himself. The miracle brings the effects that only guiltlessness can bring, and thus establishes the fact that guiltlessness must be.

W-pII.349.ti-2 - Today I let Christ's vision look upon All things for me and judge them not, but give Each one a miracle of love instead.
So would I liberate all things I see, and give to them the freedom that I seek. For thus do I obey the law of love, and give what I would find and make my own. It will be given me, because I have chosen it as the gift I want to give. Father, Your gifts are mine. Each one that I accept gives me a miracle to give. And giving as I would receive, I learn Your healing miracles belong to me.

Our Father knows our needs. He gives us grace to meet them all. And so we trust in Him to send us miracles to bless the world, and heal our minds as we return to Him.

Bible Reference - Text

Matthew 6:33 - But seek ye first the kingdom of God, and his righteousness; and all these things shall be added unto you.

Course Ref/s - Citation/s

T-03.VI.11 - There is no one who does not feel that he is imprisoned in some way. If this is the result of his own free will he must regard his will as not free, or the circular reasoning in this position would be quite apparent. Free will must lead to freedom. Judgment always imprisons because it separates segments of reality by the unstable scales of desire. Wishes are not facts. To wish is to imply that willing is not sufficient. Yet no one in his right mind believes that what is wished is as real as what is willed. Instead of "Seek ye first the Kingdom of Heaven" say, "Will ye first the Kingdom of Heaven," and you have said, "I know what I am and I accept my own inheritance."

T-07.IV.7 - Seek ye first the Kingdom of Heaven, because that is where the laws of God operate truly, and they can operate only truly because they are the laws of truth. But seek this only, because you can find nothing else. There is nothing else. God is All in all in a very literal sense. All being is in Him Who is all Being. You are therefore in Him since your being is His. Healing is a way of forgetting the sense of danger the ego has induced in you, by not recognizing its existence in your brother. This strengthens the Holy Spirit in both of you, because it is a refusal to acknowledge fear. Love needs only this invitation. It comes freely to all the Sonship, being what the Sonship is. By your awakening to it, you are merely forgetting what you are not. This enables you to remember what you are.

S-1.I.2:4-3:6 - There are decisions to make here, and they must be made whether they be illusions or not. You cannot be asked to accept answers which are beyond the level of need that you can recognize. Therefore, it is not the form of the question that matters, nor how it is asked. The form of the answer, if given by God, will suit your need as you see it. This is merely an echo of the reply of His Voice. The real sound is always a song of thanksgiving and of love.

You cannot, then, ask for the echo. It is the song that is the gift. Along with it come the overtones, the harmonics, the echoes, but these are secondary. In true prayer you hear only the song. All the rest is merely added. You have sought first the Kingdom of Heaven, and all else has indeed been given you.

Bible Reference - Text

Matthew 7:1-2 - Judge not, that ye be not judged. For with what judgment ye judge, ye shall be judged: and with what measure ye mete, it shall be measured to you again.

Course Ref/s - Citation/s

T-03.VI.1:4 - When the Bible says "Judge not that ye be not judged," it means that if you judge the reality of others you will be unable to avoid judging your own.

T-09.II.09 - To disbelieve is to side against, or to attack. To believe is to accept, and to side with. To believe is not to be credulous, but to accept and appreciate. What you do not believe you do not appreciate, and you cannot be grateful for what you do not value. There is a price you will pay for judgment, because judgment is the setting of a price. And as you set it you will pay it.

T-09.II.11 - Never forget, then, that you set the value on what you receive, and price it by what you give. To believe that it is possible to get much for little is to believe that you can bargain with God. God's laws are always fair and perfectly consistent. By giving you receive. But to receive is to accept, not to get. It is impossible not to have, but it is possible not to know you have. The recognition of having is the willingness for giving, and only by this willingness can you recognize what you have. What you give is therefore the value you put on what you have, being the exact measure of the value you put upon it. And this, in turn, is the measure of how much you want it.

T-14.V.11 - Each one you see you place within the holy circle of Atonement or leave outside, judging him fit for crucifixion or for redemption. If you bring him into the circle of purity, you will rest there with him. If you leave him without, you join him there. Judge not except in quietness which is not of you. Refuse to accept anyone as without the blessing of Atonement, and bring him into it by blessing him. Holiness must be shared, for therein lies everything that makes it holy. Come gladly to the holy circle, and look out in peace on all who think they are outside. Cast no one out, for here is what he seeks along with you. Come, let us join him in the holy place of peace which is for all of us, united as one within the Cause of peace.

T-20.V.3 - It is impossible to overestimate your brother's value. Only the ego does this, but all it means is that it wants the other for itself, and therefore values him too little. What is inestimable clearly cannot be evaluated. Do you recognize the fear that rises from the meaningless attempt to judge what lies so far beyond your judgment you cannot even see it? Judge not what is invisible to you or you will never see it, but wait in patience for its coming. It will be given you to see your brother's worth when all you want for him is peace. And what you want for him you will receive.

T-20.V.4 - How can you estimate the worth of him who offers peace to you? What would you want except his offering? His worth has been established by his Father, and you will recognize it as you receive his Father's gift through him. What is in him will shine so brightly in your grateful vision that you will merely love him and be glad. You will not think to judge him, for who would see the face of Christ and yet insist that judgment still has meaning? For this insistence is of those who do not see. Vision or judgment is your choice, but never both of these.

T-25.VIII.13 - Without impartiality there is no justice. How can specialness be just? Judge not because you cannot, not because you are a miserable sinner too. How can the special really understand that justice is the same for everyone? To take from one to give another must be an injustice to them both, since they are equal in the Holy Spirit's sight. Their Father gave the same inheritance to both. Who would have more or less is not aware that he has everything. He is no judge of what must be another's due, because he thinks he is deprived. And so must he be envious, and try to take away from whom he judges. He is not impartial, and cannot fairly see another's rights because his own have been obscured to him.

T-26.I.6 - You can lose sight of oneness, but can not make sacrifice of its reality. Nor can you lose what you would sacrifice, nor keep the Holy Spirit from His task of showing you that it has not been lost. Hear, then, the song your brother sings to you, and let the world recede, and take the rest his witness offers on behalf of peace. But judge him not, for you will hear no song of liberation for yourself, nor see what it is given him to witness to, that you may see it and rejoice with him. Make not his holiness a sacrifice to your belief in sin. You sacrifice your innocence with his, and die each time you see in him a sin deserving death.

Bible Reference - Text

Matthew 7:1-2 - Judge not, that ye be not judged....
(Continued) - (To read the full text of the above go to page 148.)

Course Ref/s - Citation/s

T-29.IX.2 - A dream of judgment came into the mind that God created perfect as Himself. And in that dream was Heaven changed to hell, and God made enemy unto His Son. How can God's Son awaken from the dream? It is a dream of judgment. So must he judge not, and he will waken. For the dream will seem to last while he is part of it. Judge not, for he who judges will have need of idols, which will hold the judgment off from resting on himself. Nor can he know the Self he has condemned. Judge not, because you make yourself a part of evil dreams, where idols are your "true" identity, and your salvation from the judgment laid in terror and in guilt upon yourself.

W-pI.151.3-4 - How can you judge? Your judgment rests upon the witness that your senses offer you. Yet witness never falser was than this. But how else do you judge the world you see? You place pathetic faith in what your eyes and ears report. You think your fingers touch reality, and close upon the truth. This is awareness that you understand, and think more real than what is witnessed to by the eternal Voice for God Himself.

Can this be judgment? You have often been urged to refrain from judging, not because it is a right to be withheld from you. You cannot judge.
You merely can believe the ego's judgments, all of which are false.
It guides your senses carefully, to prove how weak you are; how helpless and afraid, how apprehensive of just punishment, how black with sin, how wretched in your guilt.

W-pII.311.1-2 - Judgment was made to be a weapon used against the truth. It separates what it is being used against; and sets it off as if it were a thing apart. And then it makes of it what you would have it be. It judges what it cannot understand, because it cannot see totality and therefore judges falsely. Let us not use it today, but make a gift of it to Him [the Holy Spirit] Who has a different use for it. He will relieve us of the agony of all the judgments we have made against ourselves, and re-establish peace of mind by giving us God's Judgment of His Son.

Father, we wait with open mind today, to hear Your Judgment of the Son You love. We do not know him, and we cannot judge. And so we let Your Love decide what he whom You created as Your Son must be.

W-pII.312.1-2 - Perception follows judgment. Having judged, we therefore see what we would look upon. For sight can merely serve to offer us what we would have. It is impossible to overlook what we would see, and fail to see what we have chosen to behold. How surely, therefore, must the real world come to greet the holy sight of anyone who takes the Holy Spirit's purpose as his goal for seeing. And he cannot fail to look upon what Christ would have him see, and share Christ's Love for what he looks upon.

I have no purpose for today except to look upon a liberated world, set free from all the judgments I have made. Father, this is Your Will for me today. And therefore it must be my goal as well.

W-pII.349.ti-1 - Today I let Christ's vision look upon All things for me and judge them not, but give Each one a miracle of love instead.
So would I liberate all things I see, and give to them the freedom that I seek. For thus do I obey the law of love, and give what I would find and make my own. It will be given me, because I have chosen it as the gift I want to give. Father, Your gifts are mine. Each one that I accept gives me a miracle to give. And giving as I would receive, I learn Your healing miracles belong to me.

W-pII.352.ti-1 - Judgment and love are opposites. From one Come all the sorrows of the world. But from The other comes the peace of God Himself.
Forgiveness looks on sinlessness alone, and judges not. Through this I come to You. Judgment will bind my eyes and make me blind. Yet love, reflected in forgiveness here, reminds me You have given me a way to find Your peace again. I am redeemed when I elect to follow in this way. You have not left me comfortless. I have within me both the memory of

You, and One Who leads me to it. Father, I would hear Your Voice and find Your peace today. For I would love my own Identity, and find in It the memory of You.

Bible Reference - Text

Matthew 7:1-2 - Judge not, that ye be not judged....
(Continued) - (To read the full text of the above go to page 148.)

Course Ref/s - Citation/s

M-04.III.1 - God's teachers <u>do not judge</u>. To judge is to be dishonest, for to judge is to assume a position you do not have. Judgment without self-deception is impossible. Judgment implies that you have been deceived in your brothers. How, then, could you not have been deceived in yourself? Judgment implies a lack of trust, and trust remains the bedrock of the teacher of God's whole thought system. Let this be lost, and all his learning goes. Without judgment are all things equally acceptable, for who could judge otherwise? Without judgment are all men brothers, for who is there who stands apart? Judgment destroys honesty and shatters trust. No teacher of God can judge and hope to learn.

M-09.2 - As the teacher of God advances in his training, he learns one lesson with increasing thoroughness. He does not make his own decisions; he asks his Teacher [the Holy Spirit] for His answer, and it is this he follows as his guide for action. This becomes easier and easier, as the teacher of God learns to <u>give up his own judgment</u>. The giving up of judgment, the obvious prerequisite for hearing God's Voice, is usually a fairly slow process, not because it is difficult, but because it is apt to be perceived as personally insulting. The world's training is directed toward achieving a goal in direct opposition to that of our curriculum. The world trains for reliance on one's judgment as the criterion for maturity and strength. Our curriculum trains for the relinquishment of judgment as the necessary condition of salvation.

M-10.2 - It is necessary for the teacher of God to realize, not that <u>he should not judge</u>, but that he cannot. In giving up judgment, he is merely giving up what he did not have. He gives up an illusion; or better, he has an illusion of giving up. He has actually merely become more honest. Recognizing that judgment was always impossible for him, he no longer attempts it. This is no sacrifice. On the contrary, he puts himself in a position where judgment through him rather than by him can occur. And this judgment is neither "good" nor "bad." It is the only judgment there is, and it is only one: "God's Son is guiltless, and sin does not exist."

M-15.1:2-2:13 - No one can escape God's Final Judgment. Who could flee forever from the truth? But the Final Judgment will not come until it is no longer associated with fear. One day each one will welcome it, and on that very day it will be given him. He will hear his sinlessness proclaimed around and around the world, setting it free as God's Final Judgment on him is received. This is the Judgment in which salvation lies. This is the Judgment that will set him free. This is the Judgment in which all things are freed with him. Time pauses as eternity comes near, and silence lies across the world that everyone may hear this Judgment of the Son of God:

> Holy are you, eternal, free and whole, at peace forever in the Heart of God. Where is the world, and where is sorrow now?

Is this your judgment on yourself, teacher of God? Do you believe that this is wholly true? No; not yet, not yet. But this is still your goal; why you are here. It is your function to prepare yourself to hear this judgment and to recognize that it is true. One instant of complete belief in this, and you will go beyond belief to Certainty. One instant out of time can bring time's end. <u>Judge not, for you but judge yourself</u>, and thus delay this Final Judgment. What is your judgment of the world, teacher of God? Have you yet learned to stand aside and hear the Voice of Judgment [the Holy Spirit] in yourself? Or do you still attempt to take His role from Him? Learn to be quiet, for His Voice is heard in stillness. And His Judgment comes to all who stand aside in quiet listening, and wait for Him.

M-22.7 - Who can limit the power of God Himself? Who, then, can say which one can be healed of what, and what must remain beyond God's power to forgive? This is insanity indeed. It is not up to God's teachers to set limits upon Him, because it is not up to them to judge His Son. And to judge His Son is to limit his Father. Both are equally meaningless. Yet this will not be understood until God's teacher recognizes that they are the same mistake. Herein does he receive Atonement, for <u>he withdraws his judgment</u> from the Son of God, accepting him as God created him. No longer does he stand apart from God, determining where healing should be given and where it should be withheld. Now can he say with God, "This is my beloved Son, created perfect and forever so."

Bible Reference - Text

Matthew 7:1-2 - Judge not, that ye be not judged....
(Continued) - (To read the full text of the above go to page 148.)

Course Ref/s - Citation/s

P-3.II.6 - It is in the instant that the therapist <u>forgets to judge</u> the patient that healing occurs. In some relationships this point is never reached, although both patient and therapist may change their dreams in the process. Yet it will not be the same dream for both of them, and so it is not the dream of forgiveness in which both will someday wake. The good is saved; indeed is cherished. But only little time is saved. The new dreams will lose their temporary appeal and turn to dreams of fear, which is the content of all dreams. Yet no patient can accept more than he is ready to receive, and no therapist can offer more than he believes he has. And so there is a place for all relationships in this world, and they will bring as much good as each can accept and use.

P-3.II.7 - Yet it is when <u>judgment ceases</u> that healing occurs, because only then it can be understood that there is no order of difficulty in healing. This is a necessary understanding for the healed healer. He has learned that it is no harder to wake a brother from one dream than from another.
No professional therapist can hold this understanding consistently in his mind, offering it to all who come to him. There are some in this world who have come very close, but they have not accepted the gift entirely in order to stay and let their understanding remain on earth until the closing of time. They could hardly be called professional therapists. They are the Saints of God. They are the Saviors of the world. Their image remains, because they have chosen that it be so. They take the place of other images, and help with kindly dreams.

Bible Reference - Text

Matthew 7:3-5 - And why beholdest thou the mote that is in thy brother's eye, but considerest not the beam that is in thine own eye? Or how wilt thou say to thy brother, Let me pull out the mote out of thine eye; and, behold, a beam is in thine own eye? Thou hypocrite, first cast out the beam out of thine own eye; and then shalt thou see clearly to cast out the mote out of thy brother's eye.

Course Ref/s - Citation/s

T-03.III.5 - <u>The Bible tells you to know yourself</u>, or to be certain. Certainty is always of God. When you love someone you have perceived him as he is, and this makes it possible for you to know him. Until you first perceive him as he is you cannot know him. While you ask questions about him you are clearly implying that you do not know God. Certainty does not require action. When you say you are acting on the basis of knowledge, you are really confusing knowledge with perception. Knowledge provides the strength for creative thinking, but not for right doing. Perception, miracles and doing are closely related. Knowledge is the result of revelation and induces only thought. Even in its most spiritualised form perception involves the body. Knowledge comes from the altar within and is timeless because it is certain. To perceive the truth is not the same as to know it.

T-27.II.3 - To witness sin and yet forgive it is a paradox that reason cannot see. For it maintains what has been done to you deserves no pardon. And by giving it, you grant your brother mercy but retain the proof he is not really innocent. The sick remain accusers. They cannot forgive their brothers and themselves as well. For no one in whom true forgiveness rests can suffer. He holds not the proof of sin before his brother's eyes. <u>And thus he must have overlooked it and removed it from his own.</u> Forgiveness cannot be for one and not the other. Who forgives is healed. And in his healing lies the proof that he has truly pardoned, and retains no trace of condemnation that he still would hold against himself or any living thing.

Bible Reference - Text

Matthew 7:7-8 - Ask, and it shall be given you; seek, and ye shall find; knock, and it shall be opened unto you: For every one that asketh receiveth; and he that seeketh findeth; and to him that knocketh it shall be opened.

Course Ref/s - Citation/s

T-03.V.6 - <u>Prayer is a way of asking for something</u>. It is the medium of miracles. But the only meaningful prayer is for forgiveness, because those who have been forgiven have everything. Once forgiveness has been accepted, prayer in the usual sense becomes utterly meaningless. <u>The prayer for forgiveness is nothing more than a request that you may be able to recognize what you already have.</u> In electing perception instead of knowledge, you placed yourself in a position where you could resemble your Father only by perceiving miraculously. You have lost the knowledge that you yourself are a miracle of God. Creation is your Source and your only real function.

T-04.III.4:7-5:5 - Love will enter immediately into any mind that truly wants it, but it must want it truly. This means that it wants it without ambivalence, and this kind of wanting is wholly without the ego's "drive to get."

There is a kind of experience so different from anything the ego can offer that you will never want to cover or hide it again. It is necessary to repeat that your belief in darkness and hiding is why the light cannot enter. <u>The Bible gives many references to the immeasurable gifts which are for you, but for which you must ask.</u> This is not a condition as the ego sets conditions. It is the glorious condition of what you are.

T-04.III.6 - No force except your own will is strong enough or worthy enough to guide you. In this you are as free as God, and must remain so forever. <u>Let us ask the Father in my name to keep you mindful of His Love for you and yours for Him. He has never failed to answer this request, because it asks only for what He has already willed.</u> Those who call truly are always answered. Thou shalt have no other gods before Him because there are none.

T-04.III.7 - It has never really entered your mind to give up every idea you ever had that opposes knowledge. You retain thousands of little scraps of fear that prevent the Holy One from entering. Light cannot penetrate through the walls you make to block it, and it is forever unwilling to destroy what you have made. No one can see through a wall, but I [Jesus] can step around it. Watch your mind for the scraps of fear, or you will be unable to ask me to do so. I can help you only as our Father created us. I will love you and honor you and maintain complete respect for what you have made, but I will not uphold it unless it is true. I will never forsake you any more than God will, but I must wait as long as you choose to forsake yourself. Because I wait in love and not in impatience, <u>you will surely ask me truly. I will come in response to a single unequivocal call.</u>

Bible Reference - Text

Matthew 7:7-8 - Ask, and it shall be given you; seek, and....
(Continued) - (To read the full text of the above go to page 155.)

Course Ref/s - Citation/s

T-04.V.5 - This is the question that must be asked: "Where can I go for protection?" "<u>Seek and ye shall find</u>" does not mean that you should seek blindly and desperately for something you would not recognize. Meaningful seeking is consciously undertaken, consciously organised and consciously directed. The goal must be formulated clearly and kept in mind. Learning and wanting to learn are inseparable. You learn best when you believe what you are trying to learn is of value to you. However, not everything you may want to learn has lasting value. Indeed, many of the things you want to learn may be chosen because their value will not last.

T-08.III.1 - Glory to God in the highest, and to you because He has so willed it. <u>Ask and it shall be given you</u>, because it has already been given. Ask for light and learn that you are light. If you want understanding and enlightenment you will learn it, because your decision to learn it is the decision to listen to the Teacher [the Holy Spirit] Who knows of light, and can therefore teach it to you. There is no limit on your learning because there is no limit on your mind. There is no limit on His teaching because He was created to teach. Understanding His function perfectly He fulfils it perfectly, because that is His joy and yours.

T-09.II.3 - <u>The Bible emphasizes that all prayer is answered, and this is indeed true. The very fact that the Holy Spirit has been asked for anything will ensure a response.</u> Yet it is equally certain that no response given by Him will ever be one that would increase fear. It is possible that His answer will not be heard. It is impossible, however, that it will be lost. There are many answers you have already received but have not yet heard. I assure you that they are waiting for you.

T-11.VIII.05 - You may complain that this course [A Course in Miracles] is not sufficiently specific for you to understand and use. Yet perhaps you have not done what it specifically advocates. This is not a course in the play of ideas, but in their practical application. Nothing could be more specific than to be told that <u>if you ask you will receive</u>. The Holy Spirit will answer every specific problem as long as you believe that problems are specific. His answer is both many and one, as long as you believe that the One is many. You may be afraid of His specificity, for fear of what you think it will demand of you. Yet only by asking will you learn that nothing of God demands anything of you. God gives; He does not take. When you refuse to ask, it is because you believe that asking is taking rather than sharing.

T-11.VIII.07 - Little child of God, you do not understand your Father. You believe in a world that takes, because you believe that you can get by taking. And by that perception you have lost sight of the real world.
You are afraid of the world as you see it, but the real world is still yours for the asking. Do not deny it to yourself, for it can only free you. Nothing of God will enslave His Son whom He created free and whose freedom is protected by His Being. <u>Blessed are you who are willing to ask the truth of God without fear, for only thus can you learn that His answer is the release from fear.</u>

T-11.VIII.08 - Beautiful child of God, you are asking only for what I [Jesus] promised you. Do you believe I would deceive you? The Kingdom of Heaven is within you. Believe that the truth is in me, for I know that it is in you. God's Sons have nothing they do not share. <u>Ask for truth of any Son of God, and you have asked it of me. Not one of us but has the answer in him, to give to anyone who asks it of him.</u>

T-11.VIII.14 - You, my child, are afraid of your brothers and of your Father and of yourself. But you are merely deceived in them. Ask what they are of the Teacher of Reality, and hearing His answer, you too will laugh at your fears and replace them with peace. For fear lies not in reality, but in the minds of children who do not understand reality. It is only their lack of understanding that frightens them, and when they learn to perceive truly they are not afraid. And because of this they will ask for truth again when they are frightened. It is not the reality of your brothers or your Father or yourself that frightens you. You do not know what they are, and so you perceive them as ghosts and monsters and dragons. <u>Ask what their reality is from the One Who knows it, and He will tell you what they are.</u> For you do not understand them, and because you are deceived by what you see you need reality to dispel your fears.

T-12.IV.1 - The ego is certain that love is dangerous, and this is always its central teaching. It never puts it this way; on the contrary, everyone who believes that the ego is salvation seems to be intensely engaged in the search for love. Yet the ego, though encouraging the search for love very actively, makes one proviso; do not find it. Its dictates, then, can be summed up simply as: "Seek and do not find." This is the one promise the ego holds out to you, and the one promise it will keep. For the ego pursues its goal with fanatic insistence, and its judgment, though severely impaired, is completely consistent.

Bible Reference - Text

Matthew 7:7-8 - Ask, and it shall be given you; seek, and....
(Continued) - (To read the full text of the above go to page 155.)

Course Ref/s - Citation/s

T-12.IV.2 - The search the ego undertakes is therefore bound to be defeated. And since it also teaches that it is your identification, its guidance leads you to a journey which must end in perceived self-defeat. For the ego cannot love, and in its frantic search for love it is seeking what it is afraid to find. The search is inevitable because the ego is part of your mind, and because of its source the ego is not wholly split off, or it could not be believed at all. For it is your mind that believes in it and gives existence to it. Yet it is also your mind that has the power to deny the ego's existence, and you will surely do so when you realize exactly what the journey is on which the ego sets you.

T-12.IV.4 - Do you realize that the ego must set you on a journey which cannot but lead to a sense of futility and depression? To seek and not to find is hardly joyous. Is this the promise you would keep? The Holy Spirit offers you another promise, and one that will lead to joy. For His promise is always, "Seek and you will find," and under His guidance you cannot be defeated. His is the journey to accomplishment, and the goal He sets before you He will give you. For He will never deceive God's Son whom He loves with the Love of the Father.

T-12.V.7 - I have said that the ego's rule is, "Seek and do not find." Translated into curricular terms this means, "Try to learn but do not succeed." The result of this curriculum goal is obvious. Every legitimate teaching aid, every real instruction, and every sensible guide to learning will be misinterpreted, since they are all for facilitating the learning this strange curriculum is against. If you are trying to learn how not to learn, and the aim of your teaching is to defeat itself, what can you expect but confusion? Such a curriculum does not make sense. This attempt at "learning" has so weakened your mind that you cannot love, for the curriculum you have chosen is against love, and amounts to a course in how to attack yourself. A supplementary goal in this curriculum is learning how not to overcome the split that makes its primary aim believable. And you will not overcome the split in this curriculum, for all your learning will be on its behalf. Yet your mind speaks against your learning as your learning speaks against your mind, and so you fight against all learning and succeed, for that is what you want. But perhaps you do not realize, even yet, that there is something you want to learn, and that you can learn it because it *is* your choice to do so.

T-12.VII.6 - I [Jesus] am the manifestation of the Holy Spirit, and when you see me it will be because you have invited Him. For He will send you His witnesses if you will but look upon them. Remember always that you see what you seek, for <u>what you seek you will find</u>. The ego finds what it seeks, and only that. It does not find love, for that is not what it is seeking. Yet seeking and finding are the same, and if you seek for two goals you will find them, but you will recognize neither. You will think they are the same because you want both of them. The mind always strives for integration, and if it is split and wants to keep the split, it will still believe it has one goal by making it seem to be one.

T-12.VII.7 - I said before that what you project or extend is up to you, but you must do one or the other, for that is a law of mind, and you must look in before you look out. As you look in, you choose the guide for seeing. And then you look out and behold his witnesses. This is why you <u>find what you seek</u>. What you want in yourself you will make manifest, and you will accept it from the world because you put it there by wanting it. When you think you are projecting what you do not want, it is still because you do want it. This leads directly to dissociation, for it represents the acceptance of two goals, each perceived in a different place; separated from each other because you made them different. The mind then sees a divided world outside itself, but not within. This gives it an illusion of integrity, and enables it to believe that it is pursuing one goal. Yet as long as you perceive the world as split, you are not healed. For to be healed is to pursue one goal, because you have accepted only one and want but one.

T-12.VII.9 - The power of decision is your one remaining freedom as a prisoner of this world. You can decide to see it right. What you made of it is not its reality, for its reality is only what you give it. <u>You cannot really give anything but love</u> to anyone or anything, <u>nor can you really receive</u>

anything but love from them. If you think you have received anything else, it is because you have looked within and thought you saw the power to give something else within yourself. It was only this decision that determined what you found, for it was the decision for what you sought.

Bible Reference - Text

Matthew 7:7-8 - Ask, and it shall be given you; seek, and....
(Continued) - (To read the full text of the above go to page 155.)

Course Ref/s - Citation/s

T-13.I.5 - You will see me as you learn the Son of God is guiltless. He has always sought his guiltlessness, and he has found it. For everyone is seeking to escape from the prison he has made, and the way to find release is not denied him. Being in him, he has found it. When he finds it is only a matter of time, and time is but an illusion. For the Son of God is guiltless now, and the brightness of his purity shines untouched forever in God's Mind. God's Son will always be as he was created. Deny your world and judge him not, for his eternal guiltlessness is in the Mind of his Father, and protects him forever.

T-13.VI.5 - The miracle enables you to see your brother without his past, and so perceive him as born again. His errors are all past, and by perceiving him without them you are releasing him. And since his past is yours, you share in this release. Let no dark cloud out of your past obscure him from you, for truth lies only in the present, and you will find it if you seek it there. You have looked for it where it is not, and therefore have not found it. Learn, then, to seek it where it is, and it will dawn on eyes that see. Your past was made in anger, and if you use it to attack the present, you will not see the freedom that the present holds.

T-13.VII.11-12 - Everything the ego tells you that you need will hurt you. For although the ego urges you again and again to get, it leaves you nothing, for what you get it will demand of you. And even from the very hands that grasped it, it will be wrenched and hurled into the dust.
For where the ego sees salvation it sees separation, and so you lose whatever you have gotten in its name. Therefore ask not of yourself what you need, for you do not know, and your advice to yourself will hurt you. For what you think you need will merely serve to tighten up your world

against the light, and render you unwilling to question the value that this world can really hold for you.

Only the Holy Spirit knows what you need. For He will give you all things that do not block the way to light. And what else could you need? In time, He gives you all the things that you need have, and will renew them as long as you have need of them. He will take nothing from you as long as you have any need of it. And yet He knows that everything you need is temporary, and will but last until you step aside from all your needs and realize that all of them have been fulfilled. Therefore He has no investment in the things that He supplies, except to make certain that you will not use them on behalf of lingering in time. He knows that you are not at home there, and He wills no delay to wait upon your joyous homecoming.

T-14.II.1 - The Holy Spirit needs a happy learner, in whom His mission can be happily accomplished. You who are steadfastly devoted to misery must first recognize that you are miserable and not happy. The Holy Spirit cannot teach without this contrast, for you believe that misery is happiness. This has so confused you that you have undertaken to learn to do what you can never do, believing that unless you learn it you will not be happy. You do not realize that the foundation on which this most peculiar learning goal depends means absolutely nothing. Yet it may still make sense to you. Have faith in nothing and you will find the "treasure" that you seek. Yet you will add another burden to your already burdened mind. You will believe that nothing is of value, and will value it. A little piece of glass, a speck of dust, a body or a war are one to you. For if you value one thing made of nothing, you have believed that nothing can be precious, and that you can learn how to make the untrue true.

T-14.IV.3 - When you have let all that obscured the truth in your most holy mind be undone for you, and therefore stand in grace before your Father, He will give Himself to you as He has always done. Giving Himself is all He knows, and so it is all knowledge. For what He knows not cannot be, and therefore cannot be given. Ask not to be forgiven, for this has already been accomplished. Ask, rather, to learn how to forgive, and to restore what always was to your unforgiving mind. Atonement becomes real and visible to those who use it. On earth this is your only function, and you must learn that it is all you want to learn. You will feel guilty till you learn this. For in the end, whatever form it takes, your guilt arises from your failure to fulfil your function in God's Mind with all of yours. Can you escape this guilt by failing to fulfil your function here?

Bible Reference - Text

Matthew 7:7-8 - Ask, and it shall be given you; seek, and....
(Continued) - (To read the full text of the above go to page 155.)

Course Ref/s - Citation/s

T-14.VII.2 - <u>The search for truth</u> is but the honest searching out of everything that interferes with truth. Truth is. It <u>can neither be lost nor sought nor found</u>. It is there, wherever you are, being within you. Yet it can be recognized or unrecognized, real or false to you. If you hide it, it becomes unreal to you because you hid it and surrounded it with fear. Under each cornerstone of fear on which you have erected your insane system of belief, the truth lies hidden. Yet you cannot know this, for by hiding truth in fear, you see no reason to believe that the more you look at fear the less you see it, and the clearer what it conceals becomes.

T-15.III.10 - Decide with me [Jesus], who has decided to abide with you. I will as my Father wills, knowing His Will is constant and at peace forever with itself. You will be content with nothing but His Will. Accept no less, remembering that everything I learned is yours. What my Father loves I love as He does, and I can no more accept it as what it is not, than He can. And no more can you. When you have learned to accept what you are, you will make no more gifts to offer to yourself, for you will know you are complete, in need of nothing, and unable to accept anything for yourself. But you will gladly give, having received. The host of God <u>needs not seek to find</u> anything.

T-15.VI.2 - You have so little faith in yourself because you are unwilling to accept the fact that perfect love is in you. And so <u>you seek without for what you cannot find without</u>. I offer you my perfect faith in you, in place of all your doubts. But forget not that my faith must be as perfect in all your brothers as it is in you, or it would be a limited gift to you. In the holy instant we share our faith in God's Son because we recognize, together, that he is wholly worthy of it, and in our appreciation of his worth we cannot doubt his holiness. And so we love him.

T-15.VIII.3 - Relate only with what will never leave you, and what you can never leave. The loneliness of God's Son is the loneliness of his Father. Refuse not the awareness of your completion, and seek not to restore it to yourself. Fear not to give redemption over to your Redeemer's Love. He will not fail you, for He comes from One Who cannot fail. Accept your sense of failure as nothing more than a mistake in who you are. For the holy host of God is beyond failure, and nothing that he wills can be denied. You are forever in a relationship so holy that it calls to everyone to escape from loneliness, and join you in your love. And where you are must everyone <u>seek, and find</u> you there.

T-15.XI.6 - So is it that, in all your seeking for love, <u>you seek for sacrifice and find it</u>. Yet you find not love. It is impossible to deny what love is and still recognize it. The meaning of love lies in what you have cast outside yourself, and it has no meaning apart from you. It is what you prefer to keep that has no meaning, while all that you would keep away holds all the meaning of the universe, and holds the universe together in its meaning. Unless the universe were joined in you it would be apart from God, and to be without Him is to be without meaning.

T-16.IV.6 - Your task is not to seek for love, but merely <u>to seek and find</u> all of the barriers within yourself that you have built against it. It is not necessary to seek for what is true, but it is necessary to seek for what is false. Every illusion is one of fear, whatever form it takes. And the attempt to escape from one illusion into another must fail. If you seek love outside yourself you can be certain that you perceive hatred within, and are afraid of it. Yet peace will never come from the illusion of love, but only from its reality.

T-16.V.6-7 - The special relationship is a strange and unnatural ego device for joining hell and Heaven, and making them indistinguishable. And the attempt to find the imagined "best" of both worlds has merely led to fantasies of both, and to the inability to perceive either as it is. The special relationship is the triumph of this confusion. It is a kind of union from which union is excluded, and the basis for the attempt at union rests on exclusion. What better example could there be of the ego's maxim, "<u>Seek but do not find</u>"?

7 Most curious of all is the concept of the self which the ego fosters in the special relationship. This "self" <u>seeks</u> the relationship to make itself complete. Yet when it <u>finds</u> the special relationship in which it thinks it can accomplish this it gives itself away, and tries to "trade" itself for the self of another. This is not union, for there is no increase and no extension. Each partner tries to sacrifice the self he does not want for one he thinks he would prefer. And he feels guilty for the "sin" of taking, and of giving

nothing of value in return. How much value can he place upon a self that he would give away to get a "better" one?

Bible Reference - Text

Matthew 7:7-8 - Ask, and it shall be given you; seek, and....
(Continued) - (To read the full text of the above go to page 155.)

Course Ref/s - Citation/s

T-16.VII.10-11 - Remember that you always choose between truth and illusion; between the real Atonement that would heal and the ego's "atonement" that would destroy. The power of God and all His Love, without limit, will support you as you seek only your place in the plan of Atonement arising from His Love. Be an ally of God and not the ego in seeking how Atonement can come to you. His help suffices, for His Messenger understands how to restore the Kingdom to you, and to place all your investment in salvation in your relationship with Him.

Seek and find His message in the holy instant, where all illusions are forgiven. From there the miracle extends to bless everyone and to resolve all problems, be they perceived as great or small, possible or impossible. There is nothing that will not give place to Him and to His Majesty. To join in close relationship with Him is to accept relationships as real, and through their reality to give over all illusions for the reality of your relationship with God. Praise be to your relationship with Him and to no other. The truth lies there and nowhere else. You choose this or nothing.

T-17.III.6 - The ego seeks to "resolve" its problems, not at their source, but where they were not made. And thus it seeks to guarantee there will be no solution. The Holy Spirit wants only to make His resolutions complete and perfect, and so He seeks and finds the source of problems where it is, and there undoes it. And with each step in His undoing is the separation more and more undone, and union brought closer. He is not at all confused by any "reasons" for separation. All He perceives in separation is that it must be undone. Let Him uncover the hidden spark of beauty in your relationships, and show it to you. Its loveliness will so attract you that you will be unwilling ever to lose the sight of it again. And you will let this spark transform the relationship so you can see it more and more. For you will want it more and more, and become increasingly unwilling to let it be hidden from you. And you will learn to seek for and establish the conditions in which this beauty can be seen.

T-18.IV.5 - <u>You merely ask the question. The answer is given. Seek not to answer, but merely to receive the answer as it is given.</u> In preparing for the holy instant, do not attempt to make yourself holy to be ready to receive it. That is but to confuse your role with God's. Atonement cannot come to those who think that they must first atone; but only to those who offer it nothing more than simple willingness to make way for it. Purification is of God alone, and therefore for you. Rather than seek to prepare yourself for Him, try to think thus: I who am host to God am worthy of Him. He Who established His dwelling place in me created it as He would have it be. It is not needful that I make it ready for Him, but only that I do not interfere with His plan to restore to me my own awareness of my readiness, which is eternal. I need add nothing to His plan. But to receive it, I must be willing not to substitute my own in place of it.

T-19.IV.B.12 - <u>It is impossible to seek for pleasure through the body and not find pain.</u> It is essential that this relationship be understood, for it is one the ego sees as proof of sin. It is not really punitive at all. It is but the inevitable result of equating yourself with the body, which is the invitation to pain. For it invites fear to enter and become your purpose. The attraction of guilt must enter with it, and whatever fear directs the body to do is therefore painful. It will share the pain of all illusions, and the illusion of pleasure will be the same as pain.

T-19.IV.B.17 - It is not given to the ego's disciples to realize that they have dedicated themselves to death. Freedom is offered them but they have not accepted it, and what is offered must also be received, to be truly given. For the Holy Spirit, too, is a communication medium, receiving from the Father and offering His messages unto the Son. Like the ego, the Holy Spirit is both the sender and the receiver. For what is sent through Him returns to Him, <u>seeking itself along the way, and finding what it seeks</u>. So does the ego find the death it seeks, returning it to you.

T-20.VIII.2 - Do you not want to know your own Identity? Would you not happily exchange your doubts for certainty? Would you not willingly be free of misery, and learn again of joy? Your holy relationship offers all this to you. As it was given you, so will be its effects. And as its holy purpose was not made by you, the means by which its happy end is yours is also not of you. Rejoice in what is yours but for the asking, and think not that you need make either means or end. All this is given you who would but see your brother sinless. All this is given, waiting on your desire but to receive it. <u>Vision is freely given to those who ask to see.</u>

Bible Reference - Text

Matthew 7:7-8 - Ask, and it shall be given you; seek, and.... (Continued) - (To read the full text of the above go to page 155.)

Course Ref/s - Citation/s

T-21.VII.4-5 - The army of the powerless is weak indeed. It has no weapons and it has no enemy. Yes, it can overrun the world and <u>seek an enemy. But it can never find</u> what is not there. Yes, it can dream it found an enemy, but this will shift even as it attacks, so that it runs at once to find another, and never comes to rest in victory. And as it runs it turns against itself, thinking it caught a glimpse of the great enemy who always eludes its murderous attack by turning into something else. How treacherous does this enemy appear, who changes so it is impossible even to recognize him.

5 Yet hate must have a target. There can be no faith in sin without an enemy. Who that believes in sin would dare believe he has no enemy? Could he admit that no one made him powerless? Reason would surely bid him <u>seek no longer what is not there to find</u>. Yet first he must be willing to perceive a world where it is not. It is not necessary that he understand how he can see it. Nor should he try. For if he focuses on what he cannot understand, he will but emphasise his helplessness, and let sin tell him that his enemy must be himself. But let him only ask himself these questions, which he must decide, to have it done for him:

Do I desire a world I rule instead of one that rules me?

Do I desire a world where I am powerful instead of helpless?

Do I desire a world in which I have no enemies and cannot sin?

And do I want to see what I denied because it is the truth?

T-21.VIII.3 - Reason will tell you that you cannot ask for happiness inconstantly. For if what you desire you receive, and happiness is constant, then you need ask for it but once to have it always. And if you do not have it always, being what it is, you did not ask for it. For no one fails to ask for his desire of something he believes holds out some promise of the power of giving it. He may be wrong in what he asks, where, and of what. Yet he will ask because desire is a request, an asking for, and made by one whom God Himself will never fail to answer. God has already given all that he really wants. Yet what he is uncertain of, God cannot give. For he does not desire it while he remains uncertain, and <u>God's giving must be incomplete unless it is received.</u>

T-22.VI.1 - Do you want freedom of the body or of the mind? For both you cannot have. Which do you value? Which is your goal? For one you see as means; the other, end. And one must serve the other and lead to its predominance, increasing its importance by diminishing its own. Means serve the end, and as the end is reached the value of the means decreases, eclipsed entirely when they are recognized as functionless. No one but yearns for freedom and tries to find it. Yet <u>he will seek for it where he believes it is and can be found.</u> He will believe it possible of mind or body, and he will make the other serve his choice as means to find it.

T-22.VI.8 - You will see your value through your brother's eyes, and each one is released as he beholds his savior in place of the attacker who he thought was there. Through this releasing is the world released. This is your part in bringing peace. <u>For you have asked what is your function here, and have been answered. Seek not to change it, nor to substitute another goal. This one was given you, and only this.</u> Accept this one and serve it willingly, for what the Holy Spirit does with gifts you give your brother, to whom He offers them, and where and when, is up to Him. He will bestow them where they are received and welcomed. He will use every one of them for peace. Nor will one little smile or willingness to overlook the tiniest mistake be lost to anyone.

T-25.II.2 - Is it not strange that you should cherish still some hope of satisfaction from the world you see? In no respect, at any time or place, has anything but fear and guilt been your reward. How long is needed for you to realize the chance of change in this respect is hardly worth delaying change that might result in better outcome? For one thing is sure; the way you see, and long have seen, gives no support to base your future hopes, and no suggestions of success at all. To place your hopes where no hope lies must make you hopeless. Yet is this hopelessness your choice, while you would <u>seek for hope where none is ever found.</u>

T-27.VII.6 - The part you play in salvaging the world from condemnation is your own escape. Forget not that the witness to the world of evil cannot speak except for what has seen a need for evil in the world. And this is where your guilt was first beheld. In separation from your brother was the first attack upon yourself begun. And it is this the world bears witness to. Seek not another cause, nor look among the mighty legions of its witnesses for its undoing. They support its claim on your allegiance. What conceals the truth is not where you should look to *find* the truth.

Bible Reference - Text

Matthew 7:7-8 - Ask, and it shall be given you; seek, and.... (Continued) - (To read the full text of the above go to page 155.)

Course Ref/s - Citation/s

T-29.VII.1 - Seek not outside yourself. For it will fail, and you will weep each time an idol falls. Heaven cannot be found where it is not, and there can be no peace excepting there. Each idol that you worship when God calls will never answer in His place. There is no other answer you can substitute, and find the happiness His answer brings. Seek not outside yourself. For all your pain comes simply from a futile search for what you want, insisting where it must be found. What if it is not there? Do you prefer that you be right or happy? Be you glad that you are told where happiness abides, and seek no longer elsewhere. You will fail. But it is given you to know the truth, and not to seek for it outside yourself.

T-30.VIII.3 - What is temptation but a wish to make illusions real? It does not seem to be the wish that no reality be so. Yet it is an assertion that some forms of idols have a powerful appeal that makes them harder to resist than those you would not want to have reality. Temptation, then, is nothing more than this; a prayer the miracle touch not some dreams, but keep their unreality obscure and give to them reality instead. And Heaven gives no answer to the prayer, nor can a miracle be given you to heal appearances you do not like. You have established limits. What you ask is given you, but not of God Who knows no limits. You have limited yourself.

T-31.I.6:6-7:11 - Can it be your little learning, strange in outcome and incredible in difficulty will withstand the simple lessons being taught to you in every moment of each day, since time began and learning had been made?

The lessons to be learned are only two. Each has its outcome in a different world. And each world follows surely from its source. The certain outcome of the lesson that God's Son is guilty is the world you see. It is a world of terror and despair. Nor is there hope of happiness in it. There is no plan for safety you can make that ever will succeed. There is no joy that you can seek for here and hope to find. Yet this is not the only outcome which your learning can produce. However much you may have over- learned your chosen task, the lesson that reflects the Love of God is stronger still. And you will learn God's Son is innocent, and see another world.

T-31.II.9:4-10:6 - Can you make progress if you think the same, advancing only when he [your brother] would step back, and falling back when he would go ahead? For so do you forget the journey's goal, which is but to decide to walk with him, so neither leads nor follows. Thus it is a way you go together, not alone. And in this choice is learning's outcome changed, for Christ has been reborn to both of you.

An instant spent without your old ideas of who your great companion is and what he should be asking for, will be enough to let this happen.
And you will perceive his purpose is the same as yours. He asks for what you want, and needs the same as you. It takes, perhaps, a different form in him, but it is not the form you answer to. He asks and you receive, for you have come with but one purpose; that you learn you love your brother with a brother's love. And as a brother, must his Father be the same as yours, as he is like yourself in truth.

T-31.V.8 - A concept of the self is meaningless, for no one here can see what it is for, and therefore cannot picture what it is. Yet is all learning that the world directs begun and ended with the single aim of teaching you this concept of yourself, that you will choose to follow this world's laws, and never seek to go beyond its roads nor realize the way you see yourself. Now must the Holy Spirit find a way to help you see this concept of the self must be undone, if any peace of mind is to be given you. Nor can it be unlearned except by lessons aimed to teach that you are something else. For otherwise, you would be asked to make exchange of what you now believe for total loss of self, and greater terror would arise in you.

W-pI.072.11:2-7 - "What is salvation, Father?" Ask and you will be answered. Seek and you will find. We are no longer asking the ego what salvation is and where to find it. We are asking it of truth. Be certain, then, that the answer will be true because of Whom you ask.

Bible Reference - Text

Matthew 7:7-8 - Ask, and it shall be given you; seek, and....
(Continued) - (To read the full text of the above go to page 155.)

Course Ref/s - Citation/s

W-pI.076.1-2 - We have observed before how many senseless things have seemed to you to be salvation. Each has imprisoned you with laws as senseless as itself. You are not bound by them. Yet to understand that this is so, you must first realize salvation lies not there. While you would seek for it in things that have no meaning, you bind yourself to laws that make no sense. Thus do you seek to prove salvation is where it is not.

Today we will be glad you cannot prove it. For if you could, you would forever <u>seek salvation where it is not, and never find it</u>. The idea for today [I am under no laws but God's.] tells you once again how simple is salvation. Look for it where it waits for you, and there it will be found. Look nowhere else, for it is nowhere else.

W-pI.094.3:3-4:4 - I am as God created me.
    I am His Son eternally.

Now try to reach the Son of God in you. This is the Self that never sinned, nor made an image to replace reality. This is the Self that never left Its home in God to walk the world uncertainly. This is the Self that knows no fear, nor could conceive of loss or suffering or death.

Nothing is required of you to reach this goal except to lay all idols and self-images aside; go past the list of attributes, both good and bad, you have ascribed to yourself; and wait in silent expectancy for the truth. God has Himself promised that it will be revealed to all who ask for it. <u>You are asking now. You cannot fail</u> because He cannot fail.

W-pI.102.4:2-5:2 - I share God's Will for happiness for me, and I accept it as my function now.

Then <u>seek this function</u> deep within your mind, for it is there, awaiting but your choice. <u>You cannot fail to find it</u> when you learn it is your choice, and that you share God's Will.

Be happy, for your only function here is happiness. You have no need to be less loving to God's Son than He Whose Love created him as loving as Himself.

W-pI.103.3:5-7 - God, being Love, is also happiness. And it is happiness I seek today. <u>I cannot fail, because I seek the truth.</u>

W-pI.110.10 - <u>Seek Him [Christ in you] today, and find Him.</u> He will be your Savior from all idols you have made. For when you find Him, you will understand how worthless are your idols, and how false the images which you believed were you. Today we make a great advance to truth by letting idols go, and opening our hands and hearts and minds to God today.

W-pI.122.3-4 - Forgiveness lets the veil be lifted up that hides the face of Christ from those who look with unforgiving eyes upon the world. It lets you recognize the Son of God, and clears your memory of all dead thoughts so that remembrance of your Father can arise across the threshold of your mind. What would you want forgiveness cannot give? What gifts but these are worthy to be sought? What fancied value, trivial effect or transient promise, never to be kept, can hold more hope than what forgiveness brings?

Why would you seek an answer other than the answer that will answer everything? Here is the perfect answer, given to imperfect questions, meaningless requests, halfhearted willingness to hear, and less than halfway diligence and partial trust. <u>Here is the answer! Seek for it no more. You will not find another one instead.</u>

W-pI.127.6-7 - <u>Seek not within the world to find your Self.</u> Love is not found in darkness and in death. Yet it is perfectly apparent to the eyes that see and ears that hear love's Voice. Today we practice [Lesson 127: There is no love but God's.] making free your mind of all the laws you think you must obey; of all the limits under which you live, and all the changes that you think are part of human destiny. Today we take the largest single step this course requests in your advance towards its established goal.

If you achieve the faintest glimmering of what love means today, you have advanced in distance without measure and in time beyond the count of years to your release. Let us together, then, be glad to give some time to God today, and understand there is no better use for time than this.

W-pI.130.4 - Fear has made everything you think you see. All separation, all distinctions, and the multitude of differences you believe make up the world. They are not there. Love's enemy has made them up. Yet love can have no enemy, and so they have no cause, no being and no consequence. They can be valued, but remain unreal. They can be sought, but they can not be found. Today we will not seek for them, nor waste this day in <u>seeking what can not be found.</u>

Bible Reference - Text

Matthew 7:7-8 - Ask, and it shall be given you; seek, and....
(Continued) - (To read the full text of the above go to page 155.)

Course Ref/s - Citation/s

W-pI.131.1-2 - <u>Failure is all about you while you seek for goals that cannot be achieved.</u> You look for permanence in the impermanent, for love where there is none, for safety in the midst of danger; immortality within the darkness of the dream of death. Who could succeed where contradiction is the setting of his searching, and the place to which he comes to find stability?

Goals that are meaningless are not attained. There is no way to reach them, for the means by which you strive for them are meaningless as they are. Who can use such senseless means, and hope through them to gain in anything? Where can they lead? And what could they achieve that offers any hope of being real? Pursuit of the imagined leads to death because it is the search for nothingness, and while you seek for life you ask for death. You look for safety and security, while in your heart you pray for danger and protection for the little dream you made.

W-pI.131.4-5 - Be glad that search you must. Be glad as well to learn <u>you search for Heaven, and must find the goal</u> you really want. No one can fail to want this goal and reach it in the end. God's Son can not seek vainly, though he try to force delay, deceive himself and think that it is hell he seeks. When he is wrong, he finds correction. When he wanders off, he is led back to his appointed task.

5 No one remains in hell, for no one can abandon his Creator, nor affect His perfect, timeless and unchanging Love. <u>You will find Heaven. Everything you seek but this will fall away.</u> Yet not because it has been

taken from you. It will go because you do not want it. You will reach the goal you really want as certainly as God created you in sinlessness.

W-pI.131.15 - Remember often that today should be a time of special gladness, and refrain from dismal thoughts and meaningless laments. Salvation's time has come. Today is set by Heaven itself to be a time of grace for you and for the world. If you forget this happy fact, remind yourself with this:

Today I <u>seek and find</u> all that I want.

My single purpose offers it to me.

No one can fail who seeks to reach the truth.

W-pI.132.2 - Yet is salvation easily achieved, for anyone is free to change his mind, and all his thoughts change with it. Now the source of thought has shifted, for to change your mind means you have changed the source of all ideas you think or ever thought or yet will think. You free the past from what you thought before. You free the future from all ancient thoughts of <u>seeking what you do not want to find</u>.

W-pI.140.7-8 - Let us not try today to seek to cure what cannot suffer sickness. Healing must be sought but where it is, and then applied to what is sick, so that it can be cured. There is no remedy the world provides that can effect a change in anything. The mind that brings illusions to the truth is really changed. There is no change but this. For how can one illusion differ from another but in attributes that have no substance, no reality, no core, and nothing that is truly different?

Today we seek to change our minds about the source of sickness, for we seek a cure for all illusions, not another shift among them. We will try today to find the source of healing, which is in our minds because our Father placed it there for us. It is not farther from us than ourselves. It is as near to us as our own thoughts; so close it is impossible to lose. We need but <u>seek it and it must be found</u>.

W-pI.159.5:4-6:5 - Holiness has been restored to vision, and the blind can see.

This is the Holy Spirit's single gift; the treasure house to which you can appeal with perfect certainty for all the things that can contribute to your happiness. All are laid here already. <u>All can be received but for the asking.</u> Here the door is never locked, and no one is denied his least request or his most urgent need. There is no sickness not already healed, no lack unsatisfied, no need unmet within this golden treasury of Christ.

Bible Reference - Text

Matthew 7:7-8 - Ask, and it shall be given you; seek, and....
(Continued) - (To read the full text of the above go to page 155.)

Course Ref/s - Citation/s

W-pI.160.6 - <u>What does he search for now? What can he find?</u> A stranger to himself can find no home wherever he may look, for he has made return impossible. His way is lost, except a miracle will search him out and show him that he is no stranger now. The miracle will come. For in his home his Self remains. It asked no stranger in, and took no alien thought to be Itself. And It will call Its Own unto Itself in recognition of what is Its Own.

W-pI.161.8:3-9:9 - Mistake not the intensity of rage projected fear must spawn. It shrieks in wrath, and claws the air in frantic hope it can reach to its maker and devour him.

This do the body's eyes behold in one whom Heaven cherishes, the angels love and God created perfect. This is his reality. And in Christ's vision is his loveliness reflected in a form so holy and so beautiful that you could scarce refrain from kneeling at his feet. Yet you will take his hand instead, for you are like him in the sight that sees him thus. Attack on him is enemy to you, for you will not perceive that in his hands is your salvation.
<u>Ask him but for this, and he will give it to you.</u> Ask him not to symbolize your fear. Would you request that love destroy itself? Or would you have it revealed to you and set you free?

W-pI.165.4 - Deny not Heaven. It is yours today, but for the asking.
Nor need you perceive how great the gift, how changed your mind will be before it comes to you. <u>Ask to receive, and it is given you.</u> Conviction lies within it. Till you welcome it as yours, uncertainty remains. Yet God is fair. Sureness is not required to receive what only your acceptance can bestow.

W-pI.165.5 - <u>Ask with desire.</u> You need not be sure that you request the only thing you want. <u>But when you have received</u>, you will be sure you have the treasure you have always sought. What would you then exchange for it? What would induce you now to let it fade away from your ecstatic vision? For this sight proves that you have exchanged your blindness for the seeing eyes of Christ; your mind has come to lay aside denial, and accept the Thought of God as your inheritance.

W-pI.182.3 - We speak today for everyone who walks this world, for he is not at home. He goes uncertainly about in endless search, <u>seeking in darkness what he cannot find</u>; not recognizing what it is he seeks. A thousand homes he makes, yet none contents his restless mind. He does not understand he builds in vain. The home he seeks can not be made by him. There is no substitute for Heaven. All he ever made was hell.

W-pI.184.13 - <u>No one can fail who seeks</u> the meaning of the Name of God. Experience must come to supplement the Word. But first you must accept the Name for all reality, and realize the many names you gave its aspects have distorted what you see, but have not interfered with truth at all. One Name we bring into our practicing. One Name we use to unify our sight.

W-pI.185.06 - The mind which means that all it wants is peace must join with other minds, for that is how peace is obtained. And when the wish for peace is genuine, <u>the means for finding it is given, in a form each mind that seeks for it</u> in honesty can understand. Whatever form the lesson takes is planned for him in such a way that he can not mistake it, if his asking is sincere. But if he asks without sincerity, there is no form in which the lesson will meet with acceptance and be truly learned.

W-pI.185.11 - <u>No one who truly seeks the peace of God can fail to find it.</u> For he merely asks that he deceive himself no longer by denying to himself what is God's Will. Who can remain unsatisfied who asks for what he has already? Who could be unanswered who requests an answer which is his to give? The peace of God is yours.

W-pI.185.12 - <u>For you was peace created, given you by its Creator</u>, and established as His Own eternal gift. <u>How can you fail, when you but ask for what He wills for you?</u> And how could your request be limited to you alone? No gift of God can be unshared. It is this attribute that sets the gifts of God apart from every dream that ever seemed to take the place of truth.

W-pI.188.1 - Why wait for Heaven? <u>Those who seek the light are merely covering their eyes. The light is in them now.</u> Enlightenment is but a recognition, not a change at all. Light is not of the world, yet you who bear the light in you are alien here as well. The light came with you from your native home, and stayed with you because it is your own. It is the only thing you bring with you from Him Who is your Source. It shines in you because it lights your home, and leads you back to where it came from and you are at home.

Bible Reference - Text

Matthew 7:7-8 - Ask, and it shall be given you; seek, and....
(Continued) - (To read the full text of the above go to page 155.)

Course Ref/s - Citation/s

W-pI.189.7:5-8:8 - Forget this world, forget this course, and come with wholly empty hands unto your God.

Is it not He Who knows the way to you? You need not know the way to Him. Your part is simply to allow all obstacles that you have interposed between the Son and God the Father to be quietly removed forever.
God will do His part in joyful and immediate response. <u>Ask and receive.</u> But do not make demands, nor point the road to God by which He should appear to you. The way to reach Him is merely to let Him be. For in that way is your reality proclaimed as well.

W-pI.189.10 - Father, we do not know the way to You. But we have called, and You have answered us. We will not interfere. Salvation's ways are not our own, for they belong to You. And it is unto You we look for them. Our hands are open to receive Your gifts. We have no thoughts we think apart from You, and cherish no beliefs of what we are, or Who created us. Yours is the way that we would find and follow. And <u>we ask but that Your Will, which is our own as well, be done in us</u> and in the world, that it become a part of Heaven now. Amen.

W-pI.197.2 - How easily are God and guilt confused by those who know not what their thoughts can do. Deny your strength, and weakness must become salvation to you. See yourself as bound, and bars become your home. Nor will you leave the prison house, or claim your strength, until guilt and salvation are not seen as one, and freedom and salvation are perceived as joined, with strength beside them, <u>to be sought</u> and claimed, <u>and found</u> and fully recognized.

W-pI.198.4 - Forgiveness is the only road that leads out of disaster, past all suffering, and finally away from death. How could there be another way, when this one is the plan of God Himself? And why would you oppose it, quarrel with it, <u>seek to find</u> a thousand ways in which it must be wrong; a thousand other possibilities?

W-pI.199.6 - The Holy Spirit is the home of minds that seek for freedom. In Him they <u>have found what they have sought</u>. The body's purpose now is unambiguous. And it becomes perfect in the ability to serve an undivided goal. In conflict- free and unequivocal response to mind with but the thought of freedom as its goal, the body serves, and serves its purpose well. Without the power to enslave, it is a worthy servant of the freedom which the mind within the Holy Spirit seeks.

W-pI.200.01-02 - <u>Seek you no further. You will not find peace except the peace of God.</u> Accept this fact, and save yourself the agony of yet more bitter disappointments, bleak despair, and sense of icy hopelessness and doubt. Seek you no further. There is nothing else for you to find except the peace of God, unless you seek for misery and pain.

This is the final point to which each one must come at last, to lay aside all hope of finding happiness where there is none; of being saved by what can only hurt; of making peace of chaos, joy of pain, and Heaven out of hell. Attempt no more to win through losing, nor to die to live. You cannot but be asking for defeat.

W-pI.200.03-04 - Yet you can ask as easily for love, for happiness, and for eternal life in peace that has no ending. Ask for this, and you can only win. <u>To ask for what you have already must succeed.</u> To ask that what is false be true can only fail. Forgive yourself for vain imaginings, and seek no longer what you cannot find. For what could be more foolish than to seek and seek and seek again for hell, when you have but to look with open eyes to find that Heaven lies before you, through a door that opens easily to welcome you?

Come home. You have not found your happiness in foreign places and in alien forms that have no meaning to you, though you sought to make them meaningful. This world is not where you belong. You are a stranger here. But it is given you to find the means whereby the world no longer seems to be a prison house or jail for anyone.

W-pI.200.11 - <u>Today we seek no idols. Peace can not be found in them.</u> The peace of God is ours, and only this will we accept and want. Peace be to us today. For we have found a simple, happy way to leave the world of ambiguity, and to replace our shifting goals and solitary dreams with single purpose and companionship. For peace is union, if it be of God. We seek no further. We are close to home, and draw still nearer every time we say:

There is no peace except the peace of God, And I am glad and thankful it is so.

Bible Reference - Text

Matthew 7:7-8 - Ask, and it shall be given you; seek, and....
(Continued) - (To read the full text of the above go to page 155.)

Course Ref/s - Citation/s

W-pII.229.1 - I seek my own Identity, and find It in these words: "Love, which created me, is what I am." Now need I seek no more. Love has prevailed. So still It waited for my coming home, that I will turn away no longer from the holy face of Christ. And what I look upon attests the truth of the Identity I sought to lose, but which my Father has kept safe for me.

W-pII.230.2 - Father, I seek the peace You gave as mine in my creation. What was given then must be here now, for my creation was apart from time, and still remains beyond all change. The peace in which Your Son was born into Your Mind is shining there unchanged. I am as You created me. I need but call on You to find the peace You gave. It is Your Will that gave it to Your Son.

W-pII.231.1-2 - What can I seek for, Father, but Your Love? Perhaps I think I seek for something else; a something I have called by many names. Yet is Your Love the only thing I seek, or ever sought. For there is nothing else that I could ever really want to find. Let me remember You. What else could I desire but the truth about myself?

This is your will, my brother. And you share this will with me [Jesus], and with the One as well Who is our Father. To remember Him is Heaven. This we seek. And only this is what it will be given us to find.

W-pII.251.ti-1 - I am in need of nothing but the truth.

I sought for many things, and found despair. Now do I seek but one, for in that one is all I need, and only what I need. All that I sought before I needed not, and did not even want. My only need I did not recognize. But now I see that I need only truth. In that all needs are satisfied, all cravings end, all hopes are finally fulfilled and dreams are gone. Now have

I everything that I could need. Now have I everything that I could want. And now at last I find myself at peace.

W-pII.261.2 - <u>Let me not seek for idols.</u> I would come, my Father, home to You today. I choose to be as You created me, <u>and find the Son whom You created</u> as my Self.

W-pII.262.1-2 - Father, You have one Son. And it is he that I would look upon today. He is Your one creation. Why should I perceive a thousand forms in what remains as one? Why should I give this one a thousand names, when only one suffices? For Your Son must bear Your Name, for You created him. Let me not see him as a stranger to his Father, nor as stranger to myself. For he is part of me and I of him, and we are part of You Who are our Source, eternally united in Your Love; eternally the holy Son of God.

We who are one would recognize this day the truth about ourselves. We would come home, and rest in unity. For there is peace, and nowhere else can peace be <u>sought and found</u>.

W-pII.275.1 - Let us today attend the Voice for God [the Holy Spirit], which speaks an ancient lesson, no more true today than any other day. Yet has this day been chosen as the time when we <u>will seek</u> and hear and learn and understand. Join me [Jesus] in hearing. For the Voice for God tells us of things we cannot understand alone, nor learn apart. It is in this that all things are protected. And in this the healing of the Voice for God <u>is found</u>.

W-pII.287.1-2 - Where would I go but Heaven? What could be a substitute for happiness? What gift could I prefer before the peace of God? What treasure would <u>I seek and find</u> and keep that can compare with my Identity? And would I rather live with fear than love?

You are my goal, my Father. What but You could I desire to have? What way but that which leads to You could I desire to walk? And what except the memory of You could signify to me the end of dreams and futile substitutions for the truth? You are my only goal. Your Son would be as You created him. What way but this could I expect to recognize my Self, and be at one with my Identity?

W-pII.292.1 - God's promises make no exceptions. And He guarantees that only joy can be the final outcome found for everything. Yet it is up to us when this is reached; how long we let an alien will appear to be opposing His. And while we think this will is real, we will not find the end He has appointed as the outcome of all problems we perceive, all trials we see, and every situation that we meet. Yet is the ending certain. For God's Will is done in earth and Heaven. <u>We will seek and we will find</u> according to His Will, which guarantees that our will is done.

Bible Reference - Text

Matthew 7:7-8 - Ask, and it shall be given you; seek, and....
(Continued) - (To read the full text of the above go to page 155.)

Course Ref/s - Citation/s

W-pII.296.ti-2 - The Holy Spirit speaks through me today.

The Holy Spirit needs my voice today, that all the world may listen to Your Voice, and hear Your Word through me. I am resolved to let You speak through me, for I would use no words but Yours, and have no thoughts which are apart from Yours, for only Yours are true. I would be savior to the world I made. For having damned it I would set it free, that I may find escape, and hear the Word Your holy Voice will speak to me today.

We teach today what we would learn, and that alone. And so our learning goal becomes an unconflicted one, and possible of easy reach and quick accomplishment. How gladly does the Holy Spirit come to rescue us from hell, when we allow His teaching to persuade the world, through us, to <u>seek and find</u> the easy path to God.

W-pII.3.2-3 - The world was made as an attack on God. It symbolizes fear. And what is fear except love's absence? Thus the world was meant to be a place where God could enter not, and where His Son could be apart from Him. Here was perception born, for knowledge could not cause such insane thoughts. But eyes deceive, and ears hear falsely. Now mistakes become quite possible, for certainty has gone.

The mechanisms of illusion have been born instead. And now they go <u>to find what has been given them to seek</u>. Their aim is to fulfil the purpose which the world was made to witness and make real. They see in its illusions but a solid base where truth exists, upheld apart from lies. Yet everything that they report is but illusion which is kept apart from truth.

W-pII.318.1 - In me, God's holy Son, are reconciled all parts of Heaven's plan to save the world. What could conflict, when all the parts have but one purpose and one aim? How could there be a single part that stands alone, or one of more or less importance than the rest? I am the means by which God's Son is saved, because salvation's purpose is to find the sinlessness that God has placed in me. I was created as the thing I seek. I am the goal the world is searching for. I am God's Son, His one eternal Love. I am salvation's means and end as well.

W-pII.321.1 - I did not understand what made me free, nor what my freedom is, nor where to look to find it. Father, I have searched in vain until I heard Your Voice directing me. Now I would guide myself no more. For I have neither made nor understood the way to find my freedom. But I trust in You. You Who endowed me with my freedom as Your holy Son will not be lost to me. Your Voice directs me, and the way to You is opening and clear to me at last. Father, my freedom is in You alone. Father, it is my will that I return.

W-pII.325.ti-2 - All things I think I see reflect ideas.

This is salvation's keynote: What I see reflects a process in my mind, which starts with my idea of what I want. From there, the mind makes up an image of the thing the mind desires, judges valuable, and therefore seeks to find. These images are then projected outward, looked upon, esteemed as real and guarded as one's own. From insane wishes comes an insane world. From judgment comes a world condemned. And from forgiving thoughts a gentle world comes forth, with mercy for the holy Son of God, to offer him a kindly home where he can rest a while before he journeys on, and help his brothers walk ahead with him, and find the way to Heaven and to God.

Our Father, Your ideas reflect the truth, and mine apart from Yours but make up dreams. Let me behold what only Yours reflect, for Yours and Yours alone establish truth.

W-pII.334.ti-2 - Today I claim the gifts forgiveness gives.

I will not wait another day to find the treasures that my Father offers me. Illusions are all vain, and dreams are gone even while they are woven out of thoughts that rest on false perceptions. Let me not accept such meager gifts again today. God's Voice is offering the peace of God to all who hear and choose to follow Him. This is my choice today. And so I go to find the treasures God has given me.

I seek but the eternal. For Your Son can be content with nothing less than
this. What, then, can be his solace but what You are offering to his
bewildered mind and frightened heart, to give him certainty and bring him
peace? Today I would behold my brother sinless. This Your Will for me,
for so will I behold my sinlessness.

Bible Reference - Text

Matthew 7:7-8 - Ask, and it shall be given you; seek, and....
(Continued) - (To read the full text of the above go to page 155.)

Course Ref/s - Citation/s

W-pII.346.1 - Father, I wake today with miracles correcting my perception
of all things. And so begins the day I share with You as I will share
eternity, for time has stepped aside today. I do not seek the things of time,
and so I will not look upon them. What I seek today transcends all laws of
time and things perceived in time. I would forget all things except Your
Love. I would abide in You, and know no laws except Your law of love.
And I would find the peace which You created for Your Son, forgetting all
the foolish toys I made as I behold Your glory and my own.

**W-pII.349.ti-1 - Today I let Christ's vision look upon All things for me
and judge them not, but give Each one a miracle of love instead.**
So would I liberate all things I see, and give to them the freedom that I
seek. For thus do I obey the law of love, and give what I would find and
make my own. It will be given me, because I have chosen it as the gift I
want to give. Father, Your gifts are mine. Each one that I accept gives me a
miracle to give. And giving as I would receive, I learn Your healing
miracles belong to me.

W-pII.6.4-5 - The Holy Spirit reaches from the Christ in you to all your
dreams, and bids them come to Him, to be translated into truth. He will
exchange them for the final dream which God appointed as the end of
dreams. For when forgiveness rests upon the world and peace has come to
every Son of God, what could there be to keep things separate, for what
remains to see except Christ's face?

And how long will this holy face be seen, when it is but the symbol that the
time for learning now is over, and the goal of the Atonement has been

reached at last? So therefore let us <u>seek to find</u> Christ's face and look on nothing else. As we behold His glory, will we know we have no need of learning or perception or of time, or anything except the holy Self, the Christ Whom God created as His Son.

W-pII.ep.1 - This course [A Course in Miracles] is a beginning, not an end. Your Friend [the Holy Spirit] goes with you. You are not alone. No one who calls on Him can call in vain. Whatever troubles you, be certain that He has the answer, and will gladly give it to you, if you simply turn to Him and ask it of Him. He will not withhold all answers that you need for anything that seems to trouble you. He knows the way to solve all problems, and resolve all doubts. His certainty is yours. <u>You need but ask it of Him, and it will be given you.</u>

M-04.IX.1:4-2:12 - Faithfulness is the teacher of God's trust in the Word of God to set all things right; not some, but all. Generally, his faithfulness begins by resting on just some problems, remaining carefully limited for a time. To give up all problems to one Answer is to reverse the thinking of the world entirely. And that alone is faithfulness. Nothing but that really deserves the name. Yet each degree, however small, is worth achieving. Readiness, as the text notes, is not mastery.

True faithfulness, however, does not deviate. Being consistent, it is wholly honest. Being unswerving, it is full of trust. Being based on fearlessness, it is gentle. Being certain, it is joyous. And being confident, it is tolerant. Faithfulness, then, combines in itself the other attributes of God's teachers. It implies acceptance of the Word of God and His definition of His Son. It is to Them that faithfulness in the true sense is always directed. Toward Them it looks, <u>seeking until it finds</u>. And having found, it rests in quiet certainty on that alone to which all faithfulness is due.

M-13.2:5-3:7 - Think a while about what the world calls sacrifice. Power, fame, money, physical pleasure; who is the "hero" to whom all these things belong? Could they mean anything except to a body? Yet a body cannot evaluate. By seeking after such things the mind associates itself with the body, obscuring its Identity and losing sight of what it really is.

Once this confusion has occurred, it becomes impossible for the mind to understand that all the "pleasures" of the world are nothing. But what a sacrifice,-and it is sacrifice indeed!-all this entails. Now has the mind condemned itself to <u>seek without finding</u>; to be forever dissatisfied and discontented; to know not what it really wants to find. Who can escape this self-condemnation? Only through God's Word could this be possible.

For self- condemnation is a decision about identity, and no one doubts what he believes he is. He can doubt all things, but never this.

Bible Reference - Text

Matthew 7:7-8 - Ask, and it shall be given you; seek, and....
(Continued) - (To read the full text of the above go to page 155.)

Course Ref/s - Citation/s

M-13.5 - What is the real meaning of sacrifice? It is the cost of believing in illusions. It is the price that must be paid for the denial of truth. There is no pleasure of the world that does not demand this, for otherwise the pleasure would be seen as pain, and no one asks for pain if he recognizes it. It is the idea of sacrifice that makes him blind. He does not see what he is asking for. And so he seeks it in a thousand ways and in a thousand places, each time believing it is there, and each time disappointed in the end. "Seek but do not find" remains this world's stern decree, and no one who pursues the world's goal can do otherwise.

M-20.2:2-3:12 - God's peace is recognized at first by just one thing; in every way it is totally unlike all previous experiences. It calls to mind nothing that went before. It brings with it no past associations. It is a new thing entirely. There is a contrast, yes, between this thing and all the past. But strangely, it is not a contrast of true differences. The past just slips away, and in its place is everlasting quiet. Only that. The contrast first perceived has merely gone. Quiet has reached to cover everything.

How is this quiet found? No one can fail to find it who but seeks out its conditions. God's peace can never come where anger is, for anger must deny that peace exists. Who sees anger as justified in any way or any circumstance proclaims that peace is meaningless, and must believe that it cannot exist. In this condition, peace cannot be found. Therefore, forgiveness is the necessary condition for finding the peace of God. More than this, given forgiveness there must be peace. For what except attack will lead to war? And what but peace is opposite to war? Here the initial contrast stands out clear and apparent. Yet when peace is found, the war is meaningless. And it is conflict now that is perceived as nonexistent and unreal.

M-21.1 - Strictly speaking, words play no part at all in healing. The motivating factor is prayer, or asking. <u>What you ask for you receive.</u> But this refers to the prayer of the heart, not to the words you use in praying. Sometimes the words and the prayer are contradictory; sometimes they agree. It does not matter. God does not understand words, for they were made by separated minds to keep them in the illusion of separation. Words can be helpful, particularly for the beginner, in helping concentration and facilitating the exclusion, or at least the control, of extraneous thoughts. Let us not forget, however, that words are but symbols of symbols. They are thus twice removed from reality.

M-29.6:9-7:11 - A loving father does not let his child harm himself, or choose his own destruction. He may ask for injury, but his father will protect him still. And how much more than this does your Father love His Son?

Remember you are His completion and His Love. Remember your weakness is His strength. But do not read this hastily or wrongly. If His strength is in you, what you perceive as your weakness is but illusion. And He has given you the means to prove it so. <u>Ask all things of His Teacher [the Holy Spirit], and all things are given you</u>. Not in the future but immediately; now. God does not wait, for waiting implies time and He is timeless. Forget your foolish images, your sense of frailty and your fear of harm, your dreams of danger and selected "wrongs." God knows but His Son, and as he was created so he is. In confidence I [Jesus] place you in His hands, and I give thanks for you that this is so.

P-2.IV.1-2 - As all therapy is psychotherapy, so all illness is mental illness. It is a judgment on the Son of God, and judgment is a mental activity. Judgment is a decision, made again and again, against creation and its Creator. It is a decision to perceive the universe as you would have created it. It is a decision that truth can lie and must be lies. What, then, can illness be except an expression of sorrow and of guilt? And who could weep but for his innocence?

Once God's Son is seen as guilty, illness becomes inevitable. <u>It has been asked for and will be received</u>. And all who ask for illness have now condemned themselves to seek for remedies that cannot help, because their faith is in the illness and not in salvation. There can be nothing that a change of mind cannot affect, for all external things are only shadows of a decision already made. Change the decision, and how can its shadow be unchanged? Illness can be but guilt's shadow, grotesque and ugly since it mimics deformity. If a deformity is seen as real, what could its shadow be except deformed.

Bible Reference - Text

Matthew 7:7-8 - Ask, and it shall be given you; seek, and....
(Continued) - (To read the full text of the above go to page 155.)

Course Ref/s - Citation/s

P-2.V.5-6 - <u>A brother seeking aid</u> can bring us gifts beyond the heights perceived in any dream. He offers us salvation, for he comes to us as Christ and Savior. <u>What he asks is asked by God through him.</u> And what we do for him becomes the gift we give to God. The sacred calling of God's holy Son for help in his perceived distress can be but answered by his Father. Yet He needs a voice through which to speak His holy Word; a hand to reach His Son and touch his heart. In such a process, who could not be healed? This holy interaction is the plan of God Himself, by which His Son is saved.

For two have joined. And now God's promises are kept by Him. The limits laid on both the patient and the therapist will count as nothing, for the healing has begun. What they must start their Father will complete. For He has never asked for more than just the smallest willingness, the least advance, the tiniest of whispers of His Name. To ask for help, whatever form it takes, is but to call on Him. And He will send His Answer through the therapist who best can serve His Son in all his present needs. Perhaps the answer does not seem to be a gift from Heaven. It may even seem to be a worsening and not a help. Yet let the outcome not be judged by us.

S-1.I.1-3 - Prayer is a way offered by the Holy Spirit to reach God. It is not merely a question or an entreaty. It cannot succeed until you realize that it asks for nothing. How else could it serve its purpose? It is impossible to pray for idols and hope to reach God. True prayer must avoid the pitfall of asking to entreat. <u>Ask, rather, to receive what is already given</u>; to accept what is already there.

You have been told to ask the Holy Spirit for the answer to any specific problem, and that you will receive a specific answer if such is your need. You have also been told that there is only one problem and one answer.

In prayer this is not contradictory. There are decisions to make here, and they must be made whether they be illusions or not. You cannot be asked to accept answers which are beyond the level of need that you can recognize. Therefore, it is not the form of the question that matters, nor how it is asked. The form of the answer, if given by God, will suit your need as you see it. This is merely an echo of the reply of His Voice. The real sound is always a song of thanksgiving and of Love.

You cannot, then, ask for the echo. It is the song that is the gift. Along with it come the overtones, the harmonics, the echoes, but these are secondary. In true prayer you hear only the song. All the rest is merely added.
You have sought first the Kingdom of Heaven, and all else has indeed been given you.

S-1.II.1-2 - Prayer has no beginning and no end. It is a part of life. But it does change in form, and grow with learning until it reaches its formless state, and fuses into total communication with God. In its asking form it need not, and often does not, make appeal to God, or even involve belief in Him. At these levels prayer is merely wanting, out of a sense of scarcity and lack.

These forms of prayer, or asking-out-of-need, always involve feelings of weakness and inadequacy, and could never be made by a Son of God who knows Who he is. No one, then, who is sure of his Identity could pray in these forms. Yet it is also true that no one who is uncertain of his Identity can avoid praying in this way. And prayer is as continual as life. Everyone prays without ceasing. <u>Ask and you have received</u>, for you have established what it is you want.

S-2.I.6-7 - Forgiveness, truly given, is the way in which your only hope of freedom lies. Others will make mistakes and so will you, as long as this illusion of a world appears to be your home. Yet God Himself has given all His Sons a remedy for all illusions that they think they see. Christ's vision does not use your eyes, but you can look through His and learn to see like Him. Mistakes are tiny shadows, quickly gone, that for an instant only seem to hide the face of Christ, which still remains unchanged behind them all. His constancy remains in tranquil silence and in perfect peace. He does not know of shadows. His the eyes that look past error to the Christ in you.

Ask, then, His help, and ask Him how to learn forgiveness as His vision lets it be. <u>You are in need of what He gives</u>, and your salvation rests on learning this of Him. Prayer cannot be released to Heaven while forgiveness-to- destroy remains with you. God's mercy would remove this withering and poisoned thinking from your holy mind. Christ has forgiven you, and in His sight the world becomes as holy as Himself. Who sees no evil in it sees like Him. For what He has forgiven has not sinned, and guilt can be no more. Salvation's plan is made complete, and sanity has come.

Bible Reference - Text

Matthew 7:7-8 - Ask, and it shall be given you; seek, and....
(Continued) - (To read the full text of the above go to page 155.)

Course Ref/s - Citation/s

S-2.III.1 - Forgiveness-for-Salvation has one form, and only one. It does not ask for proof of innocence, nor pay of any kind. It does not argue, nor evaluate the errors that it wants to overlook. It does not offer gifts in treachery, nor promise freedom while it asks for death. Would God deceive you? He but asks for trust and willingness to learn how to be free. <u>He gives His Teacher to whoever asks,</u> and seeks to understand the Will of God. His readiness to give lies far beyond your understanding and your simple grasp. Yet He has willed you learn the way to Him, and in His willing there is certainty.

Bible Reference - Text

Matthew 7:9-11 - Or what man is there of you, whom if his son ask bread, will he give him a stone? Or if he ask a fish, will he give him a serpent? If ye then, being evil, know how to give good gifts unto your children, how much more shall your Father which is in heaven give good things to them that ask him?

Course Ref/s - Citation/s

T-13.III.10 - You who prefer separation to sanity cannot obtain it in your right mind. You were at peace until you asked for special favor. <u>And God did not give it for the request was alien to Him, and you could not ask this of a Father Who truly loved His Son.</u> Therefore you made of Him an unloving father, demanding of Him what only such a father could give. And the peace of God's Son was shattered, for he no longer understood his Father. He feared what he had made, but still more did he fear his real Father, having attacked his own glorious equality with Him.

M-29.6 - Never forget that the Holy Spirit does not depend on your words. He understands the requests of your heart, and answers them. Does this mean that, while attack remains attractive to you, He will respond with evil? Hardly! For God has given Him the power to translate your prayers of the heart into His language. He understands that an attack is a call for help. And He responds with help accordingly. God would be cruel if He let your words replace His Own. <u>A loving father does not let his child harm himself, or choose his own destruction. He may ask for injury, but his father will protect him still. And how much more than this does your Father love His Son?</u>

Bible Reference - Text

Matthew 7:12 - Therefore all things whatsoever ye would that men should do to you, do ye even so to them: for this is the law and the prophets.

Course Ref/s - Citation/s

T-01.III.6:2-7 - <u>The Golden Rule asks you to do unto others as you would have them do unto you.</u> This means that the perception of both must be accurate. The Golden Rule is the rule for appropriate behavior. You cannot behave appropriately unless you perceive correctly. Since you and your neighbor are equal members of one family, as you perceive both so you will do to both. You should look out from the perception of your own holiness to the holiness of others.

T-27.VIII.6:5-8:7 - It is a joke to think that time can come to circumvent eternity, which means there is no time.

A timelessness in which is time made real; a part of God that can attack itself; a separate brother as an enemy; a mind within a body all are forms of circularity whose ending starts at its beginning, ending at its cause.
The world you see depicts exactly what you thought you did. Except that now you think that <u>what you did is being done to you.</u> The guilt for what you thought is being placed outside yourself, and on a guilty world that

dreams your dreams and thinks your thoughts instead of you. It brings its vengeance, not your own. It keeps you narrowly confined within a body, which it punishes because of all the sinful things the body does within its dream. You have no power to make the body stop its evil deeds because you did not make it, and cannot control its actions nor its purpose nor its fate.

The world but demonstrates an ancient truth; <u>you will believe that others do to you exactly what you think you did to them</u>. But once deluded into blaming them you will not see the cause of what they do, because you want the guilt to rest on them. How childish is the petulant device to keep your innocence by pushing guilt outside yourself, but never letting go! It is not easy to perceive the jest when all around you do your eyes behold its heavy consequences, but without their trifling cause. Without the cause do its effects seem serious and sad indeed. Yet they but follow. And it is their cause that follows nothing and is but a jest.

Bible Reference - Text

Matthew 7:15-16 - Beware of false prophets, which come to you in sheep's clothing, but inwardly they are ravening wolves. Ye shall know them by their fruits. Do men gather grapes of thorns, or figs of thistles?

Course Ref/s - Citation/s

T-09.V.9 - This course [A Course in Miracles] offers a very direct and a very simple learning situation, and provides the Guide [the Holy Spirit] Who tells you what to do. If you do it, you will see that it works. Its results are more convincing than its words. They will convince you that the words are true. By following the right Guide, you will learn the simplest of all lessons: <u>By their fruits ye shall know them</u>, and they shall know themselves.

T-16.III.2 - You may have taught freedom, but you have not learned how to be free. I said earlier, "<u>By their fruits ye shall know them</u>, and they shall know themselves." For it is certain that you judge yourself according to your teaching. The ego's teaching produces immediate results, because its decisions are immediately accepted as your choice. And this acceptance means that you are willing to judge yourself accordingly. Cause and effect are very clear in the ego's thought system, because all your learning has been directed toward establishing the relationship between them. And would you not have faith in what you have so diligently taught yourself to believe? Yet remember how much care you have exerted in choosing its witnesses, and in avoiding those which spoke for the cause of truth and its effects.

Bible Reference - Text

Matthew 7:21 - "Not everyone who says to Me, 'Lord, Lord,' shall enter the kingdom of heaven, but he who does the will of My Father in heaven.

Course Ref/s - Citation/s

T-05.II.1:5-7 - <u>Your will is still in you because God placed it in your mind,</u> and although you can keep it asleep you cannot obliterate it. God Himself keeps your will alive by transmitting it from His Mind to yours as long as there is time. The miracle itself is a reflection of this union of will between Father and Son.

T-08.III.3 - <u>The Will of the Father</u> and of the Son are one, by their extension. Their extension is the result of Their oneness, holding Their unity together by extending Their joint Will. This is perfect creation by the perfectly created, in union with the Perfect Creator. The Father must give fatherhood to His Son, because His Own Fatherhood must be extended outward. You who belong in God have the holy function of extending His Fatherhood by placing no limits upon it. Let the Holy Spirit teach you how to do this, for you can know what it means only of God Himself.

T-09.I.9 - Ultimately everyone must remember <u>the Will of God,</u> because ultimately everyone must recognize himself. This recognition is the recognition that his will and God's are one. In the presence of truth, there are no unbelievers and no sacrifices. In the security of reality, fear is totally meaningless. To deny what is can only seem to be fearful. Fear cannot be real without a cause, and God is the only Cause. God is Love and you do want Him. This <u>is your will.</u> Ask for this and you will be answered, because you will be asking only for what belongs to you.

T-11.III.3 - <u>O my child, if you knew what God wills for you, your joy would be complete!</u> And what He wills has happened, for it was always true. When the light comes and you have said, "God's Will is mine," you will see such beauty that you will know it is not of you. Out of your joy you will create beauty in His Name, for your joy could no more be contained than His. The bleak little world will vanish into nothingness, and your heart will be so filled with joy that it will leap into Heaven, and into the Presence of God. I cannot tell you what this will be like, for your heart is not ready. Yet I can tell you, and remind you often, that what God wills for Himself He wills for you, and what He wills for you is yours.

T-12.II.6 - You still want what God wills, and no nightmare can defeat a child of God in his purpose. <u>For your purpose was given you by God, and you must accomplish it because it is His Will</u>. Awake and remember your purpose, for it is your will to do so. What has been accomplished for you must be yours. Do not let your hatred stand in the way of love, for nothing can withstand the Love of Christ for His Father, or His Father's Love for Him.

Bible Reference - Text

Matthew 7:24-27 - Therefore whosoever heareth these sayings of mine, and doeth them, I will liken him unto a wise man, which built his house upon a rock: And the rain descended, and the floods came, and the winds blew, and beat upon that house; and it fell not: for it was founded upon a rock. And every one that heareth these sayings of mine, and doeth them not, shall be likened unto a foolish man, which built his house upon the sand: And the rain descended, and the floods came, and the winds blew, and beat upon that house; and it fell: and great was the fall of it.

Course Ref/s - Citation/s

T-04.I.11 - <u>The ego has built a shabby and unsheltering home for you,</u> because it cannot build otherwise. Do not try to make this impoverished house stand. Its weakness is your strength. <u>Only God could make a home that is worthy of His creations</u>, who have chosen to leave it empty by their own dispossession. Yet His home will stand forever, and is ready for you when you choose to enter it. Of this you can be wholly certain. God is as incapable of creating the perishable as the ego is of making the eternal.

T-14.II.6 - If you would be a happy learner, you must give everything you have learned to the Holy Spirit, to be unlearned for you. And then begin to learn the joyous lessons that come quickly on the <u>firm foundation</u> that truth is true. For <u>what is builded there</u> is true, and built on truth. The universe of learning will open up before you in all its gracious simplicity. With truth before you, you will not look back.

T-24.III.3 - It is not you who are so vulnerable and open to attack that just a word, a little whisper that you do not like, a circumstance that suits you not, or an event that you did not anticipate upsets your world, and hurls it into chaos. Truth is not frail. Illusions leave it perfectly unmoved and undisturbed. But specialness is not the truth in you. It can be thrown off balance by anything. <u>What rests on nothing never can be stable.</u> However large and overblown it seems to be, it still must rock and turn and whirl about with every breeze.

T-24.III.4 - <u>Without foundation nothing is secure.</u> Would God have left His Son in such a state, where safety has no meaning? No, His Son is safe, resting on Him. It is your specialness that is attacked by everything that walks and breathes, or creeps or crawls, or even lives at all. Nothing is safe from its attack, and it is safe from nothing. It will forevermore be unforgiving, for that is what it is; a secret vow that what God wants for you will never be, and that you will oppose His Will forever. Nor is it possible the two can ever be the same, while specialness stands like a flaming sword of death between them, and makes them enemies.

T-28.VII.3 - Either there is a gap between you and your brother, or you are as one. There is no in between, no other choice, and no allegiance to be split between the two. A split allegiance is but faithlessness to both, and merely sets you spinning round, to grasp uncertainly at any straw that seems to hold some promise of relief. Yet <u>who can build his home upon a straw</u>, and count on it as shelter from the wind? The body can be made a home like this, because it lacks foundation in the truth. And yet, because it does, it can be seen as not your home, but merely as an aid to help you reach the home where God abides.

T-28.VII.5 - But never you alone. This world is but the dream that you can be alone, and think without affecting those apart from you. To be alone must mean you are apart, and if you are, you cannot but be sick. This seems to prove that you must be apart. Yet all it means is that you tried to keep a promise to be true to faithlessness. Yet faithlessness is sickness. It is like <u>the house set upon straw</u>. It seems to be quite solid and substantial in itself. Yet its stability cannot be judged apart from its foundation. If it rests on straw, there is no need to bar the door and lock the windows and make fast the bolts. <u>The wind will topple it, and rain will come and carry it into oblivion.</u>

T-28.VII.7 - Your home is built upon your brother's health, upon his happiness, his sinlessness, and everything his Father promised him. No secret promise you have made instead has shaken the Foundation of his home. <u>The winds will blow upon it and the rain will beat against it, but with no effect.</u> The world will wash away and yet this house will stand forever, for its strength lies not within itself alone. It is an ark of safety, resting on God's promise that His Son is safe forever in Himself. What gap can interpose itself between the safety of this shelter and its Source? From here the body can be seen as what it is, and neither less nor more in worth than the extent to which it can be used to liberate God's Son unto his home. And with this holy purpose is it made a home of holiness a little while, because it shares your Father's Will with you.

Bible Reference - Text

Matthew 8:21-22 - And another of his disciples said unto him, Lord, suffer me first to go and bury my father. But Jesus said unto him, Follow me; and let the dead bury their dead.

Course Ref/s - Citation/s

T-26.V.10 - Would God allow His Son to lose his way along a road long since a memory of time gone by? This course [A Course in Miracles] will teach you only what is now. A dreadful instant in a distant past, now perfectly corrected, is of no concern nor value. <u>Let the dead and gone be peacefully forgotten.</u> Resurrection has come to take its place. And now you are a part of resurrection, not of death. No past illusions have the power to keep you in a place of death, a vault God's Son entered an instant, to be instantly restored unto His Father's perfect Love. And how can he be kept in chains long since removed and gone forever from his mind?

Bible Reference - Text

Matthew 8:26 - And he saith unto them, Why are ye fearful, O ye of little faith? Then he arose, and rebuked the winds and the sea; and there was a great calm.

Course Ref/s - Citation/s

T-17.VII.7 - The power set in you in whom the Holy Spirit's goal has been established is so far beyond your little conception of the infinite that you have no idea how great the strength that goes with you. And you can use this in perfect safety. Yet for all its might, so great it reaches past the stars and to the universe that lies beyond them, <u>your little faithlessness</u> can make it useless, if you would use the faithlessness instead.

Bible Reference - Text

Matthew 9:2 - And, behold, they brought to him a man sick of the palsy, lying on a bed: and Jesus seeing their faith said unto the sick of the palsy; Son, be of good cheer; thy sins be forgiven thee.

Course Ref/s - Citation/s

T-26.IX.1-2 - Think but how holy you must be from whom the Voice for God calls lovingly unto your brother, that you may awake in him the Voice that answers to your call! And think how holy he must be when in him sleeps your own salvation, with his freedom joined! However much you wish he be condemned, God is in him. And never will you know He is in you as well while you attack His chosen home, and battle with His host. Regard him gently. Look with loving eyes on him who carries Christ within him, that you may behold his glory and rejoice that Heaven is not separate from you.
2 Is it too much to ask a little trust for him who carries Christ to you, that <u>you may be forgiven all your sins</u>, and left without a single one you cherish still? Forget not that a shadow held between your brother and yourself obscures the face of Christ and memory of God. And would you trade Them for an ancient hate? The ground whereon you stand is holy ground because of Them Who, standing there with you, have blessed it with Their innocence and peace.

W-pI.158.9-10 - <u>Thus are his sins forgiven him</u>, for Christ has vision that has power to overlook them all. In His forgiveness are they gone. Unseen by One they merely disappear, because a vision of the holiness that lies beyond them comes to take their place. It matters not what form they took,

nor how enormous they appeared to be, nor who seemed to be hurt by them. They are no more. And all effects they seemed to have are gone with them, undone and never to be done.
10 Thus do you learn to give as you receive. And thus Christ's vision looks on you as well. This lesson is not difficult to learn, if you remember in your brother you but see yourself. If he be lost in sin, so must you be, if you see light in him, <u>your sins have been forgiven</u> by yourself. Each brother whom you meet today provides another chance to let Christ's vision shine on you, and offer you the peace of God.

W-pII.1.1 - Forgiveness recognizes what you thought your brother did to you has not occurred. It does not pardon sins and make them real. It sees there was no sin. And in that view are <u>all your sins forgiven</u>. What is sin, except a false idea about God's Son? Forgiveness merely sees its falsity, and therefore lets it go. What then is free to take its place is now the Will of God.

W-pII.304.1 - I can obscure my holy sight, if I intrude my world upon it. Nor can I behold the holy sights Christ looks upon, unless it is His vision that I use. Perception is a mirror, not a fact. And what I look on is my state of mind, reflected outward. I would bless the world by looking on it through the eyes of Christ. And I will look upon the certain signs that <u>all my sins have been forgiven me</u>.

C-5.3-4 - In his complete identification with the Christ--the perfect Son of God, His one creation and His happiness, forever like Himself and one with Him--Jesus became what all of you must be. He led the way for you to follow him. He leads you back to God because he saw the road before him, and he followed it. He made a clear distinction, still obscure to you, between the false and true. He offered you a final demonstration that it is impossible to kill God's Son; nor can his life in any way be changed by sin and evil, malice, fear or death.
4 And therefore all <u>your sins have been forgiven</u> because they carried no effects at all. And so they were but dreams. Arise with him who showed you this because you owe him this who shared your dreams that they might be dispelled. And shares them still, to be at one with you.

M-18.4 - In order to heal, it thus becomes essential for the teacher of God to let all his own mistakes be corrected. If he senses even the faintest hint of irritation in himself as he responds to anyone, let him instantly realize that he has made an interpretation that is not true. Then let him turn within to his Eternal Guide, and let Him judge what the response should be. So is he healed, and in his healing is his pupil healed with him. The sole responsibility of God's teacher is to accept the Atonement for himself. Atonement means correction, or the undoing of errors. When this has been accomplished, the teacher of God becomes a miracle worker by definition. His sins have been forgiven him, and he no longer condemns himself. How can he then condemn anyone? And who is there whom his forgiveness can fail to heal?

Bible Reference - Text

Matthew 9:2 - And, behold, they brought to him a man sick of the .... (Continued) - (To read the full text of the above go to page 196.)

Course Ref/s - Citation/s

P-2.V.8 - Let us stand silently before God's Will, and do what it has chosen that we do. There is one way alone by which we come to where all dreams began. And it is there that we will lay them down, to come away in peace forever. Hear a brother call for help and answer him. It will be God to Whom you answer, for you called on Him. There is no other way to hear His Voice. There is no other way to seek His Son. There is no other way to find your Self. Holy is healing, for the Son of God returns to Heaven through its kind embrace. For healing tells him, in the Voice for God, that all his sins have been forgiven him.

P-2.VII.3 - The process that takes place in this relationship is actually one in which the therapist in his heart tells the patient that all his sins have been forgiven him, along with his own. What could be the difference between healing and forgiveness? Only Christ forgives, knowing His sinlessness. His vision heals perception and sickness disappears. Nor will it return again, once its cause has been removed. This, however, needs the help of a very advanced therapist, capable of joining with the patient in a holy relationship in which all sense of separation finally is overcome.

P-3.II.4 - God is said to have looked on all He created and pronounced it good. No, He declared it perfect, and so it was. And since His creations do not change and last forever, so it is now. Yet neither a perfect therapist nor a perfect patient can possibly exist. Both must have denied their perfection, for their very need for each other implies a sense of lack. A one-to-one relationship is not one Relationship. Yet it is the means of return; the way God chose for the return of His Son. In that strange dream a strange correction must enter, for only that is the call to awake. And what else should therapy be? Awake and be glad, for all <u>your sins have been forgiven you</u>. This is the only message that any two should ever give each other.

Bible Reference - Text

Matthew 9:6 - But that ye may know that the Son of man hath power on earth to forgive sins, (then saith he to the sick of the palsy,) Arise, take up thy bed, and go unto thine house.

Course Ref/s - Citation/s

T-25.VIII.8-9 - Yet justice cannot punish those who ask for punishment, but have a Judge Who knows that they are wholly innocent in truth. In justice He is bound to set them free, and give them all the honor they deserve and have denied themselves because they are not fair, and cannot understand that they are innocent. Love is not understandable to sinners because they think that justice is split off from love, and stands for something else. And thus is love perceived as weak, and vengeance strong. For love has lost when judgment left its side, and is too weak to save from punishment. But vengeance without love has gained in strength by being separate and apart from love. And what but vengeance now can help and save, while love stands feebly by with helpless hands, bereft of justice and vitality, and powerless to save?

What can Love ask of you who think that all of this is true? Could He, in justice and in love, believe in your confusion you have much to give? You are not asked to trust Him far. No more than what you see He offers you, and what you recognize you could not give yourself. In God's Own justice does He recognize all you deserve, but understands as well that you cannot accept it for yourself. It is His special function to hold out to you the gifts the innocent deserve. And every one that you accept brings joy to Him as well as you. He knows that Heaven is richer made by each one you accept. And God rejoices as His Son receives what loving justice knows to be his due. For love and justice are not different. Because they are the same does mercy stand at God's right Hand, and gives <u>the Son of God the power to forgive himself of sin</u>.

Bible Reference - Text

Matthew 9:20-22 - And, behold, a woman, which was diseased with an issue of blood twelve years, came behind him, and touched the hem of his garment: For she said within herself, If I may but touch his garment, I shall be whole. But Jesus turned him about, and when he saw her, he said, Daughter, be of good comfort; thy faith hath made thee whole. And the woman was made whole from that hour.

Course Ref/s - Citation/s

T-10.III.7 - When a brother is sick it is because he is not asking for peace, and therefore does not know he has it. The acceptance of peace is the denial of illusion, and sickness is an illusion. Yet every Son of God has the power to deny illusions anywhere in the Kingdom, merely by denying them completely in himself. I can heal you because I know you. I know your value for you, and it is this value that makes you whole. A whole mind is not idolatrous, and does not know of conflicting laws. I will heal you merely because I have only one message, and it is true. <u>Your faith in it will make you whole when you have faith in me.</u>

W-pI.110.8 - Seek Him within you Who is <u>Christ</u> in you, the Son of God and brother to the world; <u>the Savior Who has been forever saved, with power to save whoever touches Him, however lightly</u>, asking for the Word that tells him he is brother unto Him.

Bible Reference - Text

Matthew 10:8 - Heal the sick, cleanse the lepers, raise the dead, cast out devils: freely ye have received, freely give.

Course Ref/s - Citation/s

T-01.I.24 - Miracles enable you to <u>heal the sick and raise the dead</u> because you made sickness and death yourself, and can therefore abolish both. You are a miracle, capable of creating in the likeness of your Creator. Everything else is your own nightmare, and does not exist. Only the creations of light are real.

T-05.VII.2 - There have been many healers who did not heal themselves. They have not moved mountains by their faith because their faith was not whole. Some of them <u>have healed the sick</u> at times, but they have not <u>raised the dead</u>. Unless the healer heals himself, he cannot believe that there is no order of difficulty in miracles. He has not learned that every mind God created is equally worthy of being healed because God created it whole. You are merely asked to return to God the mind as He created it. He asks you only for what He gave, knowing that this giving will heal you. Sanity is wholeness, and the sanity of your brothers is yours.

T-30.I.17 - It needs but two who would have happiness this day to promise it to all the world. It needs but two to understand that they cannot decide alone, to guarantee the joy they asked for will be wholly shared. For they have understood the basic law that makes decision powerful, and gives it all effects that it will ever have. It needs but two. These two are joined before there can be a decision. Let this be the one reminder that you keep in mind, and you will have the day you want, and give it to the world by having it yourself. Your judgment has been lifted from the world by your decision for a happy day. And <u>as you have received, so must you give</u>.

Bible Reference - Text

Matthew 10:19-20 - But when they deliver you up, do not worry about how or what you should speak. For it will be given to you in that hour what you should speak; for it is not you who speak, but the Spirit of your Father who speaks in you.

Course Ref/s - Citation/s

T-02.V.18 - You can do much on behalf of your own healing and that of others if, in a situation calling for help, you think of it this way: I am here only to be truly helpful. I am here to represent Him Who sent me. <u>I do not have to worry about what to say</u> or what to do, because He Who sent me will direct me. I am content to be wherever He wishes, knowing He goes there with me. I will be healed as I let Him teach me to heal.

Bible Reference - Text

Matthew 10:34 - Think not that I am come to send peace on earth: I came not to send peace, but a sword.

Course Ref/s - Citation/s

T-06.I.15:1-3 - These are some of the examples of upside-down thinking in the New Testament, although its gospel is really only the message of love. If the Apostles had not felt guilty, they never could have quoted me as saying, "<u>I come not to bring peace but a sword.</u>" This is clearly the opposite of everything I taught.

Bible Reference - Text

Matthew 11:3-5 - And said unto him, Art thou he that should come, or do we look for another? Jesus answered and said unto them, Go and shew John again those things which ye do hear and see: The blind receive their sight, and the lame walk, the lepers are cleansed, and the deaf hear, the dead are raised up, and the poor have the gospel preached to them.

Course Ref/s - Citation/s

W-pI.159.5 - Christ's vision is the bridge between the worlds. And in its power can you safely trust to carry you from this world into one made holy by forgiveness. Things which seem quite solid here are merely shadows there; transparent, faintly seen, at times forgot, and never able to obscure the light that shines beyond them. Holiness has been restored to vision, and <u>the blind can see.</u>

W-pI.183.3 - Repeat God's Name, and all the world responds by laying down illusions. Every dream the world holds dear has suddenly gone by, and where it seemed to stand you find a star; a miracle of grace. The sick arise, healed of their sickly thoughts. <u>The blind can see; the deaf can hear.</u>

The sorrowful cast off their mourning, and the tears of pain are dried as happy laughter comes to bless the world.

Bible Reference - Text

Matthew 11:15 - He that hath ears to hear, let him hear.

Course Ref/s - Citation/s

T-24.V.5 - Rejoice you have no eyes with which to see; no ears to listen, and no hands to hold nor feet to guide. Be glad that only Christ can lend you His, while you have need of them. They are illusions, too, as much as yours. And yet because they serve a different purpose, the strength their purpose holds is given them. And what they see and hear and hold and lead is given light, that you may lead as you were led.

W-pI.127.6 - Seek not within the world to find your Self. Love is not found in darkness and in death. Yet it is perfectly apparent to the eyes that see and ears that hear love's Voice. Today we practice making free your mind of all the laws you think you must obey; of all the limits under which you live, and all the changes that you think are part of human destiny. Today we take the largest single step this course requests in your advance towards its established goal.

M-18.2-3 - God's teachers' major lesson is to learn how to react to magic thoughts wholly without anger. Only in this way can they proclaim the truth about themselves. Through them, the Holy Spirit can now speak of the reality of the Son of God. Now He can remind the world of sinlessness, the one unchanged, unchangeable condition of all that God created. Now He can speak the Word of God to listening ears, and bring Christ's vision to eyes that see. Now is He free to teach all minds the truth of what they are, so they will gladly be returned to Him. And now is guilt forgiven, overlooked completely in His sight and in God's Word.
3 Anger but screeches, "Guilt is real"! Reality is blotted out as this insane belief is taken as replacement for God's Word. The body's eyes now "see"; its ears alone can "hear." Its little space and tiny breath become the measure of reality. And truth becomes diminutive and meaningless. Correction has one answer to all this, and to the world that rests on this: You but mistake interpretation for the truth. And you are wrong. But a

mistake is not a sin, nor has reality been taken from its throne by your mistakes. God reigns forever, and His laws alone prevail upon you and upon the world. His Love remains the only thing there is. Fear is illusion, for you are like Him.

Bible Reference - Text

Matthew 11:21-22 - Woe unto thee, Chorazin! Woe unto thee, Bethsaida! For if the mighty works, which were done in you, had been done in Tyre and Sidon, they would have repented long ago in sackcloth and ashes. But I say unto you, It shall be more tolerable for Tyre and Sidon at the day of judgment, than for you.

Course Ref/s - Citation/s

T-02.VIII.1 - One of the ways in which you can correct the magic-miracle confusion is to remember that you did not create yourself. You are apt to forget this when you become egocentric, and this puts you in a position where a belief in magic is virtually inevitable. Your will to create was given you by your Creator, Who was expressing the same Will in His Creation. Since creative ability rests in the mind, everything you create is necessarily a matter of will. It also follows that whatever you alone make is real in your own sight, though not in the Mind of God. This basic distinction leads directly into the real meaning of the Last Judgment.

T-02.VIII.2 - The Last Judgment is one of the most threatening ideas in your thinking. This is because you do not understand it. judgment is not an attribute of God. It was brought into being only after the separation [the Fall], when it became one of the many learning devices to be built into the overall plan. Just as the separation occurred over millions of years, the Last Judgment will extend over a similarly long period, and perhaps an even longer one. Its length, however, can be greatly shortened by miracles, the device for shortening but not abolishing time. If a sufficient number become truly miracle-minded, this shortening process can be virtually immeasurable. It is essential, however, that you free yourself from fear quickly, because you must emerge from the conflict if you are to bring peace to other minds.

T-02.VIII.3 - The Last Judgment is generally thought of as a procedure undertaken by God. Actually it will be undertaken by my brothers with my help. It is a final healing rather than a meting out of punishment, however much you may think that punishment is deserved. Punishment is a concept totally opposed to right-mindedness, and the aim of the Last Judgment is to restore right-mindedness to you. The Last Judgment might be called a process of right evaluation. It simply means that everyone will finally come to understand what is worthy and what is not. After this, the ability to choose can be directed rationally. Until this distinction is made, however, the vacillations between free and imprisoned will cannot but continue.

T-02.VIII.5 - The term "Last Judgment" is frightening not only because it has been projected onto God, but also because of the association of "last" with death. This is an outstanding example of upside-down perception. If the meaning of the Last Judgment is objectively examined, it is quite apparent that it is really the doorway to life. No one who lives in fear is really alive. Your own last judgment cannot be directed toward yourself, because you are not your own creation. You can, however, apply it meaningfully and at any time to everything you have made, and retain in your memory only what is creative and good. This is what your right-mindedness cannot but dictate. The purpose of time is solely to "give you time" to achieve this judgment. It is your own perfect judgment of your own perfect creations. When everything you retain is loveable, there is no reason for fear to remain with you. This is your part in the Atonement.

T-03.VI.1 - We have already discussed the Last Judgment, but in insufficient detail. After the Last Judgment there will be no more. Judgment is symbolic because beyond perception there is no judgment. When the Bible says "Judge not that ye be not judged," it means that if you judge the reality of others you will be unable to avoid judging your own.

T-09.IV.9 - The ego literally lives on borrowed time, and its days are numbered. Do not fear the Last Judgment, but welcome it and do not wait, for the ego's time is "borrowed" from your eternity. This is the Second Coming that was made for you as the First was created. The Second Coming is merely the return of sense. Can this possibly be fearful?

T-26.III.4 - Nothing the Son of God believes can be destroyed. But what is truth to him must be brought to the last comparison that he will ever make; the last evaluation that will be possible, the final judgment upon this world. It is the judgment of the truth upon illusion, of knowledge on perception: "It has no meaning, and does not exist." This is not your decision. It is but a simple statement of a simple fact. But in this world there are no simple facts, because what is the same and what is different remain unclear. The one essential thing to make a choice at all is this distinction. And herein lies the difference between the worlds. In this one, choice is made impossible. In the real world is choosing simplified.

Bible Reference - Text

Matthew 11:21-22 - Woe unto thee, Chorazin! Woe unto thee.... (Continued) - (To read the full text of the above go to page 204.)

Course Ref/s - Citation/s

W-pII.10 - Christ's Second Coming gives the Son of God this gift: to hear the Voice for God proclaim that what is false is false, and what is true has never changed. And this the judgment is in which perception ends. At first you see a world that has accepted this as true, projected from a now corrected mind. And with this holy sight, perception gives a silent blessing and then disappears, its goal accomplished and its mission done.
2 The final judgment on the world contains no condemnation. For it sees the world as totally forgiven, without sin and wholly purposeless. Without a cause, and now without a function in Christ's sight, it merely slips away to nothingness. There it was born, and there it ends as well. And all the figures in the dream in which the world began go with it. Bodies now are useless, and will therefore fade away, because the Son of God is limitless.
3 You who believed that God's Last Judgment would condemn the world to hell along with you, accept this holy truth: God's Judgment is the gift of the Correction He bestowed on all your errors, freeing you from them, and all effects they ever seemed to have. To fear God's saving grace is but to fear complete release from suffering, return to peace, security and happiness, and union with your own Identity.
4 God's Final Judgment is as merciful as every step in His appointed plan to bless His Son, and call him to return to the eternal peace He shares with him. Be not afraid of love. For it alone can heal all sorrow, wipe away all tears, and gently waken from his dream of pain the Son whom God acknowledges as His. Be not afraid of this. Salvation asks you give it welcome. And the world awaits your glad acceptance, which will set it free.
5 This is God's Final Judgment: "You are still My holy Son, forever

innocent, forever loving and forever loved, as limitless as your Creator, and completely changeless and forever pure. Therefore awaken and return to Me. I am Your Father and you are My Son."

W-pII.9.3 - The Second Coming ends the lessons that the Holy Spirit teaches, making way for the Last Judgment, in which learning ends in one last summary that will extend beyond itself, and reaches up to God. The Second Coming is the time in which all minds are given to the hands of Christ, to be returned to spirit in the name of true creation and the Will of God.

M-15 - Indeed, yes! No one can escape God's Final Judgment. Who could flee forever from the truth? But the Final Judgment will not come until it is no longer associated with fear. One day each one will welcome it, and on that very day it will be given him. He will hear his sinlessness proclaimed around and around the world, setting it free as God's Final Judgment on him is received. This is the Judgment in which salvation lies. This is the Judgment that will set him free. This is the Judgment in which all things are freed with him. Time pauses as eternity comes near, and silence lies across the world that everyone may hear this Judgment of the Son of God: Holy are you, eternal, free and whole, at peace forever in the Heart of God. Where is the world, and where is sorrow now?
2 Is this your judgment on yourself, teacher of God? Do you believe that this is wholly true? No; not yet, not yet. But this is still your goal; why you are here. It is your function to prepare yourself to hear this judgment and to recognize that it is true. One instant of complete belief in this, and you will go beyond belief to Certainty. One instant out of time can bring time's end. Judge not, for you but judge yourself, and thus delay this Final Judgment. What is your judgment of the world, teacher of God? Have you yet learned to stand aside and hear the Voice of Judgment in yourself? Or do you still attempt to take His role from Him? Learn to be quiet, for His Voice is heard in stillness. And His Judgment comes to all who stand aside in quiet listening, and wait for Him.
3 You who are sometimes sad and sometimes angry; who sometimes feel your just due is not given you, and your best efforts meet with lack of appreciation and even contempt; give up these foolish thoughts! They are too small and meaningless to occupy your holy mind an instant longer. God's Judgment waits for you to set you free. What can the world hold out to you, regardless of your judgments on its gifts, that you would rather have? You will be judged, and judged in fairness and in honesty. There is no deceit in God. His promises are sure. Only remember that. His promises

have guaranteed His Judgment, and His alone, will be accepted in the end. It is your function to make that end be soon. It is your, function to hold it to your heart, and offer it to all the world to keep it safe.

Bible Reference - Text

Matthew 11:21-22 - Woe unto thee, Chorazin! Woe unto thee.... (Continued) - (To read the full text of the above go to page 204.)

Course Ref/s - Citation/s

M-28.5-6 - Now there are no distinctions. Differences have disappeared and Love looks on Itself. What further sight is needed? What remains that vision could accomplish? We have seen the face of Christ, His sinlessness, His Love behind all forms, beyond all purposes. Holy are we because His Holiness has set us free indeed! And we accept His Holiness as ours; as it is. As God created us so will we be forever and forever, and we wish for nothing but His Will to be our own. Illusions of another will are lost, for unity of purpose has been found.
6 These things await us all, but we are not prepared as yet to welcome them with joy. As long as any mind remains possessed of evil dreams, the thought of hell is real. God's teachers have the goal of wakening the minds of those asleep, and seeing there the vision of Christ's face to take the place of what they dream. The thought of murder is replaced with blessing. Judgment is laid by, and given Him Whose function judgment is. And in His <u>Final Judgment</u> is restored the truth about the holy Son of God. He is redeemed, for he has heard God's Word and understood its meaning. He is free because he let God's Voice proclaim the truth. And all he sought before to crucify are resurrected with him, by his side, as he prepares with them to meet his God.

Bible Reference - Text

Matthew 11:25 - At that time Jesus answered and said, I thank thee, O Father, Lord of heaven and earth, because thou hast hid these things from the wise and prudent, and hast revealed them unto babes.

Course Ref/s - Citation/s

T-13.X.11:10-12:6 - Behold the Son of God, and look upon his purity and be still. In quiet look upon his holiness, and offer thanks unto his Father that no guilt has ever touched him.

No illusion that you have ever held against him has touched his innocence in any way. His shining purity, wholly untouched by guilt and wholly loving, is bright within you. Let us look upon him together and love him. For in love of him is your guiltlessness. But look upon yourself, and gladness and appreciation for what you see will banish guilt forever.
I thank You, Father, for the purity of Your most holy Son, whom You have created guiltless forever.

T-13.X.13 - Like you, my faith and my belief are centered on what I treasure. The difference is that I love only what God loves with me, and because of this I treasure you beyond the value that you set on yourself, even unto the worth that God has placed upon you. I love all that He created, and all my faith and my belief I offer unto it. My faith in you is as strong as all the love I give my Father. My trust in you is without limit, and without the fear that you will hear me not. I thank the Father for your loveliness, and for the many gifts that you will let me offer to the Kingdom in honor of its wholeness that is of God.

T-28.IV.9 - I thank You, Father, knowing You will come to close each little gap that lies between the broken pieces of Your holy Son. Your Holiness, complete and perfect, lies in every one of them. And they are joined because what is in one is in them all. How holy is the smallest grain of sand, when it is recognized as being part of the completed picture of God's Son! The forms the broken pieces seem to take mean nothing.
For the whole is in each one. And every aspect of the Son of God is just the same as every other part.

T-30.VI.9 - God's Son is perfect, or he cannot be God's Son. Nor will you know him, if you think he does not merit the escape from guilt in all its consequences and its forms. There is no way to think of him but this, if you would know the truth about yourself. I thank You, Father, for Your perfect Son, and in his glory will I see my own. Here is the joyful statement that there are no forms of evil that can overcome the Will of God; the glad acknowledgement that guilt has not succeeded by your wish to make illusions real. And what is this except a simple statement of the truth?

T-31.VIII.10 - <u>I thank You, Father</u>, for these holy ones who are my brothers as they are Your Sons. My faith in them is Yours. I am as sure that they will come to me as You are sure of what they are, and will forever be. They will accept the gift I offer them, because You gave it me on their behalf. And as I would but do Your holy Will, so will they choose. And I give thanks for them. Salvation's song will echo through the world with every choice they make. For we are one in purpose, and the end of hell is near.

Bible Reference - Text

Matthew 11:27 - All things are delivered unto me of my Father: and no man knoweth the Son, but the Father; neither knoweth any man the Father, save the Son, and he to whomsoever the Son will reveal him.

Course Ref/s - Citation/s

T-13.V.10 - You have but two emotions, and one you made and one was given you. Each is a way of seeing, and different worlds arise from their different sights. See through the vision that is given you, for through Christ's vision He beholds Himself. And seeing what He is, <u>He knows His Father</u>. Beyond your darkest dreams He sees God's guiltless Son within you, shining in perfect radiance that is undimmed by your dreams. And this you will see as you look with Him, for His vision is His gift of love to you, given Him of the Father for you.

Bible Reference - Text

Matthew 11:28 - Come unto me, all ye that labour and are heavy laden, and I will give you rest.

Course Ref/s - Citation/s

T-07.V.11 - <u>Come therefore unto me</u>, and learn of the truth in you. The mind we share is shared by all our brothers, and as we see them truly they will be healed. Let your mind shine with mine upon their minds, and by our gratitude to them make them aware of the light in them. This light will shine back upon you and on the whole Sonship, because this is your proper gift to God. He will accept it and give it to the Sonship, because it is acceptable to Him and therefore to His Sons. This is true communion with the Holy Spirit, Who sees the altar of God in everyone, and by bringing it to your appreciation, He calls upon you to love God and His creation. You can appreciate the Sonship only as one. This is part of the law of creation, and therefore governs all thought.

T-11.IV.6 - Christ is at God's altar, waiting to welcome His Son. But come wholly without condemnation, for otherwise you will believe that the door is barred and you cannot enter. The door is not barred, and it is impossible that you cannot enter the place where God would have you be. But love yourself with the Love of Christ, for so does your Father love you. You can refuse to enter, but you cannot bar the door that Christ holds open. <u>Come unto me</u> who holds it open for you, for while I live it cannot be shut, and I live forever. God is my life and yours, and nothing is denied by God to His Son.

T-19.III.11 - Look upon your Redeemer, and behold what He would show you in your brother, and let not sin arise again to blind your eyes. For sin would keep you separate from him, but your Redeemer would have you look upon your brother as yourself. Your relationship is now a temple of healing; a place where all the weary ones can <u>come and rest</u>. Here is the rest that waits for all, after the journey. And it is brought nearer to all by your relationship.

T-19.IV.1-2 - As peace extends from deep inside yourself to embrace all the Sonship and give it rest, it will encounter many obstacles. Some of them you will try to impose. Others will seem to arise from elsewhere; from your brothers, and from various aspects of the world outside. Yet peace will gently cover them, extending past completely unencumbered. The extension of the Holy Spirit's purpose from your relationship to others, to bring them gently in, is the way in which He will bring means and goal in line. The peace He lay, deep within you and your brother, will quietly extend to every aspect of your life, surrounding you and your brother with glowing happiness and the calm awareness of complete protection. And you will carry its message of love and safety and freedom to everyone who draws nigh unto your temple, where healing waits for him. You will not wait to give him this, for <u>you will call to him</u> and he will answer you, recognizing in your call the Call for God. And you will draw him in <u>and give him rest</u>, as it was given you.

All this will you do. Yet the peace that already lies deeply within must first expand, and flow across the obstacles you placed before it. This will you do, for nothing undertaken with the Holy Spirit remains unfinished.
You can indeed be sure of nothing you see outside you, but of this you can be sure: The Holy Spirit asks that you offer Him a resting place where you will rest in Him. He answered you, and entered your relationship. Would you not now return His graciousness, and enter into a relationship with Him? For it is He who offered your relationship the gift of holiness, without which it would have been forever impossible to appreciate your brother.

Bible Reference - Text

Matthew 11:29 - Take my yoke upon you, and learn of me; for I am meek and lowly in heart: and ye shall find rest unto your souls.

Course Ref/s - Citation/s

T-03.IV.7:3-16 - I was a man who remembered spirit and its knowledge. As a man I did not attempt to counteract error with knowledge, but to correct error from the bottom up. I demonstrated both the powerlessness of the body and the power of the mind. By uniting my will with that of my Creator, I naturally remembered spirit and its real purpose. I cannot unite your will with God's for you, but I can erase all misperceptions from your mind if you will bring it under my guidance. Only your misperceptions stand in your way. Without them your choice is certain. Sane perception induces sane choosing. I cannot choose for you, but I can help you make your own right choice. "Many are called but few are chosen" should be, "All are called but few choose to listen." Therefore, they do not choose right. The "chosen ones" are merely those who choose right sooner. Right minds can do this now, and they will find rest unto their souls. God knows you only in peace, and this *is* your reality.

T-06.I.19 - Remember that the Holy Spirit is the communication link between God the Father and His separated Sons. If you will listen to His Voice you will know that you cannot either hurt or be hurt, and that many need your blessing to help them hear this for themselves. When you perceive only this need in them, and do not respond to any other, you will have learned of me and will be as eager to share your learning as I am.

Bible Reference - Text

Matthew 11:30 - For my yoke is easy, and my burden is light.

Course Ref/s - Citation/s

T-05.II.11 - When you are tempted by the wrong voice, call on me to remind you how to heal by sharing my decision and making it stronger. As we share this goal, we increase its power to attract the whole Sonship, and to bring it back into the oneness in which it was created. Remember that "yoke" means "join together," and "burden" means "message." Let us restate "<u>My yoke is easy and my burden light</u>" in this way; "Let us join together, for my message is light."

Bible Reference - Text

Matthew 12:24-25 - But when the Pharisees heard it, they said, This fellow doth not cast out devils, but by Beelzebub the prince of the devils. And Jesus knew their thoughts, and said unto them, Every kingdom divided against itself is brought to desolation; and every city or house divided against itself shall not stand:

Course Ref/s - Citation/s

T-23.I.11 - How can the resting place of God turn on itself, and seek to overcome the One Who dwells there? And think what happens <u>when the house of God perceives itself divided</u>. The altar disappears, the light grows dim, the temple of the Holy One becomes a house of sin. And nothing is remembered except illusions. Illusions can conflict, because their forms are different. And they do battle only to establish which form is true.

T-25.VIII.1-2 - The Holy Spirit can use all that you give to Him for your salvation. But He cannot use what you withhold, for He cannot take it from you without your willingness. For if He did, you would believe He wrested it from you against your will. And so you would not learn it is your will to be without it. You need not give it to Him wholly willingly, for if you could you had no need of Him. But this He needs; that you prefer He take it than that you keep it for yourself alone, and recognize that what brings loss to no one you would not know. This much is necessary to add to the idea no one can lose for you to gain. And nothing more.

Here is the only principle salvation needs. Nor is it necessary that your faith in it be strong, unswerving, and without attack from all beliefs opposed to it. You have no fixed allegiance. But remember salvation is not needed by the saved. You are not called upon to do what <u>one divided still against himself</u> would find impossible. Have little faith that wisdom could be found in such a state of mind. But be you thankful that only little faith is asked of you. What but a little faith remains to those who still believe in sin? What could they know of Heaven and the justice of the saved?

Bible Reference - Text

Matthew 12:30 - He that is not with me is against me; and he that gathereth not with me scattereth abroad.

Course Ref/s - Citation/s

T-20.II.4:1-6 - I have great need for lilies, for the Son of God has not forgiven me. And can I offer him forgiveness when he offers thorns to me? For he who offers thorns to anyone <u>is against me</u> still, and who is whole without him? Be you his friend for me, that I may be forgiven and you may look upon the Son of God as whole. But look you first upon the altar in your chosen home, and see what you have laid upon it to offer me. If it be thorns whose points gleam sharply in a blood-red light, the body is your chosen home and it is separation that you offer me.

T-21.VII.1 - Do you not see that all your misery comes from the strange belief that you are powerless? Being helpless is the cost of sin. Helplessness is sin's condition; the one requirement that it demands to be believed. Only the helpless could believe in it. Enormity has no appeal save to the little. And only those who first believe that they are little could see attraction there. Treachery to the Son of God is the defense of those who do not identify with him. And <u>you are for him or against him</u>; either you love him or attack him, protect his unity or see him shattered and slain by your attack.

Bible Reference - Text

Matthew 13:12 - For whosoever hath, to him shall be given, and he shall have more abundance: but whosoever hath not, from him shall be taken away even that he hath.

Course Ref/s - Citation/s

P-3.III.5- It has well been said that to him who hath shall be given. Because he has, he can give. And because he gives, he shall be given. This is the law of God, and not of the world. So it is with God's healers. They give because they have heard His Word and understood it. All that they need will thus be given them. But they will lose this understanding unless they remember that all they have comes only from God. If they believe they need anything from a brother, they will recognize him as a brother no longer. And if they do this, a light goes out even in Heaven. Where God's Son turns against himself, he can look only upon darkness. He has himself denied the light, and cannot see.

Bible Reference - Text

Matthew 13:44-46 - Again, the kingdom of heaven is like unto treasure hid in a field; the which when a man hath found, he hideth, and for joy thereof goeth and selleth all that he hath, and buyeth that field. Again, the kingdom of heaven is like unto a merchant man, seeking goodly pearls: Who, when he had found one pearl of great price, went and sold all that he had, and bought it.

Course Ref/s - Citation/s

T-12.IV.6 - Behold the Guide your Father gave you, that you might learn you have eternal life. For death is not your Father's Will nor yours, and whatever is true is the Will of the Father. You pay no price for life for that was given you, but you do pay a price for death, and a very heavy one. If death is your treasure, you will sell everything else to purchase it. And you will believe that you have purchased it, because you have sold everything else. Yet you cannot sell the Kingdom of Heaven. Your inheritance can neither be bought nor sold. There can be no disinherited parts of the Sonship, for God is whole and all His extensions are like Him.

T-23.II.10-11- All of the mechanisms of madness are seen emerging here: the "enemy" made strong by keeping hidden the valuable inheritance that should be yours; your justified position and attack for what has been withheld; and the inevitable loss the enemy must suffer to save yourself. Thus do the guilty ones protest their "innocence." Were they not forced into this foul attack by the unscrupulous behavior of the enemy, they would respond with only kindness. But in a savage world the kind cannot survive, so they must take or else be taken from.

11 And now there is a vague unanswered question, not yet "explained." What is this precious thing, this priceless pearl, this hidden secret treasure, to be wrested in righteous wrath from this most treacherous and cunning enemy? It must be what you want but never found. And now you "understand" the reason why you found it not. For it was taken from you by this enemy, and hidden where you would not think to look. He hid it in his body, making it the cover for his guilt, the hiding place for what belongs to you. Now must his body be destroyed and sacrificed, that you may have that which belongs to you. His treachery demands his death, that you may live. And you attack only in self-defense.

Bible Reference - Text

Matthew 16:18 - And I say also unto thee, That thou art Peter, and upon this rock I will build my church; and the gates of hell shall not prevail against it.

Course Ref/s - Citation/s

T-04.III.1 - It is hard to understand what "The Kingdom of Heaven is within you" really means. This is because it is not understandable to the ego, which interprets it as if something outside is inside, and this does not mean anything. The word "within" is unnecessary. The Kingdom of Heaven is you. What else but you did the Creator create, and what else but you is His Kingdom? This is the whole message of the Atonement; a message which in its totality transcends the sum of its parts. You, too, have a Kingdom that your spirit created. It has not ceased to create because of

the ego's illusions. Your creations are no more fatherless than you are. Your ego and your spirit will never be co-creators, but your spirit and your Creator will always be. Be confident that your creations are as safe as you are.
The Kingdom is perfectly united and perfectly protected, and the ego <u>will not prevail against it</u>. Amen.

T-05.IV.1 - What fear has hidden still is part of you. Joining the Atonement is the way out of fear. The Holy Spirit will help you reinterpret everything that you perceive as fearful, and teach you that only what is loving is true. Truth is beyond your ability to destroy, but entirely within your ability to accept. It belongs to you because, as an extension of God, you created it with Him. It is yours because it is part of you, just as you are part of God because He created you. Nothing that is good can be lost because it comes from the Holy Spirit, the Voice for creation. Nothing that is not good was ever created, and therefore cannot be protected. The Atonement is the guarantee of the safety of the Kingdom, and the union of the Sonship is its protection. The ego <u>cannot prevail against</u> the Kingdom because the Sonship is united. In the presence of those who hear the Holy Spirit's Call to be as one, the ego fades away and is undone.

T-06.I.8 - I [Jesus] am sorry when my brothers do not share my decision to hear only one Voice, because it weakens them as teachers and as learners. Yet I know they cannot really betray themselves or me, and that it is still on them that <u>I must build my church</u>. There is no choice in this, because only you can be the foundation of God's church. A church is where an altar is, and the presence of the altar is what makes the church holy. A church that does not inspire love has a hidden altar that is not serving the purpose for which God intended it. I must found His church on you, because those who accept me as a model are literally my disciples. Disciples are followers, and if the model they follow has chosen to save them pain in all respects, they are unwise not to follow him.

T-06.II.10 - The Holy Spirit uses time, but does not believe in it. Coming from God He uses everything for good, but He does not believe in what is not true. Since the Holy Spirit is in your mind, your mind can also believe only what is true. The Holy Spirit can speak only for this, because He speaks for God. He tells you to return your whole mind to God, because it has never left Him. If it has never left Him, you need only perceive it as it is to be returned. The full awareness of the Atonement, then, is the recognition that the separation never occurred. The ego <u>cannot prevail against</u> this because it is an explicit statement that the ego never occurred.

Bible Reference - Text

Matthew 16:18 - And I say also unto thee, That thou art Peter....
(Continued) - (To read the full text of the above go to page 216.)

Course Ref/s - Citation/s

T-07.IX.2 - Spirit knows that the awareness of all its brothers is included in its own, as it is included in God. The power of the whole Sonship and of its Creator is therefore spirit's own fullness, rendering its creations equally whole and equal in perfection. The ego <u>cannot prevail against</u> a totality that includes God, and any totality must include God. Everything He created is given all His power, because it is part of Him and shares His Being with Him. Creating is the opposite of loss, as blessing is the opposite of sacrifice. Being must be extended. That is how it retains the knowledge of itself. Spirit yearns to share its being as its Creator did. Created by sharing, its will is to create. It does not wish to contain God, but wills to extend His Being.

T-13.XI.7 - Have faith in only this one thing, and it will be sufficient: God wills you be in Heaven, and nothing can keep you from it, or it from you. Your wildest misperceptions, your weird imaginings, your blackest nightmares all mean nothing. They <u>will not prevail against</u> the peace God wills for you. The Holy Spirit will restore your sanity because insanity is not the Will of God. If that suffices Him, it is enough for you. You will not keep what God would have removed, because it breaks communication with you with whom He would communicate. His Voice will be heard.

T-17.VI.5 - The goal of truth has further practical advantages. If the situation is used for truth and sanity, its outcome must be peace. And this is quite apart from what the outcome is. If peace is the condition of truth and sanity, and cannot be without them, where peace is they must be. Truth comes of itself. If you experience peace, it is because the truth has come to you and you will see the outcome truly, for deception <u>cannot prevail against</u> you. You will recognize the outcome because you are at peace.

Here again you see the opposite of the ego's way of looking, for the ego believes the situation brings the experience. The Holy Spirit knows that the situation is as the goal determines it, and is experienced according to the goal.

T-22.III.4 - Only the form of error attracts the ego. Meaning it does not recognize, and does not see if it is there or not. Everything the body's eyes can see is a mistake, an error in perception, a distorted fragment of the whole without the meaning that the whole would give. And yet mistakes, regardless of their form, can be corrected. Sin is but error in a special form the ego venerates. It would preserve all errors and make them sins. For here is its own stability, its heavy anchor in the shifting world it made; <u>the rock on which its church is built</u>, and where its worshippers are bound to bodies, believing the body's freedom is their own.

T-24.II.13 - The hope of specialness makes it seem possible God made the body as the prison house that keeps His Son from Him. For it demands a special place God cannot enter, and a hiding place where none is welcome but your tiny self. Nothing is sacred here but unto you, and you alone, apart and separate from all your brothers; safe from all intrusions of sanity upon illusions; safe from God and safe for conflict everlasting. Here are <u>the gates of hell</u> you closed upon yourself, to rule in madness and in loneliness your special kingdom, apart from God, away from truth and from salvation.

T-25.VII.12 - Salvation is rebirth of the idea no one can lose for anyone to gain. And everyone must gain, if anyone would be a gainer. Here is sanity restored. And <u>on this single rock</u> of truth can faith in God's eternal saneness rest in perfect confidence and perfect peace. Reason satisfied, for all insane beliefs can be corrected here. And sin must be impossible, if this is true. This is the rock on which salvation rests, the vantage point from which the Holy Spirit gives meaning and direction to the plan in which your special function has a part. For here your special function is made whole, because it shares the function of the whole.

T-31.VIII.4 - The images you make <u>cannot prevail against</u> what God Himself would have you be. Be never fearful of temptation, then, but see it as it is; another chance to choose again, and let Christ's strength prevail in every circumstance and every place you raised an image of yourself before. For what appears to hide the face of Christ is powerless before His majesty, and disappears before His holy sight. The saviors of the world, who see like Him, are merely those who choose His strength instead of their own weakness, seen apart from Him. They will redeem the world, for they are joined in all the power of the Will of God. And what they will is only what He wills.

Bible Reference - Text

Matthew 16:18 - And I say also unto thee, That thou art Peter.... (Continued) - (To read the full text of the above go to page 216.)

Course Ref/s - Citation/s

W-pI.53.5:2-7 - Whatever I see reflects my thoughts. It is my thoughts that tell me where I am and what I am. The fact that I see a world in which there is suffering and loss and death shows me that I am seeing only the representation of my insane thoughts, and am not allowing my real thoughts to cast their beneficent light on what I see. Yet God's way is sure. The images I have made <u>cannot prevail against</u> Him because it is not my will that they do so. My will is His, and I will place no other gods before Him.

W-pI.73.7 - We will succeed today if you remember that you want salvation for yourself. You want to accept God's plan because you share in it. You have no will that can really oppose it, and you do not want to do so. Salvation is for you. Above all else, you want the freedom to remember who you really are. Today it is the ego that stands powerless before your will. Your will is free, and <u>nothing can prevail against it</u>.

Bible Reference - Text

Matthew 16:19 - And I will give unto thee the keys of the kingdom of heaven: and whatsoever thou shalt bind on earth shall be bound in heaven: and whatsoever thou shalt loose on earth shall be loosed in heaven.

Course Ref/s - Citation/s

T-08.III.5 - The goal of the curriculum, regardless of the teacher you choose, is "Know thyself." There is nothing else to seek. Everyone is looking for himself and for the power and glory he thinks he has lost. Whenever you are with anyone, you have another opportunity to find them. Your power and glory are in him because they are yours. The ego tries to find them in yourself alone, because it does not know where to look. The Holy Spirit teaches you that if you look only at yourself you cannot find yourself, because that is not what you are. Whenever you are with a brother, you are learning what you are because you are teaching what you are. He will respond either with pain or with joy, depending on which teacher you are following. He will be <u>imprisoned or released according to your decision</u>, and so will you. Never forget your responsibility to him, because it is your responsibility to yourself. Give him his place in the Kingdom and you will have yours.

T-14.III.6 - No penalty is ever asked of God's Son except by himself and of himself. Every chance given him to heal is another opportunity to replace darkness with light and fear with love. If he refuses it he <u>binds</u> himself to darkness, because he did not choose to free his brother and enter light with him. By giving power to nothing, he throws away the joyous opportunity to learn that nothing has no power. And by not dispelling darkness, he became afraid of darkness and of light. The joy of learning that darkness has no power over the Son of God is the happy lesson the Holy Spirit teaches, and would have you teach with Him. It is His joy to teach it, as it will be yours.

T-15.III.11 - If you are wholly willing to leave salvation to the plan of God and unwilling to attempt to grasp for peace yourself, salvation will be given you. Yet think not you can substitute your plan for His. Rather, join with me [Jesus] in His, that we may <u>release all those who would be bound,</u> proclaiming together that the Son of God is host to Him. Thus will we let no one forget what you would remember. And thus will you remember it.

T-15.VI.5 - In the world of scarcity, love has no meaning and peace is impossible. For gain and loss are both accepted, and so no one is aware that perfect love is in him. In the holy instant you recognize the idea of love in you, and unite this idea with the Mind that thought it, and could not relinquish it. By holding it within itself, there is no loss. The holy instant thus becomes a lesson in how to hold all of your brothers in your mind, experiencing not loss but completion. From this it follows you can only give. And this is love, for this alone is natural under the laws of God. In the holy instant the laws of God prevail, and only they have meaning.

The laws of this world cease to hold any meaning at all. When the Son of God accepts the laws of God as what he gladly wills, it is impossible that he <u>be bound, or limited</u> in any way. In that instant he is as free as God would have him be. For the instant he refuses to be bound, he is not bound.

Bible Reference - Text

Matthew 16:19 - And I will give unto thee the keys of the ....
(Continued) - (To read the full text of the above go to page 220.)

Course Ref/s - Citation/s

T-16.VII.9 - There is nothing you can hold against reality. All that must be forgiven are the illusions you have held against your brothers. Their reality has no past, and only illusions can be forgiven. God holds nothing against anyone, for He is incapable of illusions of any kind. <u>Release your brothers</u> from the slavery of their illusions by forgiving them for the illusions you perceive in them. Thus will you learn that you have been forgiven, for it is you who offered them illusions. In the holy instant this is done for you in time, to bring you the true condition of Heaven.

T-19.IV.C.1 - To you and your brother, in whose special relationship the Holy Spirit entered, it is given <u>to release and be released</u> from the dedication to death. For it was offered you, and you accepted. Yet you must learn still more about this strange devotion, for it contains the third obstacle that peace must flow across. No one can die unless he chooses death. What seems to be the fear of death is really its attraction. Guilt, too, is feared and fearful. Yet it could have no hold at all except on those who are attracted to it and seek it out. And so it is with death. Made by the ego, its dark shadow falls across all living things, because the ego is the "enemy" of life.

T-19.IV.C.3 - From the ego came sin and guilt and death, in opposition to life and innocence, and to the Will of God Himself. Where can such opposition lie but in the sick minds of the insane, dedicated to madness and set against the peace of Heaven? One thing is sure; <u>God, Who created neither sin nor death, wills not that you be bound by them</u>. He knows of neither sin nor its results. The shrouded figures in the funeral procession march not in honor of their Creator, Whose Will it is they live. They are not following His Will; they are opposing it.

T-24.II.07 - You who have chained your savior to your specialness, and given it his place, remember this: He has not lost the power to forgive you all the sins you think you placed between him and the function of salvation given him for you. Nor will you change his function, any more than you can change the truth in him and in yourself. But be you certain that the truth is just the same in both. It gives no different messages, and has one meaning. And it is one you and your brother both can understand, and one that brings release to both of you. Here stands your brother with <u>the key to Heaven</u> in his hand, held out to you. Let not the dream of specialness remain between you. What is one is joined in truth.

T-24.IV.5 - Do not defend this senseless dream [of specialness], in which God is bereft of what He loves, and you remain beyond salvation. Only this is certain in this shifting world that has no meaning in reality: When peace is not with you entirely, and when you suffer pain of any kind, you have beheld some sin within your brother, and have rejoiced at what you thought was there. Your specialness seemed safe because of it. And thus <u>you saved what you appointed to be your savior, and crucified the one whom God has given you instead. So are you bound with him</u>, for you are one. And so is specialness his "enemy," and yours as well.

T-24.VI.5 - Look on your brother, and behold in him the whole reversal of the laws that seem to rule this world. See in his freedom yours, for such it is. Let not his specialness obscure the truth in him, for not one law of death <u>you bind him</u> to will you escape. And not one sin you see in him but keeps you both in hell. Yet will his perfect sinlessness release you both, for holiness is quite impartial, with one judgment made for all it looks upon. And that is made, not of itself, but through the Voice that speaks for God in everything that lives and shares His Being.

W-pI.046.1 - God does not forgive because He has never condemned. And there must be condemnation before forgiveness is necessary. Forgiveness is the great need of this world, but that is because it is a world of illusions. <u>Those who forgive are thus releasing themselves from illusions, while those who withhold forgiveness are binding themselves to them.</u> As you condemn only yourself, so do you forgive only yourself.

W-pI.110.11 - We will remember Him throughout the day with thankful hearts and loving thoughts for all who meet with us today. For it is thus that we remember Him. And we will say, that we may be reminded of His Son, our holy Self, the Christ in each of us: I am as God created me. Let us declare this truth as often as we can. This is the Word of God that sets you free. This is <u>the key that opens up the gate of Heaven</u>, and that lets you enter in the peace of God and His eternity.

Bible Reference - Text

Matthew 16:19 - And I will give unto thee the keys of the .... (Continued) - (To read the full text of the above go to page 220.)

Course Ref/s - Citation/s

W-pI.115.1 - Salvation is my only function here. My function here is to forgive the world for all the errors I have made. <u>For thus am I released from them with all the world.</u>

W-pI.191.10:7-11:8 - Look about the world, and see the suffering there. Is not your heart willing to bring your weary brothers rest?

<u>They must await your own release. They stay in chains till you are free.</u> They cannot see the mercy of the world until you find it in yourself. They suffer pain until you have denied its hold on you. They die till you accept your own eternal life. You are the holy Son of God Himself. Remember this, and all the world is free. Remember this, and earth and Heaven are one.

W-pI.192.8-9 - Who can be born again in Christ but him who has forgiven everyone he sees or thinks of or imagines? Who could be set free while he imprisons anyone? <u>A jailer is not free, for he is bound together with his prisoner.</u> He must be sure that he does not escape, and so he spends his time in keeping watch on him. The bars that limit him become the world in which his jailer lives, along with him. And it is on his freedom that the way to liberty depends for both of them.

Therefore, hold no one prisoner. <u>Release instead of bind, for thus are you made free.</u> The way is simple. Every time you feel a stab of anger, realize you hold a sword above your head. And it will fall or be averted as you choose to be condemned or free. Thus does each one who seems to tempt you to be angry represent your savior from the prison house of death. And so you owe him thanks instead of pain.

W-pI.195.4 - You do not offer God your gratitude because your brother is more slave than you, nor could you sanely be enraged if he seems freer.

Love makes no comparisons. And gratitude can only be sincere if it be joined to love. We offer thanks to God our Father that in us all things will find their freedom. It will never be that <u>some are loosed while others still are bound.</u> For who can bargain in the name of love?

W-pI.197.2 - How easily are God and guilt confused by those who know not what their thoughts can do. Deny your strength, and weakness must become salvation to you. <u>See yourself as bound, and bars become your home.</u> Nor will you leave the prison house, or claim your strength, until guilt and salvation are not seen as one, and freedom and salvation are perceived as joined, with strength beside them, to be sought and claimed, and found and fully recognized.

W-pI.197.3 - <u>The world must thank you when you offer it release</u> from your illusions. Yet your thanks belong to you as well, for its release can only mirror yours. Your gratitude is all your gifts require, that they be a lasting offering of a thankful heart, released from hell forever. Is it this you would undo by taking back your gifts, because they were not honored? It is you who honor them and give them fitting thanks, for it is you who have received the gifts.

W-pI.199.7 - Be free today. And carry freedom as your gift to those who still believe they are enslaved within a body. Be you free, so that the Holy Spirit can <u>make use of your escape from bondage, to set free the many who perceive themselves as bound</u> and helpless and afraid. Let love replace their fears through you. Accept salvation now, and give your mind to Him Who calls to you to make this gift to Him. For He would give you perfect freedom, perfect joy, and hope that finds its full accomplishment in God.

W-pI.200.5 - Freedom is given you where you beheld but chains and iron doors. But you must change your mind about the purpose of the world, if you would find escape. <u>You will be bound till all the world is seen by you as blessed, and everyone made free</u> of your mistakes and honored as he is. You made him not; no more yourself. And as you free the one, the other is accepted as he is.

W-pII.277.ti-2 - Let me not bind Your Son with laws I made.

<u>Your Son is free</u>, my Father. Let me not imagine I have bound him with the laws I made to rule the body. He is not subject to any laws I made by which I try to make the body more secure. He is not changed by what is changeable. He is not slave to any laws of time. He is as You created him, because he knows no law except the law of love.

Let us not worship idols, nor believe in any law idolatry would make to hide the freedom of the Son of God. <u>He is not bound</u> except by his beliefs. Yet what he is, is far beyond his faith in slavery or freedom. <u>He is free</u> because he is his Father's Son. And he cannot be bound unless God's truth can lie, and God can will that He deceive Himself.

Bible Reference - Text

Matthew 16:19 - And I will give unto thee the keys of the ....
(Continued) - (To read the full text of the above go to page 220.)

Course Ref/s - Citation/s

W-pII.332.ti-2 - <u>**Fear binds the world. Forgiveness sets it free.**</u>

The ego makes illusions. Truth undoes its evil dreams by shining them away. Truth never makes attack. It merely is. And by its presence is the mind recalled from fantasies, awaking to the real. Forgiveness bids this presence enter in, and take its rightful place within the mind. <u>Without forgiveness is the mind in chains</u>, believing in its own futility. <u>Yet with forgiveness does the light shine through the dream of darkness, offering it hope, and giving it the means to realize the freedom</u> that is its inheritance.

<u>We would not bind the world</u> again today. Fear holds it prisoner. And yet <u>Your Love has given us the means to set it free</u>. Father, we would release it now. For as we offer freedom, it is given us. And we would not remain as prisoners, while You are holding freedom out to us.

Bible Reference - Text

Matthew 16:26 - For what is a man profited, if he shall gain the whole world, and lose his own soul? or what shall a man give in exchange for his soul?

Course Ref/s - Citation/s

T-03.VI.10 & VII.2 - Peace is a natural heritage of spirit. Everyone is free to refuse to accept his inheritance, but he is not free to establish what his inheritance is. The problem everyone must decide is the fundamental question of authorship. All fear comes ultimately, and sometimes by way of very devious routes, from the denial of Authorship. The offense is never to God, but only to those who deny Him. To deny His Authorship is to deny yourself the reason for your peace, so that you see yourself only in segments. This strange perception is the authority problem.

You cannot resolve the authority problem by depreciating the power of your mind. To do so is to deceive yourself, and this will hurt you because you really understand the strength of the mind. You also realize that you cannot weaken it, any more than you can weaken God. The "devil" is a frightening concept because he seems to be extremely powerful and extremely active. He is perceived as a force in combat with God, battling Him for possession of His creations. The devil deceives by lies, and builds kingdoms in which everything is in direct opposition to God. Yet he attracts men rather than repels them, and they are willing <u>to "sell" him their souls</u> in return for gifts of no real worth. This makes absolutely no sense.

T-05.II.7 - The Voice of the Holy Spirit does not command, because it is incapable of arrogance. It does not demand, because It does not seek control. It does not overcome, because It does not attack. It merely reminds. It is compelling only because of what it reminds you of. It brings to your mind the other way, remaining quiet even in the midst of the turmoil you may make. The Voice for God is always quiet, because It speaks of peace. Peace is stronger than war because it heals. War is division, not increase. No one gains from strife. <u>What profiteth it a man if he gain the whole world and lose his own soul?</u> If you listen to the wrong voice you have lost sight of your soul. You cannot lose it, but you can not know it. It is therefore "lost" to you until you choose right.

T-12.VI.1 - The ego is trying to teach you how <u>to gain the whole world and lose your own soul</u>. The Holy Spirit teaches that you cannot lose your soul and there is no gain in the world, for of itself it profits nothing.
To invest without profit is surely to impoverish yourself, and the overhead is high. Not only is there no profit in the investment, but the cost to you is enormous. For this investment costs you the world's reality by denying yours, and gives you nothing in return. You cannot sell your soul, but you can sell your awareness of it. You cannot perceive your soul, but you will not know it while you perceive something else as more valuable.

Bible Reference - Text

Matthew 16:27 - For the Son of man shall come in the glory of his Father with his angels; and then he shall reward every man according to his works.

Course Ref/s - Citation/s

W-pI.191.7-8 - Be glad today how very easily is hell undone. You need but tell yourself:

I am the holy Son of God Himself. I cannot suffer, cannot be in pain; I cannot suffer loss, nor fail to do all that salvation asks.

And in that thought is everything you look on wholly changed.

A miracle has lighted up all dark and ancient caverns, where the rites of death echoed since time began. For time has lost its hold upon the world. The Son of God has come in glory to redeem the lost, to save the helpless, and to give the world the gift of his forgiveness. Who could see the world as dark and sinful, when God's Son has come again at last to set it free?

Bible Reference - Text

Matthew 17:1-2 - And after six days Jesus taketh Peter, James, and John his brother, and bringeth them up into an high mountain apart, And was transfigured before them: and his face did shine as the sun, and his raiment was white as the light.

Course Ref/s - Citation/s

W-pI.151.15:4-16:4 - No one can fail to listen, when you hear the Voice for God give honor to God's Son. And everyone will share the thoughts with you which He has retranslated in your mind.

Such is your Eastertide. And so you lay the gift of snow-white lilies on the world, replacing witnesses to sin and death. Through your transfiguration is the world redeemed, and joyfully released from guilt. Now do we lift our resurrected minds in gladness and in gratitude to Him Who has restored our sanity to us.

Bible Reference - Text

Matthew 17:20 - So Jesus said to them, "Because of your unbelief; for assuredly, I say to you, if you have faith as a mustard seed, you will say to this mountain, 'Move from here to there,' and it will move; and nothing will be impossible for you.

Course Ref/s - Citation/s

T-02.VI.9 - Everyone experiences fear. Yet it would take very little right thinking to realize why fear occurs. Few appreciate the real power of the mind, and no one remains fully aware of it all the time. However, if you hope to spare yourself from fear there are some things you must realize, and realize fully. The mind is very powerful, and never loses its creative force. It never sleeps. Every instant it is creating. It is hard to recognize that thought and belief combine into a power surge that can literally <u>move mountains</u>. It appears at first glance that to believe such power about yourself is arrogant, but that is not the real reason you do not believe it. You prefer to believe that your thoughts cannot exert real influence because you are actually afraid of them. This may allay awareness of the guilt, but at the cost of perceiving the mind as impotent. If you believe that what you think is ineffectual you may cease to be afraid of it, but you are hardly likely to respect it. There are no idle thoughts. All thinking produces form at some level.

T-05.VII.2 - There have been many healers who did not heal themselves. <u>They have not moved mountains by their faith</u> because their faith was not whole. Some of them have healed the sick at times, but they have not raised the dead. Unless the healer heals himself, he cannot believe that there is no order of difficulty in miracles. He has not learned that every mind God created is equally worthy of being healed because God created it whole. You are merely asked to return to God the mind as He created it. He asks you only for what He gave, knowing that this giving will heal you. Sanity is wholeness, and the sanity of your brothers is yours.

T-21.III.2:6-3:7 - <u>The power of faith</u> is never recognized if it is placed in sin. But it is always recognized if it is placed in love.

Why is it strange to you that faith can move mountains? This is indeed a little feat for such a power. For faith can keep the Son of God in chains as long as he believes he is in chains. And when he is released from them it will be simply because he no longer believes in them, withdrawing faith that they can hold him, and placing it in his freedom instead. It is impossible to place equal faith in opposite directions. What faith you give to sin you take away from holiness. And what you offer holiness has been removed from sin.

T-21.III.5 - It is impossible that the Son of God lack faith, but he can choose where he would have it be. Faithlessness is not a lack of faith, but faith in nothing. Faith given to illusions does not lack power, for by it does the Son of God believe that he is powerless. Thus is he faithless to himself, but strong in faith in his illusions about himself. For faith, perception and belief you made, as means for losing certainty and finding sin. This mad direction was your choice, and by your faith in what you chose, you made what you desired.

T-25.VIII.1:7-2:9 - This much is necessary to add to the idea no one can lose for you to gain. And nothing more.

Here is the only principle salvation needs. Nor is it necessary that your faith in it be strong, unswerving, and without attack from all beliefs opposed to it. You have no fixed allegiance. But remember salvation is not needed by the saved. You are not called upon to do what one divided still against himself would find impossible. Have little faith that wisdom could be found in such a state of mind. But be you thankful that only little faith is asked of you. What but a little faith remains to those who still believe in sin? What could they know of Heaven and the justice of the saved?

Bible Reference - Text

Matthew 18:3 - And said, Verily I say unto you, Except ye be converted, and become as little children, ye shall not enter into the kingdom of heaven.

Course Ref/s - Citation/s

T-01.V.3 - When the Atonement has been completed, all talents will be shared by all the Sons of God. God is not partial. All His children have His total Love, and all His gifts are freely given to everyone alike. "Except ye become as little children" means that unless you fully recognize your complete dependence on God, you cannot know the real power of the Son in his true relationship with the Father. The specialness of God's Sons does not stem from exclusion but from inclusion. All my brothers are special. If they believe they are deprived of anything, their perception becomes distorted. When this occurs the whole family of God, or the Sonship, is impaired in its relationships.

T-11.VIII.02 - The Bible tells you to become as little children. Little children recognize that they do not understand what they perceive, and so they ask what it means. Do not make the mistake of believing that you understand what you perceive, for its meaning is lost to you. Yet the Holy Spirit has saved its meaning for you, and if you will let Him interpret it, He will restore to you what you have thrown away. Yet while you think you know its meaning, you will see no need to ask it of Him.

T-12.II.4 - Remember what was said about the frightening perceptions of little children, which terrify them because they do not understand them. If they ask for enlightenment and accept it, their fears vanish. But if they hide their nightmares they will keep them. It is easy to help an uncertain child, for he recognizes that he does not understand what his perceptions mean. Yet you believe that you do understand yours. Little child, you are hiding your head under the cover of the heavy blankets you have laid upon yourself. You are hiding your nightmares in the darkness of your own false certainty, and refusing to open your eyes and look at them.

Bible Reference - Text

Matthew 18:11 - For the Son of man is come to save that which was lost.

Course Ref/s - Citation/s

W-pI.191.7-8 - Be glad today how very easily is hell undone. You need but tell yourself:

> I am the holy Son of God Himself. I cannot suffer, cannot be in pain; I cannot suffer loss, nor fail to do all that salvation asks.

And in that thought is everything you look on wholly changed.

A miracle has lighted up all dark and ancient caverns, where the rites of death echoed since time began. For time has lost its hold upon the world. <u>The Son of God has come in glory to redeem the lost, to save the helpless,</u> and to give the world the gift of his forgiveness. Who could see the world as dark and sinful, when God's Son has come again at last to set it free?

Bible Reference - Text

Matthew 18:19-20 - Again I say unto you, That if two of you shall agree on earth as touching any thing that they shall ask, it shall be done for them of my Father which is in heaven. For where two or three are gathered together in my name, there am I in the midst of them.

Course Ref/s - Citation/s

T-04.IV.11:1-6 - I do not attack your ego. I do work with your higher mind, the home of the Holy Spirit, whether you are asleep or awake, just as your ego does with your lower mind, which is its home. I am your vigilance in this, because you are too confused to recognize your own hope. I am not mistaken. Your mind will elect to join with mine, and together we are invincible. <u>You and your brother will yet come together in my name</u>, and your sanity will be restored.

T-14.X.08-09 - The ego is incapable of understanding content, and is totally unconcerned with it. To the ego, if the form is acceptable the content must be. Otherwise it will attack the form. If you believe you understand something of the "dynamics" of the ego, let me assure you that you understand nothing of it. For of yourself you could not understand it. The study of the ego is not the study of the mind. In fact, the ego enjoys studying itself, and thoroughly approves the undertakings of students who would "analyze" it, thus approving its importance. Yet they but study form with meaningless content. For their teacher is senseless, though careful to conceal this fact behind impressive sounding words, but which lack any consistent sense when they are put together.

This is characteristic of the ego's judgments. Separately, they seem to hold, but put them together and the system of thought that arises from joining them is incoherent and utterly chaotic. For form is not enough for meaning, and the underlying lack of content makes a cohesive system impossible. Separation therefore remains the ego's chosen condition. For no one alone can judge the ego truly. Yet <u>when two or more join together</u> in searching for truth, the ego can no longer defend its lack of content. The fact of union tells them it is not true.

T-14.X.10 - It is impossible to remember God in secret and alone. For remembering Him means you are not alone, and are willing to remember it. Take no thought for yourself, for no thought you hold is for yourself. If you would remember your Father, let the Holy Spirit order your thoughts and give only the answer with which He answers you. Everyone seeks for love as you do, but knows it not <u>unless he joins with you</u> in seeking it. If you undertake the search together, you bring with you a light so powerful that what you see is given meaning. The lonely journey fails because it has excluded what it would find.

T-16.II.4 - You have done miracles, but it is quite apparent that you have not done them alone. You have succeeded whenever you have reached another mind and joined with it. <u>When two minds join as one</u> and share one idea equally, the first link in the awareness of the Sonship as one has been made. When you have made this joining as the Holy Spirit bids you, and have offered it to Him to use as He sees fit, His natural perception of your gift enables Him to understand it, and you to use His understanding on your behalf. It is impossible to convince you of the reality of what has clearly been accomplished through your willingness while you believe that you must understand it or else it is not real.

T-22.I.7 - So in each holy relationship is the ability to communicate instead of separate reborn. Yet a holy relationship, so recently reborn itself from an unholy relationship, and yet more ancient than the old illusion it has replaced, is like a baby now in its rebirth. Still in this infant is your vision returned to you, and he will speak the language you can understand. He is not nurtured by the "something else" you thought was you. He was not given there, nor was received by anything except yourself. <u>For no two brothers can unite except through Christ</u>, Whose vision sees them one.

W-pI.185.2-3 - No one can mean these words [I want the peace of God.] and not be healed. He cannot play with dreams, nor think he is himself a dream. He cannot make a hell and think it real. He wants the peace of God, and it is given him. For that is all he wants, and that is all he will receive. Many have said these words. But few indeed have meant them. You have but to look upon the world you see around you to be sure how very few they are. The world would be completely changed, <u>should any two agree</u> these words express the only thing they want.

Two minds with one intent become so strong that what they will becomes the Will of God. For minds can only join in truth. In dreams, no two can share the same intent. To each, the hero of the dream is different; the outcome wanted not the same for both. Loser and gainer merely shift about in changing patterns, as the ratio of gain to loss and loss to gain takes on a different aspect or another form.

Bible Reference - Text

Matthew 18:19-20 - Again I say unto you, That if two of you shall.... (Continued) - (To read the full text of the above go to page 232.)

Course Ref/s - Citation/s

W-pI.185.6 - The mind which means that all it wants is peace must join with other minds, for that is how peace is obtained. And when the wish for peace is genuine, the means for finding it is given, in a form each mind that seeks for it in honesty can understand. Whatever form the lesson takes is planned for him in such a way that he can not mistake it, if his asking is sincere. But if he asks without sincerity, there is no form in which the lesson will meet with acceptance and be truly learned.

M-2.5 - When pupil and teacher come together, a teaching-learning situation begins. For the teacher is not really the one who does the teaching. God's Teacher speaks to any two who join together for learning purposes. The relationship is holy because of that purpose, and God has promised to send His Spirit into any holy relationship. In the teaching-learning situation, each one learns that giving and receiving are the same. The demarcations they have drawn between their roles, their minds, their bodies, their needs, their interests, and all the differences they thought separated them from one another, fade and grow dim and disappear. Those who would learn the same course share one interest and one goal. And thus he who was the learner becomes a teacher of God himself, for he has made the one decision that gave his teacher to him. He has seen in another person the same interests as his own.

P-2.II.6 - If healing is an invitation to God to enter into His Kingdom, what difference does it make how the invitation is written? Does the paper matter, or the ink, or the pen? Or is it he who writes that gives the invitation? God comes to those who would restore His world, for they have found the way to call to Him. <u>If any two are joined, He must be there.</u> It does not matter what their purpose is, but they must share it wholly to succeed. It is impossible to share a goal not blessed by Christ, for what is unseen through His eyes is too fragmented to be meaningful.

Bible Reference - Text

Matthew 19:6 - Wherefore they are no more twain, but one flesh. What therefore God hath joined together, let not man put asunder.

Course Ref/s - Citation/s

T-08.VI.9 - I share with God the knowledge of the value He puts upon you. My devotion to you is of Him, being born of my knowledge of myself and Him. We cannot be separated. <u>Whom God has joined cannot be separated</u>, and God has joined all His Sons with Himself. Can you be separated from your life and your being? The journey to God is merely the reawakening of the knowledge of where you are always, and what you are forever. It is a journey without distance to a goal that has never changed. Truth can only be experienced. It cannot be described and it cannot be explained. I can make you aware of the conditions of truth, but the experience is of God. Together we can meet its conditions, but truth will dawn upon you of itself.

T-17.III.7:3-8 - <u>Whom God has joined as one, the ego cannot put asunder.</u> The spark of holiness must be safe, however hidden it may be, in every relationship. For the Creator of the one relationship has left no part of it without Himself. This is the only part of the relationship the Holy Spirit sees, because He knows that only this is true. You have made the relationship unreal, and therefore unholy, by seeing it where it is not and as it is not. Give the past to Him Who can change your mind about t for you.

T-18.I.2 - The Holy Spirit never uses substitutes. Where the ego perceives one person as a replacement for another, the Holy Spirit sees them joined and indivisible. He does not judge between them, knowing they are one. Being united, they are one because they are the same. Substitution is clearly a process in which they are perceived as different. One would unite; the other separate. <u>Nothing can come between what God has joined and what the Holy Spirit sees as one.</u> But everything seems to come between the fragmented relationships the ego sponsors to destroy.

T-22.In.1 - Take pity on yourself, so long enslaved. Rejoice <u>whom God hath joined have come together and need no longer look on sin apart.</u> No two can look on sin together, for they could never see it in the same place and time. Sin is a strictly individual perception, seen in the other yet believed by each to be within himself. And each one seems to make a different error, and one the other cannot understand. Brother, it is the same, made by the same, and forgiven for its maker in the same way.
The holiness of your relationship forgives you and your brother, undoing the effects of what you both believed and saw. And with their going is the need for sin gone with them.

T-22.V.3 - Yet how can peace be so fragmented? It is still whole, and nothing has been taken from it. See how the means and the material of evil dreams are nothing. In truth you and your brother stand together, with nothing in between. God holds your hands, and <u>what can separate whom He has joined as one</u> with Him? It is your Father Whom you would defend against. Yet it remains impossible to keep love out. God rests with you in quiet, undefended and wholly undefending, for in this quiet state alone is strength and power. Here can no weakness enter, for here is no attack and therefore no illusions. Love rests in certainty. Only uncertainty can be defensive. And all uncertainty is doubt about yourself.

T-22.V.4 - How weak is fear; how little and how meaningless.
How insignificant before the quiet strength of those <u>whom love has joined</u>! This is your "enemy"-a frightened mouse that would attack the universe. How likely is it that it will succeed? Can it be difficult to disregard its feeble squeaks that tell of its omnipotence, and would drown out the hymn of praise to its Creator that every heart throughout the universe forever sings as one? Which is the stronger? Is it this tiny mouse or everything that God created? You and your brother are not joined together by this mouse, but by the Will of God. And can a mouse betray whom God has joined?

T-28.IV.7 - The Holy Spirit is in both your [your's and your brother's] minds, and He is One because there is no gap that separates His Oneness from Itself. The gap between your bodies matters not, for <u>what is joined in Him is always one</u>. No one is sick if someone else accepts his union with him. His desire to be a sick and separated mind can not remain without a witness or a cause. And both are gone if someone wills to be united with him. He has dreams that he was separated from his brother who, by sharing not his dream, has left the space between them vacant. And the Father comes to join His Son the Holy Spirit joined.

Bible Reference - Text

Matthew 19:6 - Wherefore they are no more twain, but one.... (Continued) - (To read the full text of the above go to page 235.)

Course Ref/s - Citation/s

T-28.VII.2 - The beautiful relationship you have with all your brothers is a part of you because it is a part of God Himself. Are you not sick, if you deny yourself your wholeness and your health, the Source of help, the Call to healing and the Call to heal? Your savior waits for healing, and the world waits with him. Nor are you apart from it. For healing will be one or not at all, its oneness being where the healing is. What could correct for separation but its opposite? There is no middle ground in any aspect of salvation. You accept it wholly or accept it not. What is unseparated must be joined. And <u>what is joined cannot be separate</u>.

W-pI.160.8 - God's certainty suffices. Who He knows to be His Son belongs where He has set His Son forever. He has answered you who ask, "Who is the stranger?" Hear His Voice assure you, quietly and sure, that you are not a stranger to your Father, nor is your Creator stranger made to you. <u>Whom God has joined remain forever one</u>, at home in Him, no stranger to Himself.

Bible Reference - Text

Matthew 19:14 - But Jesus said, Suffer little children, and forbid them not, to come unto me: for of such is the kingdom of heaven.

Course Ref/s - Citation/s

T-05.IV.3 - Every loving thought held in any part of the Sonship belongs to every part. It is shared because it is loving. Sharing is God's way of creating, and also yours. The ego can keep you in exile from the Kingdom, but in the Kingdom itself it has no power. Ideas of the spirit do not leave the mind that thinks them, nor can they conflict with each other. However, ideas of the ego can conflict because they occur at different levels and also include opposite thoughts at the same level. It is impossible to share opposing thoughts. You can share only the thoughts that are of God and that He keeps for you. And of <u>such is the Kingdom of Heaven</u>. The rest remains with you until the Holy Spirit has reinterpreted them in the light of the Kingdom, making them, too, worthy of being shared. When they have been sufficiently purified He lets you give them away. The decision to share them is their purification.

W-pI.50.5 - For ten minutes, twice today, morning and evening, let the idea for today [I am sustained by the Love of God.] sink deep into your consciousness. Repeat it, think about it, let related thoughts come to help you recognize its truth, and allow peace to flow over you like a blanket of protection and surety. Let no idle and foolish thoughts enter to disturb the holy mind of the Son of God. <u>Such is the Kingdom of Heaven.</u> Such is the resting place where your Father has placed you forever.

S-3.IV.5-6 - Never forget this; it is you who are God's Son, and as you choose to be to him so are you to yourself, and God to you. Nor will your judgment fail to reach to God, for you will give the role to Him you see in His creation. Do not choose amiss, or you will think that it is you who are creator in His place, and He is then no longer Cause but only an effect. Now healing is impossible, for He is blamed for your deception and your guilt. He Who is Love becomes the source of fear, for only fear can now be justified. Vengeance is His. His great destroyer, death. And sickness, suffering and grievous loss become the lot of everyone on earth, which He abandoned to the devil's care, swearing He will deliver it no more.

<u>Come unto Me, My children</u>, once again, without such twisted thoughts upon your hearts. You still are holy with the Holiness which fathered you in perfect sinlessness, and still surrounds you with the Arms of peace. Dream now of healing. Then arise and lay all dreaming down forever. You are he your Father loves, who never left his home, nor wandered in a savage world with feet that bleed, and with a heavy heart made hard against the love that is the truth in you. Give all your dreams to Christ and let Him be your Guide to healing, leading you in prayer beyond the sorry reaches of the world.

Bible Reference - Text

Matthew 19:18-21 - He saith unto him, Which? Jesus said, Thou shalt do no murder, Thou shalt not commit adultery, Thou shalt not steal, Thou shalt not bear false witness, Honour thy father and thy mother: and, Thou shalt love thy neighbour as thyself. The young man saith unto him, All these things have I kept from my youth up: what lack I yet? Jesus said unto him, If thou wilt be perfect, go and sell that thou hast, and give to the poor, and thou shalt have treasure in heaven: and come and follow me.

Course Ref/s - Citation/s

T-12.III.01 - I once asked you to sell all you have and give to the poor and follow me. This is what I meant: If you have no investment in anything in this world, you can teach the poor where their treasure is. The poor are merely those who have invested wrongly, and they are poor indeed! Because they are in need it is given you to help them, since you are among them. Consider how perfectly your lesson would be learned if you were unwilling to share their poverty. For poverty is lack, and there is but one lack since there is but one need.

T-12.IV.7 - The Atonement is not the price of your wholeness, but it is the price of your awareness of your wholeness. For what you chose to "sell" had to be kept for you, since you could not "buy" it back. Yet you must invest in it, not with money but with spirit. For spirit is will, and will is the "price" of the Kingdom. Your inheritance awaits only the recognition that you have been redeemed. The Holy Spirit guides you into life eternal, but you must relinquish your investment in death, or you will not see life though it is all around you.

T-13.IX.2 - Release from guilt is the ego's whole undoing. Make no one fearful, for his guilt is yours, and by obeying the ego's harsh commandments you bring its condemnation on yourself, and you will not escape the punishment it offers those who obey it. The ego rewards fidelity to it with pain, for faith in it is pain. And faith can be rewarded only in terms of the belief in which the faith was placed. Faith makes the power of belief, and where it is invested determines its reward. For faith is always given what is treasured, and what is treasured is returned to you.

W-pI.193.11 - Give all you can, and give a little more. For now we would arise in haste and go unto our Father's house. We have been gone too long, and we would linger here no more. And as we practice [All things are lessons God would have me learn.], let us think about all things we saved to settle by ourselves, and kept apart from healing. Let us give them all to Him Who knows the way to look upon them so that they will disappear.

Truth is His message; truth His teaching is. His are the lessons God would have us learn.

Bible Reference - Text

Matthew 19:24-26 - And again I say unto you, It is easier for a camel to go through the eye of a needle, than for a rich man to enter into the kingdom of God. When his disciples heard it, they were exceedingly amazed, saying, Who then can be saved? But Jesus beheld them, and said unto them, With men this is impossible; but with God all things are possible.

Course Ref/s - Citation/s

T-pr.HIC.1 - A Course in Miracles began with the sudden decision of two people to join in a common goal. Their names were Helen Schucman and William Thetford, Professors of Medical Psychology at Columbia University's College of Physicians and Surgeons in New York City. It does not matter who they were, except that the story shows that <u>with God all things are possible</u>. They were anything but spiritual. Their relationship with each other was difficult and often strained, and they were concerned with personal and professional acceptance and status. In general, they had considerable investment in the values of the world. Their lives were hardly in accord with anything that the Course advocates. Helen, the one who received the material, describes herself: Psychologist, educator, conservative in theory and atheistic in belief, I was working in a prestigious and highly academic setting. And then something happened that triggered a chain of events I could never have predicted. The head of my department unexpectedly announced that he was tired of the angry and aggressive feelings our attitudes reflected, and concluded that, "there must be another way." As if on cue I agreed to help him find it. Apparently this Course is the other way.

T-11.VI.10 - God's Son is saved. Bring only this awareness to the Sonship, and you will have a part in the redemption as valuable as mine. For your part must be like mine if you learn it of me. If you believe that yours is limited, you are limiting mine. There is no order of difficulty in miracles because all of God's Sons are of equal value, and their equality is their oneness. The whole power of God is in every part of Him, and nothing contradictory to His Will is either great or small. What does not exist has no size and no measure. To God all things are possible. And to Christ it is given to be like the Father.

W-pI.71.6:4-7:4 - Only God's plan for salvation will work. There can be no real conflict about this, because there is no possible alternative to God's plan that will save you. His is the only plan that is certain in its outcome. His is the only plan that must succeed.

Let us practice recognizing this certainty today. And let us rejoice that there is an answer to what seems to be a conflict with no resolution possible. All things are possible to God. Salvation must be yours because of His plan, which cannot fail.

W-pI.91.3-5 - To be told that what you do not see is there sounds like insanity. It is very difficult to become convinced that it is insanity not to see what is there, and to see what is not there instead. You do not doubt that the body's eyes can see. You do not doubt the images they show you are reality. Your faith lies in the darkness, not the light. How can this be reversed? For you it is impossible, but you are not alone in this.

Your efforts, however little they may be, have strong support. Did you but realize how great this strength, your doubts would vanish. Today we will devote ourselves to the attempt to let you feel this strength. When you have felt the strength in you, which makes all miracles within your easy reach, you will not doubt. The miracles your sense of weakness hides will leap into awareness as you feel the strength in you.

Three times today, set aside about ten minutes for a quiet time in which you try to leave your weakness behind. This is accomplished very simply, as you instruct yourself that you are not a body. Faith goes to what you want, and you instruct your mind accordingly. Your will remains your teacher, and your will has all the strength to do what it desires. You can escape the body if you choose. You can experience the strength in you.

Bible Reference - Text

Matthew 20:16 - So the last shall be first, and the first last: for many be called, but few chosen.

Course Ref/s - Citation/s

T-03.IV.7:3-16 - I [Jesus] was a man who remembered spirit and its knowledge. As a man I did not attempt to counteract error with knowledge, but to correct error from the bottom up. I demonstrated both the powerlessness of the body and the power of the mind. By uniting my will with that of my Creator, I naturally remembered spirit and its real purpose. I cannot unite your will with God's for you, but I can erase all misperceptions from your mind if you will bring it under my guidance. Only your misperceptions stand in your way. Without them your choice is certain. Sane perception induces sane choosing. I cannot choose for you, but I can help you make your own right choice. "<u>Many are called but few are chosen" should be</u>, "All are called but few choose to listen." Therefore, they do not choose right. The "chosen ones" are merely those who choose right sooner. Right minds can do this now, and they will find rest unto their souls. God knows you only in peace, and this *is* your reality.

W-pI.153.11 - It is the function of God's ministers to help their brothers choose as they have done. <u>God has elected all, but few have come</u> to realize His Will is but their own. And while you fail to teach what you have learned, salvation waits and darkness holds the world in grim imprisonment. Nor will you learn that light has come to you, and your escape has been accomplished. For you will not see the light, until you offer it to all your brothers. As they take it from your hands, so will you recognize it as your own.

W-pI.185.2 - No one can mean these words [I want the peace of God.] and not be healed. He cannot play with dreams, nor think he is himself a dream. He cannot make a hell and think it real. He wants the peace of God, and it is given him. For that is all he wants, and that is all he will receive. <u>Many have said these words. But few indeed have meant them.</u> You have but to look upon the world you see around you to be sure how very few they are. The world would be completely changed, should any two agree these words express the only thing they want.

M-1.1-2 - A teacher of God is anyone who chooses to be one.
His qualifications consist solely in this; somehow, somewhere he has made a deliberate choice in which he did not see his interests as apart from someone else's. Once he has done that, his road is established and his direction is sure. A light has entered the darkness. It may be a single light, but that is enough. He has entered an agreement with God even if he does not yet believe in Him. He has become a bringer of salvation. He has become a teacher of God.

They come from all over the world. They come from all religions and from no religion. They are the ones who have answered. The Call is universal. It goes on all the time everywhere. It calls for teachers to speak for It and redeem the world. <u>Many hear It, but few will answer</u>. Yet it is all a matter of time. Everyone will answer in the end, but the end can be a long, long way off. It is because of this that the plan of the teachers was established. Their function is to save time. Each one begins as a single light, but with the Call at its center it is a light that cannot be limited. And each one saves a thousand years of time as the world judges it.

Bible Reference - Text

Matthew 20:16 - So the last shall be first, and the first last: for many be called, but few chosen. (Continued)

Course Ref/s - Citation/s

M-12.3 - Why is the illusion of many necessary? Only because reality is not understandable to the deluded. <u>Only very few can hear God's Voice</u> at all, and even they cannot communicate His messages directly through the Spirit which gave them. They need a medium through which communication becomes possible to those who do not realize that they are spirit. A body they can see. A voice they understand and listen to, without the fear that truth would encounter in them. Do not forget that truth can come only where it is welcomed without fear. So do God's teachers need a body, for their unity could not be recognized directly.

Bible Reference - Text

Matthew 20:18-19 - Behold, we go up to Jerusalem; and the Son of man shall be betrayed unto the chief priests and unto the scribes, and they shall condemn him to death, And shall deliver him to the Gentiles to mock, and to scourge, and to crucify him: and the third day he shall rise again.

Course Ref/s - Citation/s

T-19.IV.D.18 - Free your brother here, as I [Jesus] freed you. Give him the self-same gift, nor look upon him with condemnation of any kind. See him as guiltless as I look on you, and overlook the sins he thinks he sees within himself. Offer your brother freedom and complete release from sin, here in the garden of seeming agony and death. So will we prepare together the way unto the resurrection of God's Son, and let him rise again to glad remembrance of his Father, Who knows no sin, no death, but only life eternal.

Bible Reference - Text

Matthew 20:28 - Even as the Son of man came not to be ministered unto, but to minister, and to give his life a ransom for many.

Course Ref/s - Citation/s

M-12.ti-2 - HOW MANY TEACHERS OF GOD ARE NEEDED TO SAVE THE WORLD?

The answer to this question is-one. One wholly perfect teacher, whose learning is complete, suffices. This one, sanctified and redeemed, becomes the Self Who is the Son of God. He who was always wholly spirit now no longer sees himself as a body, or even as in a body. Therefore he is limitless. And being limitless, his thoughts are joined with God's forever and ever. His perception of himself is based upon God's judgment, not his own. Thus does he share God's Will, and bring His Thoughts to still deluded minds. He is forever one, because he is as God created him.
He has accepted Christ; and he is saved.

Thus does the son of man become the Son of God. It is not really a change; it is a change of mind. Nothing external alters, but everything internal now reflects only the Love of God. God can no longer be feared, for the mind sees no cause for punishment. God's teachers appear to be many, for that is what is the world's need. Yet being joined in one purpose, and one they share with God, how could they be separate from each other? What does it matter if they then appear in many forms? Their minds are one; their joining is complete. And God works through them now as one, for that is what they are.

Bible Reference - Text

Matthew 21:22 - And all things, whatsoever ye shall ask in prayer, believing, ye shall receive.

Course Ref/s - Citation/s

T-09.II.3 - <u>The Bible emphasizes that all prayer is answered</u>, and this is indeed true. The very fact that the Holy Spirit has been asked for anything will ensure a response. Yet it is equally certain that no response given by Him will ever be one that would increase fear. It is possible that His answer will not be heard. It is impossible, however, that it will be lost. There are many answers you have already received but have not yet heard. I assure you that they are waiting for you.

Bible Reference - Text

Matthew 22:19-21 - Shew me the tribute money. And they brought unto him a penny. And he saith unto them, Whose is this image and superscription? They say unto him, Caesar's. Then saith he unto them, Render therefore unto Caesar the things which are Caesar's; and unto God the things that are God's.

Course Ref/s - Citation/s

T-05.IV.6 - The Holy Spirit atones in all of us by undoing, and thus lifts the burden you have placed in your mind. By following Him you are led back to God where you belong, and how can you find the way except by taking your brother with you? My part in the Atonement is not complete until you join it and give it away. As you teach so shall you learn. I will never leave you or forsake you, because to forsake you would be to forsake myself and God Who created me. You forsake yourself and God if you forsake any of your brothers. You must learn to see them as they are, and understand they belong to God as you do. How could you treat your brother better than by <u>rendering unto God the things that are God's</u>?

T-25.V.2-3 - Attack makes Christ your enemy, and God along with Him. Must you not be afraid with "enemies" like these? And must you not be fearful of yourself? For you have hurt yourself, and made your Self your "enemy." And now you must believe you are not you, but something alien to yourself and "something else," a "something" to be feared instead of loved. Who would attack whatever he perceives as wholly innocent? And who, because he wishes to attack, can fail to think he must be guilty to maintain the wish, while wanting innocence? For who could see the Son of God as innocent and wish him dead? Christ stands before you, each time you look upon your brother. He has not gone because your eyes are closed. But what is there to see by searching for your Savior, seeing Him through sightless eyes?

It is not Christ you see by looking thus. It is the "enemy," confused with Christ, you look upon. And hate because there is no sin in him for you to see. Nor do you hear his plaintive call, unchanged in content in whatever form the call is made, that you unite with him, and join with him in innocence and peace. And yet, beneath the ego's senseless shrieks, such is the call that God has given him, that you might hear in him His Call to you, and answer by <u>returning unto God what is His Own</u>.

T-25.V.4 - The Son of God asks only this of you; that you <u>return to him what is his due</u>, that you may share in it with him. Alone does neither have it. So must it remain useless to both. Together, it will give to each an equal strength to save the other, and save himself along with him. Forgiven by you, your savior offers you salvation. Condemned by you, he offers death to you. In everyone you see but the reflection of what you choose to have him be to you. If you decide against his proper function, the only one he has in truth, you are depriving him of all the joy he would have found if he fulfilled the role God gave to him. But think not Heaven is lost to him alone. Nor can it be regained unless the way is shown to him through you, that you may find it, walking by his side.

Bible Reference - Text

Matthew 22:29 - Jesus answered and said unto them, Ye do err, not knowing the scriptures, nor the power of God.

Course Ref/s - Citation/s

T-15.III.4 - There is no doubt about what your function is, for the Holy Spirit knows what it is. There is no doubt about its magnitude, for it reaches you through Him from Magnitude. You do not have to strive for it, because you have it. All your striving must be directed against littleness, for it does require vigilance to protect your magnitude in this world. To hold your magnitude in perfect awareness in a world of littleness is a task the little cannot undertake. Yet it is asked of you, in tribute to your magnitude and not your littleness. Nor is it asked of you alone. The power of God will support every effort you make on behalf of His dear Son. Search for the little, and you deny yourself His power. God is not willing that His Son be content with less than everything. For He is not content without His Son, and His Son cannot be content with less than His Father has given him.

T-15.VI.8 - In the holy instant God is remembered, and the language of communication with all your brothers is remembered with Him. For communication is remembered together, as is truth. There is no exclusion in the holy instant because the past is gone, and with it goes the whole basis for exclusion. Without its source exclusion vanishes. And this permits your Source, and that of all your brothers, to replace it in your awareness. God and the power of God will take Their rightful place in you, and you will experience the full communication of ideas with ideas. Through your ability to do this you will learn what you must be, for you will begin to understand what your Creator is, and what His creation is along with Him.

T-26.VII.18 - To use the power God has given you as He would have it used is natural. It is not arrogant to be as He created you, nor to make use of what He gave to answer all His Son's mistakes and set him free. But it is arrogant to lay aside the power that He gave, and choose a little senseless wish instead of what He wills. The gift of God to you is limitless. There is no circumstance it cannot answer, and no problem which is not resolved within its gracious light.

W-pI.69.8 - Have confidence in your Father today, and be certain that He has heard you and answered you. You may not recognize His answer yet, but you can indeed be sure that it is given you and you will yet receive it. Try, as you attempt to go through the clouds to the light, to hold this confidence in your mind. Try to remember that you are at last joining your will to God's. Try to keep the thought clearly in mind that what you undertake with God must succeed. Then let the power of God work in you and through you, that His Will and yours be done.

Bible Reference - Text

Matthew 24:35 - Heaven and earth shall pass away, but my words shall not pass away.

Course Ref/s - Citation/s

T-01.III.2 - "Heaven and earth shall pass away" means that they will not continue to exist as separate states. My word, which is the resurrection and the life, shall not pass away because life is eternal. You are the work of God, and His work is wholly loveable and wholly loving. This is how a man must think of himself in his heart, because this is what he is.

T-29.VI.4 - Change is the greatest gift God gave to all that you would make eternal, to ensure that only Heaven would not pass away. You were not born to die. You cannot change, because your function has been fixed by God. All other goals are set in time and change that time might be preserved, excepting one. Forgiveness does not aim at keeping time, but at its ending, when it has no use. Its purpose ended, it is gone. And where it once held seeming sway is now restored the function God established for His Son in full awareness. Time can set no end to its fulfilment nor its changelessness. There is no death because the living share the function their Creator gave to them. Life's function cannot be to die. It must be life's extension, that it be as one forever and forever, without end.

Bible Reference - Text

Matthew 25:35 - For I was an hungred, and ye gave me meat: I was thirsty, and ye gave me drink: I was a stranger, and ye took me in:

Course Ref/s - Citation/s

T-01.III.7 - Miracles arise from a mind that is ready for them. By being united this mind goes out to everyone, even without the awareness of the miracle worker himself. The impersonal nature of miracles is because the Atonement itself is one, uniting all creations with their Creator. As an expression of what you truly are, the miracle places the mind in a state of grace. The mind then naturally welcomes the Host within and the stranger without. <u>When you bring in the stranger</u>, he becomes your brother.

T-20.I.4 - Easter is not the celebration of the cost of sin but of its end. If you see glimpses of the face of Christ behind the veil, looking between the snow white petals of the lilies you have received and given as your gift, you will behold your brother's face and recognize it. <u>I was a stranger and you took me in</u>, not knowing who I was. Yet for your gift of lilies you will know. In your forgiveness of this stranger, alien to you and yet your ancient Friend, lies his release and your redemption with him. The time of Easter is a time of joy, and not of mourning. Look on your risen Friend, and celebrate his holiness along with me. For Easter is the time of your salvation, along with mine.

Bible Reference - Text

Matthew 25:40 - And the King shall answer and say unto them, Verily I say unto you, Inasmuch as ye have done it unto one of the least of these my brethren, ye have done it unto me.

Course Ref/s - Citation/s

T-01.III.1:1-4 - I [Jesus] am in charge of the process of Atonement, which I undertook to begin. <u>When you offer a miracle to any of my brothers, you do it to yourself and me.</u> The reason you come before me is that I do not need miracles for my own Atonement, but I stand at the end in case you fail temporarily. My part in the Atonement is the cancelling out of all errors that you could not otherwise correct.

T-09.VI.2 - It seems to you that the Holy Spirit does not produce joy consistently in you only because you do not consistently arouse joy in others. Their reactions to you are your evaluations of His consistency. When you are inconsistent you will not always give rise to joy, and so you will not always recognize His consistency. <u>What you offer to your brother you offer to Him</u>, because He cannot go beyond your offering in His giving. This is not because He limits His giving, but simply because you have limited your receiving. The decision to receive is the decision to accept.

T-09.VI.3 - If your brothers are part of you, will you accept them? Only they can teach you what you are, for your learning is the result of what you taught them. What you call upon in them you call upon in yourself. And as you call upon it in them it becomes real to you. God has but one Son, knowing them all as one. Only God Himself is more than they but they are not less than He is. Would you know what this means? If <u>what you do to my brother you do to me</u>, and if you do everything for yourself because we are part of you, everything we do belongs to you as well. Everyone God created is part of you and shares His glory with you. His Glory belongs to Him, but it is equally yours. You cannot, then, be less glorious than He is.

Bible Reference - Text

Matthew 25:44-45 - Then shall they also answer him, saying, Lord, when saw we thee an hungred, or athirst, or a stranger, or naked, or sick, or in prison, and did not minister unto thee? Then shall he answer them, saying, Verily I say unto you, Inasmuch as ye did it not to one of the least of these, ye did it not to me.

Course Ref/s - Citation/s

W-pI.160.10 - Not one does Christ forget. Not one He fails to give you to remember, that your home may be complete and perfect as it was established. He has not forgotten you. But you will not remember Him until you look on all as He does. <u>Who denies his brother is denying Him</u>, and thus refusing to accept the gift of sight by which his Self is clearly recognized, his home remembered and salvation come.

Bible Reference - Text

Matthew 26:14-15 - Then one of the twelve, called Judas Iscariot, went unto the chief priests, And said unto them, What will ye give me, and I will deliver him unto you? And they covenanted with him for thirty pieces of silver.

Course Ref/s - Citation/s

T-30.V.9 - An ancient hate is passing from the world. And with it goes all hatred and all fear. Look back no longer, for what lies ahead is all you ever wanted in your heart. Give up the world! But not to sacrifice. You never wanted it. What happiness have you sought here that did not bring you pain? What moment of content has not been bought at fearful <u>price in coins of suffering</u>? Joy has no cost. It is your sacred right, and what you pay for is not happiness. Be speeded on your way by honesty, and let not your experiences here deceive in retrospect. They were not free from bitter cost and joyless consequence.

Bible Reference - Text

Matthew 26:24 - The Son of man goeth as it is written of him: but woe unto that man by whom the Son of man is betrayed! it had been good for that man if he had not been born.

Course Ref/s - Citation/s

T-06.I.15 - These are some of the examples of upside-down thinking in the New Testament, although its gospel is really only the message of love. If the Apostles had not felt guilty, they never could have quoted me as saying, "I come not to bring peace but a sword." This is clearly the opposite of everything I taught. Nor could they have described my reactions to Judas as they did, if they had really understood me. I could not have said, "<u>Betrayest thou the Son of man with a kiss?</u>" unless I believed in betrayal. The whole message of the crucifixion was simply that I did not. The "punishment" I was said to have called forth upon Judas was a similar mistake. Judas was my brother and a Son of God, as much a part of the Sonship as myself. Was it likely that I would condemn him when I was ready to demonstrate that condemnation is impossible?

Bible Reference - Text

Matthew 26:26-29 - And as they were eating, Jesus took bread, and blessed it, and brake it, and gave it to the disciples, and said, Take, eat; this is my body. And he took the cup, and gave thanks, and gave it to them, saying, Drink ye all of it; For this is my blood of the new testament, which is shed for many for the remission of sins. But I say unto you, I will not drink henceforth of this fruit of the vine, until that day when I drink it new with you in my Father's kingdom.

Course Ref/s - Citation/s

T-19.IV.A.16 - Love, too, would set a feast before you, on a table covered with a spotless cloth, set in a quiet garden where no sound but singing and a softly joyous whispering is ever heard. This is a feast that honors your holy relationship, and at which everyone is welcomed as an honored guest. And in a holy instant grace is said by everyone together, as they join in gentleness before the table of communion. And I will join you there, as long ago I promised and promise still. For in your new relationship am I made welcome. And where I am made welcome, there I am.

T-23.II.4 - The second law of chaos, dear indeed to every worshipper of sin, is that each one must sin, and therefore deserves attack and death. This principle, closely related to the first ["the truth is different for everyone"], is the demand that errors, call for punishment and not correction. For the destruction of the one who makes the error places him beyond correction and beyond forgiveness. What he has done is thus interpreted as an irrevocable sentence upon himself, which God Himself is powerless to overcome. Sin cannot be remitted, being the belief the Son of God can make mistakes for which his own destruction becomes inevitable.

Bible Reference - Text

Matthew 26:63-65 - But Jesus held his peace, And the high priest answered and said unto him, I adjure thee by the living God, that thou tell us whether thou be the Christ, the Son of God. Jesus saith unto him, Thou hast said: nevertheless I say unto you, Hereafter shall ye see the Son of man sitting on the right hand of power, and coming in the clouds of heaven. Then the high priest rent his clothes, saying, He hath spoken blasphemy; what further need have we of witnesses? Behold, now ye have heard his blasphemy.

Course Ref/s - Citation/s

T-10.V.01 - The rituals of the god of sickness are strange and very demanding. Joy is never permitted, for depression is the sign of allegiance to him. Depression means that you have forsworn God. Many are afraid of blasphemy, but they do not understand what it means. They do not realize that to deny God is to deny their own Identity, and in this sense the wages of sin is death. The sense is very literal; denial of life perceives its opposite, as all forms of denial replace what is with what is not. No one can really do this, but that you think you can and believe you have is beyond dispute.

T-10.V.03 - Allegiance to the denial of God is the ego's religion. The god of sickness obviously demands the denial of health, because health is in direct opposition to its own survival. But consider what this means to you. Unless you are sick you cannot keep the gods you made, for only in sickness could you possibly want them. Blasphemy, then, is self-destructive, not God-destructive. It means that you are willing not to know yourself in order to be sick. This is the offering your god demands because, having made him out of your insanity, he is an insane idea. He has many forms, but although he may seem to be many different things he is but one idea;-the denial of God.

T-10.V.08 - Do not look to the god of sickness for healing but only to the God of love, for healing is the acknowledgement of Him. When you acknowledge Him you will know that He has never ceased to acknowledge you, and that in His acknowledgement of you lies your being. You are not sick and you cannot die. But you can confuse yourself with things that do. Remember, though, that to do this is blasphemy, for it means that you are looking without love on God and His creation, from which He cannot be separated.

T-10.V.12 - If God knows His children as wholly sinless, it is blasphemous to perceive them as guilty. If God knows His children as wholly without pain, it is blasphemous to perceive suffering anywhere. If God knows His children to be wholly joyous, it is blasphemous to feel depressed. All of these illusions, and the many other forms that blasphemy may take, are refusals to accept creation as it is. If God created His Son perfect, that is how you must learn to see him to learn of his reality. And as part of the Sonship, that is how you must see yourself to learn of yours.

Bible Reference - Text

Matthew 27:29 - And when they had platted a crown of thorns, they put it upon his head, and a reed in his right hand: and they bowed the knee before him, and mocked him, saying, Hail, King of the Jews!

Course Ref/s - Citation/s

T-11.VI.7 - You will not find peace until you have removed the nails from the hands of God's Son, and taken the last <u>thorn from his forehead</u>.
The Love of God surrounds His Son whom the god of crucifixion condemns. Teach not that I died in vain. Teach rather that I did not die by demonstrating that I live in you. For the undoing of the crucifixion of God's Son is the work of the redemption, in which everyone has a part of equal value. God does not judge His guiltless Son. Having given Himself to him, how could it be otherwise?

T-11.VI.8 - You have nailed yourself to a cross, and <u>placed a crown of thorns</u> upon your own head. Yet you cannot crucify God's Son, for the Will of God cannot die. His Son has been redeemed from his own crucifixion, and you cannot assign to death whom God has given eternal life. The dream of crucifixion still lies heavy on your eyes, but what you see in dreams is not reality. While you perceive the Son of God as crucified, you are asleep. And as long as you believe that you can crucify him, you are only having nightmares. You who are beginning to wake are still aware of dreams, and have not yet forgotten them. The forgetting of dreams and the awareness of Christ come with the awakening of others to share your redemption.

T-27.I.1 - The wish to be unfairly treated is a compromise attempt that would combine attack and innocence. Who can combine the wholly incompatible, and make a unity of what can never join? Walk you the gentle way, and you will fear no evil and no shadows in the night.
But place no terror symbols on your path, or you will weave <u>a crown of thorns</u> from which your brother and yourself will not escape. You cannot crucify yourself alone. And if you are unfairly treated, he must suffer the unfairness that you see. You cannot sacrifice yourself alone. For sacrifice is total. If it could occur at all it would entail the whole of God's creation, and the Father with the sacrifice of His beloved Son.

W-pI.161.11 - Select one brother, symbol of the rest, and ask salvation of him. See him first as clearly as you can, in that same form to which you are accustomed. See his face, his hands and feet, his clothing. Watch him smile, and see familiar gestures which he makes so frequently. Then think of this: What you are seeing now conceals from you the sight of one who can forgive you all your sins; whose sacred hands can take away the nails which pierce your own, and lift <u>the crown of thorns</u> which you have placed upon your bleeding head. Ask this of him, that he may set you free: Give me your blessing, holy Son of God. I would behold you with the eyes of Christ, and see my perfect sinlessness in you.

S-3.IV.9 - Creation leans across the bars of time to lift the heavy burden from the world. Lift up your hearts to greet its advent. See the shadows fade away in gentleness; <u>the thorns fall softly from the bleeding brow of him</u> who is the holy Son of God. How lovely are you, child of Holiness! How like to Me! How lovingly I hold you in My Heart and in My Arms. How dear is every gift to Me that you have made, who healed My Son and took him from the cross. Arise and let My thanks be given you. And with My gratitude will come the gift first of forgiveness, then eternal peace.

Bible Reference - Text

Matthew 28:2 - And, behold, there was a great earthquake: for the angel of the Lord descended from heaven, and came and rolled back the stone from the door, and sat upon it.

Course Ref/s - Citation/s

C-ep.2 - You are a stranger here. But you belong to Him Who loves you as He loves Himself. Ask but my help to <u>roll the stone away</u>, and it is done according to His Will. We have begun the journey. Long ago the end was written in the stars and set into the Heavens with a shining Ray that held it safe within eternity and through all time as well. And holds it still; unchanged, unchanging and unchangeable.

Bible Reference - Text

Matthew 28:18 - And Jesus came and spake unto them, saying, All power is given unto me in heaven and in earth.

Course Ref/s - Citation/s

T-05.II.9 - My mind will always be like yours, because we were created as equals. It was only my decision that gave me <u>all power in Heaven and earth</u>. My only gift to you is to help you make the same decision. This decision is the choice to share it, because the decision itself is the decision to share. It is made by giving, and is therefore the one choice that resembles true creation. I am your model for decision. By deciding for God I showed you that this decision can be made, and that you can make it.

T-14.XI.1-2 - Yet the essential thing is learning that you do not know. Knowledge is power, and <u>all power is of God</u>. You who have tried to keep power for yourself have "lost" it. You still have the power, but you have interposed so much between it and your awareness of it that you cannot use it. Everything you have taught yourself has made your power more and more obscure to you. You know not what it is, nor where. You have made a semblance of power and a show of strength so pitiful that it must fail you. For power is not a seeming strength, and truth is beyond semblance of any kind. Yet all that stands between you and the power of God in you is but your learning of the false, and of your attempts to undo the true.

Be willing, then, for all of it to be undone, and be glad that you are not bound to it forever. For you have taught yourself how to imprison the Son of God, a lesson so unthinkable that only the insane, in deepest sleep, could even dream of it. Can God learn how not to be God? And can <u>His Son, given all power by Him</u>, learn to be powerless? What have you taught yourself that you can possibly prefer to keep, in place of what you have and what you are?

T-14.XI.4 - You who have not yet brought all of the darkness you have taught yourself into the light in you, can hardly judge the truth and value of this course [A Course in Miracles]. Yet God did not abandon you. And so you have another lesson sent from Him, already learned for every child of light by Him to Whom God gave it. This lesson shines with <u>God's glory, for in it lies His power, which He shares so gladly with His Son</u>. Learn of His happiness, which is yours. But to accomplish this, all your dark lessons must be brought willingly to truth, and joyously laid down by hands open to receive, not closed to take. Every dark lesson that you bring to Him Who teaches light He will accept from you, because you do not want it. And He will gladly exchange each one for the bright lesson He has learned for you. Never believe that any lesson you have learned apart from Him means anything.

Bible Reference - Text

Matthew 28:18 - And Jesus came and spake unto them, saying, All power is given unto me in heaven and in earth. (Continued)

Course Ref/s - Citation/s

T-26.VI.2 - Lead not your little life in solitude, with one illusion as your only friend. This is no friendship worthy of God's Son, nor one with which he could remain content. Yet God has given him a better Friend, in Whom all power in earth and Heaven rests. The one illusion that you think is friend obscures His grace and majesty from you, and keeps His friendship and forgiveness from your welcoming embrace. Without Him you are friendless. Seek not another friend to take His place. There is no other friend. What God appointed has no substitute, for what illusion can replace the truth?

W-pI.020.3 - Your decision to see is all that vision requires. What you want is yours. Do not mistake the little effort that is asked of you for an indication that our goal is of little worth. Can the salvation of the world be a trivial purpose? And can the world be saved if you are not? God has one Son, and he is the resurrection and the life. His will is done because all power is given him in Heaven and on earth. In your determination to see is vision given you.

W-pI.191.9 - You who perceive yourself as weak and frail, with futile hopes and devastated dreams, born but to die, to weep and suffer pain, hear this: All power is given unto you in earth and Heaven. There is nothing that you cannot do. You play the game of death, of being helpless, pitifully tied to dissolution in a world which shows no mercy to you. Yet when you accord it mercy, will its mercy shine on you.

W-pII.320.ti-2 - My Father gives all power unto me.

The Son of God is limitless. There are no limits on his strength, his peace, his joy, nor any attributes his Father gave in his creation. What he wills with his Creator and Redeemer must be done. His holy will can never be denied, because his Father shines upon his mind, and lays before it all the strength and love in earth and Heaven. I am he to whom all this is given. I am he in whom the power of my Father's Will abides.

Your Will can do all things in me, and then extend to all the world as well through me. There is no limit on Your Will. And so <u>all power has been given to Your Son</u>.

C-6.2 - The Holy Spirit is described throughout the course as giving us the answer to the separation and bringing the plan of the Atonement to us, establishing our particular part in it and showing us exactly what it is. He has established Jesus as the leader in carrying out His plan since he was the first to complete his own part perfectly. <u>All power in Heaven and earth is therefore given him</u> and he will share it with you when you have completed yours. The Atonement principle was given to the Holy Spirit long before Jesus set it in motion.

P-2.VII.6 - Yet it is as insane not to accept a function God has given you as to invent one He has not. The advanced therapist in no way can ever doubt the power that is in him. Nor does he doubt its Source. He understands <u>all power in earth and Heaven</u> belongs to him because of who he is. And he is this because of his Creator, Whose Love is in him and Who cannot fail. Think what this means; he has the gifts of God Himself to give away. His patients are God's saints, who call upon his sanctity to make it theirs. And as he gives it to them, they behold Christ's shining face as it looks back at them.

Bible Reference - Text

Matthew 28:19-20 - Go ye therefore, and teach all nations, baptizing them in the name of the Father, and of the Son, and of the Holy Ghost: Teaching them to observe all things whatsoever I have commanded you: and, lo, I am with you always, even unto the end of the world. Amen.

Course Ref/s - Citation/s

T-07.III.1 - The Holy Spirit teaches one lesson, and applies it to all individuals in all situations. Being conflict-free, He maximises all efforts and all results. By teaching the power of the Kingdom of God Himself, He teaches you that all power is yours. Its application does not matter. It is always maximal. Your vigilance does not establish it as yours, but it does enable you to use it always and in all ways. When I said "<u>I am with you always</u>," I meant it literally. I am not absent to anyone in any situation. Because I am always with you, you are the way, the truth and the life.

You did not make this power, any more than I did. It was created to be shared, and therefore cannot be meaningfully perceived as belonging to anyone at the expense of another. Such a perception makes it meaningless by eliminating or overlooking its real and only meaning.

T-08.III.4 - When you meet anyone, remember it is a holy encounter. As you see him you will see yourself. As you treat him you will treat yourself. As you think of him you will think of yourself. Never forget this, for in him you will find yourself or lose yourself. Whenever two Sons of God meet, they are given another chance at salvation. Do not leave anyone without giving salvation to him and receiving it yourself. For <u>I am always there with you</u>, in remembrance of *you*.

T-08.IV.2 - I am come as a light into a world that does deny itself everything. It does this simply by dissociating itself from everything. It is therefore an illusion of isolation, maintained by fear of the same loneliness that is its illusion. I said that <u>I am with you always, even unto the end of the world</u>. That is why I am the light of the world. If I am with you in the loneliness of the world, the loneliness is gone. You cannot maintain the illusion of loneliness if you are not alone. My purpose, then, is still to overcome the world. I do not attack it, but my light must dispel it because of what it is. Light does not attack darkness, but it does shine it away. If my light goes with you everywhere, you shine it away with me. The light becomes ours, and you cannot abide in darkness any more than darkness can abide wherever you go. The remembrance of me is the remembrance of yourself, and of Him Who sent me to you.

T-08.IV.3 - You were in darkness until God's Will was done completely by any part of the Sonship. When this was done, it was perfectly accomplished by all. How else could it be perfectly accomplished? My mission was simply to unite the will of the Sonship with the Will of the Father by being aware of the Father's Will myself. This is the awareness I came to give you, and your problem in accepting it is the problem of this world. Dispelling it is salvation, and in this sense I am the salvation of the world. The world must therefore despise and reject me, because the world is the belief that love is impossible. If you will accept the fact that <u>I am with you</u>, you are denying the world and accepting God. My will is His, and your decision to hear me is the decision to hear His Voice and abide in His Will. As God sent me to you so will I send you to others. And I will go to them with you, so we can teach them peace and union.

T-13.V.6-7 - As you look with open eyes upon your world, it must occur to you that you have withdrawn into insanity. You see what is not there, and you hear what makes no sound. Your manifestations of emotions are the opposite of what the emotions are. You communicate with no one, and you are as isolated from reality as if you were alone in all the universe. In your madness you overlook reality completely, and you see only your own split mind everywhere you look. God calls you and you do not hear, for you are preoccupied with your own voice. And the vision of Christ is not in your sight, for you look upon yourself alone.

Little child, would you offer this to your Father? For if you offer it to yourself, you are offering it to Him. And He will not return it, for it is unworthy of you because it is unworthy of Him. Yet He would release you from it and set you free. His sane Answer tells you what you have offered yourself is not true, but His offering to you has never changed. You who know not what you do can learn what insanity is, and look beyond it. It is given you to learn how to deny insanity, and come forth from your private world in peace. You will see all that you denied in your brothers because you denied it in yourself. For you will love them, and by drawing nigh unto them you will draw them to yourself, perceiving them as witnesses to the reality you share with God. I am with them as I am with you, and we will draw them from their private worlds, for as we are united so would we unite with them. The Father welcomes all of us in gladness, and gladness is what we should offer Him. For every Son of God is given you to whom God gave Himself. And it is God Whom you must offer them, to recognize His gift to you.

Bible Reference - Text

Matthew 28:19-20 - Go ye therefore, and teach all nations....
(Continued) - (To read the full text of the above go to page 258.)

Course Ref/s - Citation/s

T-25.I.5 - Since you believe that you are separate, Heaven presents itself to you as separate, too. Not that it is in truth, but that the link that has been given you to join the truth may reach to you through what you understand. Father and Son and Holy Spirit are as One, as all your brothers join as one in truth. Christ and His Father never have been separate, and Christ abides within your understanding, in the part of you that shares His Father's Will. The Holy Spirit links the other part-the tiny mad desire to be separate, different and special-to the Christ, to make the oneness clear to what is really one. In this world this is not understood, but can be taught.

W-pI.97.2 - We state again the truth about your Self, the holy Son of God Who rests in you, whose mind has been restored to sanity. You are the spirit lovingly endowed with all your Father's Love and peace and joy. You are the spirit which completes Himself, and shares His function as Creator. <u>He is with you always</u>, as you are with Him.

M-23.7 - This course has come from him [Jesus] because his words have reached you in a language you can love and understand. Are other teachers possible, to lead the way to those who speak in different tongues and appeal to different symbols? Certainly there are. Would God leave anyone without a very present help in time of trouble; a savior who can symbolize Himself? Yet do we need a many-faceted curriculum, not because of content differences, but because symbols must shift and change to suit the need. Jesus has come to answer yours. In him you find God's Answer. Do you, then, teach with him, for <u>he is with you; he is always here</u>.

Q. Mark

The following are the references from the Gospel of Mark that are cited in the Course:

[5:9], [8:17-18], [10:9] and [10:51-52].

Bible Reference - Text

Mark 5:9 - And he asked him, What is thy name? And he answered, saying, My name is Legion: for we are many.

Course Ref/s - Citation/s

T-06.II.13 - The Holy Spirit was given you with perfect impartiality, and only by recognizing Him impartially can you recognize Him at all. The ego is legion, but the Holy Spirit is one. No darkness abides anywhere in the Kingdom, but your part is only to allow no darkness to abide in your own mind. This alignment with light is unlimited, because it is in alignment with the light of the world. Each of us is the light of the world, and by joining our minds in this light we proclaim the Kingdom of God together and as one.

T-09.IV.11 - The impossible can happen only in fantasy. When you search for reality in fantasies you will not find it. The symbols of fantasy are of the ego, and of these you will find many. But do not look for meaning in them. They have no more meaning than the fantasies into which they are woven. Fairy tales can be pleasant or fearful, but no one calls them true. Children may believe them, and so, for a while, the tales are true for them. Yet when reality dawns, the fantasies are gone. Reality has not gone in the meanwhile. The Second Coming is the awareness of reality, not its return.

Bible Reference - Text

Mark 8:17-18 - And when Jesus knew it, he saith unto them, Why reason ye, because ye have no bread? Perceive ye not yet, neither understand? Have ye your heart yet hardened? Having eyes, see ye not? And having ears, hear ye not? And do ye not remember?

Course Ref/s - Citation/s

W-pI.92.3 - It is God's strength in you that is the light in which you see, as it is His Mind with which you think. His strength denies your weakness. It is your weakness that sees through the body's eyes, peering about in darkness to behold the likeness of itself; the small, the weak, the sickly and the dying, those in need, the helpless and afraid, the sad, the poor, the starving and the joyless. These are seen through <u>eyes that cannot see</u> and cannot bless.

Bible Reference - Text

Mark 10:9 - What therefore God hath joined together, let not man put asunder.

Course Ref/s - Citation/s

T-pr.WIS.8 - Only minds can really join, and <u>whom God has joined no man can put asunder</u> (Text, p. 356). It is, however, only at the level of Christ Mind that true union is possible, and has, in fact, never been lost. The "little I" seeks to enhance itself by external approval, external possessions and external "love." The Self That God created needs nothing. It is forever complete, safe, loved and loving. It seeks to share rather than to get; to extend rather than project. It has no needs and wants to join with others out of their mutual awareness of abundance.

T-18.I.2 - The Holy Spirit never uses substitutes. Where the ego perceives one person as a replacement for another, the Holy Spirit sees them joined and indivisible. He does not judge between them, knowing they are one. Being united, they are one because they are the same. Substitution is clearly a process in which they are perceived as different. One would unite; the other separate. <u>Nothing can come between what God has joined</u> and what the Holy Spirit sees as one. But everything seems to come between the fragmented relationships the ego sponsors to destroy.

P-2.II.6 - If healing is an invitation to God to enter into His Kingdom, what difference does it make how the invitation is written? Does the paper matter, or the ink, or the pen? Or is it he who writes that gives the invitation? God comes to those who would restore His world, for they have found the way to call to Him. If any two are joined, He must be there. It does not matter what their purpose is, but they must share it wholly to succeed. It is impossible to share a goal not blessed by Christ, for what is unseen through His eyes is too fragmented to be meaningful.

P-2.V.4 - Healing is holy. Nothing in the world is holier than helping one who asks for help. And two come very close to God in this attempt, however limited, however lacking in sincerity. Where two have joined for healing, God is there. And He has guaranteed that He will hear and answer them in truth. They can be sure that healing is a process He directs, because it is according to His Will. We have His Word to guide us, as we try to help our brothers. Let us not forget that we are helpless of ourselves, and lean upon a Strength beyond our little scope for what to teach as well as what to learn.

P-2.V.5-6 - A brother seeking aid can bring us gifts beyond the heights perceived in any dream. He offers us salvation, for he comes to us as Christ and Savior. What he asks is asked by God through him. And what we do for him becomes the gift we give to God. The sacred calling of God's holy Son for help in his perceived distress can be but answered by his Father. Yet He needs a voice through which to speak His holy Word; a hand to reach His Son and touch his heart. In such a process, who could not be healed? This holy interaction is the plan of God Himself, by which His Son is saved.

For two have joined. And now God's promises are kept by Him. The limits laid on both the patient and the therapist will count as nothing, for the healing has begun. What they must start their Father will complete. For He has never asked for more than just the smallest willingness, the least advance, the tiniest of whispers of His Name. To ask for help, whatever form it takes, is but to call on Him. And He will send His Answer through the therapist who best can serve His Son in all his present needs. Perhaps the answer does not seem to be a gift from Heaven. It may even seem to be a worsening and not a help. Yet let the outcome not be judged by us.

P-3.I.3 - Your patients need not be physically present for you to serve them in the Name of God. This may be hard to remember, but God will not have His gifts to you limited to the few you actually see. You can see others as well, for seeing is not limited to the body's eyes. Some do not need your physical presence. They need you as much, and perhaps even more, at the instant they are sent. You will recognize them in whatever way can be most helpful to both of you. It does not matter how they come. They will be sent in whatever form is most helpful; a name, a thought, a picture, an idea, or perhaps just a feeling of reaching out to someone somewhere. The joining is in the hands of the Holy Spirit. It cannot fail to be accomplished.

Bible Reference - Text

Mark 10:51-52 - And Jesus answered and said unto him, What wilt thou that I should do unto thee? The blind man said unto him, Lord, that I might receive my sight. And Jesus said unto him, Go thy way; thy faith hath made thee whole. And immediately he received his sight, and followed Jesus in the way.

Course Ref/s - Citation/s

W-pI.160.10 - Not one does Christ forget. Not one He fails to give you to remember, that your home may be complete and perfect as it was established. He has not forgotten you. But you will not remember Him until you look on all as He does. Who denies his brother is denying Him, and thus refusing to accept the gift of sight by which his Self is clearly recognized, his home remembered and salvation come.

R. Luke

There are 31 references from the Gospel of Luke that are cited in the Course. They are as follows:

>[1:19], [1:28], [1:31-33], [1:76-79], [2:7],
>
>[2:12], [2:14], [2:29-31], [5:18-25], [6:36],
>
>[6:48], [8:13], [9:49-50], [9:62], [14:16-23],
>
>[15:7], [15:11-32], [16:8], [17:5-6], [17:21],
>
>[19:1-10], [22:19], [22:34], [22:39-46], [22:48],
>
>[23:33], [23:34], [23:39-43], [23:46], [24:1-7] and
>
>[24:13-16].

Bible Reference - Text

Luke 1:19 - And the angel answering said unto him, I am Gabriel, that stand in the presence of God; and am sent to speak unto thee, and to shew thee these glad tidings.

Course Ref/s - Citation/s

T-16.II.6 - No evidence will convince you of the truth of what you do not want. Yet your relationship with Him is real. Regard this not with fear, but with rejoicing. The One you called upon is with you. Bid Him welcome, and honor the witnesses who bring you the glad tidings He has come. It is true, just as you fear, that to acknowledge Him is to deny all that you think you know. But what you think you know was never true. What gain is there to you in clinging to it, and denying the evidence for truth? For you have come too near to truth to renounce it now, and you will yield to its compelling attraction. You can delay this now, but only a little while. The Host of God has called to you, and you have heard. Never again will you be wholly willing not to listen.

T-16.II.8 - Do not interpret against God's Love, for you have many witnesses that speak of it so clearly that only the blind and deaf could fail to see and hear them. This year determine not to deny what has been given you by God. Awake and share it, for that is the only reason He has called to you. His Voice has spoken clearly, and yet you have so little faith in what you heard, because you have preferred to place still greater faith in the disaster you have made. Today, let us resolve together to accept the joyful tidings that disaster is not real and that reality is not disaster. Reality is safe and sure, and wholly kind to everyone and everything. There is no greater love than to accept this and be glad. For love asks only that you be happy, and will give you everything that makes for happiness.

T-19.I.14 - In the holy instant, you and your brother stand before the altar God has raised unto Himself and both of you. Lay faithlessness aside, and come to it together. There will you see the miracle of your relationship as it was made again through faith. And there it is that you will realize that there is nothing faith cannot forgive. No error interferes with its calm sight, which brings the miracle of healing with equal ease to all of them. For what the messengers of love are sent to do they do, returning the glad tidings that it was done to you and your brother who stand together before the altar from which they were sent forth.

W-pI.75.5- We do not want to see the ego's shadow on the world today. We see the light, and in it we see Heaven's reflection lie across the world. Begin the longer practice periods by telling yourself the glad tidings of your release:

The light has come. I have forgiven the world.

W-pII.14.5 - We are the holy messengers of God who speak for Him, and carrying His Word to everyone whom He has sent to us, we learn that it is written on our hearts. And thus our minds are changed about the aim for which we came, and which we seek to serve. We bring glad tidings to the Son of God, who thought he suffered. Now is he redeemed. And as he sees the gate of Heaven stand open before him, he will enter in and disappear into the Heart of God.

M-4.X.3 - You may have noticed that the list of attributes of God's teachers [Trust, Honesty, Tolerance, Gentleness, Joy, Defenselessness, Generosity, Patience, Faithfulness and Open-Mindedness] does not include things that are the Son of God's inheritance. Terms like love, sinlessness, perfection, knowledge and eternal truth do not appear in this context. They would be most inappropriate here. What God has given is so far beyond our curriculum that learning but disappears in its presence. Yet while its presence is obscured, the focus properly belongs on the curriculum. It is the function of God's teachers to bring true learning to the world. Properly speaking it is unlearning that they bring, for that is "true learning" in the world. It is given to the teachers of God to bring the glad tidings of complete forgiveness to the world. Blessed indeed are they, for they are the bringers of salvation.

Bible Reference - Text

Luke 1:19 - And the angel answering said unto him....
(Continued) - (To read the full text of the above go to page 266.)

Course Ref/s - Citation/s

P-3.III.8 - Physician, healer, therapist, teacher, heal thyself. Many will come to you carrying the gift of healing, if you so elect. The Holy Spirit never refuses an invitation to enter and abide with you. He will give you endless opportunities to open the door to your salvation, for such is His function. He will also tell you exactly what your function is in every circumstance and at all times. Whoever He sends you will reach you, holding out his hand to his Friend. Let the Christ in you bid him welcome, for that same Christ is in him as well. Deny him entrance, and you have denied the Christ in you. Remember the sorrowful story of the world, and the glad tidings of salvation. Remember the plan of God for the restoration of joy and peace. And do not forget how very simple are the ways of God. You were lost in the darkness of the world until you asked for light. And then God sent His Son to give it to you.

Bible Reference - Text

Luke 1:28 - And the angel came in unto her, and said, Hail, thou that art highly favoured, the Lord is with thee: blessed art thou among women.

Course Ref/s - Citation/s

T-12.II.9 - You who have tried to banish love have not succeeded, but you who choose to banish fear must succeed. The Lord is with you, but you know it not. Yet your Redeemer liveth, and abideth in you in the peace out of which He was created. Would you not exchange this awareness for the awareness of fear? When we have overcome fear—not by hiding it, not by minimizing it, and not by denying its full import in any way—this is what you will really see. You cannot lay aside the obstacles to real vision without looking upon them, for to lay aside means to judge against. If you will look, the Holy Spirit will judge, and He will judge truly. Yet He cannot shine away what you keep hidden, for you have not offered it to Him and He cannot take it from you.

Bible Reference - Text

Luke 1:31-33 - And, behold, thou shalt conceive in thy womb, and bring forth a son, and shalt call his name Jesus. He shall be great, and shall be called the Son of the Highest: and the Lord God shall give unto him the throne of his father David: And he shall reign over the house of Jacob for ever; and of his kingdom there shall be no end.

Course Ref/s - Citation/s

T-16.III.7 - This year you will begin to learn, and make learning commensurate with teaching. You have chosen this by your own willingness to teach. Though you seemed to suffer for it, the joy of teaching will yet be yours. For the joy of teaching is in the learner, who offers it to the teacher in gratitude, and shares it with him. As you learn, your gratitude to your Self, Who teaches you what He is, will grow and help you honor Him. And you will learn His power and strength and purity, and love Him as His Father does. <u>His Kingdom has no limits and no end</u>, and there is nothing in Him that is not perfect and eternal. All this is you, and nothing outside of this is you.

Bible Reference - Text

Luke 1:76-79 - And thou, child, shalt be called the prophet of the Highest: for thou shalt go before the face of the Lord to prepare his ways; To give knowledge of salvation unto his people by the remission of their sins, Through the tender mercy of our God; whereby the dayspring from on high hath visited us, To give light to them that sit in darkness and in the shadow of death, to guide our feet into the way of peace.

Course Ref/s - Citation/s

M-1.1 - A teacher of God is anyone who chooses to be one. His qualifications consist solely in this; somehow, somewhere he has made a deliberate choice in which he did not see his interests as apart from someone else's. Once he has done that, his road is established and his direction is sure. <u>A light has entered the darkness</u>. It may be a single light, but that is enough. He has entered an agreement with God even if he does not yet believe in Him. He has become a bringer of salvation. He has become a teacher of God.

Bible Reference - Text

Luke 2:7 - And she brought forth her firstborn son, and wrapped him in swaddling clothes, and laid him in a manger; because there was no room for them in the inn.

Course Ref/s - Citation/s

T-15.III.9 - Holy child of God, when will you learn that only holiness can content you and give you peace? Remember that you learn not for yourself alone, no more than I [Jesus] did. It is because I learned for you that you can learn of me. I would but teach you what is yours, so that together we can replace the shabby littleness that binds the host of God to guilt and weakness with the glad awareness of the glory that is in him. My birth in you is your awakening to grandeur. Welcome me not <u>into a manger</u>, but into the altar to holiness, where holiness abides in perfect peace.
My Kingdom is not of this world because it is in you. And you are of your Father. Let us join in honoring you, who must remain forever beyond littleness.

T-15.X.1 - It is in your power, in time, to delay the perfect union of the Father and the Son. For in this world, the attraction of guilt does stand between them. Neither time nor season means anything in eternity. But here it is the Holy Spirit's function to use them both, though not as the ego uses them. This is the season when you would celebrate <u>my birth</u> into the world. Yet you know not how to do it. Let the Holy Spirit teach you, and let me celebrate your birth through Him. The only gift I can accept of you is the gift I gave to you. Release me as I choose your own release. The time of Christ we celebrate together, for it has no meaning if we are apart.

T-15.X.3 - We who are one cannot give separately. When you are willing to accept our relationship as real, guilt will hold no attraction for you. For in our union you will accept all of our brothers. The gift of union is the only gift that <u>I was born</u> to give. Give it to me, that you may have it. The time of Christ is the time appointed for the gift of freedom, offered to everyone. And by your acceptance of it, you offer it to everyone.

T-15.XI.07 - In the holy instant the condition of love is met, for minds are joined without the body's interference, and where there is communication there is peace. The Prince of Peace was born to re-establish the condition of love by teaching that communication remains unbroken even if the body is destroyed, provided that you see not the body as the necessary means of communication. And if you understand this lesson, you will realize that to sacrifice the body is to sacrifice nothing, and communication, which must be of the mind, cannot be sacrificed. Where, then, is sacrifice? The lesson <u>I was born</u> to teach, and still would teach to all my brothers, is that sacrifice is nowhere and love is everywhere. For communication embraces everything, and in the peace it re-establishes, love comes of itself.

T-15.XI.10 - This is the time in which a new year will soon be <u>born from the time of Christ</u>. I have perfect faith in you to do all that you would accomplish. Nothing will be lacking, and you will make complete and not destroy. Say, then, to your brother: I give you to the Holy Spirit as part of myself. I know that you will be released, unless I want to use you to imprison myself. In the name of my freedom I choose your release, because I recognize that we will be released together. So will the year begin in joy and freedom. There is much to do, and we have been long delayed. Accept the holy instant as this year is born, and take your place, so long left unfulfilled, in the Great Awakening. Make this year different by making it all the same. And let all your relationships be made holy for you. This is our will. Amen.

W-pII.308.1 - I have conceived of time in such a way that I defeat my aim. If I elect to reach past time to timelessness, I must change my perception of what time is for. Time's purpose cannot be to keep the past and future one. The only interval in which I can be saved from time is now. For in this instant has forgiveness come to set me free. The birth of Christ is now, without a past or future. He has come to give His present blessing to the world, restoring it to timelessness and love. And love is ever- present, here and now.

Bible Reference - Text

Luke 2:12 - And this shall be a sign unto you; Ye shall find the babe wrapped in swaddling clothes, lying in a manger.

Course Ref/s - Citation/s

T-19.IV.C.10 - What danger can assail the wholly innocent? What can attack the guiltless? What fear can enter and disturb the peace of sinlessness? What has been given you, even in its infancy, is in full communication with God and you. In its tiny hands it holds, in perfect safety, every miracle you will perform, held out to you. The miracle of life is ageless, born in time but nourished in eternity. Behold this infant, to whom you gave a resting place by your forgiveness of your brother, and see in it the Will of God. Here is the babe of Bethlehem reborn.
And everyone who gives him shelter will follow him, not to the cross, but to the resurrection and the life.

Bible Reference - Text

Luke 2:14 - Glory to God in the highest, and on earth peace, good will toward men.

Course Ref/s - Citation/s

T-08.III.1 - Glory to God in the highest, and to you because He has so willed it. Ask and it shall be given you, because it has already been given. Ask for light and learn that you are light. If you want understanding and enlightenment you will learn it, because your decision to learn it is the decision to listen to the Teacher [the Holy Spirit] Who knows of light, and can therefore teach it to you. There is no limit on your learning because there is no limit on your mind. There is no limit on His teaching because He was created to teach. Understanding His function perfectly He fulfils it perfectly, because that is His joy and yours.

Bible Reference - Text

Luke 2:29-31 - Lord, now lettest thou thy servant depart in peace, according to thy word: For mine eyes have seen thy salvation, Which thou hast prepared before the face of all people;

Course Ref/s - Citation/s

T-05.IV.8 - How can you who are so holy suffer? All your past except its beauty is gone, and nothing is left but a blessing. I have saved all your kindnesses and every loving thought you ever had. I have purified them of the errors that hid their light, and kept them for you in their own perfect radiance. They are beyond destruction and beyond guilt. They came from the Holy Spirit within you, and we know what God creates is eternal. You can indeed <u>depart in peace</u> because I have loved you as I loved myself. You go with my blessing and for my blessing. Hold it and share it, that it may always be ours. I place the peace of God in your heart and in your hands, to hold and share. The heart is pure to hold it, and the hands are strong to give it. We cannot lose. My judgment is as strong as the wisdom of God, in Whose Heart and Hands we have our being. His quiet children are His blessed Sons. The Thoughts of God are with you.

T-13.III.11 - In peace he needed nothing and asked for nothing. In war he demanded everything and found nothing. For how could the gentleness of love respond to his demands, except by <u>departing in peace</u> and returning to the Father? If the Son did not wish to remain in peace, he could not remain at all. For a darkened mind cannot live in the light, and it must seek a place of darkness where it can believe it is where it is not. God did not allow this to happen. Yet you demanded that it happen, and therefore believed that it was so.

W-pI.61.4 - You will want to think about this idea [I am the light of the world.] as often as possible today. It is the perfect answer to all illusions, and therefore to all temptation. It brings all the images you have made about yourself to the truth, and helps you <u>depart in peace</u>, unburdened and certain of your purpose.

Bible Reference - Text

Luke 5:18-25 - And, behold, men brought in a bed a man which was taken with a palsy: and they sought means to bring him in, and to lay him before him. And when they could not find by what way they might bring him in because of the multitude, they went upon the housetop, and let him down through the tiling with his couch into the midst before Jesus. And when he saw their faith, he said unto him, Man, thy sins are forgiven thee. And the scribes and the Pharisees began to reason, saying, Who is this which speaketh blasphemies? Who can forgive sins, but God alone? But when Jesus perceived their thoughts, he answering said unto them,

What reason ye in your hearts? Whether is easier, to say, Thy sins be forgiven thee; or to say, Rise up and walk? But that ye may know that the Son of man hath power upon earth to forgive sins, (he said unto the sick of the palsy,) I say unto thee, Arise, and take up thy couch, and go into thine house. And immediately he rose up before them, and took up that whereon he lay, and departed to his own house, glorifying God.

Course Ref/s - Citation/s

T-19.IV.D.12:7-13:8 - Brother, you need forgiveness of your brother, for you will share in madness or in Heaven together. And you will raise your eyes in faith together, or not at all.

Beside you is one who offers you the chalice of Atonement, for the Holy Spirit is in him. Would you hold his sins against him, or accept his gift to you? Is this giver of salvation your friend or enemy? Choose which he is, remembering that you will receive of him according to your choice. He has in him the power to forgive your sin, as you for him. Neither can give it to himself alone. And yet your savior stands beside each one. Let him be what he is, and seek not to make of love an enemy.

Bible Reference - Text

Luke 6:36 - Be ye therefore merciful, as your Father also is merciful.

Course Ref/s - Citation/s

T-03.I.4 - Sacrifice is a notion totally unknown to God. It arises solely from fear, and frightened people can be vicious. Sacrificing in any way is a violation of my injunction that <u>you should be merciful even as your Father in Heaven is merciful</u>. It has been hard for many Christians to realize that this applies to themselves. Good teachers never terrorize their students. To terrorize is to attack, and this results in rejection of what the teacher offers. The result is learning failure.

T-30.V.10 - Do not look back except in honesty. And when an idol tempts you, think of this: There never was a time an idol brought you anything except the "gift" of guilt. Not one was bought except at cost of pain, nor was it ever paid by you alone. <u>Be merciful</u> unto your brother, then. And do not choose an idol thoughtlessly, remembering that he will pay the cost as well as you. For he will be delayed when you look back, and you will not perceive Whose loving hand you hold. Look forward, then; in confidence walk with a happy heart that beats in hope and does not pound in fear.

Bible Reference - Text

Luke 6:48 - He is like a man which built an house, and digged deep, and laid the foundation on a rock: and when the flood arose, the stream beat vehemently upon that house, and could not shake it: for it was founded upon a rock.

Course Ref/s - Citation/s

W-pI.61.7 - Today's idea [I am the light of the world.] goes far beyond the ego's petty views of what you are and what your purpose is. As a bringer of salvation, this is obviously necessary. This is the first of a number of giant steps we will take in the next few weeks. Try today to begin to <u>build a firm foundation</u> for these advances. You are the light of the world. God has built His plan for the salvation of His Son on you.

Bible Reference - Text

Luke 8:13 - They on the rock are they, which, when they hear, receive the word with joy; and these have no root, which for a while believe, and in time of temptation fall away.

Course Ref/s - Citation/s

T-1.V.6 - The miracle is a sign that the mind has chosen to be led by me in Christ's service. The abundance of Christ is the natural result of choosing to follow Him. <u>All shallow roots must be uprooted, because they are not deep enough</u> to sustain you. The illusion that shallow roots can be deepened, and thus made to hold, is one of the distortions on which the reverse of the Golden Rule rests. As these false underpinnings are given up, the equilibrium is temporarily experienced as unstable. However, nothing is less stable than an upside-down orientation. Nor can anything that holds it upside down be conducive to increased stability.

Bible Reference - Text

Luke 9:49-50 - And John answered and said, Master, we saw one casting out devils in thy name; and we forbad him, because he followeth not with us. And Jesus said unto him, Forbid him not: for he that is not against us is for us.

Course Ref/s - Citation/s

T-21.VII.1 - Do you not see that all your misery comes from the strange belief that you are powerless? Being helpless is the cost of sin. Helplessness is sin's condition; the one requirement that it demands to be believed. Only the helpless could believe in it. Enormity has no appeal save to the little. And only those who first believe that they are little could see attraction there. Treachery to the Son of God is the defense of those who do not identify with him. And <u>you are for him or against him</u>; either you love him or attack him, protect his unity or see him shattered and slain by your attack.

Bible Reference - Text

Luke 9:62 - And Jesus said unto him, No man, having put his hand to the plough, and looking back, is fit for the kingdom of God.

Course Ref/s - Citation/s

T-14.II.6 - If you would be a happy learner, you must give everything you have learned to the Holy Spirit, to be unlearned for you. And then begin to learn the joyous lessons that come quickly on the firm foundation that truth is true. For what is builded there is true, and built on truth. The universe of learning will open up before you in all its gracious simplicity. With truth before you, <u>you will not look back</u>.

Bible Reference - Text

Luke 14:16-23 - Then said he unto him, A certain man made a great supper, and bade many: And sent his servant at supper time to say to them that were bidden, Come; for all things are now ready. And they all with one consent began to make excuse. The first said unto him, I have bought a piece of ground, and I must needs go and see it: I pray thee have me excused. And another said, I have bought five yoke of oxen, and I go to prove them: I pray thee have me excused. And another said, I have married a wife, and therefore I cannot come. So that servant came, and shewed his lord these things. Then the master of the house being angry said to his servant, Go out quickly into the streets and lanes of the city, and bring in hither the poor, and the maimed, and the halt, and the blind. And the servant said, Lord, it is done as thou hast commanded, and yet there is room. And the lord said unto the servant, Go out into the highways and hedges, and compel them to come in, that my house may be filled.

Course Ref/s - Citation/s

T-28.III.8-9 - Be not afraid, my child, but let your world be gently lit by miracles. And where the little gap was seen to stand between you and your brother, join him there. And so sickness will now be seen without a cause. The dream of healing in forgiveness lies, and gently shows you that you never sinned. The miracle would leave no proof of guilt to bring you witness to what never was. And in your storehouse it will make a place of welcome for your Father and your Self. The door is open, that <u>all those</u>

may come who would no longer starve, and would enjoy the feast of plenty set before them there. And they will meet with your invited Guests the miracle has asked to come to you.

This is a feast unlike indeed to those the dreaming of the world has shown. For here, the more that anyone receives, the more is left for all the rest to share. The Guests have brought unlimited supply with Them. And no one is deprived or can deprive. Here is a feast the Father lays before His Son, and shares it equally with him. And in Their sharing there can be no gap in which abundance falters and grows thin. Here can the lean years enter not, for time waits not upon this feast, which has no end. For love has set its table in the space that seemed to keep your Guests apart from you.

Bible Reference - Text

Luke 15:7 - I say unto you, that likewise joy shall be in heaven over one sinner that repenteth, more than over ninety and nine just persons, which need no repentance.

Course Ref/s - Citation/s

T-13.II.8-9 - The Atonement has always been interpreted as the release from guilt, and this is correct if it is understood. Yet even when I interpret it for you, you may reject it and do not accept it for yourself. You have perhaps recognized the futility of the ego and its offerings, but though you do not want them, you may not yet look upon the alternative with gladness. In the extreme, you are afraid of redemption and you believe it will kill you. Make no mistake about the depth of this fear. For you believe that, in the presence of truth you might turn on yourself and destroy yourself.

Little child, this is not so. Your "guilty secret" is nothing, and if you will but bring it to the light, the light will dispel it. And then no dark cloud will remain between you and the remembrance of your Father, for you will remember His guiltless Son, who did not die because he is immortal. And you will see that you were redeemed with him, and have never been separated from him. In this understanding lies your remembering, for it is the recognition of love without fear. There will be great joy in Heaven on your homecoming, and the joy will be yours. For the redeemed son of man is the guiltless Son of God, and to recognize him is your redemption.

T-13.IX.6 - See no one, then, as guilty, and you will affirm the truth of guiltlessness unto yourself. In every condemnation that you offer the Son of God lies the conviction of your own guilt. If you would have the Holy Spirit make you free of it, accept His offer of Atonement for all your brothers. For so you learn that it is true for you. Remember always that it is impossible to condemn the Son of God in part. Those whom you see as guilty become the witnesses to guilt in you, and you will see it there, for it is there until it is undone. Guilt is always in your mind, which has condemned itself. Project it not, for while you do, it cannot be undone. With everyone whom you release from guilt great is the joy in Heaven, where the witnesses to your fatherhood rejoice.

T-26.IV.5-6 - Where sin once was perceived will rise a world that will become an altar to the truth, and you will join the lights of Heaven there, and sing their song of gratitude and praise. And as they come to you to be complete, so will you go with them. For no one hears the song of Heaven and remains without a voice that adds its power to the song, and makes it sweeter still. And each one joins the singing at the altar that was raised within the tiny spot that sin proclaimed to be its own. And what was tiny then has soared into a magnitude of song in which the universe has joined with but a single voice.

This tiny spot of sin that stands between you and your brother still is holding back the happy opening of Heaven's gate. How little is the hindrance that withholds the wealth of Heaven from you. And how great will be the joy in Heaven when you join the mighty chorus to the Love of God!

Bible Reference - Text

Luke 15:11-32 - And he said, A certain man had two sons: And the younger of them said to his father, Father, give me the portion of goods that falleth to me. And he divided unto them his living. And not many days after the younger son gathered all together, and took his journey into a far country, and there wasted his substance with riotous living. And when he had spent all, there arose a mighty famine in that land; and he began to be in want. And he went and joined himself to a citizen of that country; and he sent him into his fields to feed swine. And he would fain have filled his belly with the husks that the swine did eat: and no man gave unto him. And when he came to himself, he said, How many hired servants of my father's have bread enough and to spare, and I perish with hunger! I will arise and go to my father, and will say unto him, Father, I have sinned against heaven, and before thee, And am no more worthy to be called thy son: make me as one of thy hired servants. And he arose, and came to his father.

But when he was yet a great way off, his father saw him, and had compassion, and ran, and fell on his neck, and kissed him. And the son said unto him, Father, I have sinned against heaven, and in thy sight, and am no more worthy to be called thy son. But the father said to his servants, Bring forth the best robe, and put it on him; and put a ring on his hand, and shoes on his feet: And bring hither the fatted calf, and kill it; and let us eat, and be merry: For this my son was dead, and is alive again; he was lost, and is found. And they began to be merry.

Now his elder son was in the field: and as he came and drew nigh to the house, he heard musick and dancing. And he called one of the servants, and asked what these things meant. And he said unto him, Thy brother is come; and thy father hath killed the fatted calf, because he hath received him safe and sound. And he was angry, and would not go in: therefore came his father out, and intreated him. And he answering said to his father, Lo, these many years do I serve thee, neither transgressed I at any time thy commandment: and yet thou never gavest me a kid, that I might make merry with my friends: But as soon as this thy son was come, which hath devoured thy living with harlots, thou hast killed for him the fatted calf. And he said unto him, Son, thou art ever with me, and all that I have is thine. It was meet that we should make merry, and be glad: for this thy brother was dead, and is alive again; and was lost, and is found.

Course Ref/s - Citation/s

T-08.VI.4 - Listen to the story of the prodigal son, and learn what God's treasure is and yours: This son of a loving father left his home and thought he had squandered everything for nothing of any value, although he had not understood its worthlessness at the time. He was ashamed to return to his father, because he thought he had hurt him. Yet when he came home the father welcomed him with joy, because the son himself was his father's treasure. He wanted nothing else.

T-11.VI.6 - Resurrection must compel your allegiance gladly, because it is the symbol of joy. Its whole compelling power lies in the fact that it represents what you want to be. The freedom to leave behind everything that hurts you and humbles you and frightens you cannot be thrust upon you, but it can be offered you through the grace of God. And you can accept it by His grace, for God is gracious to His Son, accepting him without question as His Own. Who, then, is your own? The Father has given you all that is His, and He Himself is yours with them. Guard them in their resurrection, for otherwise you will not awake in God, safely surrounded by what is yours forever.

T-14.III.11 - It will never happen that you must make decisions for yourself. You are not bereft of help, and Help that knows the answer. Would you be content with little, which is all that you alone can offer yourself, when He Who gives you everything will simply offer it to you? He will never ask what you have done to make you worthy of the gift of God. Ask it not therefore of yourself. Instead, accept His answer, for He knows that you are worthy of everything God wills for you. Do not try to escape the gift of God He so freely and so gladly offers you. He offers you but what God gave Him for you. You need not decide whether or not you are deserving of it. God knows you are.

T-15.III.4 - There is no doubt about what your function is, for the Holy Spirit knows what it is. There is no doubt about its magnitude, for it reaches you through Him from Magnitude. You do not have to strive for it, because you have it. All your striving must be directed against littleness, for it does require vigilance to protect your magnitude in this world. To hold your magnitude in perfect awareness in a world of littleness is a task the little cannot undertake. Yet it is asked of you, in tribute to your magnitude and not your littleness. Nor is it asked of you alone. The power of God will support every effort you make on behalf of His dear Son. Search for the little, and you deny yourself His power. God is not willing that His Son be content with less than everything. For He is not content without His Son, and His Son cannot be content with less than His Father has given him.

T-19.IV.D.18:4-19:6 - Offer your brother freedom and complete release from sin, here in the garden of seeming agony and death. So will we prepare together the way unto the resurrection of God's Son, and let him rise again to glad remembrance of his Father, Who knows no sin, no death, but only life eternal.

Together we will disappear into the Presence beyond the veil, not to be lost but found; not to be seen but known. And knowing, nothing in the plan God has established for salvation will be left undone. This is the journey's purpose, without which is the journey meaningless. Here is the peace of God, given to you eternally by Him. Here is the rest and quiet that you seek, the reason for the journey from its beginning. Heaven is the gift you owe your brother, the debt of gratitude you offer to the Son of God in thanks for what he is, and what his Father created him to be.

Bible Reference - Text

Luke 15:11-32 - And he said, A certain man had two sons:.... (Continued) - (To read the full text of the above go to page 279.)

Course Ref/s - Citation/s

T-29.I.8:3-9:6 - Would you know that nothing stands between you and your brother? Would you know there is no gap behind which you can hide? There is a shock that comes to those who learn their savior is their enemy no more. There is a wariness that is aroused by learning that the body is not real. And there are overtones of seeming fear around the happy message, "God is Love."

Yet all that happens when the gap is gone is peace eternal. Nothing more than that, and nothing less. Without the fear of God, what could induce you to abandon Him? What toys or trinkets in the gap could serve to hold you back an instant from His Love? Would you allow the body to say "no" to Heaven's calling, were you not afraid to find a loss of self in finding God? Yet can your self be lost by being found?

W-pI.193.11 - Give all you can, and give a little more. For now we would arise in haste and go unto our Father's house. We have been gone too long, and we would linger here no more. And as we practice, let us think about all things we saved to settle by ourselves, and kept apart from healing. Let us give them all to Him Who knows the way to look upon them so that they will disappear. Truth is His message; truth His teaching is. His are the lessons God would have us learn.

W-pII.249.1-2 - Forgiveness paints a picture of a world where suffering is over, loss becomes impossible and anger makes no sense. Attack is gone, and madness has an end. What suffering is now conceivable? What loss can be sustained? The world becomes a place of joy, abundance, charity and endless giving. It is now so like to Heaven that it quickly is transformed into the light that it reflects. And so the journey which the Son of God began has ended in the light from which he came.

Father, we would return our minds to You. We have betrayed them, held them in a vice of bitterness, and frightened them with thoughts of violence and death. Now would we rest again in You, as You created us.

W-pII.fl.6 - We come in honesty to God and say we did not understand, and ask Him to help us to learn His lessons, through the Voice of His Own Teacher. Would He hurt His Son? Or would He rush to answer him, and say, "This is my Son, and all I have is his"? Be certain He will answer thus, for these are His Own Words to you. And more than that can no one ever have, for in these words is all there is, and all that there will be throughout all time and in eternity.

C-6.4 - The Holy Spirit abides in the part of your mind that is part of the Christ Mind. He represents your Self and your Creator, Who are One. He speaks for God and also for you, being joined with Both. And therefore it is He Who proves Them One. He seems to be a Voice, for in that form He speaks God's Word to you. He seems to be a Guide through a far country, for you need that form of help. He seems to be whatever meets the needs you think you have. But He is not deceived when you perceive your self entrapped in needs you do not have. It is from these He would deliver you. It is from these that He would make you safe.

M-19.5 - Pray for God's justice, and do not confuse His mercy with your own insanity. Perception can make whatever picture the mind desires to see. Remember this. In this lies either Heaven or hell, as you elect. God's justice points to Heaven just because it is entirely impartial. It accepts all evidence that is brought before it, omitting nothing and assessing nothing as separate and apart from, all the rest. From this one standpoint does it judge, and this alone. Here all attack and condemnation becomes meaningless and indefensible. Perception rests, the mind is still, and light returns again. Vision is now restored. What had been lost has now been found. The peace of God descends on all the world, and we can see. And we can see!

S-2.III.3 - Do not establish what the form should be that Christ's forgiveness takes. He knows the way to make of every call a help to you, as you arise in haste to go at last unto your Father's house. Now can He make your footsteps sure, your words sincere; not with your own sincerity, but with His Own. Let Him take charge of how you would forgive, and each occasion then will be to you another step to Heaven and to peace.

Bible Reference - Text

Luke 16:8 - And the lord commended the unjust steward, because he had done wisely: for the children of this world are in their generation wiser than the children of light.

Course Ref/s - Citation/s

T-11.III.1- <u>The children of light</u> cannot abide in darkness, for darkness is not in them. Do not be deceived by the dark comforters, and never let them enter the mind of God's Son, for they have no place in His temple. When you are tempted to deny Him remember that there are no other gods to place before Him, and accept His Will for you in peace. For you cannot accept it otherwise.

Bible Reference - Text

Luke 17:5-6 - And the apostles said unto the Lord, Increase our faith. And the Lord said, If ye had faith as a grain of mustard seed, ye might say unto this sycamine tree, Be thou plucked up by the root, and be thou planted in the sea; and it should obey you.

Course Ref/s - Citation/s

T-17.VII.3 - A situation is a relationship, being the joining of thoughts. If problems are perceived, it is because the thoughts are judged to be in conflict. But if the goal is truth, this is impossible. Some idea of bodies must have entered, for minds cannot attack. The thought of bodies is the sign of faithlessness, for bodies cannot solve anything. It is their intrusion on the relationship, an error in your thoughts about the situation, which then becomes the justification for your lack of faith. You will make this error, but be not at all concerned with that. The error does not matter. Faithlessness brought to faith will never interfere with truth.
But faithlessness used against truth will always destroy faith. <u>If you lack faith, ask that it be restored</u> where it was lost, and seek not to have it made up to you elsewhere, as if you had been unjustly deprived of it.

T-17.VII.4 - Only what you have not given can be lacking in any situation. But remember this; the goal of holiness was set for your relationship, and not by you. You did not set it because holiness cannot be seen except through faith, and your relationship was not holy because your faith in your brother was so limited and little. <u>Your faith must grow</u> to meet the goal that has been set. The goal's reality will call this forth, for you will see that peace and faith will not come separately. What situation can you be in without faith, and remain faithful to your brother?

Bible Reference - Text

Luke 17:21 - Neither shall they say, Lo here! or, lo there! for, behold, the kingdom of God is within you.

Course Ref/s - Citation/s

T-04.III.1:1-6 - It is hard to understand what "<u>The Kingdom of Heaven is within you</u>" really means. This is because it is not understandable to the ego, which interprets it as if something outside is inside, and this does not mean anything. The word "within" is unnecessary. The Kingdom of Heaven is you. What else but you did the Creator create, and what else but you is His Kingdom? This is the whole message of the Atonement; a message which in its totality transcends the sum of its parts.

T-04.III.9 - In your own mind, though denied by the ego, is the declaration of your release. God has given you everything. This one fact means the ego does not exist, and this makes it profoundly afraid. In the ego's language, "to have" and "to be" are different, but they are identical to the Holy Spirit. The Holy Spirit knows that you both have everything and are everything. Any distinction in this respect is meaningful only when the idea of "getting," which implies a lack, has already been accepted. That is why we make no distinction between having <u>the Kingdom of God</u> and being <u>the Kingdom of God</u>.

T-05.II.4 - You are <u>the Kingdom of Heaven,</u> but you have let the belief in darkness enter your mind and so you need a new light. The Holy Spirit is the radiance that you must let banish the idea of darkness. His is the glory before which dissociation falls away, and the Kingdom of Heaven breaks through into its own. Before the separation you did not need guidance. You knew as you will know again, but as you do not know now.

T-06.IV.2:1-5 - When <u>God</u> created you He made you part of Him. That is why attack <u>within the Kingdom</u> is impossible. You made the ego without love, and so it does not love you. You could not remain within the Kingdom without love, and since the Kingdom is love, you believe that you are without it. This enables the ego to regard itself as separate and outside its maker, thus speaking for the part of your mind that believes you are separate and outside the Mind of God.

T-06.IV.6 - Hear, then, the one answer of the Holy Spirit to all the questions the ego raises: <u>You are a child of God, a priceless part of His Kingdom</u>, which He created as part of Him. Nothing else exists and only this is real. You have chosen a sleep in which you have had bad dreams, but the sleep is not real and God calls you to awake. There will be nothing left of your dream when you hear Him, because you will awaken. Your dreams contain many of the ego's symbols and they have confused you. Yet that was only because you were asleep and did not know. When you wake you will see the truth around you and you will no longer believe in dreams, because they will have no reality for you. Yet the Kingdom and all that you have created there will have great reality for you, because they are beautiful and true.

T-08.III.6 - The Kingdom cannot be found alone, and <u>you who are the Kingdom</u> cannot find yourself alone. To achieve the goal of the curriculum, then, you cannot listen to the ego, whose purpose is to defeat its own goal. The ego does not know this, because it does not know anything. But you can know it, and you will know it if you are willing to look at what the ego would make of you. This is your responsibility, because once you have really looked at it you will accept the Atonement for yourself. What other choice could you make? Having made this choice you will understand why you once believed that, when you met someone else, you thought he was someone else. And every holy encounter in which you enter fully will teach you this is not so.

T-11.VIII.8 - Beautiful child of God, you are asking only for what I promised you. Do you believe I would deceive you? <u>The Kingdom of Heaven is within you.</u> Believe that the truth is in me, for I know that it is in you. God's Sons have nothing they do not share. Ask for truth of any Son of God, and you have asked it of me. Not one of us but has the answer in him, to give to anyone who asks it of him.

T-15.III.9 - <u>Holy child of God</u>, when will you learn that only holiness can content you and give you peace? Remember that you learn not for yourself alone, no more than I did. It is because I learned for you that you can learn of me. I would but teach you what is yours, so that together we can replace the shabby littleness that binds the host of God to guilt and weakness with the glad awareness of the glory that is in him. My birth in you is your awakening to grandeur. Welcome me not into a manger, but into the altar to holiness, where holiness abides in perfect peace. <u>My Kingdom</u> is not of this world because it <u>is in you</u>. And you are of your Father. Let us join in honoring you, who must remain forever beyond littleness.

Bible Reference - Text

Luke 17:21 - Neither shall they say, Lo here! or, lo there! for, behold, the kingdom of God is within you. (Continued)

Course Ref/s - Citation/s

T-18.VI.1 - There is nothing outside you. That is what you must ultimately learn, for it is the realization that <u>the Kingdom of Heaven</u> is restored to you. For God created only this, and He did not depart from it nor leave it separate from Himself. The Kingdom of Heaven is the dwelling place of the Son of God, who left not his Father and dwells not apart from Him. Heaven is not a place nor a condition. It is merely an awareness of perfect Oneness, and the knowledge that there is nothing else; nothing outside this Oneness, and nothing else within.

T-25.IV.5 - <u>In you is all of Heaven.</u> Every leaf that falls is given life in you. Each bird that ever sang will sing again in you. And every flower that ever bloomed has saved its perfume and its loveliness for you. What aim can supersede the Will of God and of His Son, that Heaven be restored to him for whom it was created as his only home? Nothing before and nothing after it. No other place; no other state nor time. Nothing beyond nor nearer. Nothing else. In any form. This can you bring to all the world, and all the thoughts that entered it and were mistaken for a little while. How better could your own mistakes be brought to truth than by your willingness to bring the light of Heaven with you, as you walk beyond the world of darkness into light?

T-29.VIII.9 - God has not many Sons, but only One. Who can have more, and who be given less? In Heaven would the Son of God but laugh, if idols could intrude upon his peace. It is for him the Holy Spirit speaks, and tells you idols have no purpose here. For more than Heaven can you never have.

If <u>Heaven is within</u>, why would you seek for idols that would make of Heaven less, to give you more than God bestowed upon your brother and on you, as one with Him? God gave you all there is. And to be sure you could not lose it, did He also give the same to every living thing as well. And thus is every living thing a part of you, as of Himself. No idol can establish you as more than God. But you will never be content with being less.

W-pI.77.3 - Today we will claim the miracles which are your right, since they belong to you. You have been promised full release from the world you made. You have been assured that <u>the Kingdom of God is within you</u>, and can never be lost. We ask no more than what belongs to us in truth. Today, however, we will also make sure that we will not content ourselves with less.

Bible Reference - Text

Luke 19:1-10 - And Jesus entered and passed through Jericho. And, behold, there was a man named Zacchaeus, which was the chief among the publicans, and he was rich. And he sought to see Jesus who he was; and could not for the press, because he was little of stature. And he ran before, and climbed up into a sycamore tree to see him: for he was to pass that way. And when Jesus came to the place, he looked up, and saw him, and said unto him, Zacchaeus, make haste, and come down; for to day I must abide at thy house.

And he made haste, and came down, and received him joyfully. And when they saw it, they all murmured, saying, That he was gone to be guest with a man that is a sinner.

And Zacchaeus stood, and said unto the Lord: Behold, Lord, the half of my goods I give to the poor; and if I have taken any thing from any man by false accusation, I restore him fourfold.

And Jesus said unto him, This day is salvation come to this house, forsomuch as he also is a son of Abraham. For the Son of man is come to seek and to save that which was lost.

Course Ref/s - Citation/s

T-pr.WIS.11 - The opposite of seeing through the body's eyes is <u>the vision of Christ</u>, which reflects strength rather than weakness, unity rather than separation, and love rather than fear. The opposite of hearing through the body's ears is communication through the Voice for God, the Holy Spirit, which abides in each of us. His Voice seems distant and difficult to hear because the ego, which speaks for the little, separated self, seems to be much louder. This is actually reversed. The Holy Spirit speaks with unmistakable clarity and overwhelming appeal. No one who does not choose to identify with the body could possibly be deaf to His messages of release and hope, nor could he fail to accept joyously the vision of Christ in glad exchange for his miserable picture of himself.

T-12.VI.4 - Correction is for all who cannot see. To open the eyes of the blind is the Holy Spirit's mission, for He knows that they have not lost their vision, but merely sleep. He would awaken them from the sleep of forgetting to the remembering of God. <u>Christ's eyes</u> are open, and He will look upon whatever you see with love if you accept His vision as yours. The Holy Spirit keeps <u>the vision of Christ</u> for every Son of God who sleeps. In His sight the Son of God is perfect, and He longs to share His vision with you. He will show you the real world because God gave you Heaven. Through Him your Father calls His Son to remember.
The awakening of His Son begins with his investment in the real world, and by this he will learn to re-invest in himself. For reality is one with the Father and the Son, and the Holy Spirit blesses the real world in Their Name.

T-13.V.6 - As you look with open eyes upon your world, it must occur to you that you have withdrawn into insanity. You see what is not there, and you hear what makes no sound. Your manifestations of emotions are the opposite of what the emotions are. You communicate with no one, and you are as isolated from reality as if you were alone in all the universe. In your madness you overlook reality completely, and you see only your own split mind everywhere you look. God calls you and you do not hear, for you are preoccupied with your own voice. And <u>the vision of Christ</u> is not in your sight, for you look upon yourself alone.

T-13.V.9 - Do not seek vision through your eyes, for you made your way of seeing that you might see in darkness, and in this you are deceived. Beyond this darkness, and yet still within you, is <u>the vision of Christ, Who looks on all in light</u>. Your "vision" comes from fear, as His from love. And He sees for you, as your witness to the real world. He is the Holy Spirit's manifestation, looking always on the real world, and calling forth its witnesses and drawing them to you. He loves what He sees within you, and He would extend it. And He will not return unto the Father until He has extended your perception even unto Him. And there perception is no more, for He has returned you to the Father with Him.

Bible Reference - Text

Luke 19:1-10 - And Jesus entered and passed through Jericho.... (Continued) - (To read the full text of the above go to page 288.)

Course Ref/s - Citation/s

T-13.VI.13 - And yet the laws of love are not suspended because you sleep. And you have followed them through all your nightmares, and have been faithful in your giving, for you were not alone. Even in sleep has Christ protected you, ensuring the real world for you when you awake. In your name He has given for you, and given you the gifts He gave. God's Son is still as loving as his Father. Continuous with his Father, he has no past apart from Him. So he has never ceased to be his Father's witness and his own. Although he slept, Christ's vision did not leave him. And so it is that he can call unto himself the witnesses that teach him that he never slept.

T-13.VIII.2 - The very real difference between perception and knowledge becomes quite apparent if you consider this: There is nothing partial about knowledge. Every aspect is whole, and therefore no aspect is separate. You are an aspect of knowledge, being in the Mind of God, Who knows you. All knowledge must be yours, for in you is all knowledge. Perception, at its loftiest, is never complete. Even the perception of the Holy Spirit, as perfect as perception can be, is without meaning in Heaven. Perception can reach everywhere under His guidance, for the vision of Christ beholds everything in light. Yet no perception, however holy, will last forever.

T-14.VII.6 - The Holy Spirit asks of you but this; bring to Him every secret you have locked away from Him. Open every door to Him, and bid Him enter the darkness and lighten it away. At your request He enters gladly. He brings the light to darkness if you make the darkness open to Him. But what you hide He cannot look upon. He sees for you, and unless you look with Him He cannot see. The vision of Christ is not for Him alone, but for Him with you. Bring, therefore, all your dark and secret thoughts to Him, and look upon them with Him. He holds the light, and you the darkness. They cannot coexist when both of you together look on them. His judgment must prevail, and He will give it to you as you join your perception to His.

T-22.I.7 - So in each holy relationship is the ability to communicate instead of separate reborn. Yet a holy relationship, so recently reborn itself from an unholy relationship, and yet more ancient than the old illusion it has replaced, is like a baby now in its rebirth. Still in this infant is your vision returned to you, and he will speak the language you can understand. He is not nurtured by the "something else" you thought was you. He was not given there, nor was received by anything except yourself. For no two brothers can unite except through <u>Christ, Whose vision</u> sees them one.

T-22.II.12-13 - Beyond the body that you interposed between you and your brother, and shining in the golden light that reaches it from the bright, endless circle that extends forever, is your holy relationship, beloved of God Himself. How still it rests, in time and yet beyond, immortal yet on earth. How great the power that lies in it. Time waits upon its will, and earth will be as it would have it be. Here is no separate will, nor the desire that anything be separate. Its will has no exceptions, and what it wills is true. Every illusion brought to its forgiveness is gently overlooked and disappears. For at its center <u>Christ</u> has been reborn, to light His home <u>with vision</u> that overlooks the world. Would you not have this holy home be yours as well? No misery is here, but only joy.

All you need do to dwell in quiet here with <u>Christ</u> is share <u>His vision</u>. Quickly and gladly is His vision given anyone who is but willing to see his brother sinless. And no one can remain beyond this willingness, if you would be released entirely from all effects of sin. Would you have partial forgiveness for yourself? Can you reach Heaven while a single sin still tempts you to remain in misery? Heaven is the home of perfect purity, and God created it for you. Look on your holy brother, sinless as yourself, and let him lead you there.

T-24.II.5 - You can defend your specialness, but never will you hear the Voice for God beside it. They speak a different language and they fall on different ears. To every special one a different message, and one with different meaning, is the truth. Yet how can truth be different to each one? The special messages the special hear convince them they are different and apart; each in his special sins and "safe" from love, which does not see his specialness at all. <u>Christ's vision</u> is their "enemy," for it sees not what they would look upon, and it would show them that the specialness they think they see is an illusion.

Bible Reference - Text

Luke 19:1-10 - And Jesus entered and passed through Jericho.... (Continued) - (To read the full text of the above go to page 288.)

Course Ref/s - Citation/s

T-24.V.7 - Yet is He [Christ] quiet, for He knows that love is in you now, and safely held in you by that same hand that holds your brother's in your own. Christ's hand holds all His brothers in Himself. He gives them vision for their sightless eyes, and sings to them of Heaven, that their ears may hear no more the sound of battle and of death. He reaches through them, holding out His hand, that everyone may bless all living things, and see their holiness. And He rejoices that these sights are yours, to look upon with Him and share His joy. His perfect lack of specialness He offers you, that you may save, all living things from death, receiving from each one the gift of life that your forgiveness offers to your Self. The sight of Christ is all there is to see. The song of Christ is all there is to hear. The hand of Christ is all there is to hold. There is no journey but to walk with Him.

T-31.VII.13 - The savior's vision is as innocent of what your brother is as it is free of any judgment made upon yourself. It sees no past in anyone at all. And thus it serves a wholly open mind, unclouded by old concepts, and prepared to look on only what the present holds. It cannot judge because it does not know. And recognizing this, it merely asks, "What is the meaning of what I behold?" Then is the answer given. And the door held open for the face of Christ to shine upon the one who asks, in innocence, to see beyond the veil of old ideas and ancient concepts held so long and dear against the vision of the Christ in you.

T-31.VIII.8 - My brothers in salvation, do not fail to hear my voice and listen to my words. I [Jesus] ask for nothing but your own release. There is no place for hell within a world whose loveliness can yet be so intense and so inclusive it is but a step from there to Heaven. To your tired eyes I bring a vision of a different world, so new and clean and fresh you will forget the pain and sorrow that you saw before. Yet this a vision is which you must share with everyone you see, for otherwise you will behold it not. To give this gift is how to make it yours. And God ordained, in loving kindness, that it be for you.

W-pI.059.3 - God is my Source. I cannot see apart from Him. I can see what God wants me to see. I cannot see anything else. Beyond His Will lie only illusions. It is these I choose when I think I can see apart from Him. It is these I choose when I try to see through the body's eyes. Yet <u>the vision of Christ</u> has been given me to replace them. It is through this vision that I choose to see.

W-pI.158.05-06 - A teacher does not give experience, because he did not learn it. It revealed itself to him at its appointed time. But vision is his gift. This he can give directly, for <u>Christ's</u> knowledge is not lost, because <u>He has a vision</u> He can give to anyone who asks. The Father's Will and His are joined in knowledge. Yet there is a vision which the Holy Spirit sees because the Mind of Christ beholds it too.

Here is the joining of the world of doubt and shadows made with the intangible. Here is a quiet place within the world made holy by forgiveness and by love. Here are all contradictions reconciled, for here the journey ends. Experience - unlearned, untaught, unseen - is merely there. This is beyond our goal, for it transcends what needs to be accomplished. Our concern is with <u>Christ's vision</u>. This we can attain.

W-pI.158.07 - <u>Christ's vision</u> has one law. It does not look upon a body, and mistake it for the Son whom God created. It beholds a light beyond the body; an idea beyond what can be touched, a purity undimmed by errors, pitiful mistakes, and fearful thoughts of guilt from dreams of sin. It sees no separation. And it looks on everyone, on every circumstance, all happenings and all events, without the slightest fading of the light it sees.

W-pI.158.8:3-9:6 - And this you give today: See no one as a body. Greet him as the Son of God he is, acknowledging that he is one with you in holiness.

Thus are his sins forgiven him, for <u>Christ has vision</u> that has power to overlook them all. In His forgiveness are they gone. Unseen by One they merely disappear, because a vision of the holiness that lies beyond them comes to take their place. It matters not what form they took, nor how enormous they appeared to be, nor who seemed to be hurt by them. They are no more. And all effects they seemed to have are gone with them, undone and never to be done.

W-pI.158.10 - Thus do you learn to give as you receive. And thus <u>Christ's vision</u> looks on you as well. This lesson is not difficult to learn, if you remember in your brother you but see yourself. If he be lost in sin, so must you be, if you see light in him, your sins have been forgiven by yourself. Each brother whom you meet today provides another chance to let Christ's vision shine on you, and offer you the peace of God.

Bible Reference - Text

Luke 19:1-10 - And Jesus entered and passed through Jericho.... (Continued) - (To read the full text of the above go to page 288.)

Course Ref/s - Citation/s

W-pI.159.3 - Christ's vision is a miracle. It comes from far beyond itself, for it reflects eternal love and the rebirth of love which never dies, but has been kept obscure. Christ's vision pictures Heaven, for it sees a world so like to Heaven that what God created perfect can be mirrored there. The darkened glass the world presents can show but twisted images in broken parts. The real world pictures Heaven's innocence.

W-pI.159.4 - Christ's vision is the miracle in which all miracles are born. It is their source, remaining with each miracle you give, and yet remaining yours. It is the bond by which the giver and receiver are united in extension here on earth, as they are one in Heaven. Christ beholds no sin in anyone. And in His sight the sinless are as one. Their holiness was given by His Father and Himself.

W-pI.159.5 - Christ's vision is the bridge between the worlds. And in its power can you safely trust to carry you from this world into one made holy by forgiveness. Things which seem quite solid here are merely shadows there; transparent, faintly seen, at times forgot, and never able to obscure the light that shines beyond them. Holiness has been restored to vision, and the blind can see.

W-pI.159.8 - Christ's vision is the holy ground in which the lilies of forgiveness set their roots. This is their home. They can be brought from here back to the world, but they can never grow in its unnourishing and shallow soil. They need the light and warmth and kindly care Christ's charity provides. They need the love with which He looks on them. And they become His messengers, who give as they received.

W-pI.161.08-09 - Who sees a brother as a body sees him as fear's symbol. And he will attack, because what he beholds is his own fear external to himself, poised to attack, and howling to unite with him again. Mistake not the intensity of rage projected fear must spawn. It shrieks in wrath, and claws the air in frantic hope it can reach to its maker and devour him.

This do the body's eyes behold in one whom Heaven cherishes, the angels love and God created perfect. This is his reality. And in <u>Christ's vision</u> is his loveliness reflected in a form so holy and so beautiful that you could scarce refrain from kneeling at his feet. Yet you will take his hand instead, for you are like him in the sight that sees him thus. Attack on him is enemy to you, for you will not perceive that in his hands is your salvation.
Ask him but for this, and he will give it to you. Ask him not to symbolize your fear. Would you request that love destroy itself? Or would you have it revealed to you and set you free?

W-pI.161.11 - Select one brother, symbol of the rest, and ask salvation of him. See him first as clearly as you can, in that same form to which you are accustomed. See his face, his hands and feet, his clothing. Watch him smile, and see familiar gestures which he makes so frequently. Then think of this: What you are seeing now conceals from you the sight of one who can forgive you all your sins; whose sacred hands can take away the nails which pierce your own, and lift the crown of thorns which you have placed upon your bleeding head. Ask this of him, that he may set you free: Give me your blessing, holy Son of God. I would behold you with <u>the eyes of Christ</u>, and see my perfect sinlessness in you.

W-pI.164.ti-1 - Now are we one with Him Who is our Source.

What time but now can truth be recognized? The present is the only time there is. And so today, this instant, now, we come to look upon what is forever there; not in our sight, but in <u>the eyes of Christ</u>. He looks past time, and sees eternity as represented there. He hears the sounds the senseless, busy world engenders, yet He hears them faintly. For beyond them all He hears the song of Heaven, and the Voice for God more clear, more meaningful, more near.

W-pI.165.4-5 - Deny not Heaven. It is yours today, but for the asking. Nor need you perceive how great the gift, how changed your mind will be before it comes to you. Ask to receive, and it is given you. Conviction lies within it. Till you welcome it as yours, uncertainty remains. Yet God is fair. Sureness is not required to receive what only your acceptance can bestow.

Ask with desire. You need not be sure that you request the only thing you want. But when you have received, you will be sure you have the treasure you have always sought. What would you then exchange for it? What would induce you now to let it fade away from your ecstatic vision? For this sight proves that you have exchanged your blindness for the seeing eyes of Christ; your mind has come to lay aside denial, and accept the Thought of God as your inheritance.

Bible Reference - Text

Luke 19:1-10 - And Jesus entered and passed through Jericho.... (Continued) - (To read the full text of the above go to page 288.)

Course Ref/s - Citation/s

W-pII.13.3 - Forgiveness is the home of miracles. The eyes of Christ deliver them to all they look upon in mercy and in love. Perception stands corrected in His sight, and what was meant to curse has come to bless. Each lily of forgiveness offers all the world the silent miracle of love. And each is laid before the Word of God, upon the universal altar to Creator and creation in the light of perfect purity and endless joy.

W-pII.14.4 - Ours are the eyes through which Christ's vision sees a world redeemed from every thought of sin. Ours are the ears that hear the Voice for God proclaim the world as sinless. Ours the minds that join together as we bless the world. And from the oneness that we have attained we call to all our brothers, asking them to share our peace and consummate our joy.

W-pII.237.ti-2 - Now would I be as God created me.

Today I will accept the truth about myself. I will arise in glory, and allow the light in me to shine upon the world throughout the day. I bring the world the tidings of salvation which I hear as God my Father speaks to me. And I behold the world that Christ would have me see, aware it ends the bitter dream of death; aware it is my Father's Call to me.

Christ is my eyes today, and He the ears that listen to the Voice for God today. Father, I come to You through Him Who is Your Son, and my true Self as well. Amen.

W-pII.247.ti-2 - Without forgiveness I will still be blind.

Sin is the symbol of attack. Behold it anywhere, and I will suffer.
For forgiveness is the only means whereby Christ's vision comes to me.
Let me accept what His sight shows me as the simple truth, and I am
healed completely. Brother, come and let me look on you. Your loveliness
reflects my own. Your sinlessness is mine. You stand forgiven, and I stand
with you.

So would I look on everyone today. My brothers are Your Sons. Your
Fatherhood created them, and gave them all to me as part of You, and my
own Self as well. Today I honor You through them, and thus I hope this
day to recognize my Self.

W-pII.263.ti-2 - My holy vision sees all things as pure.

Father, Your Mind created all that is, Your Spirit entered into it, Your
Love gave life to it. And would I look upon what You created as if it could
be made sinful? I would not perceive such dark and fearful images.
A madman's dream is hardly fit to be my choice, instead of all the
loveliness with which You bless creation; all its purity, its joy, and its
eternal, quiet home in You.

And while we still remain outside the gate of Heaven, let us look on all we
see through holy vision and the eyes of Christ. Let all appearances seem
pure to us, that we may pass them by in innocence, and walk together to
our Father's house as brothers and the holy Sons of God.

W-pII.270.ti-2 - I will not use the body's eyes today.

Father, Christ's vision is Your gift to me, and it has power to translate all
that the body's eyes behold into the sight of a forgiven world. How glorious
and gracious is this world! Yet how much more will I perceive in it than
sight can give. The world forgiven signifies Your Son acknowledges his
Father, lets his dreams be brought to truth, and waits expectantly the one
remaining instant more of time which ends forever, as Your memory
returns to him. And now his will is one with Yours. His function now is
but Your Own, and every thought except Your Own is gone.

The quiet of today will bless our hearts, and through them peace will come
to everyone. Christ is our eyes today. And through His sight we offer
healing to the world through Him, the holy Son whom God created whole;
the holy Son whom God created one.

W-pII.290.1 - Unless I look upon what is not there, my present happiness
is all I see. Eyes that begin to open see at last. And I would have Christ's
vision come to me this very day. What I perceive without God's Own

Correction for the sight I made is frightening and painful to behold. Yet I would not allow my mind to be deceived by the belief the dream I made is real an instant longer. This the day I seek my present happiness, and look on nothing else except the thing I seek.

Bible Reference - Text

Luke 19:1-10 - And Jesus entered and passed through Jericho.... (Continued) - (To read the full text of the above go to page 288.)

Course Ref/s - Citation/s

W-pII.291.1 - Christ's vision looks through me today. His sight shows me all things forgiven and at peace, and offers this same vision to the world. And I accept this vision in its name, both for myself and for the world as well. What loveliness we look upon today! What holiness we see surrounding us! And it is given us to recognize it is a holiness in which we share; it is the Holiness of God Himself.

W-pII.295.1-2 - Christ asks that He may use my eyes today, and thus redeem the world. He asks this gift that He may offer peace of mind to me, and take away all terror and all pain. And as they are removed from me, the dreams that seemed to settle on the world are gone. Redemption must be one. As I am saved, the world is saved with me. For all of us must be redeemed together. Fear appears in many different forms, but love is one.

My Father, Christ has asked a gift of me, and one I give that it be given me. Help me to use the eyes of Christ today, and thus allow the Holy Spirit's Love to bless all things which I may look upon, that His forgiving Love may rest on me.

W-pII.302.1-2 - Father, our eyes are opening at last. Your holy world awaits us, as our sight is finally restored and we can see. We thought we suffered. But we had forgot the Son whom You created. Now we see that darkness is our own imagining, and light is there for us to look upon. Christ's vision changes darkness into light, for fear must disappear when love has come. Let me forgive Your holy world today, that I may look upon its holiness and understand it but reflects my own.

Our Love awaits us as we go to Him, and walks beside us showing us the way. He fails in nothing. He the End we seek, and He the Means by which we go to Him.

W-pII.304.1 - I can obscure my holy sight, if I intrude my world upon it. Nor can I behold <u>the holy sights Christ</u> looks upon, unless it is <u>His vision</u> that I use. Perception is a mirror, not a fact. And what I look on is my state of mind, reflected outward. I would bless the world by looking on it through <u>the eyes of Christ</u>. And I will look upon the certain signs that all my sins have been forgiven me.

W-pII.305.1 - Who uses but <u>Christ's vision</u> finds a peace so deep and quiet, undisturbable and wholly changeless, that the world contains no counterpart. Comparisons are still before this peace. And all the world departs in silence as this peace envelops it, and gently carries it to truth, no more to be the home of fear. For love has come, and healed the world by giving it Christ's peace.

W-pII.306.1 - What but <u>Christ's vision</u> would I use today, when it can offer me a day in which I see a world so like to Heaven that an ancient memory returns to me? Today I can forget the world I made. Today I can go past all fear, and be restored to love and holiness and peace. Today I am redeemed, and born anew into a world of mercy and of care; of loving kindness and the peace of God.

W-pII.312.1-2 - Perception follows judgment. Having judged, we therefore see what we would look upon. For sight can merely serve to offer us what we would have. It is impossible to overlook what we would see, and fail to see what we have chosen to behold. How surely, therefore, must the real world come to greet the holy sight of anyone who takes the Holy Spirit's purpose as his goal for seeing. And he cannot fail to look upon <u>what Christ would have him see</u>, and share Christ's Love for what he looks upon.

I have no purpose for today except to look upon a liberated world, set free from all the judgments I have made. Father, this is Your Will for me today. And therefore it must be my goal as well.

W-pII.313.1-2 - Father, there is a vision which beholds all things as sinless, so that fear has gone, and where it was is love invited in. And love will come wherever it is asked. This vision is Your gift. <u>The eyes of Christ</u> look on a world forgiven. In His sight are all its sins forgiven, for He sees no sin in anything He looks upon. Now let His true perception come to me, that I may waken from the dream of sin and look within upon my sinlessness, which You have kept completely undefiled upon the altar to Your holy Son, the Self with which I would identify.

Let us today behold each other in the sight of Christ. How beautiful we are! How holy and how loving! Brother, come and join with me today. We save the world when we have joined. For in our vision it becomes as holy as the light in us.

Bible Reference - Text

Luke 19:1-10 - And Jesus entered and passed through Jericho.... (Continued) - (To read the full text of the above go to page 288.)

Course Ref/s - Citation/s

W-pII.340.1 - Father, I thank You for today, and for the freedom I am certain it will bring. This day is holy, for today Your Son will be redeemed. His suffering is done. For he will hear Your Voice directing him to find Christ's vision through forgiveness, and be free forever from all suffering. Thanks for today, my Father. I was born into this world but to achieve this day, and what it holds in joy and freedom for Your holy Son and for the world he made, which is released along with him today.

W-pII.349.ti-1 - Today I let Christ's vision look upon All things for me and judge them not, but give Each one a miracle of love instead.
So would I liberate all things I see, and give to them the freedom that I seek. For thus do I obey the law of love, and give what I would find and make my own. It will be given me, because I have chosen it as the gift I want to give. Father, Your gifts are mine. Each one that I accept gives me a miracle to give. And giving as I would receive, I learn Your healing miracles belong to me.

W-pII.In.6 - I am so close to you we cannot fail. Father, we give these holy times to You, in gratitude to Him Who taught us how to leave the world of sorrow in exchange for its replacement, given us by You.
We look not backward now. We look ahead, and fix our eyes upon the journey's end. Accept these little gifts of thanks from us, as through Christ's vision we behold a world beyond the one we made, and take that world to be the full replacement of our own.

C-1.5 - The mind can be right or wrong, depending on the voice to which it listens. Right-mindedness listens to the Holy Spirit, forgives the world, and through <u>Christ's vision</u> sees the real world in its place. This is the final vision, the last perception, the condition in which God takes the final step Himself. Here time and illusions end together.

C-5.5 - Is he [Jesus] the Christ? O yes, along with you. His little life on earth was not enough to teach the mighty lesson that he learned for all of you. He will remain with you to lead you from the hell you made to God. And when you join your will with his, <u>your sight will be his vision, for the eyes of Christ are shared</u>. Walking with him is just as natural as walking with a brother whom you knew since you were born, for such indeed he is. Some bitter idols have been made of him who would be only brother to the world. Forgive him your illusions, and behold how dear a brother he would be to you. For he will set your mind at rest at last and carry it with you unto your God.

C-6.3 - The Holy Spirit is described as the remaining Communication Link between God and His separated Sons. In order to fulfil this special function the Holy Spirit has assumed a dual function. He knows because He is part of God; He perceives because He was sent to save humanity. He is the great correction principle; the bringer of true perception, the inherent power of <u>the vision of Christ</u>. He is the light in which the forgiven world is perceived; in which the face of Christ alone is seen. He never forgets the Creator or His creation. He never forgets the Son of God. He never forgets you. And He brings the Love of your Father to you in an eternal shining that will never be obliterated because God has put it there.

M-18.2 - God's teachers' major lesson is to learn how to react to magic thoughts wholly without anger. Only in this way can they proclaim the truth about themselves. Through them, the Holy Spirit can now speak of the reality of the Son of God. Now He can remind the world of sinlessness, the one unchanged, unchangeable condition of all that God created.
Now He can speak the Word of God to listening ears, and <u>bring Christ's vision to eyes that see</u>. Now is He free to teach all minds the truth of what they are, so they will gladly be returned to Him. And now is guilt forgiven, overlooked completely in His sight and in God's Word.

P-2.II.5 - Different teaching aids appeal to different people. Some forms of religion have nothing to do with God, and some forms of psychotherapy have nothing to do with healing. Yet if pupil and teacher join in sharing one goal, God will enter into their relationship because He has been invited to come in. In the same way, a union of purpose between patient and therapist restores the place of God to ascendance, first through Christ's vision and then through the memory of God Himself. The process of psychotherapy is the return to sanity. Teacher and pupil, therapist and patient, are all insane or they would not be here. Together they can find a pathway out, for no one will find sanity alone.

Bible Reference - Text

Luke 19:1-10 - And Jesus entered and passed through Jericho.... (Continued) - (To read the full text of the above go to page 288.)

Course Ref/s - Citation/s

P-2.II.6 - If healing is an invitation to God to enter into His Kingdom, what difference does it make how the invitation is written? Does the paper matter, or the ink, or the pen? Or is it he who writes that gives the invitation? God comes to those who would restore His world, for they have found the way to call to Him. If any two are joined, He must be there. It does not matter what their purpose is, but they must share it wholly to succeed. It is impossible to share a goal not blessed by Christ, for what is unseen through His eyes is too fragmented to be meaningful.

P-2.VII.2-3 - Think carefully, teacher and therapist, for whom you pray, and who is in need of healing. For therapy is prayer, and healing is its aim and its result. What is prayer except the joining of minds in a relationship which Christ can enter? This is His home, into which psychotherapy invites Him. What is symptom cure, when another is always there to choose? But once Christ enters in, what choice is there except to have Him stay? There is no need for more than this, for it is everything. Healing is here, and happiness and peace. These are the "symptoms" of the ideal patient-therapist relationship, replacing those with which the patient came to ask for help.

The process that takes place in this relationship is actually one in which the therapist in his heart tells the patient that all his sins have been forgiven him, along with his own. What could be the difference between healing and forgiveness? Only Christ forgives, knowing His sinlessness. His vision heals perception and sickness disappears. Nor will it return again, once its cause has been removed. This, however, needs the help of a very advanced therapist, capable of joining with the patient in a holy relationship in which all sense of separation finally is overcome.

S-2.I.6-7 - Forgiveness, truly given, is the way in which your only hope of freedom lies. Others will make mistakes and so will you, as long as this illusion of a world appears to be your home. Yet God Himself has given all His Sons a remedy for all illusions that they think they see. Christ's vision does not use your eyes, but you can look through His and learn to see like Him. Mistakes are tiny shadows, quickly gone, that for an instant only seem to hide the face of Christ, which still remains unchanged behind them all. His constancy remains in tranquil silence and in perfect peace. He does not know of shadows. His the eyes that look past error to the Christ in you.

Ask, then, His help, and ask Him how to learn forgiveness as His vision lets it be. You are in need of what He gives, and your salvation rests on learning this of Him. Prayer cannot be released to Heaven while forgiveness-to- destroy remains with you. God's mercy would remove this withering and poisoned thinking from your holy mind. Christ has forgiven you, and in His sight the world becomes as holy as Himself. Who sees no evil in it sees like Him. For what He has forgiven has not sinned, and guilt can be no more. Salvation's plan is made complete, and sanity has come.

S-2.III.2 - You child of God, the gifts of God are yours, not by your plans but by His holy Will. His Voice will teach you what forgiveness is, and how to give it as He wills it be. Do not, then, seek to understand what is beyond you yet, but let it be a way to draw you up to where the eyes of Christ become the sight you choose. Give up all else, for there nothing else. When someone calls for help in any form, He is the One to answer for you. All that you need do is to step back and not to interfere. Forgiveness-for- Salvation is His task, and it is He Who will respond for you.

S-2.III.5 - "What should I do for him, Your holy Son?" should be the only thing you ever ask when help is needed and forgiveness sought. The form the seeking takes you need not judge. And let it not be you who sets the form in which forgiveness comes to save God's Son. The light of Christ in him is his release, and it is this that answers to his call. Forgive him as the Christ decides you should, and be His eyes through which you look on him, and speak for Him as well. He knows the need; the question and the answer. He will say exactly what to do, in words that you can understand and you can also use. Do not confuse His function with your own. He is the Answer. You the one who hears.

Bible Reference - Text

Luke 22:19 - And he took bread, and gave thanks, and brake it, and gave unto them, saying, This is my body which is given for you: this do in remembrance of me.

Course Ref/s - Citation/s

T-02.V.17 - The injunction "Be of one mind" is the statement for revelation-readiness. My request "<u>Do this in remembrance of me</u>" is the appeal for cooperation from miracle workers. The two statements are not in the same order of reality. Only the latter involves an awareness of time, since to remember is to recall the past in the present. Time is under my direction, but timelessness belongs to God. In time we exist for and with each other. In timelessness we coexist with God.

T-05.III.11 - The ego made the world as it perceives it, but the Holy Spirit, the re-interpreter of what the ego made, sees the world as a teaching device for bringing you home. The Holy Spirit must perceive time, and reinterpret it into the timeless. He must work through opposites, because He must work with and for a mind that is in opposition. Correct and learn, and be open to learning. You have not made truth, but truth can still set you free. Look as the Holy Spirit looks, and understand as He understands. His understanding looks back to God <u>in remembrance of me</u>. He is in communion with God always, and He is part of you. He is your Guide to salvation, because He holds the remembrance of things past and to come, and brings them to the present. He holds this gladness gently in your mind, asking only that you increase it in His Name by sharing it to increase His joy in you.

T-07.V.10 - You cannot forget the Father because I am with you, and I cannot forget Him. To forget me is to forget yourself and Him Who created you. Our brothers are forgetful. That is why they need your <u>remembrance of me</u> and of Him Who created me. Through this remembrance, you can change their minds about themselves, as I can change yours. Your mind is so powerful a light that you can look into theirs and enlighten them, as I can enlighten yours. I do not want to share my body in communion because this is to share nothing. Would I try to share an illusion with the most holy children of a most holy Father? Yet I do want to share my mind with you because we are of one Mind, and that Mind is ours. See only this

Mind everywhere, because only this is everywhere and in everything. It is everything because it encompasses all things within itself. Blessed are you who perceive only this, because you perceive only what is true.

T-08.III.4 - When you meet anyone, remember it is a holy encounter. As you see him you will see yourself. As you treat him you will treat yourself. As you think of him you will think of yourself. Never forget this, for in him you will find yourself or lose yourself. Whenever two Sons of God meet, they are given another chance at salvation. Do not leave anyone without giving salvation to him and receiving it yourself. For I am always there with you, <u>in remembrance</u> of you.

T-08.IV.2 - I am come as a light into a world that does deny itself everything. It does this simply by dissociating itself from everything. It is therefore an illusion of isolation, maintained by fear of the same loneliness that is its illusion. I said that I am with you always, even unto the end of the world. That is why I am the light of the world. If I am with you in the loneliness of the world, the loneliness is gone. You cannot maintain the illusion of loneliness if you are not alone. My purpose, then, is still to overcome the world. I do not attack it, but my light must dispel it because of what it is. Light does not attack darkness, but it does shine it away. If my light goes with you everywhere, you shine it away with me. The light becomes ours, and you cannot abide in darkness any more than darkness can abide wherever you go. <u>The remembrance of me</u> is the remembrance of yourself, and of Him Who sent me to you.

T-08.IV.7 - If your will were not mine it would not be our Father's. This would mean you have imprisoned yours, and have not let it be free. Of yourself you can do nothing, because of yourself you are nothing. I am nothing without the Father and you are nothing without me, because by denying the Father you deny yourself. I will always remember you, and <u>in my remembrance</u> of you lies your remembrance of yourself. In our remembrance of each other lies our remembrance of God. And in this remembrance lies your freedom because your freedom is in Him. Join, then, with me in praise of Him and you whom He created. This is our gift of gratitude to Him, which He will share with all His creations, to whom He gives equally whatever is acceptable to Him. Because it is acceptable to Him it is the gift of freedom, which is His Will for all His Sons. By offering freedom you will be free.

Bible Reference - Text

Luke 22:34 - And he said, I tell thee, Peter, the cock shall not crow this day, before that thou shalt thrice deny that thou knowest me.

Course Ref/s - Citation/s

T-14.XI.10 - He [the Holy Spirit] Who has freed you from the past would teach you are free of it. He would but have you accept His accomplishments as yours, because He did them for you. And because He did, they are yours. He has made you free of what you made. <u>You can deny Him</u>, but you cannot call on Him in vain. He always gives His gifts in place of yours. He would establish His bright teaching so firmly in your mind, that no dark lesson of guilt can abide in what He has established as holy by His Presence. Thank God that He is there and works through you. And all His works are yours. He offers you a miracle with every one you let Him do through you.

Bible Reference - Text

Luke 22:39-46 - And he came out, and went, as he was wont, to the mount of Olives; and his disciples also followed him. And when he was at the place, he said unto them, Pray that ye enter not into temptation.

And he was withdrawn from them about a stone's cast, and kneeled down, and prayed, Saying, Father, if thou be willing, remove this cup from me: nevertheless not my will, but thine, be done. And there appeared an angel unto him from heaven, strengthening him. And being in an agony he prayed more earnestly: and his sweat was as it were great drops of blood falling down to the ground.

And when he rose up from prayer, and was come to his disciples, he found them sleeping for sorrow, And said unto them, Why sleep ye? Rise and pray, lest ye enter into temptation.

Course Ref/s - Citation/s

T-06.I.7 - Your resurrection is your reawakening. I am the model for rebirth, but rebirth itself is merely the dawning on your mind of what is

already in it. God placed it there Himself, and so it is true forever.
I believed in it, and therefore accepted it as true for me. Help me to teach it to our brothers in the name of the Kingdom of God, but first believe that it is true for you, or you will teach amiss. <u>My brothers slept during the so-called "agony in the garden,"</u> but I could not be angry with them because I knew I could not be abandoned.

T-19.IV.D.18 - Free your brother here, as I freed you. Give him the self-same gift, nor look upon him with condemnation of any kind. See him as guiltless as I look on you, and overlook the sins he thinks he sees within himself. Offer your brother freedom and complete release from sin, here in <u>the garden of seeming agony</u> and death. So will we prepare together the way unto the resurrection of God's Son, and let him rise again to glad remembrance of his Father, Who knows no sin, no death, but only life eternal.

Bible Reference - Text

Luke 22:48 - But Jesus said unto him, Judas, betrayest thou the Son of man with a kiss?

Course Ref/s - Citation/s

T-06.I.15:1-6 - These are some of the examples of upside-down thinking in the New Testament, although its gospel is really only the message of love. If the Apostles had not felt guilty, they never could have quoted me as saying, "I come not to bring peace but a sword." This is clearly the opposite of everything I taught. Nor could they have described my reactions to Judas as they did, if they had really understood me. I could not have said, "<u>Betrayest thou the Son of man with a kiss?</u>" unless I believed in betrayal. The whole message of the crucifixion was simply that I did not.

T-17.I.1 - <u>The betrayal of the Son of God</u> lies only in illusions, and all his "sins" are but his own imagining. His reality is forever sinless. He need not be forgiven but awakened. In his dreams he has betrayed himself, his brothers and his God. Yet what is done in dreams has not been really done. It is impossible to convince the dreamer that this is so, for dreams are what they are because of their illusion of reality. Only in waking is the full release from them, for only then does it become perfectly apparent that they had no effect upon reality at all, and did not change it. Fantasies change reality. That is their purpose. They cannot do so in reality, but they can do so in the mind that would have reality be different.

Bible Reference - Text

Luke 23:33 - And when they were come to the place, which is called Calvary, there they crucified him, and the malefactors, one on the right hand, and the other on the left.

Course Ref/s - Citation/s

T-06.I.03-04 - You have probably reacted for years as if you were being crucified. This is a marked tendency of the separated, who always refuse to consider what they have done to themselves. Projection means anger, anger fosters assault, and assault promotes fear. The real meaning of the crucifixion lies in the apparent intensity of the assault of some of the Sons of God upon another. This, of course, is impossible, and must be fully understood as impossible. Otherwise, I cannot serve as a model for learning.

Assault can ultimately be made only on the body. There is little doubt that one body can assault another, and can even destroy it. Yet if destruction itself is impossible, anything that is destructible cannot be real. Its destruction, therefore, does not justify anger. To the extent to which you believe that it does, you are accepting false premises and teaching them to others. The message the crucifixion was intended to teach was that it is not necessary to perceive any form of assault in persecution, because you cannot be persecuted. If you respond with anger, you must be equating yourself with the destructible, and are therefore regarding yourself insanely.

T-06.I.06 - As I have said before, "As you teach so shall you learn." If you react as if you are persecuted, you are teaching persecution. This is not a lesson a Son of God should want to teach if he is to realize his own salvation. Rather, teach your own perfect immunity, which is the truth in you, and realize that it cannot be assailed. Do not try to protect it yourself, or you are believing that it is assailable. You are not asked to be crucified, which was part of my own teaching contribution. You are merely asked to follow my example in the face of much less extreme temptations to misperceive, and not to accept them as false justifications for anger. There can be no justification for the unjustifiable. Do not believe there is, and do not teach that there is. Remember always that what you believe you will teach. Believe with me, and we will become equal as teachers.

T-06.I.11 - You are not persecuted, nor was I. You are not asked to repeat my experiences because the Holy Spirit, Whom we share, makes this unnecessary. To use my experiences constructively, however, you must still follow my example in how to perceive them. My brothers and yours are constantly engaged in justifying the unjustifiable. My one lesson, which I must teach as I learned it, is that no perception that is out of accord with the judgment of the Holy Spirit can be justified. I undertook to show this was true in an extreme case [crucifixion], merely because it would serve as a good teaching aid to those whose temptation to give in to anger and assault would not be so extreme. I will with God that none of His Sons should suffer.

T-06.I.12-14 - The crucifixion cannot be shared because it is the symbol of projection, but the resurrection is the symbol of sharing because the reawakening of every Son of God is necessary to enable the Sonship to know its wholeness. Only this is knowledge.

The message of the crucifixion is perfectly clear:

> Teach only love, for that is what you are.

If you interpret the crucifixion in any other way, you are using it as a weapon for assault rather than as the call for peace for which it was intended. The Apostles often misunderstood it, and for the same reason that anyone misunderstands it. Their own imperfect love made them vulnerable to projection, and out of their own fear they spoke of the "wrath of God" as His retaliatory weapon. Nor could they speak of the crucifixion entirely without anger, because their sense of guilt had made them angry.

T-06.I.16 - As you read the teachings of the Apostles, remember that I told them myself that there was much they would understand later, because they were not wholly ready to follow me at the time. I do not want you to allow any fear to enter into the thought system toward which I am guiding you. I do not call for martyrs but for teachers. No one is punished for sins, and the Sons of God are not sinners. Any concept of punishment involves the projection of blame, and reinforces the idea that blame is justified. The result is a lesson in blame, for all behaviour teaches the beliefs that motivate it. The crucifixion was the result of clearly opposed thought systems; the perfect symbol of the "conflict" between the ego and the Son of God. This conflict seems just as real now, and its lessons must be learned now as well as then.

Bible Reference - Text

Luke 23:33 - And when they were come to the place....
(Continued) - (To read the full text of the above go to page 308.)

Course Ref/s - Citation/s

T-11.VI.5 - Do not underestimate the power of the devotion of God's Son, nor the power the god he worships has over him. For he places himself at the altar of his god, whether it be the god he made or the God Who created him. That is why his slavery is as complete as his freedom, for he will obey only the god he accepts. The god of <u>crucifixion</u> demands that he crucify, and his worshippers obey. In his name they crucify themselves, believing that the power of the Son of God is born of sacrifice and pain. The God of resurrection demands nothing, for He does not will to take away. He does not require obedience, for obedience implies submission. He would only have you learn your will and follow it, not in the spirit of sacrifice and submission, but in the gladness of freedom.

T-11.VI.7 - You will not find peace until you have removed the nails from the hands of God's Son, and taken the last thorn from his forehead. The Love of God surrounds His Son whom the god of <u>crucifixion</u> condemns. Teach not that I died in vain. Teach rather that I did not die by demonstrating that I live in you. For the undoing of the crucifixion of God's Son is the work of the redemption, in which everyone has a part of equal value. God does not judge His guiltless Son. Having given Himself to him, how could it be otherwise?

T-11.VI.8 - You have nailed yourself to a cross, and placed a crown of thorns upon your own head. Yet you cannot crucify God's Son, for the Will of God cannot die. His Son has been redeemed from his own <u>crucifixion,</u> and you cannot assign to death whom God has given eternal life.
The dream of crucifixion still lies heavy on your eyes, but what you see in dreams is not reality. While you perceive the Son of God as crucified, you are asleep. And as long as you believe that you can crucify him, you are only having nightmares. You who are beginning to wake are still aware of dreams, and have not yet forgotten them. The forgetting of dreams and the

awareness of Christ come with the awakening of others to share your redemption.

T-14.V.10 - The crucifixion had no part in the Atonement. Only the resurrection became my part in it. That is the symbol of the release from guilt by guiltlessness. Whom you perceive as guilty you would crucify. Yet you restore guiltlessness to whomever you see as guiltless. Crucifixion is always the ego's aim. It sees everyone as guilty, and by its condemnation it would kill. The Holy Spirit sees only guiltlessness, and in His gentleness He would release from fear and re-establish the reign of love. The power of love is in His gentleness, which is of God and therefore cannot crucify nor suffer crucifixion. The temple you restore becomes your altar, for it was rebuilt through you. And everything you give to God is yours. Thus He creates, and thus must you restore.

T-17.VIII.4-5 - To you who have acknowledged the Call of your Redeemer, the strain of not responding to His Call seems to be greater than before. This is not so. Before, the strain was there, but you attributed it to something else, believing that the "something else" produced it. This was never true. For what the "something else" produced was sorrow and depression, sickness and pain, darkness and dim imaginings of terror, cold fantasies of fear and fiery dreams of hell. And it was nothing but the intolerable strain of refusing to give faith to truth, and see its evident reality.

Such was the crucifixion of the Son of God. His faithlessness did this to him. Think carefully before you let yourself use faithlessness against him. For he is risen, and you have accepted the Cause of his awakening as yours. You have assumed your part in his redemption, and you are now fully responsible to him. Fail him not now, for it has been given you to realize what your lack of faith in him must mean to you. His salvation is your only purpose. See only this in every situation, and it will be a means for bringing only this.

T-26.VII.17 - In crucifixion is redemption laid, for healing is not needed where there is no pain or suffering. Forgiveness is the answer to attack of any kind. So is attack deprived of its effects, and hate is answered in the name of love. To you to whom it has been given to save the Son of God from crucifixion and from hell and death, all glory be forever. For you have power to save the Son of God because his Father willed that it be so. And in your hands does all salvation lie, to be both offered and received as one.

Bible Reference - Text

Luke 23:33 - And when they were come to the place....
(Continued) - (To read the full text of the above go to page 308.)

Course Ref/s - Citation/s

T-27.I.3 - Whenever you consent to suffer pain, to be deprived, unfairly treated or in need of anything, you but accuse your brother of attack upon God's Son. You hold a picture of your <u>crucifixion</u> before his eyes, that he may see his sins are writ in Heaven in your blood and death, and go before him, closing off the gate and damning him to hell. Yet this is writ in hell and not in Heaven, where you are beyond attack and prove his innocence. The picture of yourself you offer him you show yourself, and give it all your faith. The Holy Spirit offers you, to give to him, a picture of yourself in which there is no pain and no reproach at all. And what was martyred to his guilt becomes the perfect witness to his innocence.

W-pI.196.ti-1 - It can be but myself I <u>crucify</u>.

When this is firmly understood and kept in full awareness, you will not attempt to harm yourself, nor make your body slave to vengeance.
You will not attack yourself, and you will realize that to attack another is but to attack yourself. You will be free of the insane belief that to attack a brother saves yourself. And you will understand his safety is your own, and in his healing you are healed.

W-pI.196.5 - The dreary, hopeless thought that you can make attacks on others and escape yourself <u>has nailed you to the cross</u>. Perhaps, it seemed to be salvation. Yet it merely stood for the belief the fear of God is real. And what is that but hell? Who could believe his Father is his deadly enemy, separate from him, and waiting to destroy his life and blot him from the universe, without the fear of hell upon his heart?

Bible Reference - Text

Luke 23:34 - Then said Jesus, Father, forgive them; for they know not what they do. And they parted his raiment, and cast lots.

Course Ref/s - Citation/s

T-01.VII.3 - Fantasy is a distorted form of vision. Fantasies of any kind are distortions, because they always involve twisting perception into unreality. Actions that stem from distortions are literally the reactions of those who know not what they do. Fantasy is an attempt to control reality according to false needs. Twist reality in any way and you are perceiving destructively. Fantasies are a means of making false associations and attempting to obtain pleasure from them. But although you can perceive false associations, you can never make them real except to yourself. You believe in what you make. If you offer miracles, you will be equally strong in your belief in them. The strength of your conviction will then sustain the belief of the miracle receiver. Fantasies become totally unnecessary as the wholly satisfying nature of reality becomes apparent to both giver and receiver. Reality is "lost" through usurpation, which produces tyranny. As long as a single "slave" remains to walk the earth, your release is not complete. Complete restoration of the Sonship is the only goal of the miracle-minded.

T-02.V.16 - Miracle-minded forgiveness is only correction. It has no element of judgment at all. The statement "Father forgive them for they know not what they do" in no way evaluates what they do. It is an appeal to God to heal their minds. There is no reference to the outcome of the error. That does not matter.

T-11.II.2:4-3:7 - Every miracle that you accomplish speaks to you of the Fatherhood of God. Every healing thought that you accept, either from your brother or in your own mind, teaches you that you are God's Son. In every hurtful thought you hold, wherever you perceive it, lies the denial of God's Fatherhood and of your Sonship.

And denial is as total as love. You cannot deny part of yourself, because the rest will seem to be separate and therefore without meaning. And being without meaning to you, you will not understand it. To deny meaning is to fail to understand. You can heal only yourself, for only God's Son needs healing. You need it because you do not understand yourself, and therefore know not what you do. Having forgotten your will, you do not know what you really want.

T-11.III.2 - God's Son is indeed in need of comfort, for <u>he knows not what he does</u>, believing his will is not his own. The Kingdom is his, and yet he wanders homeless. At home in God he is lonely, and amid all his brothers he is friendless. Would God let this be real, when He did not will to be alone Himself? And if your will is His it cannot be true of you, because it is not true of Him.

T-13.V.6-7 - As you look with open eyes upon your world, it must occur to you that you have withdrawn into insanity. You see what is not there, and you hear what makes no sound. Your manifestations of emotions are the opposite of what the emotions are. You communicate with no one, and you are as isolated from reality as if you were alone in all the universe. In your madness you overlook reality completely, and you see only your own split mind everywhere you look. God calls you and you do not hear, for you are preoccupied with your own voice. And the vision of Christ is not in your sight, for you look upon yourself alone.

Little child, would you offer this to your Father? For if you offer it to yourself, you are offering it to Him. And He will not return it, for it is unworthy of you because it is unworthy of Him. Yet He would release you from it and set you free. His sane Answer tells you what you have offered yourself is not true, but His offering to you has never changed. <u>You who know not what you do</u> can learn what insanity is, and look beyond it. It is given you to learn how to deny insanity, and come forth from your private world in peace. You will see all that you denied in your brothers because you denied it in yourself. For you will love them, and by drawing nigh unto them you will draw them to yourself, perceiving them as witnesses to the reality you share with God. I am with them as I am with you, and we will draw them from their private worlds, for as we are united so would we unite with them. The Father welcomes all of us in gladness, and gladness is what we should offer Him. For every Son of God is given you to whom God gave Himself. And it is God Whom you must offer them, to recognize His gift to you.

T-14.V.2- Everyone has a special part to play in the Atonement, but the message given to each one is always the same; God's Son is guiltless. Each one teaches the message differently, and learns it differently. Yet until he teaches it and learns it, he will suffer the pain of dim awareness that his true function remains unfulfilled in him. The burden of guilt is heavy, but God would not have you bound by it. His plan for your awaking is as perfect as yours is fallible. <u>You know not what you do</u>, but He Who knows is with you. His gentleness is yours, and all the love you share with God

He holds in trust for you. He would teach you nothing except how to be happy

Bible Reference - Text

Luke 23:34 - Then said Jesus, Father, forgive them; for they.... (Continued) - (To read the full text of the above go to page 313.)

Course Ref/s - Citation/s

T-21.VII.2 - No one believes the Son of God is powerless. And those who see themselves as helpless must believe that they are not the Son of God. What can they be except his enemy? And what can they do but envy him his power, and by their envy make themselves afraid of it? These are the dark ones, silent and afraid, alone and not communicating, fearful the power of the Son of God will strike them dead, and raising up their helplessness against him. They join the army of the powerless, to wage their war of vengeance, bitterness and spite on him, to make him one with them. Because they do not know that they are one with him, they know not whom they hate. They are indeed a sorry army, each one as likely to attack his brother or turn upon himself as to remember that they thought they had a common cause.

T-25.IX.1 - What can it be but arrogance to think your little errors cannot be undone by Heaven's justice? And what could this mean except that they are sins and not mistakes, forever uncorrectable, and to be met with vengeance, not with justice? Are you willing to be released from all effects of sin? You cannot answer this until you see all that the answer must entail. For if you answer "yes" it means you will forego all values of this world in favor of the peace of Heaven. Not one sin would you retain. And not one doubt that this is possible will you hold dear that sin be kept in place. You mean that truth has greater value now than all illusions. And you recognize that truth must be revealed to you, because you know not what it is.

T-27.VII.1 - Suffering is an emphasis upon all that the world has done to injure you. Here is the world's demented version of salvation clearly shown. Like to a dream of punishment, in which the dreamer is unconscious of what brought on the attack against himself, he sees himself attacked unjustly and by something not himself. He is the victim of this "something else," a thing outside himself, for which he has no reason to be held responsible. He must be innocent because <u>he knows not what he does</u>, but what is done to him. Yet is his own attack upon himself apparent still, for it is he who bears the suffering. And he cannot escape because its source is seen outside himself.

W-pI.153.4-5 - Defenses are the costliest of all the prices which the ego would exact. In them lies madness in a form so grim that hope of sanity seems but to be an idle dream, beyond the possible. The sense of threat the world encourages is so much deeper, and so far beyond the frenzy and intensity of which you can conceive, that you have no idea of all the devastation it has wrought.

You are its slave. <u>You know not what you do</u>, in fear of it. You do not understand how much you have been made to sacrifice, who feel its iron grip upon your heart. You do not realize what you have done to sabotage the holy peace of God by your defensiveness. For you behold the Son of God as but a victim to attack by fantasies, by dreams, and by illusions he has made; yet helpless in their presence, needful only of defense by still more fantasies, and dreams by which illusions of his safety comfort him.

W-pI.197.2 - How easily are God and guilt confused by <u>those who know not what their thoughts can do</u>. Deny your strength, and weakness must become salvation to you. See yourself as bound, and bars become your home. Nor will you leave the prison house, or claim your strength, until guilt and salvation are not seen as one, and freedom and salvation are perceived as joined, with strength beside them, to be sought and claimed, and found and fully recognized.

Bible Reference - Text

Luke 23:39-43 - And one of the malefactors which were hanged railed on him, saying, If thou be Christ, save thyself and us. But the other answering rebuked him, saying, Dost not thou fear God, seeing thou art in the same condemnation? And we indeed justly; for we receive the due reward of our deeds: but this man hath done nothing amiss. And he said unto Jesus, Lord, remember me when thou comest into thy kingdom. And Jesus said unto him, Verily I say unto thee, Today shalt thou be with me in paradise.

Course Ref/s - Citation/s

T-20.III.9 - Prisoners bound with heavy chains for years, starved and emaciated, weak and exhausted, and with eyes so long cast down in darkness they remember not the light, do not leap up in joy the instant they are made free. It takes a while for them to understand what freedom is. You groped but feebly in the dust and found your brother's hand, uncertain whether to let it go or to take hold on life so long forgotten. Strengthen your hold and raise your eyes unto your strong companion, in whom the meaning of your freedom lies. <u>He seemed to be crucified beside you.</u> And yet his holiness remained untouched and perfect, and <u>with him beside you, you shall this day enter with him to Paradise</u>, and know the peace of God.

W-pII.266.1-2 - Father, You gave me all Your Sons, to be my saviors and my counsellors in sight; the bearers of Your holy Voice to me. In them are You reflected, and in them does Christ look back upon me from my Self. Let not Your Son forget Your holy Name. Let not Your Son forget his holy Source. Let not Your Son forget his Name is Yours.

<u>This day we enter into Paradise</u>, calling upon God's Name and on our own, acknowledging our Self in each of us; united in the holy Love of God. How many saviors God has given us! How can we lose the way to Him, when He has filled the world with those who point to Him, and given us the sight to look on them?

Bible Reference - Text

Luke 23:46 - And when Jesus had cried with a loud voice, he said, Father, into thy hands I commend my spirit: and having said thus, he gave up the ghost.

Course Ref/s - Citation/s

T-03.II.5 - Nothing can prevail against <u>a Son of God who commends his Spirit into the Hands of his Father</u>. By doing this the mind awakens from its sleep and remembers its Creator. All sense of separation disappears. The Son of God is part of the Holy Trinity, but the Trinity Itself is one. There is no confusion within Its Levels, because They are of one Mind and one Will. This single purpose creates perfect integration and establishes the peace of God. Yet this vision can be perceived only by the truly innocent. Because their hearts are pure, the innocent defend true perception instead of defending themselves against it. Understanding the lesson of the Atonement they are without the wish to attack, and therefore they see truly. This is what the Bible means when it says, "When he shall appear (or be perceived) we shall be like him, for we shall see him as he is."

T-05.VII.3 - Why should you listen to the endless insane calls you think are made upon you, when you can know the Voice for God is in you? <u>God commended His Spirit to you, and asks that you commend yours to Him.</u> He wills to keep it in perfect peace, because you are of one mind and spirit with Him. Excluding yourself from the Atonement is the ego's last-ditch defense of its own existence. It reflects both the ego's need to separate, and your willingness to side with its separateness. This willingness means that you do not want to be healed.

Bible Reference - Text

Luke 24:1-7 - Now upon the first day of the week, very early in the morning, they came unto the sepulchre, bringing the spices which they had prepared, and certain others with them. And they found the stone rolled away from the sepulchre. And they entered in, and found not the body of the Lord Jesus. And it came to pass, as they were much perplexed thereabout, behold, two men stood by them in shining garments: And as they were afraid, and bowed down their faces to the earth, they said unto them, Why seek ye the living among the dead? He is not here, but is risen: remember how he spake unto you when he was yet in Galilee, Saying, The Son of man must be delivered into the hands of sinful men, and be crucified, and the third day rise again.

Course Ref/s - Citation/s

T-03.I.1-2 - A further point must be perfectly clear before any residual fear still associated with miracles can disappear. <u>The crucifixion did not establish the Atonement; the resurrection did.</u> Many sincere Christians have misunderstood this. No one who is free of the belief in scarcity could possibly make this mistake. If the crucifixion is seen from an upside-down point of view, it does appear as if God permitted and even encouraged one of His Sons to suffer because he was good. This particularly unfortunate interpretation, which arose out of projection, has led many people to be bitterly afraid of God. Such anti-religious concepts enter into many religions. Yet the real Christian should pause and ask, "How could this be?" Is it likely that God Himself would be capable of the kind of thinking which His Own words have clearly stated is unworthy of His Son?

The best defense, as always, is not to attack another's position, but rather to protect the truth. It is unwise to accept any concept if you have to invert a whole frame of reference in order to justify it. This procedure is painful in its minor applications and genuinely tragic on a wider scale. Persecution frequently results in an attempt to "justify" the terrible misperception that God Himself persecuted His Own Son on behalf of salvation. The very words are meaningless. It has been particularly difficult to overcome this because, although the error itself is no harder to correct than any other, many have been unwilling to give it up in view of its prominent value as a defense. In milder forms a parent says, "This hurts me more than it hurts you," and feels exonerated in beating a child. Can you believe our Father really thinks this way? It is so essential that all such thinking be dispelled that we must be sure that nothing of this kind remains in your mind. I was not "punished" because you were bad. The wholly benign lesson the Atonement teaches is lost if it is tainted with this kind of distortion in any form.

T-06.I.07:1-5 - <u>Your resurrection is your reawakening.</u> I am the model for rebirth, but rebirth itself is merely the dawning on your mind of what is already in it. God placed it there Himself, and so it is true forever.
I believed in it, and therefore accepted it as true for me. Help me to teach it to our brothers in the name of the Kingdom of God, but first believe that it is true for you, or you will teach amiss.

T-06.I.12-13 - The crucifixion cannot be shared because it is the symbol of projection, but <u>the resurrection is the symbol of sharing</u> because the reawakening of every Son of God is necessary to enable the Sonship to know its wholeness. Only this is knowledge.

The message of the crucifixion is perfectly clear:

> Teach only love, for that is what you are.

T-11.VI.1 - It is impossible not to believe what you see, but it is equally impossible to see what you do not believe. Perceptions are built up on the basis of experience, and experience leads to beliefs. It is not until beliefs are fixed that perceptions stabilise. In effect, then, what you believe you do see. That is what I meant when I said, "Blessed are ye who have not seen and still believe," for those who believe in the resurrection will see it. <u>The resurrection is the complete triumph of Christ over the ego</u>, not by attack but by transcendence. For Christ does rise above the ego and all its works, and ascends to the Father and His Kingdom.

Bible Reference - Text

Luke 24:1-7 - Now upon the first day of the week, very....
(Continued) - (To read the full text of the above go to page 318.)

Course Ref/s - Citation/s

T-11.VI.4 - I am your resurrection and your life. You live in me because you live in God. And everyone lives in you, as you live in everyone. Can you, then, perceive unworthiness in a brother and not perceive it in yourself? And can you perceive it in yourself and not perceive it in God? Believe in the resurrection because it has been accomplished, and it has been accomplished in you. This is as true now as it will ever be, for the resurrection is the Will of God, which knows no time and no exceptions. But make no exceptions yourself, or you will not perceive what has been accomplished for you. For we ascend unto the Father together, as it was in the beginning, is now and ever shall be, for such is the nature of God's Son as his Father created him.

T-11.VI.5 - Do not underestimate the power of the devotion of God's Son, nor the power the god he worships has over him. For he places himself at the altar of his god, whether it be the god he made or the God Who created him. That is why his slavery is as complete as his freedom, for he will obey only the god he accepts. The god of crucifixion demands that he crucify, and his worshippers obey. In his name they crucify themselves, believing that the power of the Son of God is born of sacrifice and pain. The God of resurrection demands nothing, for He does not will to take away. He does not require obedience, for obedience implies submission. He would only have you learn your will and follow it, not in the spirit of sacrifice and submission, but in the gladness of freedom.

T-11.VI.6 - Resurrection must compel your allegiance gladly, because it is the symbol of joy. Its whole compelling power lies in the fact that it represents what you want to be. The freedom to leave behind everything that hurts you and humbles you and frightens you cannot be thrust upon you, but it can be offered you through the grace of God. And you can accept it by His grace, for God is gracious to His Son, accepting him without question as His Own. Who, then, is your own? The Father has given you all that is His, and He Himself is yours with them. Guard them in their resurrection, for otherwise you will not awake in God, safely surrounded by what is yours forever.

T-11.VI.7 - You will not find peace until you have removed the nails from the hands of God's Son, and taken the last thorn from his forehead.
The Love of God surrounds His Son whom the god of crucifixion condemns. Teach not that I died in vain. Teach rather that I did not die by demonstrating that I live in you. For the undoing of the crucifixion of God's Son is the work of the redemption, in which everyone has a part of equal value. God does not judge His guiltless Son. Having given Himself to him, how could it be otherwise?

T-11.VI.8 - You have nailed yourself to a cross, and placed a crown of thorns upon your own head. Yet you cannot crucify God's Son, for the Will of God cannot die. His Son has been redeemed from his own crucifixion, and you cannot assign to death whom God has given eternal life.
The dream of crucifixion still lies heavy on your eyes, but what you see in dreams is not reality. While you perceive the Son of God as crucified, you are asleep. And as long as you believe that you can crucify him, you are only having nightmares. You who are beginning to wake are still aware of dreams, and have not yet forgotten them. The forgetting of dreams and the awareness of Christ come with the awakening of others to share your redemption.

T-11.VI.9 - You will awaken to your own call, for the Call to awake is within you. If I live in you, you are awake. Yet you must see the works I do through you, or you will not perceive that I have done them unto you. Do not set limits on what you believe I can do through you, or you will not accept what I can do for you. Yet it is done already, and unless you give all that you have received you will not know that your Redeemer liveth, and that you have awakened with him. Redemption is recognized only by sharing it.

T-12.II.7 - A little while and you will see me, for I am not hidden because you are hiding. I will awaken you as surely as I awakened myself, for I awoke for you. In my resurrection is your release. Our mission is to escape from crucifixion, not from redemption. Trust in my help, for I did not walk alone, and I will walk with you as our Father walked with me. Do you not know that I walked with Him in peace? And does not that mean that peace goes with us on the journey?

Bible Reference - Text

Luke 24:1-7 - Now upon the first day of the week, very....
(Continued) - (To read the full text of the above go to page 318.)

Course Ref/s - Citation/s

T-14.V.10 - The crucifixion had no part in the <u>Atonement. Only the resurrection became my part in it</u>. That is the symbol of the release from guilt by guiltlessness. Whom you perceive as guilty you would crucify. Yet you restore guiltlessness to whomever you see as guiltless. Crucifixion is always the ego's aim. It sees everyone as guilty, and by its condemnation it would kill. The Holy Spirit sees only guiltlessness, and in His gentleness He would release from fear and re-establish the reign of love. The power of love is in His gentleness, which is of God and therefore cannot crucify nor suffer crucifixion. The temple you restore becomes your altar, for it was rebuilt through you. And everything you give to God is yours. Thus He creates, and thus must you restore.

T-17.VIII.4-5 - To you who have acknowledged the Call of your Redeemer, the strain of not responding to His Call seems to be greater than before. This is not so. Before, the strain was there, but you attributed it to something else, believing that the "something else" produced it. This was never true. For what the "something else" produced was sorrow and depression, sickness and pain, darkness and dim imaginings of terror, cold fantasies of fear and fiery dreams of hell. And it was nothing but the intolerable strain of refusing to give faith to truth, and see its evident reality.

Such was the crucifixion of the Son of God. His faithlessness did this to him. Think carefully before you let yourself use faithlessness against him. For <u>he is risen</u>, and you have accepted the Cause of his awakening as yours. You have assumed your part in his redemption, and you are now fully responsible to him. Fail him not now, for it has been given you to realize what your lack of faith in him must mean to you. His salvation is your only purpose. See only this in every situation, and it will be a means for bringing only this.

T-19.IV.D.17 - Give faith to your brother, for faith and hope and mercy are yours to give. Into the hands that give, the gift is given. Look on your

brother, and see in him the gift of God you would receive. It is almost
Easter, the time of resurrection. Let us give redemption to each other and
share in it, that we may rise as one in resurrection, not separate in death.
Behold the gift of freedom that I gave the Holy Spirit for you. And be you
and your brother free together, as you offer to the Holy Spirit this same
gift. And giving it, receive it of Him in return for what you gave.
He leadeth you and me together, that we might meet here in this holy
place, and make the same decision.

T-20.I.1 - This is Palm Sunday, the celebration of victory and the
acceptance of the truth. Let us not spend this holy week brooding on the
crucifixion of God's Son, but happily in the celebration of his release.
For Easter is the sign of peace, not pain. A slain Christ has no meaning.
But a risen Christ becomes the symbol of the Son of God's forgiveness on
himself; the sign he looks upon himself as healed and whole.

T-20.I.2 - This week begins with palms and ends with lilies, the white and
holy sign the Son of God is innocent. Let no dark sign of crucifixion
intervene between the journey and its purpose; between the acceptance of
the truth and its expression. This week we celebrate life, not death. And we
honor the perfect purity of the Son of God, and not his sins. Offer your
brother the gift of lilies, not the crown of thorns; the gift of love and not
the "gift" of fear. You stand beside your brother, thorns in one hand and
lilies in the other, uncertain which to give. Join now with me and throw
away the thorns, offering the lilies to replace them. This Easter I would
have the gift of your forgiveness offered by you to me, and returned by me
to you. We cannot be united in crucifixion and in death. Nor can the
resurrection be complete till your forgiveness rests on Christ, along with
mine.

T-20.I.3 - A week is short, and yet this holy week is the symbol of the
whole journey the Son of God has undertaken. He started with the sign of
victory, the promise of the resurrection, already given him. Let him not
wander into the temptation of crucifixion, and delay him there. Help him to
go in peace beyond it, with the light of his own innocence lighting his way
to his redemption and release. Hold him not back with thorns and nails
when his redemption is so near. But let the whiteness of your shining gift
of lilies speed him on his way to resurrection.

T-20.I.4 - Easter is not the celebration of the cost of sin but of its end.
If you see glimpses of the face of Christ behind the veil, looking between
the snow white petals of the lilies you have received and given as your gift,
you will behold your brother's face and recognize it. I was a stranger and

you took me in, not knowing who I was. Yet for your gift of lilies you will know. In your forgiveness of this stranger, alien to you and yet your ancient Friend, lies his release and your redemption with him. The time of Easter is a time of joy, and not of mourning. Look on <u>your risen Friend</u>, and celebrate his holiness along with me. For Easter is the time of your salvation, along with mine.

Bible Reference - Text

Luke 24:1-7 - Now upon the first day of the week, very....
(Continued) - (To read the full text of the above go to page 318.)

Course Ref/s - Citation/s

T-26.V.10 - Would God allow His Son to lose his way along a road long since a memory of time gone by? This course will teach you only what is now. A dreadful instant in a distant past, now perfectly corrected, is of no concern nor value. Let the dead and gone be peacefully forgotten. Resurrection has come to take its place. And now <u>you are a part of resurrection, not of death</u>. No past illusions have the power to keep you in a place of death, a vault God's Son entered an instant, to be instantly restored unto His Father's perfect Love. And how can he be kept in chains long since removed and gone forever from his mind?

W-pI.151.11-12 - He [the Holy Spirit] will select the elements in them which represent the truth, and disregard those aspects which reflect but idle dreams. And He will reinterpret all you see, and all occurrences, each circumstance, and every happening that seems to touch on you in any way from His one frame of reference, wholly unified and sure. And you will see the love beyond the hate, the constancy in change, the pure in sin, and only Heaven's blessing on the world.

Such is your <u>resurrection</u>, for your life is not a part of anything you see. It stands beyond the body and the world, past every witness for unholiness, within the Holy, holy as Itself. In everyone and everything His Voice would speak to you of nothing but your Self and your Creator, Who is one with Him. So will you see the holy face of Christ in everything, and hear in everything no sound except the echo of God's Voice.

W-pI.rV.7 - <u>My resurrection comes again</u> each time I lead a brother safely to the place at which the journey ends and is forgot. I am renewed each time a brother learns there is a way from misery and pain. I am reborn each time a brother's mind turns to the light in him and looks for me. I have forgotten no one. Help me now to lead you back to where the journey was begun, to make another choice with me.

C-ep.2 - You are a stranger here. But you belong to Him Who loves you as He loves Himself. Ask but my help <u>to roll the stone away</u>, and it is done according to His Will. We have begun the journey. Long ago the end was written in the stars and set into the Heavens with a shining Ray that held it safe within eternity and through all time as well. And holds it still; unchanged, unchanging and unchangeable.

M-28.1 - Very simply, <u>the resurrection is the overcoming or surmounting of death</u>. It is a re-awakening or a rebirth; a change of mind about the meaning of the world. It is the acceptance of the Holy Spirit's interpretation of the world's purpose; the acceptance of the Atonement for oneself. It is the end of dreams of misery, and the glad awareness of the Holy Spirit's final dream. It is the recognition of the gifts of God. It is the dream in which the body functions perfectly, having no function except communication. It is the lesson in which learning ends, for it is consummated and surpassed with this. It is the invitation to God to take His final step. It is the relinquishment of all other purposes, all other interests, all other wishes and all other concerns. It is the single desire of the Son for the Father.

M-28.2 - <u>The resurrection is the denial of death</u>, being the assertion of life. Thus is all the thinking of the world reversed entirely. Life is now recognized as salvation, and pain and misery of any kind perceived as hell. Love is no longer feared, but gladly welcomed. Idols have disappeared, and the remembrance of God shines unimpeded across the world. Christ's face is seen in every living thing, and nothing is held in darkness, apart from the light of forgiveness. There is no sorrow still upon the earth. The joy of Heaven has come upon it.

Bible Reference - Text

Luke 24:13-16 - And, behold, two of them went that same day to a village called Emmaus, which was from Jerusalem about threescore furlongs. And they talked together of all these things which had happened. And it came to pass, that, while they communed together and reasoned, Jesus himself drew near, and went with them. But their eyes were holden that they should not know him.

Course Ref/s - Citation/s

T-18.III.3 - Truth has rushed to meet you since you called upon it. <u>If you knew Who walks beside you</u> on the way that you have chosen, fear would be impossible. You do not know because the journey into darkness has been long and cruel, and you have gone deep into it. A little flicker of your eyelids, closed so long, has not yet been sufficient to give you confidence in yourself, so long despised. You go toward love still hating it, and terribly afraid of its judgment upon you. And you do not realize that you are not afraid of love, but only of what you have made of it. You are advancing to love's meaning, and away from all illusions in which you have surrounded it. When you retreat to the illusion your fear increases, for there is little doubt that what you think it means is fearful. Yet what is that to us who travel surely and very swiftly away from fear?

S. John

There are 54 references from the Gospel of John which are cited in the Course. They are:

[1:1-5], [1:7-8], [1:14], [1:29-34], [3:3],
[3:6], [3:16], [3:35], [3:36], [4:10],
[5:30], [6:19-20], [6:68-69], [7:24], [8:12],
[8:16], [8:31-32], [8:51], [8:58], [10:30],
[11:1-4], [11:11], [11:25], [11:43-44], [12:12-15],

[12:46], [14:1], [14:2-3], [14:5-6], [14:7-9],
[14:13-14], [14:16], [14:18], [14:26], [14:27],
[14:28], [15:2], [15:5], [15:11], [15:12-15],
[15:18], [15:19], [16:12], [16:16], [16:32-33],
[17:16-17], [18:36], [18:37], [18:38], [19:5],

[20:17], [20:19], [20:25] and [20:29].

Bible Reference - Text

John 1:1-5 - In the beginning was the Word, and the Word was with God, and the Word was God. The same was in the beginning with God.
All things were made by him; and without him was not any thing made that was made. In him was life; and the life was the light of men. And the light shineth in darkness; and the darkness comprehended it not.

Course Ref/s - Citation/s

T-06.II.7 - The perfect equality of the Holy Spirit's perception is the reflection of the perfect equality of God's knowing. The ego's perception has no counterpart in God, but the Holy Spirit remains the bridge between perception and knowledge. By enabling you to use perception in a way that reflects knowledge, you will ultimately remember it. The ego would prefer to believe that this memory is impossible, yet it is your perception the Holy

Spirit guides. Your perception will end where it began. Everything meets in God, because everything was created by Him and in Him.

T-14.II.4 - Like you, the Holy Spirit did not make truth. Like God, He knows it to be true. He brings the light of truth into the darkness, and lets it shine on you. And as it shines your brothers see it, and realizing that this light is not what you have made, they see in you more than you see. They will be happy learners of the lesson this light brings to them, because it teaches them release from nothing and from all the works of nothing. The heavy chains that seem to bind them to despair they do not see as nothing, until you bring the light to them. And then they see the chains have disappeared, and so they must have been nothing. And you will see it with them. Because you taught them gladness and release, they will become your teachers in release and gladness.

T-18.III.1 - You who have spent your life in bringing truth To illusion, reality to fantasy, have walked the way of dreams. For you have gone from waking to sleeping, and on and on to a yet deeper sleep. Each dream has led to other dreams, and every fantasy that seemed to bring a light into the darkness but made the darkness deeper. Your goal was darkness, in which no ray of light could enter. And you sought a blackness so complete that you could hide from truth forever, in complete insanity. What you forgot was simply that God cannot destroy Himself. The light is in you. Darkness can cover it, but cannot put it out.

W-pI.12.5:1-8 - What is meaningless is neither good nor bad. Why, then, should a meaningless world upset you? If you could accept the world as meaningless and let the truth be written upon it for you, it would make you indescribably happy. But because it is meaningless; you are impelled to write upon it what you would have it be. It is this you see in it. It is this that is meaningless in truth. Beneath your words is written the Word of God. The truth upsets you now, but when your words have been erased, you will see His.

W-pI.198.4-6 - Forgiveness is the only road that leads out of disaster, past all suffering, and finally away from death. How could there be another way, when this one is the plan of God Himself? And why would you oppose it, quarrel with it, seek to find a thousand ways in which it must be wrong; a thousand other possibilities?

Is it not wiser to be glad you hold the answer to your problems in your hand? Is it not more intelligent to thank the One Who gives salvation, and accept His gift with gratitude? And is it not a kindness to yourself to hear

His Voice and learn the simple lessons He would teach, instead of trying to dismiss His words, and substitute your own in place of His?

His words will work. His words will save. His words contain all hope, all blessing and all joy that ever can be found upon this earth. His words are born in God, and come to you with Heaven's love upon them. Those who hear His words have heard the song of Heaven. For these are the words in which all merge as one at last. And as this one will fade away, the Word of God will come to take its place, for it will be remembered then and loved.

Bible Reference - Text

John 1:1-5 - In the beginning was the Word, and the Word....
(Continued) - (To read the full text of the above go to page 327.)

Course Ref/s - Citation/s

M-01.1 - A teacher of God is anyone who chooses to be one.
His qualifications consist solely in this; somehow, somewhere he has made a deliberate choice in which he did not see his interests as apart from someone else's. Once he has done that, his road is established and his direction is sure. A light has entered the darkness. It may be a single light, but that is enough. He has entered an agreement with God even if he does not yet believe in Him. He has become a bringer of salvation. He has become a teacher of God.

M-04.IX.1:4-2:12 - Faithfulness is the teacher of God's trust in the Word of God to set all things right; not some, but all. Generally, his faithfulness begins by resting on just some problems, remaining carefully limited for a time. To give up all problems to one Answer is to reverse the thinking of the world entirely. And that alone is faithfulness. Nothing but that really deserves the name. Yet each degree, however small, is worth achieving. Readiness, as the text notes, is not mastery.

True faithfulness, however, does not deviate. Being consistent, it is wholly honest. Being unswerving, it is full of trust. Being based on fearlessness, it is gentle. Being certain, it is joyous. And being confident, it is tolerant. Faithfulness, then, combines in itself the other attributes of God's teachers. It implies acceptance of the Word of God and His definition of His Son. It is to Them that faithfulness in the true sense is always directed. Toward

Them it looks, seeking until it finds. And having found, it rests in quiet certainty on that alone to which all faithfulness is due.

M-11.ti-2 - HOW IS PEACE POSSIBLE IN THIS WORLD?

This is a question everyone must ask. Certainly peace seems to be impossible here. Yet the Word of God promises other things that seem impossible, as well as this. His Word has promised peace. It has also promised that there is no death, that resurrection must occur, and that rebirth is man's inheritance. The world you see cannot be the world God loves, and yet His Word assures us that He loves the world. God's Word has promised that peace is possible here, and what He promises can hardly be impossible. But it is true that the world must be looked at differently, if His promises are to be accepted. What the world is, is but a fact. You cannot choose what this should be. But you can choose how you would see it. Indeed, you must choose this.

Again we come to the question of judgment. This time ask yourself whether your judgment or the Word of God is more likely to be true. For they say different things about the world, and things so opposite that it is pointless to try to reconcile them. God offers the world salvation; your judgment would condemn it. God says there is no death; your judgment sees but death as the inevitable end of life. God's Word assures you that He loves the world; your judgment says it is unlovable. Who is right? For one of you is wrong. It must be so.

M-22.1 - Healing and Atonement are not related; they are identical. There is no order of difficulty in miracles because there are no degrees of Atonement. It is the one complete concept possible in this world, because it is the source of a wholly unified perception. Partial Atonement is a meaningless idea, just as special areas of hell in Heaven are inconceivable. Accept Atonement and you are healed. Atonement is the Word of God. Accept His Word and what remains to make sickness possible? Accept His Word and every miracle has been accomplished. To forgive is to heal. The teacher of God has taken accepting the Atonement for himself as his only function. What is there, then, he cannot heal? What miracle can be withheld from him?

Bible Reference - Text

John 1:7-8 - The same came for a witness, to bear witness of the Light, that all men through him might believe.

⁸ He was not that Light, but was sent to bear witness of that Light.

Course Ref/s - Citation/s

T-1.I.14 - Miracles bear witness to truth. They are convincing because they arise from conviction. Without conviction they deteriorate into magic, which is mindless and therefore destructive; or rather, the uncreative use of mind.

T-18.IX.3 - From the world of bodies, made by insanity, insane messages seem to be returned to the mind that made it. And these messages bear witness to this world, pronouncing it as true. For you sent forth these messengers to bring this back to you. Everything these messages relay to you is quite external. There are no messages that speak of what lies underneath, for it is not the body that could speak of this. Its eyes perceive it not; its senses remain quite unaware of it; its tongue cannot relay its messages. Yet God can bring you there, if you are willing to follow the Holy Spirit through seeming terror, trusting Him not to abandon you and leave you there. For it is not His purpose to frighten you, but only yours. You are severely tempted to abandon Him at the outside ring of fear, but He would lead you safely through and far beyond.

W-pI.121.5 - The unforgiving mind is in despair, without the prospect of a future which can offer anything but more despair. Yet it regards its judgment of the world as irreversible, and does not see it has condemned itself to this despair. It thinks it cannot change, for what it sees bears witness that its judgment is correct. It does not ask, because it thinks it knows. It does not question, certain it is right.

W-pI.169.4 - We have perhaps appeared to contradict our statement that the revelation of the Father and the Son as one has been already set. But we have also said the mind determines when that time will be, and has determined it. And yet we urge you to bear witness to the Word of God to hasten the experience of truth, and speed its advent into every mind that recognizes truth's effects on you.

W-pI.169.6-7 - We cannot speak nor write nor even think of this at all. It comes to every mind when total recognition that its will is God's has been completely given and received completely. It returns the mind into the endless present, where the past and future cannot be conceived. It lies beyond salvation; past all thought of time, forgiveness and the holy face of

Christ. The Son of God has merely disappeared into His Father, as His Father has in him. The world has never been at all. Eternity remains a constant state.

7 This is beyond experience we try to hasten. Yet forgiveness, taught and learned, brings with it the experiences which <u>bear witness</u> that the time the mind itself determined to abandon all but this is now at hand. We do not hasten it, in that what you will offer was concealed from Him Who teaches what forgiveness means.

W-pII.255.1 - It does not seem to me that I can choose to have but peace today. And yet, my God assures me that His Son is like Himself. Let me this day have faith in Him Who says I am God's Son. And let the peace I choose be mine today <u>bear witness</u> to the truth of what He says. God's Son can have no cares, and must remain forever in the peace of Heaven. In His Name, I give today to finding what my Father wills for me, accepting it as mine, and giving it to all my Father's Sons, along with me.

Bible Reference - Text

John 1:14 - And the Word was made flesh, and dwelt among us, (and we beheld his glory, the glory as of the only begotten of the Father,) full of grace and truth.

Course Ref/s - Citation/s

T-08.VII.07 - <u>The Bible says, "The Word (or thought) was made flesh."</u> Strictly speaking this is impossible, since it seems to involve the translation of one order of reality into another. Different orders of reality merely appear to exist, just as different orders of miracles do. Thought cannot be made into flesh except by belief, since thought is not physical. Yet thought is communication, for which the body can be used. This is the only natural use to which it can be put. To use the body unnaturally is to lose sight of the Holy Spirit's purpose, and thus to confuse the goal of His curriculum.

T-08.VII.14 - You are not limited by the body, and <u>thought cannot be made flesh</u>. Yet mind can be manifested through the body if it goes beyond it and does not interpret it as limitation. Whenever you see another as limited to or by the body, you are imposing this limit on yourself. Are you willing to accept this, when your whole purpose for learning should be to escape from limitations? To conceive of the body as a means of attack and to believe that joy could possibly result, is a clear-cut indication of a poor learner. He has accepted a learning goal in obvious contradiction to the unified purpose of the curriculum, and one that is interfering with his ability to accept its purpose as his own.

W-pII.276.ti-1 - The Word of God is given me to speak.

What is the Word of God? "My Son is pure and holy as Myself." And thus did God become the Father of the Son He loves, for thus was he created. This the Word His Son did not create with Him, because in this His Son was born. Let us accept His Fatherhood, and all is given us. Deny we were created in His Love and we deny our Self, to be unsure of Who we are, of Who our Father is, and for what purpose we have come. And yet, we need but to acknowledge Him Who gave His Word to us in our creation, to remember Him and so recall our Self.

Bible Reference - Text

John 1:29-34 - The next day John seeth Jesus coming unto him, and saith, Behold the Lamb of God, which taketh away the sin of the world. This is he of whom I said, After me cometh a man which is preferred before me: for he was before me. And I knew him not: but that he should be made manifest to Israel, therefore am I come baptizing with water.

And John bare record, saying, I saw the Spirit descending from heaven like a dove, and it abode upon him. And I knew him not: but he that sent me to baptize with water, the same said unto me, Upon whom thou shalt see the Spirit descending, and remaining on him, the same is he which baptizeth with the Holy Ghost. And I saw, and bare record that this is the Son of God.

Course Ref/s - Citation/s

T-03.I.5 - I have been correctly referred to as "the lamb of God who taketh away the sins of the world," but those who represent the lamb as bloodstained do not understand the meaning of the symbol. Correctly understood, it is a very simple symbol that speaks of my innocence. The lion and the lamb lying down together symbolize that strength and innocence are not in conflict, but naturally live in peace. "Blessed are the pure in heart for they shall see God" is another way of saying the same thing. A pure mind knows the truth and this is its strength. It does not confuse destruction with innocence because it associates innocence with strength, not with weakness.

T-03.I.6 - Innocence is incapable of sacrificing anything, because the innocent mind has everything and strives only to protect its wholeness. It cannot project. It can only honor other minds, because honor is the natural greeting of the truly loved to others who are like them. The lamb "taketh away the sins of the world" in the sense that the state of innocence, or grace, is one in which the meaning of the Atonement is perfectly apparent. The Atonement is entirely unambiguous. It is perfectly clear because it exists in light. Only the attempts to shroud it in darkness have made it inaccessible to those who do not choose to see.

T-29.V.5 - There is no gift the Father asks of you but that you see in all creation but the shining glory of His gift to you. Behold His Son, His perfect gift, in whom his Father shines forever, and to whom is all creation given as his own. Because he has it is it given you, and where it lies in him behold your peace. The quiet that surrounds you dwells in him, and from this quiet come the happy dreams in which your hands are joined in innocence. These are not hands that grasp in dreams of pain. They hold no sword, for they have left their hold on every vain illusion of the world. And being empty they receive, instead, a brother's hand in which completion lies.

Bible Reference - Text

John 3:3 - Jesus answered and said unto him, Verily, verily, I say unto thee, Except a man be born again, he cannot see the kingdom of God.

Course Ref/s - Citation/s

T-13.VI.3:2-7 - The Christ as revealed to you now has no past, for He is changeless, and in His changelessness lies your release. For if He is as He was created, there is no guilt in Him. No cloud of guilt has risen to obscure Him, and He stands revealed in everyone you meet because you see Him through Himself. To be born again is to let the past go, and look without condemnation upon the present. The cloud that obscures God's Son to you is the past, and if you would have it past and gone, you must not see it now. If you see it now in your illusions, it has not gone from you, although it is not there.

T-13.VI.4 - Time can release as well as imprison, depending on whose interpretation of it you use. Past, present and future are not continuous, unless you force continuity on them. You can perceive them as continuous, and make them so for you. But do not be deceived, and then believe that this is how it is. For to believe reality is what you would have it be according to your use for it is delusional. You would destroy time's continuity by breaking it into past, present and future for your own purposes. You would anticipate the future on the basis of your past experience, and plan for it accordingly. Yet by doing so you are aligning past and future, and not allowing the miracle, which could intervene between them, to free you to be born again.

T-13.VI.5 - The miracle enables you to see your brother without his past, and so perceive him as born again. His errors are all past, and by perceiving him without them you are releasing him. And since his past is yours, you share in this release. Let no dark cloud out of your past obscure him from you, for truth lies only in the present, and you will find it if you seek it there. You have looked for it where it is not, and therefore have not found it. Learn, then, to seek it where it is, and it will dawn on eyes that see. Your past was made in anger, and if you use it to attack the present, you will not see the freedom that the present holds.

T-13.X.5 - Determine, then, to be not as you were. Use no relationship to hold you to the past, but with each one each day be born again. A minute, even less, will be enough to free you from the past, and give your mind in peace over to the Atonement. When everyone is welcome to you as you would have yourself be welcome to your Father, you will see no guilt in you. For you will have accepted the Atonement, which shone within you all the while you dreamed of guilt, and would not look within and see it.

T-26.I.6-7 - You can lose sight of oneness, but can not make sacrifice of its reality. Nor can you lose what you would sacrifice, nor keep the Holy Spirit from His task of showing you that it has not been lost. Hear, then, the song your brother sings to you, and let the world recede, and take the rest his witness offers on behalf of peace. But judge him not, for you will hear no song of liberation for yourself, nor see what it is given him to witness to, that you may see it and rejoice with him. Make not his holiness a sacrifice to your belief in sin. You sacrifice your innocence with his, and die each time you see in him a sin deserving death.

Yet every instant can you be reborn, and given life again. His holiness gives life to you, who cannot die because his sinlessness is known to God; and can no more be sacrificed by you than can the light in you be blotted out because he sees it not. You who would make a sacrifice of life, and make your eyes and ears bear witness to the death of God and of His holy Son, think not that you have power to make of Them what God willed not They be. In Heaven, God's Son is not imprisoned in a body, nor is sacrificed in solitude to sin. And as he is in Heaven, so must he be eternally and everywhere. He is the same forever. Born again each instant, untouched by time, and far beyond the reach of any sacrifice of life or death. For neither did he make, and only one was given him by One Who knows His gifts can never suffer sacrifice and loss.

Bible Reference - Text

John 3:3 - Jesus answered and said unto him, Verily....
(Continued) - (To read the full text of the above go to page 334.)

Course Ref/s - Citation/s

T-26.VII.16 - The miracle but calls your ancient Name, which you will recognize because the truth is in your memory. And to this Name your brother calls for his release and yours. Heaven is shining on the Son of God. Deny him not, that you may be released. Each instant is the Son of God reborn until he chooses not to die again. In every wish to hurt he chooses death instead of what his Father wills for him. Yet every instant offers life to him because his Father wills that he should live.

T-31.I.13 - Be innocent of judgment, unaware of any thoughts of evil or of good that ever crossed your mind of anyone. Now do you know him not. But you are free to learn of him, and learn of him anew. Now is he born again to you, and you are born again to him, without the past that sentenced him to die, and you with him. Now is he free to live as you are free, because an ancient learning passed away, and left a place for truth to be reborn.

T-31.II.9 - Forgive your brother all appearances, that are but ancient lessons you have taught yourself about the sinfulness in you. Hear but his call for mercy and release from all the fearful images he holds of what he is and of what you must be. He is afraid to walk with you, and thinks perhaps a bit behind, a bit ahead would be a safer place for him to be. Can you make progress if you think the same, advancing only when he would step back, and falling back when he would go ahead? For so do you forget the journey's goal, which is but to decide to walk with him, so neither leads nor follows. Thus it is a way you go together, not alone. And in this choice is learning's outcome changed, for Christ has been <u>reborn</u> to both of you.

W-pI.109.2 - "I rest in God." This thought will bring to you the rest and quiet, peace and stillness, and the safety and the happiness you seek. "I rest in God." This thought has power to wake the sleeping truth in you, whose vision sees beyond appearances to that same truth in everyone and everything there is. Here is the end of suffering for all the world, and everyone who ever came and yet will come to linger for a while. Here is the thought in which the Son of God is <u>born again</u>, to recognize himself.

W-pI.109.6 - Each hour that you take your rest today, a tired mind is suddenly made glad, a bird with broken wings begins to sing, a stream long dry begins to flow again. The world is <u>born again</u> each time you rest, and hourly remember that you came to bring the peace of God into the world, that it might take its rest along with you.

W-pI.182.10 - Christ is <u>reborn</u> as but a little Child each time a wanderer would leave his home. For he must learn that what he would protect is but this Child, Who comes defenseless and Who is protected by defenselessness. Go home with Him from time to time today. You are as much an alien here as He.

W-pI.192.8 - Who can <u>be born again</u> in Christ but him who has forgiven everyone he sees or thinks of or imagines? Who could be set free while he imprisons anyone? A jailer is not free, for he is bound together with his prisoner. He must be sure that he does not escape, and so he spends his time in keeping watch on him. The bars that limit him become the world in which his jailer lives, along with him. And it is on his freedom that the way to liberty depends for both of them.

W-pI.rV.7 - My resurrection comes again each time I lead a brother safely to the place at which the journey ends and is forgot. I am renewed each time a brother learns there is a way from misery and pain. I am <u>reborn</u> each time a brother's mind turns to the light in him and looks for me. I have forgotten no one. Help me now to lead you back to where the journey was begun, to make another choice with me.

Bible Reference - Text

John 3:3 - Jesus answered and said unto him, Verily....
(Continued) - (To read the full text of the above go to page 334.)

Course Ref/s - Citation/s

W-pII.303.1-2 - Watch with me, angels, watch with me today. Let all God's holy Thoughts surround me, and be still with me while Heaven's Son is born. Let earthly sounds be quiet, and the sights to which I am accustomed disappear. Let Christ be welcomed where He is at home. And let Him hear the sounds He understands, and see but sights that show His Father's Love. Let Him no longer be a stranger here, for He is <u>born again</u> in me today.

Your Son is welcome, Father. He has come to save me from the evil self I made. He is the Self that You have given me. He is but what I really am in truth. He is the Son You love above all things. He is my Self as You created me. It is not Christ that can be crucified. Safe in Your Arms let me receive Your Son.

W-pII.306.1 - What but Christ's vision would I use today, when it can offer me a day in which I see a world so like to Heaven that an ancient memory returns to me? Today I can forget the world I made. Today I can go past all fear, and be restored to love and holiness and peace. Today I am redeemed, and <u>born anew</u> into a world of mercy and of care; of loving kindness and the peace of God.

C-ep.5 - Let us go out and meet the newborn world, knowing that Christ has been <u>reborn</u> in it, and that the holiness of this <u>rebirth</u> will last forever. We had lost our way but He has found it for us. Let us go and bid Him welcome Who returns to us to celebrate salvation and the end of all we thought we made. The morning star of this new day looks on a different world where God is welcomed and His Son with Him. We who complete Him offer thanks to Him, as He gives thanks to us. The Son is still, and in the quiet God has given him enters his home and is at peace at last.

Bible Reference - Text

John 3:6 - That which is born of the flesh is flesh; and that which is born of the Spirit is spirit.

Course Ref/s - Citation/s

T-31.VI.1 - <u>You see the flesh or recognize the spirit</u>. There is no compromise between the two. If one is real the other must be false, for what is real denies its opposite. There is no choice in vision but this one. What you decide in this determines all you see and think is real and hold as true. On this one choice does all your world depend, for here have you established what you are, as flesh or spirit in your own belief. If you choose flesh, you never will escape the body as your own reality, for you have chosen that you want it so. But choose the spirit, and all Heaven bends to touch your eyes and bless your holy sight, that you may see the world of flesh no more except to heal and comfort and to bless.

Bible Reference - Text

John 3:16 - For God so loved the world, that he gave his only begotten Son, that whosoever believeth in him should not perish, but have everlasting life.

Course Ref/s - Citation/s

T-02.VII.5 - Nothing and everything cannot coexist. To believe in one is to deny the other. Fear is really nothing and love is everything. Whenever light enters darkness, the darkness is abolished. What you believe is true for you. In this sense the separation has occurred, and to deny it is merely to use denial inappropriately. However, to concentrate on error is only a further error. The initial corrective procedure is to recognize temporarily that there is a problem, but only as an indication that immediate correction is needed. This establishes a state of mind in which the Atonement can be accepted without delay. It should be emphasized, however, that ultimately no compromise is possible between everything and nothing. Time is essentially a device by which all compromise in this respect can be given up. It only seems to be abolished by degrees, because time itself involves intervals that do not exist. Miscreation made this necessary as a corrective device. The statement "<u>For God so loved the world that He gave His only begotten Son, that whosoever believeth in Him should not perish but have</u>

everlasting life" needs only one slight correction to be meaningful in this context; "He gave it *to* His only begotten Son."

T-12.III.8 - I said before that God so loved the world that He gave it to His only begotten Son. God does love the real world, and those who perceive its reality cannot see the world of death. For death is not of the real world, in which everything reflects the eternal. God gave you the real world in exchange for the one you made out of your split mind, and which is the symbol of death. For if you could really separate yourself from the Mind of God you would die.

Bible Reference - Text

John 3:35 - The Father loveth the Son, and hath given all things into his hand.

Course Ref/s - Citation/s

T-04.III.9 - In your own mind, though denied by the ego, is the declaration of your release. God has given you everything. This one fact means the ego does not exist, and this makes it profoundly afraid. In the ego's language, "to have" and "to be" are different, but they are identical to the Holy Spirit. The Holy Spirit knows that you both have everything and are everything. Any distinction in this respect is meaningful only when the idea of "getting," which implies a lack, has already been accepted. That is why we make no distinction between having the Kingdom of God and being the Kingdom of God.

T-04.VII.5 - God, Who encompasses all being, created beings who have everything individually, but who want to share it to increase their joy. Nothing real can be increased except by sharing. That is why God created you. Divine Abstraction takes joy in sharing. That is what creation means. "How," "what" and "to whom" are irrelevant, because real creation gives everything, since it can create only like itself. Remember that in the Kingdom there is no difference between having and being, as there is in existence. In the state of being the mind gives everything always.

Bible Reference - Text

John 3:36 - He that believeth on the Son hath everlasting life: and he that believeth not the Son shall not see life; but the wrath of God abideth on him.

Course Ref/s - Citation/s

T-06.I.13-14 - The message of the crucifixion is perfectly clear:

> Teach only love, for that is what you are.

If you interpret the crucifixion in any other way, you are using it as a weapon for assault rather than as the call for peace for which it was intended. The Apostles often misunderstood it, and for the same reason that anyone misunderstands it. Their own imperfect love made them vulnerable to projection, and out of their own fear they spoke of the "wrath of God" as His retaliatory weapon. Nor could they speak of the crucifixion entirely without anger, because their sense of guilt had made them angry.

T-25.VIII.6 - It is extremely hard for those who still believe sin meaningful to understand the Holy Spirit's justice. They must believe He shares their own confusion, and cannot avoid the vengeance that their own belief in justice must entail. And so they fear the Holy Spirit, and perceive the "wrath" of God in Him. Nor can they trust Him not to strike them dead with lightning bolts torn from the "fires" of Heaven by God's Own angry Hand. They do believe that Heaven is hell, and are afraid of love. And deep suspicion and the chill of fear comes over them when they are told that they have never sinned. Their world depends on sin's stability. And they perceive the "threat" of what God knows as justice to be more destructive to themselves and to their world than vengeance, which they understand and love.

Bible Reference - Text

John 4:10 - Jesus answered and said unto her, If thou knewest the gift of God, and who it is that saith to thee, Give me to drink; thou wouldest have asked of him, and he would have given thee living water.

Course Ref/s - Citation/s

T-18.VIII.9 - The Thought of God surrounds your little kingdom, waiting at the barrier you built to come inside and shine upon the barren ground. See how life springs up everywhere! The desert becomes a garden, green and deep and quiet, offering rest to those who lost their way and wander in the dust. Give them a place of refuge, prepared by love for them where once a desert was. And everyone you welcome will bring love with him from Heaven for you. They enter one by one into this holy place, but they will not depart as they had come, alone. The love they brought with them will stay with them, as it will stay with you. And under its beneficence your little garden will expand, and reach out to everyone who thirsts for living water, but has grown too weary to go on alone.

Bible Reference - Text

John 5:30 - I can of mine own self do nothing: as I hear, I judge: and my judgment is just; because I seek not mine own will, but the will of the Father which hath sent me.

Course Ref/s - Citation/s

T-04.I.12:1-3 - Of your ego you can do nothing to save yourself or others, but of your spirit you can do everything for the salvation of both. Humility is a lesson for the ego, not for the spirit. Spirit is beyond humility, because it recognizes its radiance and gladly sheds its light everywhere.

T-08.IV.7 - If your will were not mine it would not be our Father's. This would mean you have imprisoned yours, and have not let it be free. Of yourself you can do nothing, because of yourself you are nothing. I am nothing without the Father and you are nothing without me, because by denying the Father you deny yourself. I will always remember you, and in my remembrance of you lies your remembrance of yourself. In our remembrance of each other lies our remembrance of God. And in this remembrance lies your freedom because your freedom is in Him. Join, then, with me in praise of Him and you whom He created. This is our gift of gratitude to Him, which He will share with all His creations, to whom He gives equally whatever is acceptable to Him. Because it is acceptable to Him it is the gift of freedom, which is His Will for all His Sons. By offering freedom you will be free.

T-08.VII.6 - Rejoice, then, that <u>of yourself you can do nothing</u>. You are not of yourself. He of Whom you are has willed your power and glory for you, with which you can perfectly accomplish His holy Will for you when you accept it for yourself. He has not withdrawn His gifts from you, but you believe you have withdrawn them from Him. Let no Son of God remain hidden for His Name's sake, because His Name is yours.

T-10.V.5 - I said before that <u>of yourself you can do nothing</u>, but you are not of yourself. If you were, what you have made would be true, and you could never escape. It is because you did not make yourself that you need be troubled over nothing. Your gods are nothing, because your Father did not create them. You cannot make creators who are unlike your Creator, any more than He could have created a Son who was unlike Him.
If creation is sharing, it cannot create what is unlike itself. It can share only what it is. Depression is isolation, and so it could not have been created.

T-12.V.5 - You have learning handicaps in a very literal sense. There are areas in your learning skills that are so impaired that you can progress only under constant, clear-cut direction, provided by a Teacher [the Holy Spirit] Who can transcend your limited resources. He becomes your Resource because <u>of yourself you cannot learn</u>. The learning situation in which you placed yourself is impossible, and in this situation you clearly require a special Teacher and a special curriculum. Poor learners are not good choices as teachers, either for themselves or for anyone else. You would hardly turn to them to establish the curriculum by which they can escape from their limitations. If they understood what is beyond them, they would not be handicapped.

T-24.IV.2 - What could the purpose of the body be but specialness? And it is this that makes it frail and helpless in its own defense. It was conceived to make you frail and helpless. The goal of separation is its curse.
Yet bodies have no goal. Purpose is of the mind. And mind's can change as they desire. What they are, and all their attributes, they cannot change. But what they hold as purpose can be changed, and body states must shift accordingly. <u>Of itself the body can do nothing</u>. See it as means to hurt, and it is hurt. See it as means to heal, and it is healed.

W-pI.47.ti-2 - God is the strength in which I trust.

If you are trusting in your own strength, you have every reason to be apprehensive, anxious and fearful. What can you predict or control? What is there in you that can be counted on? What would give you the ability to be aware of all the facets of any problem, and to resolve them in such a way that only good can come of it? What is there in you that gives you the recognition of the right solution, and the guarantee that it will be accomplished?

<u>Of yourself you can do none of these things.</u> To believe that you can is to put your trust where trust is unwarranted, and to justify fear, anxiety, depression, anger and sorrow. Who can put his faith in weakness and feel safe? Yet who can put his faith in strength and feel weak?

Bible Reference - Text

John 5:30 - I can of mine own self do nothing: as I hear, I....
(Continued) - (To read the full text of the above go to page 342.)

Course Ref/s - Citation/s

M-29.4 - Here again is the paradox often referred to in the course. To say, "<u>Of myself I can do nothing</u>" is to gain all power. And yet it is but a seeming paradox. As God created you, you have all power. The image you made of yourself has none. The Holy Spirit knows the truth about you. The image you made does not. Yet, despite its obvious and complete ignorance, this image assumes it knows all things because you have given that belief to it. Such is your teaching, and teaching of the world that was made to uphold it. But the Teacher Who knows the truth has not forgotten it. His decisions bring benefit to all, being wholly devoid of attack. And therefore incapable of arousing guilt.

Bible Reference - Text

John 6:19-20 - So when they had rowed about five and twenty or thirty furlongs, they see Jesus walking on the sea, and drawing nigh unto the ship: and they were afraid. But he saith unto them, It is I; be not afraid.

Course Ref/s - Citation/s

T-11.V.2 - What is healing but the removal of all that stands in the way of knowledge? And how else can one dispel illusions except by looking at them directly, without protecting them? Be not afraid, therefore, for what you will be looking at is the source of fear, and you are beginning to learn that fear is not real. You are also learning that its effects can be dispelled merely by denying their reality. The next step is obviously to recognize that what has no effects does not exist. Laws do not operate in a vacuum, and what leads to nothing has not happened. If reality is recognized by its extension, what leads to nothing could not be real. Do not be afraid, then, to look upon fear, for it cannot be seen. Clarity undoes confusion by definition, and to look upon darkness through light must dispel it.

T-27.V.4 - There is no sadness where a miracle has come to heal. And nothing more than just one instant of your love without attack is necessary that all this occur. In that one instant you are healed, and in that single instant is all healing done. What stands apart from you, when you accept the blessing that the holy instant brings? Be not afraid of blessing, for the One Who blesses you loves all the world, and leaves nothing within the world that could be feared. But if you shrink from blessing, will the world indeed seem fearful, for you have withheld its peace and comfort, leaving it to die.

T-28.III.8 - Be not afraid, my child, but let your world be gently lit by miracles. And where the little gap was seen to stand between you and your brother, join him there. And sickness will now be seen without a cause. The dream of healing in forgiveness lies, and gently shows you that you never sinned. The miracle would leave no proof of guilt to bring you witness to what never was. And in your storehouse it will make a place of welcome for your Father and your Self. The door is open, that all those may come who would no longer starve, and would enjoy the feast of plenty set before them there. And they will meet with your invited Guests the miracle has asked to come to you.

W-pI.153.20 - Your practicing will now begin to take the earnestness of love, to help you keep your mind from wandering from its intent. Be not afraid nor timid. There can be no doubt that you will reach your final goal. The ministers of God can never fail, because the love and strength and peace that shine from them to all their brothers come from Him. These are His gifts to you. Defenselessness is all you need to give Him in return. You lay aside but what was never real, to look on Christ and see His sinlessness.

W-pII.10.4 - God's Final Judgment is as merciful as every step in His appointed plan to bless His Son, and call him to return to the eternal peace He shares with him. Be not afraid of love. For it alone can heal all sorrow, wipe away all tears, and gently waken from his dream of pain the Son whom God acknowledges as His. Be not afraid of this. Salvation asks you give it welcome. And the world awaits your glad acceptance, which will set it free.

C-ep.3 - <u>Be not afraid.</u> We only start again an ancient journey long ago begun that but seems new. We have begun again upon a road we travelled on before and lost our way a little while. And now we try again. Our new beginning has the certainty the journey lacked till now. Look up and see His Word among the stars, where He has set your Name along with His. Look up and find your certain destiny the world would hide but God would have you see.

Bible Reference - Text

John 6:68-69 - Then Simon Peter answered him, Lord, to whom shall we go? Thou hast the words of eternal life. And we believe and are sure that thou art that Christ, the Son of the living God.

Course Ref/s - Citation/s

T-07.VII.5 - The gift of life is yours to give, because it was given you. You are unaware of your gift because you do not give it. You cannot make nothing live, since nothing cannot be enlivened. Therefore, you are not extending the gift you both have and are, and so you do not know your being. All confusion comes from not extending life, because that is not the Will of your Creator. You can do nothing apart from Him, and you do do nothing apart from Him. Keep His way to remember yourself, and teach His way lest you forget yourself. Give only honour to <u>the Sons of the living God</u>, and count yourself among them gladly.

Bible Reference - Text

John 7:24 - Judge not according to the appearance, but judge righteous judgment.

Course Ref/s - Citation/s

M-10.3 - The aim of our curriculum [A Course in Miracles], unlike the goal of the world's learning, is the recognition that judgment in the usual sense is impossible. This is not an opinion but a fact. In order to <u>judge anything rightly</u>, one would have to be fully aware of an inconceivably wide range of things; past, present and to come. One would have to recognize in advance all the effects of his judgments on everyone and everything involved in them in any way. And one would have to be certain there is no distortion in his perception, so that his judgment would be wholly fair to everyone on whom it rests now and in the future. Who is in a position to do this? Who except in grandiose fantasies would claim this for himself?

Bible Reference - Text

John 8:12 - Then spake Jesus again unto them, saying, I am the light of the world: he that followeth me shall not walk in darkness, but shall have the light of life.

Course Ref/s - Citation/s

T-08.IV.2 - <u>I am come as a light into a world</u> that does deny itself everything. It does this simply by dissociating itself from everything. It is therefore an illusion of isolation, maintained by fear of the same loneliness that is its illusion. I said that I am with you always, even unto the end of the world. That is why <u>I am the light of the world</u>. If I am with you in the loneliness of the world, the loneliness is gone. You cannot maintain the illusion of loneliness if you are not alone. My purpose, then, is still to overcome the world. I do not attack it, but my light must dispel it because of what it is. Light does not attack darkness, but it does shine it away. If my light goes with you everywhere, you shine it away with me. The light becomes ours, and you cannot abide in darkness any more than darkness can abide wherever you go. The remembrance of me is the remembrance of yourself, and of Him Who sent me to you.

T-13.V.11 - <u>The Holy Spirit is the light in which Christ stands</u> revealed. And all who would behold Him can see Him, for they have asked for light. Nor will they see Him alone, for He is no more alone than they are. Because they saw the Son, they have risen in Him to the Father. And all this will they understand, because they looked within and saw beyond the darkness the Christ in them, and recognized Him. In the sanity of His vision they looked upon themselves with love, seeing themselves as the Holy Spirit sees them. And with this vision of the truth in them came all the beauty of the world to shine upon them.

T-13.VI.7 - The present offers you your brothers in the light that would unite you with them, and free you from the past. Would you, then, hold the past against them? For if you do, you are choosing to remain in the darkness that is not there, and refusing to accept the light that is offered you. For <u>the light of perfect vision</u> is freely given as it is freely received, and can be accepted only without limit. In this one, still dimension of time that does not change, and where there is no sight of what you were, you look at Christ and call His witnesses to shine on you because you called them forth. And they will not deny the truth in you, because you looked for it in them and found it there.

T-13.VIII.4-5 - Apart from the Father and the Son, the Holy Spirit has no function. He is not separate from Either, being in the Mind of Both, and knowing that Mind is One. He is a Thought of God, and God has given Him to you because He has no Thoughts He does not share. His message speaks of timelessness in time, and that is why Christ's vision looks on everything with love. Yet even Christ's vision is not His reality. The golden aspects of reality that spring to light under His loving gaze are partial glimpses of the Heaven that lies beyond them.

This is the miracle of creation; that it is one forever. Every miracle you offer to the Son of God is but the true perception of one aspect of the whole. Though every aspect is the whole, you cannot know this until you see that every aspect is the same, perceived in the same light and therefore one. Everyone seen without the past thus brings you nearer to the end of time by bringing healed and healing sight into the darkness, and enabling the world to see. <u>For light must come into the darkened world to make Christ's vision possible even here. Help Him to give His gift of light to all who think they wander in the darkness</u>, and let Him gather them into His quiet sight that makes them one.

T-14.II.7 - The happy learner meets the conditions of learning here, as he meets the conditions of knowledge in the Kingdom. All this lies in the Holy Spirit's plan to free you from the past, and open up the way to freedom for you. For truth is true. What else could ever be, or ever was? This simple lesson holds the key to the dark door that you believe is locked forever. You made this door of nothing, and behind it is nothing. The key is only the light that shines away the shapes and forms and fears of nothing. Accept this key to freedom from the hands of Christ Who gives it to you, that you may join Him in the holy task of bringing light. For, like your brothers, you do not realize <u>the light has come and freed you from the sleep of darkness</u>.

Bible Reference - Text

John 8:12 - Then spake Jesus again unto them, saying....
(Continued) - (To read the full text of the above go to page 347.)

Course Ref/s - Citation/s

W-pI.61.3-4 - True humility requires that you accept today's idea [<u>I am the light of the world.</u>] because it is God's Voice which tells you it is true. This is a beginning step in accepting your real function on earth. It is a giant stride toward taking your rightful place in salvation. It is a positive assertion of your right to be saved, and an acknowledgment of the power that is given you to save others.

You will want to think about this idea as often as possible today. It is the perfect answer to all illusions, and therefore to all temptation. It brings all the images you have made about yourself to the truth, and helps you depart in peace, unburdened and certain of your purpose.

W-pI.81.1 - <u>I am the light of the world.</u>

How holy am I, who have been given the function of lighting up the world! Let me be still before my holiness. In its calm light let all my conflicts disappear. In its peace let me remember who I am.

W-pI.81.3 - <u>Forgiveness is my function as the light of the world.</u>

It is through accepting my function that I will see the light in me. And in this light will my function stand clear and perfectly unambiguous before my sight. My acceptance does not depend on my recognizing what my function is, for I do not yet understand forgiveness. Yet I will trust that, in the light, I will see it as it is.

W-pI.82.1 - <u>The light of the world brings peace to every mind through my forgiveness.</u>

My forgiveness is the means by which the light of the world finds expression through me. My forgiveness is the means by which I become aware of the light of the world in me. My forgiveness is the means by which the world is healed, together with myself. Let me, then, forgive the world, that it may be healed along with me.

M-1.1-2 - A teacher of God is anyone who chooses to be one. His qualifications consist solely in this; somehow, somewhere he has made a deliberate choice in which he did not see his interests as apart from someone else's. Once he has done that, his road is established and his direction is sure. <u>A light has entered the darkness</u>. It may be a single light, but that is enough. He has entered an agreement with God even if he does not yet believe in Him. He has become a bringer of salvation. He has become a teacher of God.

2 They come from all over the world. They come from all religions and from no religion. They are the ones who have answered. The Call is universal. It goes on all the time everywhere. It calls for teachers to speak for It and redeem the world. Many hear It, but few will answer. Yet it is all a matter of time. Everyone will answer in the end, but the end can be a long, long way off. It is because of this that the plan of the teachers was established. Their function is to save time. Each one begins as a single light, but with the Call at its center it is <u>a light that cannot be limited</u>. And each one saves a thousand years of time as the world judges it. To the Call Itself time has no meaning.

Bible Reference - Text

John 8:16 - And yet if I judge, my judgment is true: for I am not alone, but I and the Father that sent me.

Course Ref/s - Citation/s

T-08.IV.3 - You were in darkness until God's Will was done completely by any part of the Sonship. When this was done, it was perfectly accomplished by all. How else could it be perfectly accomplished?
My mission was simply to unite the will of the Sonship with the Will of the Father by being aware of the Father's Will myself. This is the awareness I came to give you, and your problem in accepting it is the problem of this world. Dispelling it is salvation, and in this sense I am the salvation of the

world. The world must therefore despise and reject me, because the world is the belief that love is impossible. If you will accept the fact that I am with you, you are denying the world and accepting God. My will is His, and your decision to hear me is the decision to hear His Voice and abide in His Will. As <u>God sent me</u> to you so will I send you to others. And I will go to them with you, so we can teach them peace and union.

Bible Reference - Text

John 8:31-32 - Then said Jesus to those Jews which believed on him, If ye continue in my word, then are ye my disciples indeed; And ye shall know the truth, and the truth shall make you free.

Course Ref/s - Citation/s

T-02.I.4 - All fear is ultimately reducible to the basic misperception that you have the ability to usurp the power of God. Of course, you neither can nor have been able to do this. Here is the real basis for your escape from fear. The escape is brought about by your acceptance of the Atonement, which enables you to realize that your errors never really occurred. Only after the deep sleep fell upon Adam could he experience nightmares. If a light is suddenly turned on while someone is dreaming a fearful dream, he may initially interpret the light itself as part of his dream and be afraid of it. However, when he awakens, the light is correctly perceived as the release from the dream, which is then no longer accorded reality. This release does not depend on illusions. <u>The knowledge that illuminates not only sets you free, but also shows you clearly that you are free.</u>

T-03.V.5 - Knowing is not open to interpretation. You may try to "interpret" meaning, but this is always open to error because it refers to the perception of meaning. Such incongruities are the result of attempts to regard yourself as separated and unseparated at the same time. It is impossible to make so fundamental a confusion without increasing your overall confusion still further. Your mind may have become very ingenious, but as always happens when method and content are separated, it is utilized in a futile attempt to escape from an inescapable impasse. Ingenuity is totally divorced from knowledge, because knowledge does not require ingenuity. Ingenious thinking is not <u>the truth that shall set you free</u>, but you are free of the need to engage in it when you are willing to let it go.

T-05.III.11 - The ego made the world as it perceives it, but the Holy Spirit, the re-interpreter of what the ego made, sees the world as a teaching device for bringing you home. The Holy Spirit must perceive time, and reinterpret it into the timeless. He must work through opposites, because He must work with and for a mind that is in opposition. Correct and learn, and be open to learning. You have not made truth, but <u>truth can still set you free</u>. Look as the Holy Spirit looks, and understand as He understands. His understanding looks back to God in remembrance of me. He is in communion with God always, and He is part of you. He is your Guide to salvation, because He holds the remembrance of things past and to come, and brings them to the present. He holds this gladness gently in your mind, asking only that you increase it in His Name by sharing it to increase His joy in you.

T-05.IV.2 - What the ego makes it keeps to itself, and so it is without strength. Its existence is unshared. It does not die; it was merely never born. Physical birth is not a beginning; it is a continuing. Everything that continues has already been born. It will increase as you are willing to return the unhealed part of your mind to the higher part, returning it undivided to creation. I have come to give you the foundation, so your own <u>thoughts can make you really free</u>. You have carried the burden of unshared ideas that are too weak to increase, but having made them you did not realize how to undo them. You cannot cancel out your past errors alone. They will not disappear from your mind without the Atonement, a remedy not of your making. The Atonement must be understood as a pure act of sharing. That is what I meant when I said it is possible even in this world to listen to one Voice. If you are part of God and the Sonship is one, you cannot be limited to the self the ego sees.

T-06.III.4 - Since you cannot not teach, your salvation lies in teaching the exact opposite of everything the ego believes. This is how you will learn <u>the truth that will set you free</u>, and will keep you free as others learn it of you. The only way to have peace is to teach peace. By teaching peace you must learn it yourself, because you cannot teach what you still dissociate. Only thus can you win back the knowledge that you threw away. An idea that you share you must have. It awakens in your mind through the conviction of teaching it. Everything you teach you are learning. Teach only love, and learn that love is yours and you are love.

T-14.III.13 - The One Who knows the plan of God that God would have you follow can teach you what it is. Only His wisdom is capable of guiding you to follow it. Every decision you undertake alone but signifies that you

would define what salvation is, and what you would be saved from.
The Holy Spirit knows that all salvation is escape from guilt. You have no other "enemy," and against this strange distortion of the purity of the Son of God the Holy Spirit is your only Friend. He is the strong protector of <u>the innocence that sets you free</u>. And it is His decision to undo everything that would obscure your innocence from your unclouded mind.

Bible Reference - Text

John 8:31-32 - Then said Jesus to those Jews which believed....
(Continued) - (To read the full text of the above go to page 351.)

Course Ref/s - Citation/s

T-18.I.7 - When you seem to see some twisted form of the original error rising to frighten you, say only, "God is not fear, but Love," and it will disappear. <u>The truth will save you.</u> It has not left you, to go out into the mad world and so depart from you. Inward is sanity; insanity is outside you. You but believe it is the other way; that truth is outside, and error and guilt within. Your little, senseless substitutions, touched with insanity and swirling lightly off on a mad course like feathers dancing insanely in the wind, have no substance. They fuse and merge and separate, in shifting and totally meaningless patterns that need not be judged at all. To judge them individually is pointless. Their tiny differences in form are no real differences at all. None of them matters. That they have in common and nothing else. Yet what else is necessary to make them all the same?

W-pI.076.7 - The laws of God can never be replaced. We will devote today to rejoicing that this is so. It is no longer a truth we would hide. We realize instead it is <u>a truth that keeps us free</u> forever. Magic imprisons, but the laws of God make free. The light has come because there are no laws but His.

W-pI.110.05 - The healing power of today's idea [I am as God created me.] is limitless. It is the birthplace of all miracles, the great restorer of the truth to the awareness of the world. Practice today's idea with gratitude. This is <u>the truth that comes to set you free</u>. This is the truth that God has promised you. This is the Word in which all sorrow ends.

W-pI.110.11 - We will remember Him throughout the day with thankful hearts and loving thoughts for all who meet with us today. For it is thus that we remember Him. And we will say, that we may be reminded of His Son, our holy Self, the Christ in each of us: I am as God created me. Let us declare this truth as often as we can. <u>This is the Word of God that sets you free.</u> This is the key that opens up the gate of Heaven, and that lets you enter in the peace of God and His eternity.

W-pI.136.14-15 - Truth has a power far beyond defense, for no illusions can remain where truth has been allowed to enter. And it comes to any mind that would lay down its arms, and cease to play with folly. It is found at any time; today, if you will choose to practice giving welcome to the truth.

15 This is our aim today. And we will give a quarter of an hour twice to ask <u>the truth to come to us and set us free</u>. And truth will come, for it has never been apart from us. It merely waits for just this invitation which we give today. We introduce it with a healing prayer, to help us rise above defensiveness, and let truth be as it has always been:

Sickness is a defense against the truth. I will accept the truth of what I am, and let my mind be wholly healed today.

W-pI.161.8:3-9:9 - Mistake not the intensity of rage projected fear must spawn. It shrieks in wrath, and claws the air in frantic hope it can reach to its maker and devour him.

This do the body's eyes behold in one whom Heaven cherishes, the angels love and God created perfect. This is his reality. And in Christ's vision is his loveliness reflected in a form so holy and so beautiful that you could scarce refrain from kneeling at his feet. Yet you will take his hand instead, for you are like him in the sight that sees him thus. Attack on him is enemy to you, for you will not perceive that in his hands is your salvation.
Ask him but for this, and he will give it to you. Ask him not to symbolize your fear. Would you request that <u>love</u> destroy itself? Or would you have it revealed to you and <u>set you free</u>?

W-pI.161.11 - Select one brother, symbol of the rest, and ask salvation of him. See him first as clearly as you can, in that same form to which you are accustomed. See his face, his hands and feet, his clothing. Watch him smile, and see familiar gestures which he makes so frequently. Then think of this: What you are seeing now conceals from you the sight of one who can forgive you all your sins; whose sacred hands can take away the nails which pierce your own, and lift the crown of thorns which you have placed upon your bleeding head. Ask this of him, that <u>he may set you free</u>: Give me your blessing, holy Son of God. I would behold you with the eyes of Christ, and see my perfect sinlessness in you.

Bible Reference - Text

John 8:51 - Verily, verily, I say unto you, If a man keep my saying, he shall never see death.

Course Ref/s - Citation/s

W-pI.162.2 - Here is the Word [I am as God created me.] by which the Son became his Father's happiness, His Love and His completion. Here creation is proclaimed, and honored as it is. There is no dream these words will not dispel; no thought of sin and no illusion which the dream contains that will not fade away before their might. They are the trumpet of awakening that sounds around the world. The dead awake in answer to its call. And those who live and hear this sound <u>will never look on death</u>.

Bible Reference - Text

John 8:58 - Jesus said unto them, Verily, verily, I say unto you, Before Abraham was, I am.

Course Ref/s - Citation/s

T-03.III.6 - Right perception is necessary before God can communicate directly to His altars, which He established in His Sons. There He can communicate His certainty, and His knowledge will bring peace without question. God is not a stranger to His Sons, and His Sons are not strangers to each other. Knowledge preceded both perception and time, and will ultimately replace them. That is the real meaning of "Alpha and Omega, the beginning and the end" and "<u>Before Abraham was I am.</u>" Perception can and must be stabilised, but knowledge is stable. "Fear God and keep His commandments" becomes "Know God and accept His certainty."

Bible Reference - Text

John 10:30 - I and my Father are one.

Course Ref/s - Citation/s

T-01.II.4 - "No man cometh unto the Father but by me" does not mean that I am in any way separate or different from you except in time, and time does not really exist. The statement is more meaningful in terms of a vertical rather than a horizontal axis. You stand below me and I stand below God. In the process of "rising up," I am higher because without me the distance between God and man would be too great for you to encompass. I bridge the distance as an elder brother to you on the one hand, and as a Son of God on the other. My devotion to my brothers has placed me in charge of the Sonship, which I render complete because I share it. This may appear to contradict the statement "<u>I and my Father are one</u>," but there are two parts to the statement in recognition that the Father is greater.

T-08.III.3 - <u>The Will of the Father and of the Son are one</u>, by their extension. Their extension is the result of Their oneness, holding Their unity together by extending Their joint Will. This is perfect creation by the perfectly created, in union with the Perfect Creator. The Father must give fatherhood to His Son, because His Own Fatherhood must be extended outward. You who belong in God have the holy function of extending His Fatherhood by placing no limits upon it. Let the Holy Spirit teach you how to do this, for you can know what it means only of God Himself.

T-11.I.02 - To be alone is to be separated from infinity, but how can this be if infinity has no end? No one can be beyond the limitless, because what has no limits must be everywhere. There are no beginnings and no endings in God, Whose universe is Himself. Can you exclude yourself from the universe, or from God Who is the universe? <u>I and my Father are one</u> with you, for you are part of Us. Do you really believe that part of God can be missing or lost to Him?

T-11.I.07 - Could any part of God be without His Love, and could any part of His Love be contained? God is your heritage, because His one gift is Himself. How can you give except like Him if you would know His gift to you? Give, then, without limit and without end, to learn how much He has given you. Your ability to accept Him depends on your willingness to give as He gives. Your fatherhood and your Father are one. God wills to create, and your will is His. It follows, then, that you will to create, since your will follows from His. And being an extension of His Will, yours must be the same.

T-11.I.11 - You are asked to trust the Holy Spirit only because He speaks for you. He is the Voice for God, but never forget that God did not will to be alone. He shares His Will with you; He does not thrust it upon you. Always remember that what He gives He keeps, so that nothing He gives can contradict Him. You who share His life must share it to know it, for sharing is knowing. Blessed are you who learn that to hear the Will of your Father is to know your own. For it is your will to be like Him, Whose Will it is that it be so. God's Will is that His Son be one, and united with Him in His Oneness. That is why healing is the beginning of the recognition that your will is His.

T-11.II.1 - If sickness is separation, the decision to heal and to be healed is the first step toward recognizing what you truly want. Every attack is a step away from this, and every healing thought brings it closer. The Son of God has both Father and Son, because he is both Father and Son. To unite having and being is to unite your will with His, for He wills you Himself. And you will yourself to Him because, in your perfect understanding of Him, you know there is but one Will. Yet when you attack any part of God and His Kingdom your understanding is not perfect, and what you really want is therefore lost to you.

T-14.XI.05 - You have one test, as sure as God, by which to recognize if what you learned is true. If you are wholly free of fear of any kind, and if all those who meet or even think of you share in your perfect peace, then you can be sure that you have learned God's lesson, and not your own. Unless all this is true, there are dark lessons in your mind that hurt and hinder you, and everyone around you. The absence of perfect peace means but one thing: You think you do not will for God's Son what his Father wills for him. Every dark lesson teaches this, in one form or another. And each bright lesson with which the Holy Spirit will replace the dark ones you do not accept, teaches you that you will with the Father and His Son.

T-14.XI.11 - God's Son will always be indivisible. As we are held as one in God, so do we learn as one in Him. God's Teacher is as like to His Creator as is His Son, and through His Teacher does God proclaim His Oneness and His Son's. Listen in silence, and do not raise your voice against Him. For He teaches the miracle of oneness, and before His lesson division disappears. Teach like Him here, and you will remember that you have always created like your Father. The miracle of creation has never ceased, having the holy stamp of immortality upon it. This is the Will of God for all creation, and all creation joins in willing this.

Bible Reference - Text

John 10:30 - I and my Father are one. (Continued)

Course Ref/s - Citation/s

T-15.XI.09 - God offers thanks to the holy host who would receive Him, and lets Him enter and abide where He would be. And by your welcome does He welcome you into Himself, for what is contained in you who welcome Him is returned to Him. And we but celebrate His Wholeness as we welcome Him into ourselves. Those who receive the Father are one with Him, being host to Him Who created them. And by allowing Him to enter, the remembrance of the Father enters with Him, and with Him they remember the only relationship they ever had, and ever want to have.

W-pI.158.1-2 - What has been given you? The knowledge that you are a mind, in Mind and purely mind, sinless forever, wholly unafraid, because you were created out of love. Nor have you left your Source, remaining as you were created. This was given you as knowledge which you cannot lose. It was given as well to every living thing, for by that knowledge only does it live.

You have received all this. No one who walks the world but has received it. It is not this knowledge which you give, for that is what creation gave. All this cannot be learned. What, then, are you to learn to give today? Our lesson yesterday [Into His Presence would I enter now.] evoked a theme found early in the text. Experience cannot be shared directly, in the way that vision can. The revelation that the Father and the Son are one will come in time to every mind. Yet is that time determined by the mind itself, not taught.

W-pI.169.4-5 - We have perhaps appeared to contradict our statement that the revelation of the Father and the Son as one has been already set. But we have also said the mind determines when that time will be, and has determined it. And yet we urge you to bear witness to the Word of God to hasten the experience of truth, and speed its advent into every mind that recognizes truth's effects on you.

Oneness is simply the idea God is. And in His Being, He encompasses all things. No mind holds anything but Him. We say "God is," and then we cease to speak, for in that knowledge words are meaningless. There are no lips to speak them, and no part of mind sufficiently distinct to feel that it is now aware of something not itself. It has united with its Source. And like its Source Itself, it merely is.

W-pI.195.6 - We thank our Father for one thing alone; that <u>we are</u> separate from no living thing, and therefore <u>one with Him</u>. And we rejoice that no exceptions ever can be made which would reduce our wholeness, nor impair or change our function to complete the One Who is Himself completion. We give thanks for every living thing, for otherwise we offer thanks for nothing, and we fail to recognize the gifts of God to us.

W-pI.198.3 - Forgiveness sweeps all other dreams away, and though it is itself a dream, it breeds no others. All illusions save this one must multiply a thousand fold. But this is where illusions end. Forgiveness is the end of dreams, because it is a dream of waking. It is not itself the truth. Yet does it point to where the truth must be, and gives direction with the certainty of God Himself. It is a dream in which <u>the Son of God awakens to his Self and to his Father, knowing They are one</u>.

Bible Reference - Text

John 11:1-4 - Now a certain man was sick, named Lazarus, of Bethany, the town of Mary and her sister Martha. (It was that Mary which anointed the Lord with ointment, and wiped his feet with her hair, whose brother Lazarus was sick.) Therefore his sisters sent unto him, saying, Lord, behold, he whom thou lovest is sick. When Jesus heard that, he said, This sickness is not unto death, but for the glory of God, that the Son of God might be glorified thereby.

Course Ref/s - Citation/s

T-08.IX.3 - Wholeness heals because it is of the mind. All forms of <u>sickness, even unto death</u>, are physical expressions of the fear of awakening. They are attempts to reinforce sleeping out of fear of waking.

This is a pathetic way of trying not to see by rendering the faculties for seeing ineffectual. "Rest in peace" is a blessing for the living, not the dead, because rest comes from waking, not from sleeping. Sleep is withdrawing; waking is joining. Dreams are illusions of joining, because they reflect the ego's distorted notions about what joining is. Yet the Holy Spirit, too, has use for sleep, and can use dreams on behalf of waking if you will let Him.

Bible Reference - Text

John 11:11 - These things said he: and after that he saith unto them, Our friend Lazarus sleepeth; but I go, that I may awake him out of sleep.

Course Ref/s - Citation/s

T-24.III.7 - <u>The special ones are all asleep</u>, surrounded by a world of loveliness they do not see. Freedom and peace and joy stand there, beside the bier on which they sleep, <u>and call them to come forth and waken from their dream of death</u>. Yet they hear nothing. They are lost in dreams of specialness. They hate the call that would awaken them, and they curse God because He did not make their dream reality. Curse God and die, but not by Him Who made not death; but only in the dream. Open your eyes a little; see the savior God gave to you that you might look on him, and give him back his birthright. It is yours.

Bible Reference - Text

John 11:25 - Jesus said unto her, I am the resurrection, and the life: he that believeth in me, though he were dead, yet shall he live:

Course Ref/s - Citation/s

T-1.III.2 - "Heaven and earth shall pass away" means that they will not continue to exist as separate states. My word, which is <u>the resurrection and the life</u>, shall not pass away because life is eternal. You are the work of God, and His work is wholly loveable and wholly loving. This is how a man must think of himself in his heart, because this is what he is.

T-11.VI.4 - <u>I am your resurrection and your life.</u> You live in me because you live in God. And everyone lives in you, as you live in everyone. Can you, then, perceive unworthiness in a brother and not perceive it in yourself? And can you perceive it in yourself and not perceive it in God? Believe in the resurrection because it has been accomplished, and it has been accomplished in you. This is as true now as it will ever be, for the resurrection is the Will of God, which knows no time and no exceptions. But make no exceptions yourself, or you will not perceive what has been accomplished for you. For we ascend unto the Father together, as it was in the beginning, is now and ever shall be, for such is the nature of God's Son as his Father created him.

T-19.IV.C.10 - What danger can assail the wholly innocent? What can attack the guiltless? What fear can enter and disturb the peace of sinlessness? What has been given you, even in its infancy, is in full communication with God and you. In its tiny hands it holds, in perfect safety, every miracle you will perform, held out to you. The miracle of life is ageless, born in time but nourished in eternity. Behold this infant, to whom you gave a resting place by your forgiveness of your brother, and see in it the Will of God. Here is the babe of Bethlehem reborn.
And everyone who gives him shelter will follow him, not to the cross, but to <u>the resurrection and the life.</u>

W-pI.20.3 - Your decision to see is all that vision requires. What you want is yours. Do not mistake the little effort that is asked of you for an indication that our goal is of little worth. Can the salvation of the world be a trivial purpose? And can the world be saved if you are not? <u>God has one Son, and he is the resurrection and the life.</u> His will is done because all power is given him in Heaven and on earth. In your determination to see is vision given you.

Bible Reference - Text

John 11:43-44 - And when he thus had spoken, he cried with a loud voice, Lazarus, come forth. And he that was dead came forth, bound hand and foot with grave clothes: and his face was bound about with a napkin. Jesus saith unto them, Loose him, and let him go.

Course Ref/s - Citation/s

T-04.IV.11 - I do not attack your ego. I do work with your higher mind, the home of the Holy Spirit, whether you are asleep or awake, just as your ego does with your lower mind, which is its home. I am your vigilance in this, because you are too confused to recognize your own hope. I am not mistaken. Your mind will elect to join with mine, and together we are invincible. You and your brother will yet come together in my name, and your sanity will be restored. <u>I raised the dead</u> by knowing that life is an eternal attribute of everything that the living God created. Why do you believe it is harder for me to inspire the dis-spirited or to stabilise the unstable? I do not believe that there is an order of difficulty in miracles; you do. I have called and you will answer. I understand that miracles are natural, because they are expressions of love. My calling you is as natural as your answer, and as inevitable.

T-29.VI.5-6 - This world will <u>bind your feet and tie your hands</u> and kill your body only if you think that it was made to crucify God's Son.
For even though it was a dream of death, you need not let it stand for this to you. Let this be changed, and nothing in the world but must be changed as well. For nothing here but is defined as what you see it for.

How lovely is the world whose purpose is forgiveness of God's Son! How free from fear, how filled with blessing and with happiness! And what a joyous thing it is to dwell a little while in such a happy place! Nor can it be forgot, in such a world, it is a little while till timelessness comes quietly to take the place of time.

Bible Reference - Text

John 12:12-15 - On the next day much people that were come to the feast, when they heard that Jesus was coming to Jerusalem,
[13] Took branches of palm trees, and went forth to meet him, and cried, Hosanna: Blessed is the King of Israel that cometh in the name of the Lord.
[14] And Jesus, when he had found a young ass, sat thereon; as it is written,
[15] Fear not, daughter of Sion: behold, thy King cometh, sitting on an ass's colt.

Course Ref/s - Citation/s

T-20.I.1.1 - <u>This is Palm Sunday</u>, the celebration of victory and the acceptance of the truth. Let us not spend this holy week brooding on the crucifixion of God's Son, but happily in the celebration of his release. For Easter is the sign of peace, not pain. A slain Christ has no meaning. But a risen Christ becomes the symbol of the Son of God's forgiveness on himself; the sign he looks upon himself as healed and whole.

T-20.I.1.2 - <u>This week begins with palms</u> and ends with lilies, the white and holy sign the Son of God is innocent. Let no dark sign of crucifixion intervene between the journey and its purpose; between the acceptance of the truth and its expression. This week we celebrate life, not death. And we honor the perfect purity of the Son of God, and not his sins. Offer your brother the gift of lilies, not the crown of thorns; the gift of love and not the "gift" of fear. You stand beside your brother, thorns in one hand and lilies in the other, uncertain which to give. Join now with me and throw away the thorns, offering the lilies to replace them. This Easter I would have the gift of your forgiveness offered by you to me, and returned by me to you. We cannot be united in crucifixion and in death. Nor can the resurrection be complete till your forgiveness rests on Christ, along with mine.

T-20.I.1.3 - <u>A week is short, and yet this holy week is the symbol of the whole journey the Son of God has undertaken.</u> He started with the sign of victory, the promise of the resurrection, already given him. Let him not wander into the temptation of crucifixion, and delay him there. Help him to go in peace beyond it, with the light of his own innocence lighting his way to his redemption and release. Hold him not back with thorns and nails when his redemption is so near. But let the whiteness of your shining gift of lilies speed him on his way to resurrection.

T-20.I.1.4 - Easter is not the celebration of the cost of sin but of its end. If you see glimpses of the face of Christ behind the veil, looking between the snow white petals of the lilies you have received and given as your gift, you will behold your brother's face and recognize it. I was a stranger and you took me in, not knowing who I was. Yet for your gift of lilies you will know. In your forgiveness of this stranger, alien to you and yet your ancient Friend, lies his release and your redemption with him. <u>The time of Easter is a time of joy, and not of mourning. Look on your risen Friend, and celebrate his holiness along with me. For Easter is the time of your salvation, along with mine.</u>

T-20.II.1.6 - This <u>Easter</u>, look with different eyes upon your brother. You have forgiven me. And yet I cannot use your gift of lilies while you see them not. Nor can you use what I have given unless you share it. The Holy Spirit's vision is no idle gift, no plaything to be tossed about a while and laid aside. Listen and hear this carefully, nor think it but a dream, a careless thought to play with, or a toy you would pick up from time to time and then put by. For if you do, so will it be to you.

Bible Reference - Text

John 12:46 - I am come a light into the world, that whosoever believeth on me should not abide in darkness.

Course Ref/s - Citation/s

T-05.VI.11 - When I said "I am come as a light into the world," I meant that I came to share the light with you. Remember my reference to the ego's dark glass, and remember also that I said, "Do not look there." It is still true that where you look to find yourself is up to you. Your patience with your brother is your patience with yourself. Is not a child of God worth patience? I have shown you infinite patience because my will is that of our Father, from Whom I learned of infinite patience. His Voice was in me as It is in you, speaking for patience towards the Sonship in the Name of Its Creator.

T-08.IV.2 - I am come as a light into a world that does deny itself everything. It does this simply by dissociating itself from everything. It is therefore an illusion of isolation, maintained by fear of the same loneliness that is its illusion. I said that I am with you always, even unto the end of the world. That is why I am the light of the world. If I am with you in the loneliness of the world, the loneliness is gone. You cannot maintain the illusion of loneliness if you are not alone. My purpose, then, is still to overcome the world. I do not attack it, but my light must dispel it because of what it is. Light does not attack darkness, but it does shine it away. If my light goes with you everywhere, you shine it away with me. The light becomes ours, and you cannot abide in darkness any more than darkness can abide wherever you go. The remembrance of me is the remembrance of yourself, and of Him Who sent me to you.

Bible Reference - Text

John 14:1 - Let not your heart be troubled: ye believe in God, believe also in me.

Course Ref/s - Citation/s

T-10.V.5 - I said before that of yourself you can do nothing, but you are not of yourself. If you were, what you have made would be true, and you could never escape. It is because you did not make yourself that <u>you need be troubled over nothing</u>. Your gods are nothing, because your Father did not create them. You cannot make creators who are unlike your Creator, any more than He could have created a Son who was unlike Him. If creation is sharing, it cannot create what is unlike itself. It can share only what it is. Depression is isolation, and so it could not have been created.

Bible Reference - Text

John 14:2-3 - In my Father's house are many mansions: if it were not so, I would have told you. I go to prepare a place for you. And if I go and prepare a place for you, I will come again, and receive you unto myself; that where I am, there ye may be also.

Course Ref/s - Citation/s

T-20.II.8 - <u>Your chosen home is on the other side</u>, beyond the veil. <u>It has been carefully prepared for you, and it is ready to receive you now.</u> You will not see it with the body's eyes. Yet all you need you have. Your home has called to you since time began, nor have you ever failed entirely to hear. You heard, but knew not how to look, nor where. And now you know. In you the knowledge lies, ready to be unveiled and freed from all the terror that kept it hidden. There is no fear in love. The song of Easter is the glad refrain the Son of God was never crucified. Let us lift up our eyes together, not in fear but faith. And there will be no fear in us, for in our vision will be no illusions; only a pathway to the open door of Heaven, the home we share in quietness and where we live in gentleness and peace, as one together.

T-29.V.6 - If you but knew the glorious goal that lies beyond forgiveness, you would not keep hold on any thought, however light the touch of evil

on it may appear to be. For you would understand how great the cost of holding anything God did not give in minds that can direct the hand to bless, and lead God's Son unto his <u>Father's house</u>. Would you not want to be a friend to him, created by his Father as His home? If God esteems him worthy of Himself, would you attack him with the hands of hate?
Who would lay bloody hands on Heaven itself, and hope to find its peace? Your brother thinks he holds the hand of death. Believe him not. But learn, instead, how blessed are you who can release him, just by offering him yours.

T-30.V.8 - How light and easy is the step across the narrow boundaries of the world of fear when you have recognized Whose hand you hold! Within your hand is everything you need to walk with perfect confidence away from fear forever, and to go straight on, and quickly reach the gate of Heaven itself. For He Whose hand you hold was waiting but for you to join Him. Now that you have come, would He delay in showing you the way that He must walk with you? His blessing lies on you as surely as His Father's Love rests upon Him. His gratitude to you is past your understanding, for you have enabled Him to rise from chains and go with you, together, to <u>His Father's house</u>.

T-31.VIII.12 - And now we say "Amen." For <u>Christ has come to dwell in the abode You set for Him before time was</u>, in calm eternity. The journey closes, ending at the place where it began. No trace of it remains. Not one illusion is accorded faith, and not one spot of darkness still remains to hide the face of Christ from anyone. Thy Will is done, complete and perfectly, and all creation recognizes You, and knows You as the only Source it has. Clear in Your likeness does the light shine forth from everything that lives and moves in You. For we have reached where all of us are one, and <u>we are home, where You would have us be</u>.

W-pI.156.2 - We are not inconsistent in the thoughts that we present in our curriculum. Truth must be true throughout, if it be true. It cannot contradict itself, nor be in parts uncertain and in others sure. You cannot walk the world apart from God, because you could not be without Him. He is what your life is. <u>Where you are He is.</u> There is one life. That life you share with Him. Nothing can be apart from Him and live.

W-pI.182.4 - Perhaps you think it is your childhood home that you would find again. The childhood of your body, and its place of shelter, are a memory now so distorted that you merely hold a picture of a past that never happened. Yet there is a Child in you Who seeks <u>His Father's house</u>, and knows that He is alien here. This childhood is eternal, with an innocence that will endure forever. Where this Child shall go is holy ground. It is His Holiness that lights up Heaven, and that brings to earth the pure reflection of the light above, wherein are earth and Heaven joined as one.

Bible Reference - Text

John 14:2-3 - In my Father's house are many mansions: if it....
(Continued) - (To read the full text of the above go to page 365.)

Course Ref/s - Citation/s

W-pI.193.11 - Give all you can, and give a little more. For now we would arise in haste and <u>go unto our Father's house</u>. We have been gone too long, and we would linger here no more. And as we practice, let us think about all things we saved to settle by ourselves, and kept apart from healing. Let us give them all to Him Who knows the way to look upon them so that they will disappear. Truth is His message; truth His teaching is. His are the lessons God would have us learn.

W-pII.263.ti-2 - My holy vision sees all things as pure.

Father, Your Mind created all that is, Your Spirit entered into it, Your Love gave life to it. And would I look upon what You created as if it could be made sinful? I would not perceive such dark and fearful images. A madman's dream is hardly fit to be my choice, instead of all the loveliness with which You bless creation; all its purity, its joy, and its eternal, quiet home in You. And while we still remain outside the gate of Heaven, let us look on all we see through holy vision and the eyes of Christ. Let all appearances seem pure to us, that we may pass them by in innocence, and walk together to our <u>Father's house</u> as brothers and the holy Sons of God.

S-2.III.3 - Do not establish what the form should be that Christ's forgiveness takes. He knows the way to make of every call a help to you, as you arise in haste to <u>go at last unto your Father's house</u>. Now can He make your footsteps sure, your words sincere; not with your own sincerity, but with His Own. Let Him take charge of how you would forgive, and each occasion then will be to you another step to Heaven and to peace.

Bible Reference - Text

John 14:5-6 - Thomas saith unto him, Lord, we know not whither thou goest; and how can we know the way? Jesus saith unto him, I am the way, the truth, and the life: no man cometh unto the Father, but by me.

Course Ref/s - Citation/s

T-01.II.4:1-5 - "No man cometh unto the Father but by me" does not mean that I am in any way separate or different from you except in time, and time does not really exist. The statement is more meaningful in terms of a vertical rather than a horizontal axis. You stand below me and I stand below God. In the process of "rising up," I am higher because without me the distance between God and man would be too great for you to encompass. I bridge the distance as an elder brother to you on the one hand, and as a Son of God on the other.

T-06.I.10 - We are still equal as learners, although we do not need to have equal experiences. The Holy Spirit is glad when you can learn from mine, and be reawakened by them. That is their only purpose, and that is the only way in which I can be perceived as the way, the truth and the life. When you hear only one Voice you are never called on to sacrifice. On the contrary, by being able to hear the Holy Spirit in others you can learn from their experiences, and can gain from them without experiencing them directly yourself. That is because the Holy Spirit is one, and anyone who listens is inevitably led to demonstrate His way for all.

T-07.III.1 - The Holy Spirit teaches one lesson, and applies it to all individuals in all situations. Being conflict-free, He maximises all efforts and all results. By teaching the power of the Kingdom of God Himself, He teaches you that all power is yours. Its application does not matter. It is always maximal. Your vigilance does not establish it as yours, but it does enable you to use it always and in all ways. When I said "I am with you always," I meant it literally. I am not absent to anyone in any situation. Because I am always with you, you are the way, the truth and the life. You did not make this power, any more than I did. It was created to be shared, and therefore cannot be meaningfully perceived as belonging to anyone at the expense of another. Such a perception makes it meaningless by eliminating or overlooking its real and only meaning.

T-16.I.6:7-7:9 - Only the Holy Spirit recognizes foolish needs as well as real ones. And He will teach you how to meet both without losing either.

You will attempt to do this only in secrecy. And you will think that by meeting the needs of one you do not jeopardise another, because you keep them separate and secret from each other. <u>That is not the way, for it leads not to life and truth.</u> No needs will long be left unmet if you leave them all to Him Whose function is to meet them. That is His function, and not yours. He will not meet them secretly, for He would share everything you give through Him. That is why He gives it. What you give through Him is for the whole Sonship, not for part of it. Leave Him His function, for He will fulfil it if you but ask Him to enter your relationships, and bless them for you.

T-20.III.11 - Your gift unto your brother has given me the certainty our union will be soon. Share, then, this faith with me, and know that it is justified. There is no fear in perfect love because it knows no sin, and it must look on others as on itself. Looking with charity within, what can it fear without? The innocent see safety, and the pure in heart see God within His Son, and look unto <u>the Son to lead them to the Father</u>. And where else would they go but where they will to be? You and your brother now will lead the other to the Father as surely as God created His Son holy, and kept him so. In your brother is the light of God's eternal promise of your immortality. See him as sinless, and there can *be* no fear in you.

W-pI.189.7:5-8:8 - Forget this world, forget this course, and come with wholly empty hands unto your God.

<u>Is it not He Who knows the way</u> to you? You need not know the way to Him. Your part is simply to allow all obstacles that you have interposed between the Son and God the Father to be quietly removed forever.
God will do His part in joyful and immediate response. Ask and receive. But do not make demands, nor point the road to God by which He should appear to you. The way to reach Him is merely to let Him be. For in that way is your reality proclaimed as well.

W-pII.302.1-2 - Father, our eyes are opening at last. Your holy world awaits us, as our sight is finally restored and we can see. We thought we suffered. But we had forgot the Son whom You created. Now we see that darkness is our own imagining, and light is there for us to look upon. Christ's vision changes darkness into light, for fear must disappear when love has come. Let me forgive Your holy world today, that I may look upon its holiness and understand it but reflects my own.

Our Love awaits us as <u>we go to Him, and walks beside us showing us the way</u>. He fails in nothing. He the End we seek, and He the Means by which we go to Him.

Bible Reference - Text

John 14:5-6 - Thomas saith unto him, Lord, we know not ….
(Continued) - (To read the full text of the above go to page 368.)

Course Ref/s - Citation/s

W-pII.324.ti-2 - I merely follow, for I would not lead.

Father, You are the One Who gave the plan for my salvation to me. You have set the way I am to go, the role to take, and every step in my appointed path. I cannot lose the way. I can but choose to wander off a while, and then return. Your loving Voice will always call me back, and guide my feet aright. My brothers all can follow in the way I lead them. Yet I merely follow in the way to You, as You direct me and would have me go.

<u>So let us follow One Who knows the way.</u> We need not tarry, and we cannot stray except an instant from His loving Hand. We walk together, for we follow Him. And it is He Who makes the ending sure, and guarantees a safe returning home.

W-pII.fl.3:5-4:5 - For all that we forgive we will not fail to recognize as part of God Himself. And thus His memory is given back, completely and complete.

It is our function to remember Him on earth, as it is given us to be His Own completion in reality. So let us not forget our goal is shared, for it is that remembrance which contains the memory of God, and points <u>the way to Him</u> and to the Heaven of His peace. And shall we not forgive our brother, who can offer this to us? <u>He is the way, the truth and life that shows the way</u> to us. In him resides salvation, offered us through our forgiveness, given unto him.

P-1.1.2 - What better purpose could any relationship have than to invite the Holy Spirit to enter into it and give it His Own great gift of rejoicing? What higher goal could there be for anyone than to learn to call upon God and hear His Answer? And what more transcendent aim can there be than to recall <u>the Way, the Truth and the Life</u>, and to remember God? To help in this is the proper purpose of psychotherapy. Could anything be holier? For psychotherapy, correctly understood, teaches forgiveness and helps the patient to recognize and accept it. And in his healing is the therapist forgiven with him.

Bible Reference - Text

John 14:7-9 - If ye had known me, ye should have known my Father also: and from henceforth ye know him, and have seen him. Philip saith unto him, Lord, show us the Father, and it sufficeth us. Jesus saith unto him, Have I been so long time with you, and yet hast thou not known me, Philip? He that hath seen me hath seen the Father; and how sayest thou then, Show us the Father?

Course Ref/s - Citation/s

W-pI.198.10-12 - Accept the one illusion which proclaims there is no condemnation in God's Son, and Heaven is remembered instantly; the world forgotten, all its weird beliefs forgotten with it, as the face of Christ appears unveiled at last in this one dream. This is the gift the Holy Spirit holds for you from God your Father. Let today be celebrated both on earth and in your holy home as well. Be kind to both, as you forgive the trespasses you thought them guilty of, and see your innocence shining upon you from the face of Christ.

Now is there silence all around the world. Now is there stillness where before there was a frantic rush of thoughts that made no sense. Now is there tranquil light across the face of earth, made quiet in a dreamless sleep. And now the Word of God alone remains upon it. Only that can be perceived an instant longer. Then are symbols done, and everything you ever thought you made completely vanished from the mind that God forever knows to be His only Son.

There is no condemnation in him. He is perfect in his holiness. He needs no thoughts of mercy. Who could give him gifts when everything is his? And who could dream of offering forgiveness to <u>the Son</u> of Sinlessness Itself, <u>so like to Him Whose Son he is, that to behold the Son is to perceive no more, and only know the Father</u>? In this vision of the Son, so brief that not an instant stands between this single sight and timelessness itself, you see the vision of yourself, and then you disappear forever into God.

W-pII.354.ti-1 - We stand together, Christ and I, in peace And certainty of purpose. And in Him Is His Creator, as He is in me.
My oneness with the Christ establishes me as Your Son, beyond the reach of time, and wholly free of every law but Yours. I have no self except the Christ in me. I have no purpose but His Own. And He is like His Father. Thus must I be one with You as well as Him. For who is Christ except Your Son as You created Him? And what am I except the Christ in me?

Bible Reference - Text

John 14:13-14 - And whatsoever ye shall ask in my name, that will I do, that the Father may be glorified in the Son. If ye shall ask any thing in my name, I will do it.

Course Ref/s - Citation/s

T-04.III.6 - No force except your own will is strong enough or worthy enough to guide you. In this you are as free as God, and must remain so forever. Let us ask the Father in my name to keep you mindful of His Love for you and yours for Him. He has never failed to answer this request, because it asks only for what He has already willed. Those who call truly are always answered. Thou shalt have no other gods before Him because there are none.

T-08.IX.7 - The Bible enjoins you to be perfect, to heal all errors, to take no thought of the body as separate and to accomplish all things in my name. This is not my name alone, for ours is a shared identification. The Name of God's Son is one, and you are enjoined to do the works of love because we share this Oneness. Our minds are whole because they are one. If you are sick you are withdrawing from me. Yet you cannot withdraw from me alone. You can only withdraw from yourself and me.

M-23.1-3 - God's gifts can rarely be received directly. Even the most advanced of God's teachers will give way to temptation in this world. Would it be fair if their pupils were denied healing because of this? The Bible says, "Ask in the name of Jesus Christ." Is this merely an appeal to magic? A name does not heal, nor does an invocation call forth any special power. What does it mean to call on Jesus Christ? What does calling on his name confer? Why is the appeal to him part of healing?

We have repeatedly said that one who has perfectly accepted the Atonement for himself can heal the world. Indeed, he has already done so. Temptation may recur to others, but never to this One. He has become the risen Son of God. He has overcome death because he has accepted life. He has recognized himself as God created him, and in so doing he has recognized all living things as part of him. There is now no limit on his power, because it is the Power of God. So has his name become the Name of God, for he no longer sees himself as separate from Him.

What does this mean for you? It means that in remembering Jesus you are remembering God. The whole relationship of the Son to the Father lies in him. His part in the Sonship is also yours, and his completed learning guarantees your own success. Is he still available for help? What did he say about this? Remember his promises, and ask yourself honestly whether it is likely that he will fail to keep them. Can God fail His Son? And can one who is one with God be unlike Him? Who transcends the body has transcended limitation. Would the greatest teacher be unavailable to those who follow him?

S-2.III.6-7 - And what is it He [Christ] speaks to you about? About salvation and the gift of peace. About the end of sin and guilt and death. About the role forgiveness has in Him. Do you but listen. <u>For He will be heard by anyone who calls upon His Name</u>, and places his forgiveness in His hands. Forgiveness has been given Him to teach, to save it from destruction and to make the means for separation, sin and death become again the holy gift of God. Prayer is His Own right Hand, made free to save as true forgiveness is allowed to come from His eternal vigilance and Love. Listen and learn, and do not judge. It is to God you turn to hear what you should do. His answer will be clear as morning, nor is His forgiveness what you think it is.

Still does He know, and that should be enough. Forgiveness has a Teacher Who will fail in nothing. Rest a while in this; do not attempt to judge forgiveness, nor to set it in an earthly frame. Let it arise to Christ, Who welcomes it as gift to Him. He will not leave you comfortless, nor fail to send His angels down to <u>answer you in His Own Name</u>. He stands beside the door to which forgiveness is the only key. Give it to Him to use instead of you, and you will see the door swing silently open upon the shining face of Christ. Behold your brother there beyond the door; the Son of God as He created him.

S. John

Bible Reference - Text

John 14:16 - And I will pray the Father, and he shall give you another Comforter, that he may abide with you for ever;

Course Ref/s - Citation/s

T-05.I.4 - The Holy Spirit is the only part of the Holy Trinity that has a symbolic function. He is referred to as the Healer, the Comforter and the Guide. He is also described as something "separate," apart from the Father and from the Son. I myself said, "If I go I will send you another Comforter and He will abide with you." His symbolic function makes the Holy Spirit difficult to understand, because symbolism is open to different interpretations. As a man and also one of God's creations, my right thinking, which came from the Holy Spirit or the Universal Inspiration, taught me first and foremost that this Inspiration is for all. I could not have It myself without knowing this. The word "know" is proper in this context, because the Holy Spirit is so close to knowledge that He calls it forth; or better, allows it to come. I have spoken before of the higher or "true" perception, which is so near to truth that God Himself can flow across the little gap. Knowledge is always ready to flow everywhere, but it cannot oppose. Therefore you can obstruct it, although you can never lose it.

T-10.III.2 - What Comforter can there be for the sick children of God except His power through you? Remember that it does not matter where in the Sonship He is accepted. He is always accepted for all, and when your mind receives Him the remembrance of Him awakens throughout the Sonship. Heal your brothers simply by accepting God for them. Your minds are not separate, and God has only one channel for healing because He has but one Son. God's remaining Communication Link with all His children joins them together, and them to Him. To be aware of this is to heal them because it is the awareness that no one is separate, and so no one is sick.

T-11.II.4 - Healing is a sign that you want to make whole. And this willingness opens your ears to the Voice of the Holy Spirit, Whose message is wholeness. He will enable you to go far beyond the healing you would undertake, for beside your small willingness to make whole He will lay His Own complete Will and make yours whole. What can the Son of

God not accomplish with the Fatherhood of God in Him? And yet the invitation must come from you, for you have surely learned that whom you invite as your guest will abide with you.

T-11.II.7 - Would you be hostage to the ego or host to God? You will accept only whom you invite. You are free to determine who shall be your guest, and how long he shall remain with you. Yet this is not real freedom, for it still depends on how you see it. The Holy Spirit is there; although He cannot help you without your invitation. And the ego is nothing, whether you invite it in or not. Real freedom depends on welcoming reality, and of your guests only the Holy Spirit is real. Know, then, Who abides with you merely by recognizing what is there already, and do not be satisfied with imaginary comforters, for the Comforter of God is in you.

T-11.III.1 - When you are weary, remember you have hurt yourself. Your Comforter will rest you, but you cannot. You do not know how, for if you did you could never have grown weary. Unless you hurt yourself you could never suffer in any way, for that is not God's Will for His Son. Pain is not of Him, for He knows no attack and His peace surrounds you silently. God is very quiet, for there is no conflict in Him. Conflict is the root of all evil, for being blind it does not see whom it attacks. Yet it always attacks the Son of God, and the Son of God is you.

T-11.III.7 - Only God's Comforter can comfort you. In the quiet of His temple, He waits to give you the peace that is yours. Give His peace, that you may enter the temple and find it waiting for you. But be holy in the Presence of God, or you will not know that you are there. For what is unlike God cannot enter His Mind, because it was not His Thought and therefore does not belong to Him. And your mind must be as pure as His, if you would know what belongs to you. Guard carefully His temple, for He Himself dwells there and abides in peace. You cannot enter God's Presence with the dark companions beside you, but you also cannot enter alone. All your brothers must enter with you, for until you have accepted them you cannot enter. For you cannot understand wholeness unless you are whole, and no part of the Son can be excluded if he would know the Wholeness of his Father.

T-12.II.9 - You who have tried to banish love have not succeeded, but you who choose to banish fear must succeed. The Lord is with you, but you know it not. Yet your Redeemer liveth, and abideth in you in the peace out of which He was created. Would you not exchange this awareness for the awareness of fear? When we have overcome fear—not by hiding it, not by minimizing it, and not by denying its full import in any way—this is what you will really see. You cannot lay aside the obstacles to real vision without looking upon them, for to lay aside means to judge against. If you will look, the Holy Spirit will judge, and He will judge truly. Yet He cannot shine away what you keep hidden, for you have not offered it to Him and He cannot take it from you.

Bible Reference - Text

John 14:16 - And I will pray the Father, and he shall give.... (Continued) - (To read the full text of the above go to page 374.)

Course Ref/s - Citation/s

T-16.VI.9 - Nothing you seek to strengthen in the special relationship is really part of you. And you cannot keep part of the thought system that taught you it was real, and understand the Thought that knows what you are. You have allowed the Thought of your reality to enter your mind, and because you invited it, it will <u>abide with you</u>. Your love for it will not allow you to betray yourself, and you could not enter into a relationship where it could not go with you, for you would not want to be apart from it.

W-pI.127.9 - Call to your Father, certain that His Voice will answer. He Himself has promised this. And He Himself will place a spark of truth within your mind wherever you give up a false belief, a dark illusion of your own reality and what love means. He will shine through your idle thoughts today, and help you understand the truth of love. In loving gentleness <u>He will abide with you</u>, as you allow His Voice to teach love's meaning to your clean and open mind. And He will bless the lesson with His Love.

W-pII.346.1 - Father, I wake today with miracles correcting my perception of all things. And so begins the day I share with You as I will share eternity, for time has stepped aside today. I do not seek the things of time, and so I will not look upon them. What I seek today transcends all laws of time and things perceived in time. I would forget all things except Your Love. I would <u>abide in You</u>, and know no laws except Your law of love. And I would find the peace which You created for Your Son, forgetting all the foolish toys I made as I behold Your glory and my own.

W-pII.351.ti – 1 - My sinless brother is my guide to peace. My sinful brother is my guide to pain. And which I choose to see I will behold.

Who is my brother but Your holy Son? And if I see him sinful I proclaim myself a sinner, not a Son of God; alone and friendless in a fearful world. Yet this perception is a choice I make, and can relinquish. I can also see my brother sinless, as Your holy Son. And with this choice I see my sinlessness, <u>my everlasting Comforter</u> and Friend beside me, and my way secure and clear. Choose, then, for me, my Father, through Your Voice. For He alone gives judgment in Your Name.

Bible Reference - Text

John 14:18 - I will not leave you comfortless: I will come to you.

Course Ref/s - Citation/s

T-05.II.6 - The Holy Spirit calls you both to remember and to forget. You have chosen to be in a state of opposition in which opposites are possible. As a result, there are choices you must make. In the holy state the will is free, so that its creative power is unlimited and choice is meaningless. Freedom to choose is the same power as freedom to create, but its application is different. Choosing depends on a split mind. The Holy Spirit is one way of choosing. <u>God did not leave His children comfortless,</u> even though they chose to leave Him. The voice they put in their minds was not the Voice for His Will, for which the Holy Spirit speaks.

T-07.X.7 - Even the relinquishment of your false decision- making prerogative, which the ego guards so jealously, is not accomplished by your wish. It was accomplished for you by the Will of <u>God, Who has not left you comfortless</u>. His Voice will teach you how to distinguish between pain and joy, and will lead you out of the confusion you have made. There is no confusion in the mind of a Son of God, whose will must be the Will of the Father, because the Father's Will is His Son.

T-17.V.9:6-10:7 - For you have chosen but the goal of God, from which your true intent was never absent.

Throughout the Sonship is the song of freedom heard, in joyous echo of your choice. You have joined with many in the holy instant, and they have joined with you. Think not your choice <u>will leave you comfortless</u>, for God Himself has blessed your holy relationship. Join in His blessing, and withhold not yours upon it. For all it needs now is your blessing, that you may see that in it rests salvation. Condemn salvation not, for it has come to you. And welcome it together, for it has come to join you and your brother together in a relationship in which all the Sonship is together blessed.

T-31.VIII.3 - Trials are but lessons that you failed to learn presented once again, so where you made a faulty choice before you now can make a better one, and thus escape all pain that what you chose before has brought to you. In every difficulty, all distress, and each perplexity <u>Christ</u> calls to you and gently says, "My brother, choose again." He would not leave one source of pain unhealed, nor any image left to veil the truth. He would remove all misery from you whom God created altar unto joy. <u>He would not leave you comfortless</u>, alone in dreams of hell, but would release your mind from everything that hides His face from you. His Holiness is yours because He is the only Power that is real in you. His strength is yours because He is the Self that God created as His only Son.

W-pII.352.ti-1 - Judgment and love are opposites. From one Come all the sorrows of the world. But from The other comes the peace of God Himself.
Forgiveness looks on sinlessness alone, and judges not. Through this I come to You. Judgment will bind my eyes and make me blind. Yet love, reflected in forgiveness here, reminds me You have given me a way to find Your peace again. I am redeemed when I elect to follow in this way.
<u>You have not left me comfortless.</u> I have within me both the memory of You, and One Who leads me to it. Father, I would hear Your Voice and find Your peace today. For I would love my own Identity, and find in It the memory of You.

W-pII.ep.6 - We trust our ways to Him [the Holy Spirit] and say "Amen." In peace we will continue in His way, and trust all things to Him.
In confidence we wait His answers, as we ask His Will in everything we do. He loves God's Son as we would love him. And He teaches us how to behold him through His eyes, and love him as He does. You do not walk alone. God's angels hover near and all about. His Love surrounds you, and of this be sure; that <u>I will never leave you comfortless</u>.

S-2.III.7:2-8 - Forgiveness has a Teacher Who will fail in nothing. Rest a while in this; do not attempt to judge forgiveness, nor to set it in an earthly frame. Let it arise to Christ, Who welcomes it as gift to Him. <u>He will not leave you comfortless</u>, nor fail to send His angels down to answer you in

His Own Name. He stands beside the door to which forgiveness is the only key. Give it to Him to use instead of you, and you will see the door swing silently open upon the shining face of Christ. Behold your brother there beyond the door; the Son of God as He created him.

Bible Reference - Text

John 14:26 - But the Comforter, which is the Holy Ghost, whom the Father will send in my name, he shall teach you all things, and bring all things to your remembrance, whatsoever I have said unto you.

Course Ref/s - Citation/s

T-05.I.4 - The Holy Spirit is the only part of the Holy Trinity that has a symbolic function. He is referred to as the Healer, the Comforter and the Guide. He is also described as something "separate," apart from the Father and from the Son. I myself said, "If I go I will send you another Comforter and He will abide with you." His symbolic function makes the Holy Spirit difficult to understand, because symbolism is open to different interpretations. As a man and also one of God's creations, my right thinking, which came from the Holy Spirit or the Universal Inspiration, taught me first and foremost that this Inspiration is for all. I could not have It myself without knowing this. The word "know" is proper in this context, because the Holy Spirit is so close to knowledge that He calls it forth; or better, allows it to come. I have spoken before of the higher or "true" perception, which is so near to truth that God Himself can flow across the little gap. Knowledge is always ready to flow everywhere, but it cannot oppose. Therefore you can obstruct it, although you can never lose it.

T-05.III.10 - The Holy Spirit is the perfect Teacher. He uses only what your mind already understands to teach you that you do not understand it. The Holy Spirit can deal with a reluctant learner without going counter to his mind, because part of it is still for God. Despite the ego's attempts to conceal this part, it is still much stronger than the ego, although the ego does not recognize it. The Holy Spirit recognizes it perfectly because it is His Own dwelling place; the place in the mind where He is at home.
You are at home there, too, because it is a place of peace, and peace is of God. You who are part of God are not at home except in His peace.
If peace is eternal, you are at home only in eternity.

T-06.I.10 - We are still equal as learners, although we do not need to have equal experiences. The Holy Spirit is glad when you can learn from mine [Jesus'], and be reawakened by them. That is their only purpose, and that is the only way in which I can be perceived as the way, the truth and the life. When you hear only one Voice you are never called on to sacrifice. On the contrary, by being able to hear the Holy Spirit in others you can learn from their experiences, and can gain from them without experiencing them directly yourself. That is because the Holy Spirit is one, and anyone who listens is inevitably led to demonstrate His way for all.

T-06.I.19 - Remember that the Holy Spirit is the communication link between God the Father and His separated Sons. If you will listen to His Voice you will know that you cannot either hurt or be hurt, and that many need your blessing to help them hear this for themselves. When you perceive only this need in them, and do not respond to any other, you will have learned of me and will be as eager to share your learning as I am.

T-07.III.1 - The Holy Spirit teaches one lesson, and applies it to all individuals in all situations. Being conflict-free, He maximises all efforts and all results. By teaching the power of the Kingdom of God Himself, He teaches you that all power is yours. Its application does not matter. It is always maximal. Your vigilance does not establish it as yours, but it does enable you to use it always and in all ways. When I said "I am with you always," I meant it literally. I am not absent to anyone in any situation. Because I am always with you, you are the way, the truth and the life. You did not make this power, any more than I did. It was created to be shared, and therefore cannot be meaningfully perceived as belonging to anyone at the expense of another. Such a perception makes it meaningless by eliminating or overlooking its real and only meaning.

T-07.VIII.6 - The Holy Spirit will teach you to perceive beyond your belief, because truth is beyond belief and His perception is true. The ego can be completely forgotten at any time, because it is a totally incredible belief, and no one can keep a belief he has judged to be unbelievable. The more you learn about the ego, the more you realize that it cannot be believed. The incredible cannot be understood because it is unbelievable. The meaninglessness of perception based on the unbelievable is apparent, but it may not be recognized as being beyond belief, because it is made by belief.

T-07.X.3 - The Holy Spirit will direct you only so as to avoid pain. Surely no one would object to this goal if he recognized it. The problem is not whether what the Holy Spirit says is true, but whether you want to listen to what He says. You no more recognize what is painful than you know what is joyful, and are, in fact, very apt to confuse the two. The Holy Spirit's main function is to teach you to tell them apart. What is joyful to you is painful to the ego, and as long as you are in doubt about what you are, you will be confused about joy and pain. This confusion is the cause of the whole idea of sacrifice. Obey the Holy Spirit, and you will be giving up the ego. But you will be sacrificing nothing. On the contrary, you will be gaining everything. If you believed this, there would be no conflict.

Bible Reference - Text

John 14:26 - But the Comforter, which is the Holy Ghost,....
(Continued) - (To read the full text of the above go to page 379.)

Course Ref/s - Citation/s

T-08.III.2 - To fulfil the Will of God perfectly is the only joy and peace that can be fully known, because it is the only function that can be fully experienced. When this is accomplished, then, there is no other experience. Yet the wish for other experience will block its accomplishment, because God's Will cannot be forced upon you, being an experience of total willingness. The Holy Spirit understands how to teach this, but you do not. That is why you need Him, and why God gave Him to you. Only His teaching will release your will to God's, uniting it with His power and glory and establishing them as yours. You share them as God shares them, because this is the natural outcome of their being.

T-08.III.3 - The Will of the Father and of the Son are one, by their extension. Their extension is the result of Their oneness, holding Their unity together by extending Their joint Will. This is perfect creation by the perfectly created, in union with the Perfect Creator. The Father must give fatherhood to His Son, because His Own Fatherhood must be extended outward. You who belong in God have the holy function of extending His Fatherhood by placing no limits upon it. Let the Holy Spirit teach you how to do this, for you can know what it means only of God Himself.

T-08.III.7 - You can encounter only part of yourself because you are part of God, Who is everything. His power and glory are everywhere, and you cannot be excluded from them. The ego teaches that your strength is in you alone. The Holy Spirit teaches that all strength is in God and therefore in you. God wills no one suffer. He does not will anyone to suffer for a wrong decision, including you. That is why He has given you the means for undoing it. Through His power and glory all your wrong decisions are undone completely, releasing you and your brother from every imprisoning thought any part of the Sonship holds. Wrong decisions have no power, because they are not true. The imprisonment they seem to produce is no more true than they are.

T-08.VIII.9 - <u>The Holy Spirit teaches you</u> to use your body only to reach your brothers, so He can teach His message through you. This will heal them and therefore heal you. Everything used in accordance with its function as the Holy Spirit sees it cannot be sick. Everything used otherwise is. Do not allow the body to be a mirror of a split mind. Do not let it be an image of your own perception of littleness. Do not let it reflect your decision to attack. Health is seen as the natural state of everything when interpretation is left to the Holy Spirit, Who perceives no attack on anything. Health is the result of relinquishing all attempts to use the body lovelessly. Health is the beginning of the proper perspective on life under the guidance of the one Teacher Who knows what life is, being the Voice for Life Itself.

T-14.III.13 - <u>The One Who knows</u> the plan of God that God would have you follow <u>can teach you</u> what it is. Only His wisdom is capable of guiding you to follow it. Every decision you undertake alone but signifies that you would define what salvation is, and what you would be saved from.
<u>The Holy Spirit knows</u> that all salvation is escape from guilt. You have no other "enemy," and against this strange distortion of the purity of the Son of God the Holy Spirit is your only Friend. He is the strong protector of the innocence that sets you free. And it is His decision to undo everything that would obscure your innocence from your unclouded mind.

T-14.III.14 - Let <u>Him [the Holy Spirit]</u>, therefore, be the only Guide that you would follow to salvation. He knows the way, and leads you gladly on it. <u>With Him you will not fail to learn</u> that what God wills for you is your will. Without His guidance you will think you know alone, and will decide against your peace as surely as you decided that salvation lay in you alone. Salvation is of Him to Whom God gave it for you. He has not forgotten it. Forget Him not and He will make every decision for you, for your salvation and the peace of God in you.

T-14.III.16 - Say to <u>the Holy Spirit only</u>, "Decide for me," and it is done. For His decisions are reflections of what God knows about you, and in this light, error of any kind becomes impossible. Why would you struggle so frantically to anticipate all you cannot know, when all knowledge lies behind every decision the Holy Spirit makes for you? <u>Learn of His wisdom and His Love</u>, and teach His answer to everyone who struggles in the dark. For you decide for them and for yourself.

Bible Reference - Text

John 14:26 - But the Comforter, which is the Holy Ghost,.... (Continued) - (To read the full text of the above go to page 379.)

Course Ref/s - Citation/s

T-14.III.19 - Whenever you are in doubt what you should do, think of <u>His Presence [the Holy Spirit]</u> in you, and tell yourself this, and only this: He leadeth me and knows the way, which I know not. Yet He will never keep from me what He would have me learn. And so I trust Him to communicate to me all that He knows for me. Then <u>let Him teach you</u> quietly how to perceive your guiltlessness, which is already there.

T-14.VI.5 - You have regarded the separation [the Fall] as a means for breaking your communication with your Father. <u>The Holy Spirit</u> reinterprets it as a means of re-establishing what was not broken, but has been made obscure. All things you made have use to Him, for His most holy purpose. He knows you are not separate from God, but He perceives much in your mind that lets you think you are. All this and nothing else would He separate from you. The power of decision, which you made in place of the power of creation, <u>He would teach you</u> how to use on your behalf. You who made it to crucify yourself must learn of Him how to apply it to the holy cause of restoration.

T-14.VI.8 - <u>The Holy Spirit</u>'s function is entirely communication. He therefore must remove whatever interferes with communication in order to restore it. Therefore, keep no source of interference from His sight, for He will not attack your sentinels. But bring them to Him and <u>let His gentleness teach you</u> that, in the light, they are not fearful, and cannot serve to guard the dark doors behind which nothing at all is carefully concealed. We must open all doors and let the light come streaming through. There are no hidden chambers in God's temple. Its gates are open wide to greet His Son. No one can fail to come where God has called him, if he close not the door himself upon his Father's welcome.

T-14.XI.09 - Do you think that what <u>the Holy Spirit</u> would have you give, He would withhold from you? You have no problems that He cannot solve by offering you a miracle. Miracles are for you. And every fear or pain or trial you have has been undone. He has brought all of them to light, having accepted them instead of you, and recognized they never were. There are no dark lessons He has not already lightened for you. <u>The lessons you would teach yourself He has corrected already.</u> They do not exist in His Mind at all. For the past binds Him not, and therefore binds not you. He does not see time as you do. And each miracle He offers you corrects your use of time, and makes it His.

T-14.XI.11 - God's Son will always be indivisible. As we are held as one in God, so do we learn as one in Him. <u>God's Teacher [the Holy Spirit]</u> is as like to His Creator as is His Son, and through His Teacher does God proclaim His Oneness and His Son's. Listen in silence, and do not raise your voice against Him. For He teaches the miracle of oneness, and before His lesson division disappears. Teach like Him here, and you will remember that you have always created like your Father. The miracle of creation has never ceased, having the holy stamp of immortality upon it. This is the Will of God for all creation, and all creation joins in willing this.

T-21.III.6 - The Holy Spirit has a use for all the means for sin by which you sought to find it. But as He uses them they lead away from sin, because His purpose lies in the opposite direction. He sees the means you use, but not the purpose for which you made them. He would not take them from you, for He sees their value as a means for what He wills for you. You made perception that you might choose among your brothers, and seek for sin with them. <u>The Holy Spirit sees perception as a means to teach you</u> that the vision of the holy relationship is all you want to see. Then will you give your faith to holiness, desiring and believing in it because of your desire.

C-6.3 - <u>The Holy Spirit</u> is described as the remaining Communication Link between God and His separated Sons. In order to fulfil this special function the Holy Spirit has assumed a dual function. He knows because He is part of God; He perceives because <u>He was sent</u> to save humanity. He is the great correction principle; the bringer of true perception, the inherent power of the vision of Christ. He is the light in which the forgiven world is perceived; in which the face of Christ alone is seen. He never forgets the Creator or His creation. He never forgets the Son of God. He never forgets you. And He brings the Love of your Father to you in an eternal shining that will never be obliterated because God has put it there.

Bible Reference - Text

John 14:27 - Peace I leave with you, my peace I give unto you: not as the world giveth, give I unto you. Let not your heart be troubled, neither let it be afraid.

Course Ref/s - Citation/s

T-10.III.6-7 - There are no idolaters in the Kingdom, but there is great appreciation for everything that God created, because of the calm knowledge that each one is part of Him. God's Son knows no idols, but he does know his Father. Health in this world is the counterpart of value in Heaven. It is not my merit that I contribute to you but my love, for you do not value yourself. When you do not value yourself you become sick, but my value of you can heal you, because the value of God's Son is one. When I said, "My peace I give unto you," I meant it. Peace comes from God through me to you. It is for you although you may not ask for it.

When a brother is sick it is because he is not asking for peace, and therefore does not know he has it. The acceptance of peace is the denial of illusion, and sickness is an illusion. Yet every Son of God has the power to deny illusions anywhere in the Kingdom, merely by denying them completely in himself. I can heal you because I know you. I know your value for you, and it is this value that makes you whole. A whole mind is not idolatrous, and does not know of conflicting laws. I will heal you merely because I have only one message, and it is true. Your faith in it will make you whole when you have faith in me.

T-13.VII.16 - In me you have already overcome every temptation that would hold you back. We walk together on the way to quietness that is the gift of God. Hold me dear, for what except your brothers can you need? We will restore to you the peace of mind that we must find together.
The Holy Spirit will teach you to awaken unto us and to yourself. This is the only real need to be fulfilled in time. Salvation from the world lies only here. My peace I give you. Take it of me in glad exchange for all the world has offered but to take away. And we will spread it like a veil of light

across the world's sad face, in which we hide our brothers from the world, and it from them.

T-26.VI.3 - Who dwells with shadows is alone indeed, and loneliness is not the Will of God. Would you allow one shadow to usurp the throne that God appointed for your Friend, if you but realized its emptiness has left yours empty and unoccupied? Make no illusion friend, for if you do, it can but take the place of Him Whom God has called your Friend. And it is He Who is your only Friend in truth. <u>He brings you gifts that are not of this world</u>, and only He to Whom they have been given can make sure that you receive them. He will place them on your throne, when you make room for Him on His.

M-20.1-3 - <u>It has been said that there is a kind of peace that is not of this world.</u> How is it recognized? How is it found? And being found, how can it be retained? Let us consider each of these questions separately, for each reflects a different step along the way.

First, how can the peace of God be recognized? God's peace is recognized at first by just one thing; in every way it is totally unlike all previous experiences. It calls to mind nothing that went before. It brings with it no past associations. It is a new thing entirely. There is a contrast, yes, between this thing and all the past. But strangely, it is not a contrast of true differences. The past just slips away, and in its place is everlasting quiet. Only that. The contrast first perceived has merely gone. Quiet has reached to cover everything.

How is this quiet found? No one can fail to find it who but seeks out its conditions. God's peace can never come where anger is, for anger must deny that peace exists. Who sees anger as justified in any way or any circumstance proclaims that peace is meaningless, and must believe that it cannot exist. In this condition, peace cannot be found. Therefore, forgiveness is the necessary condition for finding the peace of God. More than this, given forgiveness there must be peace. For what except attack will lead to war? And what but peace is opposite to war? Here the initial contrast stands out clear and apparent. Yet when peace is found, the war is meaningless. And it is conflict now that is perceived as nonexistent and unreal.

Bible Reference - Text

John 14:28 - Ye have heard how I said unto you, I go away, and come again unto you. If ye loved me, ye would rejoice, because I said, I go unto the Father: for my Father is greater than I.

Course Ref/s - Citation/s

T-1.II.4 - "No man cometh unto the Father but by me" does not mean that I am in any way separate or different from you except in time, and time does not really exist. The statement is more meaningful in terms of a vertical rather than a horizontal axis. You stand below me and I stand below God. In the process of "rising up," I am higher because without me the distance between God and man would be too great for you to encompass. I bridge the distance as an elder brother to you on the one hand, and as a Son of God on the other. My devotion to my brothers has placed me in charge of the Sonship, which I render complete because I share it. This may appear to contradict the statement "I and my Father are one," but there are two parts to the statement in recognition that the Father is greater.

T-13.V.9 - Do not seek vision through your eyes, for you made your way of seeing that you might see in darkness, and in this you are deceived. Beyond this darkness, and yet still within you, is the vision of Christ, Who looks on all in light. Your "vision" comes from fear, as His from love. And He sees for you, as your witness to the real world. He is the Holy Spirit's manifestation, looking always on the real world, and calling forth its witnesses and drawing them to you. He loves what He sees within you, and He would extend it. And He will not return unto the Father until He has extended your perception even unto Him. And there perception is no more, for He has returned you to the Father with Him.

Bible Reference - Text

John 15:2 - Every branch in me that beareth not fruit he taketh away: and every branch that beareth fruit, he purgeth it, that it may bring forth more fruit.

Course Ref/s - Citation/s

T-03.VII.6:1-8 - <u>The branch that bears no fruit will be cut off</u> and will wither away. Be glad! The light will shine from the true Foundation of life, and your own thought system will stand corrected. It cannot stand otherwise. You who fear salvation are choosing death. Life and death, light and darkness, knowledge and perception, are irreconcilable. To believe that they can be reconciled is to believe that God and His Son can not. Only the oneness of knowledge is free of conflict.

Bible Reference - Text

John 15:5 - I am the vine, ye are the branches: He that abideth in me, and I in him, the same bringeth forth much fruit: for without me ye can do nothing.

Course Ref/s - Citation/s

T-07.VII.5 - The gift of life is yours to give, because it was given you. You are unaware of your gift because you do not give it. You cannot make nothing live, since nothing cannot be enlivened. Therefore, you are not extending the gift you both have and are, and so you do not know your being. All confusion comes from not extending life, because that is not the Will of your Creator. <u>You can do nothing apart from Him, and you do do nothing apart from Him.</u> Keep His way to remember yourself, and teach His way lest you forget yourself. Give only honor to the Sons of the living God, and count yourself among them gladly.

T-14.X.8 - The ego is incapable of understanding content, and is totally unconcerned with it. To the ego, if the form is acceptable the content must be. Otherwise it will attack the form. If you believe you understand something of the "dynamics" of the ego, let me assure you that you understand nothing of it. <u>For of yourself you could not understand it.</u> The study of the ego is not the study of the mind. In fact, the ego enjoys studying itself, and thoroughly approves the undertakings of students who would "analyze" it, thus approving its importance. Yet they but study form with meaningless content. For their teacher is senseless, though careful to conceal this fact behind impressive sounding words, but which lack any consistent sense when they are put together.

T-14.XI.4 - You who have not yet brought all of the darkness you have taught yourself into the light in you, can hardly judge the truth and value of this course [A Course in Miracles]. Yet God did not abandon you. And so you have another lesson sent from Him, already learned for every child of light by Him to Whom God gave it. This lesson shines with God's glory, for in it lies His power, which He shares so gladly with His Son. Learn of His happiness, which is yours. But to accomplish this, all your dark lessons must be brought willingly to truth, and joyously laid down by hands open to receive, not closed to take. Every dark lesson that you bring to Him Who teaches light He will accept from you, because you do not want it. And He will gladly exchange each one for the bright lesson He has learned for you. <u>Never believe that any lesson you have learned apart from Him means anything.</u>

T-21.II.12 - <u>The Son's creations are like his Father's</u>. Yet in creating them the Son does not delude himself that he is independent of his Source. His union with It is the source of his creating. <u>Apart from this he has no power to create</u>, and what he makes is meaningless. It changes nothing in creation, depends entirely upon the madness of its maker, and cannot serve to justify the madness. Your brother thinks he made the world with you. Thus he denies creation. With you, he thinks the world he made, made him. Thus he denies he made it.

M-29.4 - Here again is the paradox often referred to in the course. To say, "<u>Of myself I can do nothing</u>" is to gain all power. And yet it is but a seeming paradox. As God created you, you have all power. The image you made of yourself has none. The Holy Spirit knows the truth about you. The image you made does not. Yet, despite its obvious and complete ignorance, this image assumes it knows all things because you have given that belief to it. Such is your teaching, and teaching of the world that was made to uphold it. But the Teacher Who knows the truth has not forgotten it. His decisions bring benefit to all, being wholly devoid of attack. And therefore incapable of arousing guilt.

Bible Reference - Text

John 15:11 - These things have I spoken unto you, that my joy might remain in you, and that your joy might be full.

Course Ref/s - Citation/s

T-07.I.6 - To think like God is to share His certainty of what you are, and to create like Him is to share the perfect Love He shares with you. To this the Holy Spirit leads you, <u>that your joy may be complete</u> because the Kingdom of God is whole. I have said that the last step in the reawakening of knowledge is taken by God. This is true, but it is hard to explain in words because words are symbols, and nothing that is true need be explained. However, the Holy Spirit has the task of translating the useless into the useful, the meaningless into the meaningful, and the temporary into the timeless. He can therefore tell you something about this last step.

T-11.III.3 - O my child, if you knew what God wills for you, <u>your joy would be complete</u>! And what He wills has happened, for it was always true. When the light comes and you have said, "God's Will is mine," you will see such beauty that you will know it is not of you. Out of your joy you will create beauty in His Name, for your joy could no more be contained than His. The bleak little world will vanish into nothingness, and your heart will be so filled with joy that it will leap into Heaven, and into the Presence of God. I cannot tell you what this will be like, for your heart is not ready. Yet I can tell you, and remind you often, that what God wills for Himself He wills for you, and what He wills for you is yours.

T-25.II.9 - How could the Lord of Heaven not be glad if you appreciate His masterpiece? What could He do but offer thanks to you who love His Son as He does? Would He not make known to you His Love, if you but share His praise of what He loves? God cherishes creation as the perfect Father that He is. And so <u>His joy is made complete</u> when any part of Him joins in His praise, to share His joy. This brother is His perfect gift to you. And He is glad and thankful when you thank His perfect Son for being what he is. And all His thanks and gladness shine on you who would complete His joy, along with Him. And thus is yours completed. Not one ray of darkness can be seen by those who will to make their Father's happiness complete, and theirs along with His. The gratitude of God Himself is freely offered to everyone who shares His purpose. It is not His Will to be alone. And neither is it yours.

T-25.IV.2 - Perception's basic law could thus be said, "You will rejoice at what you see because you see it to rejoice." And while you think that suffering and sin will bring you joy, so long will they be there for you to see. Nothing is harmful or beneficent apart from what you wish. It is your wish that makes it what it is in its effects on you. Because you chose it as a means to gain these same effects, believing them to be the bringers of rejoicing and of joy. Even in Heaven does this law obtain. The Son of God creates to bring him joy, sharing his Father's purpose in his own creation, that <u>this joy might be increased</u>, and God's along with his.

Bible Reference - Text

John 15:11 - These things have I spoken unto you, that my joy might remain in you, and that your joy might be full. (Continued)

Course Ref/s - Citation/s

W-pI.100.2 - God's Will for you is perfect happiness. Why should you choose to go against His Will? The part that He has saved for you to take in working out His plan is given you that you might be restored to what He wills. This part is as essential to His plan as to your happiness. <u>Your joy must be complete</u> to let His plan be understood by those to whom He sends you. They will see their function in your shining face, and hear God calling to them in your happy laugh.

W-pI.100.3 - You are indeed essential to God's plan. <u>Without your joy, His joy is incomplete</u>. Without your smile, the world cannot be saved. While you are sad, the light that God Himself appointed as the means to save the world is dim and lusterless, and no one laughs because all laughter can but echo yours.

Bible Reference - Text

John 15:12-15 - This is my commandment, That ye love one another, as I have loved you. Greater love hath no man than this, that a man lay down his life for his friends. Ye are my friends, if ye do whatsoever I command you. Henceforth I call you not servants; for the servant knoweth not what his lord doeth: but I have called you friends; for all things that I have heard of my Father I have made known unto you.

Course Ref/s - Citation/s

T-19.IV.D.14-15 - Behold <u>your Friend, the Christ</u> Who stands beside you. How holy and how beautiful He is! You thought He sinned because you cast the veil of sin upon Him to hide His loveliness. Yet still He holds forgiveness out to you, to share His holiness. This "enemy," this "stranger" still offers you salvation as His Friend. The "enemies" of Christ, the worshippers of sin, know not Whom they attack.

This is your brother, crucified by sin and waiting for release from pain. Would you not offer him forgiveness, when only he can offer it to you? For his redemption he will give you yours, as surely as God created every living thing and loves it. And he will give it truly, for it will be both offered and received. There is no grace of Heaven that you cannot offer to your brother, and receive from <u>your most holy Friend</u>. Let him withhold it not, for by receiving it you offer it to him. And he will receive of you what you received of him. Redemption has been given you to give your brother, and thus receive it. Whom you forgive is free, and what you give you share. Forgive the sins your brother thinks he has committed, and all the guilt you think you see in him.

T-20.I.4 - Easter is not the celebration of the cost of sin but of its end. If you see glimpses of the face of Christ behind the veil, looking between the snow white petals of the lilies you have received and given as your gift, you will behold your brother's face and recognize it. I was a stranger and you took me in, not knowing who I was. Yet for your gift of lilies you will know. In your forgiveness of this stranger, alien to you and yet your ancient Friend, lies his release and your redemption with him. The time of Easter is a time of joy, and not of mourning. Look on <u>your risen Friend</u>, and celebrate his holiness along with me. For Easter is the time of your salvation, along with mine.

T-26.VI.2 - Lead not your little life in solitude, with one illusion as your only friend. This is no friendship worthy of God's Son, nor one with which he could remain content. Yet <u>God has given him a better Friend</u>, in Whom all power in earth and Heaven rests. The one illusion that you think is friend obscures His grace and majesty from you, and keeps His friendship and forgiveness from your welcoming embrace. Without Him you are friendless. Seek not another friend to take His place. There is no other friend. What God appointed has no substitute, for what illusion can replace the truth?

T-26.VI.3 - Who dwells with shadows is alone indeed, and loneliness is not the Will of God. Would you allow one shadow to usurp the throne that God appointed for your Friend, if you but realized its emptiness has left yours empty and unoccupied? Make no illusion friend, for if you do, it can but <u>take the place of Him Whom God has called your Friend</u>. And it is He

Who is your only Friend in truth. He brings you gifts that are not of this world, and only He to Whom they have been given can make sure that you receive them. He will place them on your throne, when you make room for Him on His.

Bible Reference - Text

John 15:12-15 - This is my commandment, That ye love one.... (Continued) - (To read the full text of the above go to page 391.)

Course Ref/s - Citation/s

T-27.V.6:6-7:7 - Healing replaces suffering. Who looks on one cannot perceive the other, for they cannot both be there. And what you see the world will witness, and will witness to.

Thus is your healing everything the world requires, that it may be healed. It needs one lesson that has perfectly been learned. And then, when you forget it, will the world remind you gently of what you have taught. No reinforcement will its thanks withhold from you who let yourself be healed that it might live. It will call forth its witnesses to show the face of Christ to you who brought the sight to them, by which they witnessed it. The world of accusation is replaced by one in which all eyes look lovingly upon the Friend who brought them their release. And happily your brother will perceive the many friends he thought were enemies.

W-pI.182.08-09 - When you are still an instant, when the world recedes from you, when valueless ideas cease to have value in your restless mind, then will you hear His Voice. So poignantly He calls to you that you will not resist Him longer. In that instant He will take you to His home, and you will stay with Him in perfect stillness, silent and at peace, beyond all words, untouched by fear and doubt, sublimely certain that you are at home.

Rest with Him frequently today. For He was willing to become a little Child that you might learn of Him how strong is he who comes without defenses, offering only love's messages to those who think he is their enemy. He holds the might of Heaven in His hand and calls them friend, and gives His strength to them, that they may see He would be Friend to them. He asks that they protect Him, for His home is far away, and He will not return to it alone.

W-pI.182.11 - Take time today to lay aside your shield which profits nothing, and lay down the spear and sword you raised against an enemy without existence. Christ has called you friend and brother. He has even come to ask your help in letting Him go home today, completed and completely. He has come as does a little child, who must beseech his father for protection and for love. He rules the universe, and yet He asks unceasingly that you return with Him, and take illusions as your gods no more.

W-pII.274.1 - Father, today I would let all things be as You created them, and give Your Son the honor due his sinlessness; the love of brother to his brother and his Friend. Through this I am redeemed. Through this as well the truth will enter where illusions were, light will replace all darkness, and Your Son will know he is as You created him.

W-pII.351.ti-1 - My sinless brother is my guide to peace. My sinful brother is my guide to pain. And which I choose to see I will behold.

Who is my brother but Your holy Son? And if I see him sinful I proclaim myself a sinner, not a Son of God; alone and friendless in a fearful world. Yet this perception is a choice I make, and can relinquish. I can also see my brother sinless, as Your holy Son. And with this choice I see my sinlessness, my everlasting Comforter and Friend beside me, and my way secure and clear. Choose, then, for me, my Father, through Your Voice. For He alone gives judgment in Your Name.

W-pII.ep.1 - This course [A Course in Miracles] is a beginning, not an end. Your Friend goes with you. You are not alone. No one who calls on Him can call in vain. Whatever troubles you, be certain that He has the answer, and will gladly give it to you, if you simply turn to Him and ask it of Him. He will not withhold all answers that you need for anything that seems to trouble you. He knows the way to solve all problems, and resolve all doubts. His certainty is yours. You need but ask it of Him, and it will be given you.

P-3.III.8 - Physician, healer, therapist, teacher, heal thyself. Many will come to you carrying the gift of healing, if you so elect. The Holy Spirit never refuses an invitation to enter and abide with you. He will give you endless opportunities to open the door to your salvation, for such is His function. He will also tell you exactly what your function is in every circumstance and at all times. Whoever He sends you will reach you, holding out his hand to his Friend. Let the Christ in you bid him welcome, for that same Christ is in him as well. Deny him entrance, and you have denied the Christ in you. Remember the sorrowful story of the world, and the glad tidings of salvation. Remember the plan of God for the restoration of joy and peace. And do not forget how very simple are the ways of God: You were lost in the darkness of the world until you asked for light. And then God sent His Son to give it to you.

Bible Reference - Text

John 15:18 - If the world hate you, ye know that it hated me before it hated you.

Course Ref/s - Citation/s

T-08.IV.3 - You were in darkness until God's Will was done completely by any part of the Sonship. When this was done, it was perfectly accomplished by all. How else could it be perfectly accomplished? My [Jesus'] mission was simply to unite the will of the Sonship with the Will of the Father by being aware of the Father's Will myself. This is the awareness I came to give you, and your problem in accepting it is the problem of this world. Dispelling it is salvation, and in this sense I am the salvation of the world. The world must therefore despise and reject me, because the world is the belief that love is impossible. If you will accept the fact that I am with you, you are denying the world and accepting God. My will is His, and your decision to hear me is the decision to hear His Voice and abide in His Will. As God sent me to you so will I send you to others. And I will go to them with you, so we can teach them peace and union.

Bible Reference - Text

John 15:19 - If ye were of the world, the world would love his own: but because ye are not of the world, but I have chosen you out of the world, therefore the world hateth you.

Course Ref/s - Citation/s

T-7.XI.1 - The Holy Spirit will always guide you truly, because your joy is His. This is His Will for everyone because He speaks for the Kingdom of God, which is joy. <u>Following Him is therefore the easiest thing in the world</u>, and the only thing that is easy, <u>because it is not of the world</u>. It is therefore natural. The world goes against your nature, being out of accord with God's laws. The world perceives orders of difficulty in everything. This is because the ego perceives nothing as wholly desirable. By demonstrating to yourself there is no order of difficulty in miracles, you will convince yourself that, in your natural state, there is no difficulty at all because it is a state of grace.

W-pI.155.ti-3 - I will step back and let Him lead the way.

<u>There is a way of living in the world that is not here, although it seems to be.</u> You do not change appearance, though you smile more frequently. Your forehead is serene; your eyes are quiet. And the ones who walk the world as you do recognize their own. Yet those who have not yet perceived the way will recognize you also, and believe that you are like them, as you were before.

The world is an illusion. Those who choose to come to it are seeking for a place where they can be illusions, and avoid their own reality. Yet when they find their own reality is even here, then they step back and let it lead the way. What other choice is really theirs to make? To let illusions walk ahead of truth is madness. But to let illusion sink behind the truth and let the truth stand forth as what it is, is merely sanity.

This is the simple choice we make today. The mad illusion will remain awhile in evidence, for those to look upon who chose to come, and have not yet rejoiced to find they were mistaken in their choice. They cannot learn directly from the truth, because they have denied that it is so. And so they need a Teacher Who perceives their madness, but Who still can look beyond illusion to the simple truth in them.

Bible Reference - Text

John 16:12 - I have yet many things to say unto you, but ye cannot bear them now.

Course Ref/s - Citation/s

T-06.I.16:1-6 - As you read the teachings of the Apostles, remember that I told them myself that there was much they would understand later, because they were not wholly ready to follow me at the time. I do not want you to allow any fear to enter into the thought system toward which I am guiding you. I do not call for martyrs but for teachers. No one is punished for sins, and the Sons of God are not sinners. Any concept of punishment involves the projection of blame, and reinforces the idea that blame is justified. The result is a lesson in blame, for all behaviour teaches the beliefs that motivate it.

Bible Reference - Text

John 16:16 - A little while, and ye shall not see me: and again, a little while, and ye shall see me, because I go to the Father.

Course Ref/s - Citation/s

T-12.II.7 - A little while and you will see me, for I am not hidden because you are hiding. I will awaken you as surely as I awakened myself, for I awoke for you. In my resurrection is your release. Our mission is to escape from crucifixion, not from redemption. Trust in my help, for I did not walk alone, and I will walk with you as our Father walked with me. Do you not know that I walked with Him in peace? And does not that mean that peace goes with us on the journey?

Bible Reference - Text

John 16:32-33 - Behold, the hour cometh, yea, is now come, that ye shall be scattered, every man to his own, and shall leave me alone: and yet I am not alone, because the Father is with me. These things I have spoken unto you, that in me ye might have peace. In the world ye shall have tribulation: but be of good cheer; I have overcome the world.

Course Ref/s - Citation/s

T-04.I.13 - I will substitute for your ego if you wish, but never for your spirit. A father can safely leave a child with an elder brother who has shown himself responsible, but this involves no confusion about the child's origin. The brother can protect the child's body and his ego, but he does not confuse himself with the father because he does this. I can be entrusted with your body and your ego only because this enables you not to be concerned with them, and lets me teach you their unimportance. I could not understand their importance to you if I had not once been tempted to believe in them myself. Let us undertake to learn this lesson together so we can be free of them together. I need devoted teachers who share my aim of healing the mind. Spirit is far beyond the need of your protection or mine. Remember this: <u>In this world you need not have tribulation because I have overcome the world. That is why you should be of good cheer.</u>

T-08.IV.2 - I am come as a light into a world that does deny itself everything. It does this simply by dissociating itself from everything. It is therefore an illusion of isolation, maintained by fear of the same loneliness that is its illusion. I said that I am with you always, even unto the end of the world. That is why I am the light of the world. If I am with you in the loneliness of the world, the loneliness is gone. You cannot maintain the illusion of loneliness if <u>you are not alone</u>. My purpose, then, is still to <u>overcome the world</u>. I do not attack it, but my light must dispel it because of what it is. Light does not attack darkness, but it does shine it away. If my light goes with you everywhere, you shine it away with me. The light becomes ours, and you cannot abide in darkness any more than darkness can abide wherever you go. The remembrance of me is the remembrance of yourself, and of Him Who sent me to you.

T-19.IV.B.6 - Let me be to you the symbol of the end of guilt, and look upon your brother as you would look on me. Forgive me all the sins you think the Son of God committed. And in the light of your forgiveness he will remember who he is, and forget what never was. I ask for your forgiveness, for if you are guilty, so must I be. But if <u>I surmounted guilt and overcame the world</u>, you were with me. Would you see in me the symbol of guilt or the end of guilt, remembering that what I signify to you you see within yourself?

Bible Reference - Text

John 17:16-17 - They [the Apostles] are not of the world, even as I am not of the world. Sanctify them through thy truth: thy word is truth.

Course Ref/s - Citation/s

T-26.VII.4-5 - Perception's laws are opposite to truth, and what is true of knowledge is not true of anything that is apart from it. Yet has God given answer to the world of sickness, which applies to all its forms. God's answer is eternal, though it works in time, where it is needed. Yet because it is of God, the laws of time do not affect its workings. It is in this world, but not a part of it. For it is real, and dwells where all reality must be. Ideas leave not their source, and their effects but seem to be apart from them. Ideas are of the mind. What is projected out, and seems to be external to the mind, is not outside at all, but an effect of what is in, and has not left its source.

God's answer lies where the belief in sin must be, for only there can its effects be utterly undone and without cause. Perception's laws must be reversed, because they are reversals of the laws of truth. The laws of truth forever will be true, and cannot be reversed; yet can be seen as upside down. And this must be corrected where the illusion of reversal lies.

Bible Reference - Text

John 18:36 - Jesus answered, My kingdom is not of this world: if my kingdom were of this world, then would my servants fight, that I should not be delivered to the Jews: but now is my kingdom not from hence.

Course Ref/s - Citation/s

T-03.VII.6 - The branch that bears no fruit will be cut off and will wither away. Be glad! The light will shine from the true Foundation of life, and your own thought system will stand corrected. It cannot stand otherwise. You who fear salvation are choosing death. Life and death, light and darkness, knowledge and perception, are irreconcilable. To believe that they can be reconciled is to believe that God and His Son can not. Only the oneness of knowledge is free of conflict. Your kingdom is not of this world because it was given you from beyond this world. Only in this world is the idea of an authority problem meaningful. The world is not left by death but by truth, and truth can be known by all those for whom the Kingdom was created, and for whom it waits.

T-08.VI.3 - <u>Let us glorify Him Whom the world denies, for over His Kingdom the world has no power.</u> No one created by God can find joy in anything except the eternal; not because he is deprived of anything else, but because nothing else is worthy of him. What God and His Sons create is eternal, and in this and this only is their joy.

T-15.III.9 - Holy child of God, when will you learn that only holiness can content you and give you peace? Remember that you learn not for yourself alone, no more than I did. It is because I learned for you that you can learn of me. I would but teach you what is yours, so that together we can replace the shabby littleness that binds the host of God to guilt and weakness with the glad awareness of the glory that is in him. My birth in you is your awakening to grandeur. Welcome me not into a manger, but into the altar to holiness, where holiness abides in perfect peace. <u>My Kingdom is not of this world</u> because it is in you. And you are of your Father. Let us join in honoring you, who must remain forever beyond littleness.

Bible Reference - Text

John 18:37 - Pilate therefore said unto him, Art thou a king then? Jesus answered, Thou sayest that I am a king. To this end was I born, and for this cause came I into the world, that I should bear witness unto the truth. Every one that is of the truth heareth my voice.

Course Ref/s - Citation/s

T-18.IX.3 - From the world of bodies, made by insanity, insane messages seem to be returned to the mind that made it. And these messages <u>bear witness to this world, pronouncing it as true</u>. For you sent forth these messengers to bring this back to you. Everything these messages relay to you is quite external. There are no messages that speak of what lies underneath, for it is not the body that could speak of this. Its eyes perceive it not; its senses remain quite unaware of it; its tongue cannot relay its messages. Yet God can bring you there, if you are willing to follow the Holy Spirit through seeming terror, trusting Him not to abandon you and leave you there. For it is not His purpose to frighten you, but only yours.

You are severely tempted to abandon Him at the outside ring of fear, but He would lead you safely through and far beyond.

W-pI.121.5 - The unforgiving mind is in despair, without the prospect of a future which can offer anything but more despair. Yet it regards its judgment of the world as irreversible, and does not see it has condemned itself to this despair. It thinks it cannot change, for what it sees <u>bears witness</u> that its judgment is correct. It does not ask, because it thinks it knows. It does not question, certain it is right.

W-pI.169.4 - We have perhaps appeared to contradict our statement that the revelation of the Father and the Son as one has been already set. But we have also said the mind determines when that time will be, and has determined it. And yet we urge you to <u>bear witness to the Word of God to hasten the experience of truth, and speed its advent into every mind that recognizes truth's effects on you</u>.

W-pI.169.6:7-7:3 - Eternity remains a constant state.

This is beyond experience we try to hasten. Yet forgiveness, taught and learned, brings with it the experiences which <u>bear witness</u> that the time the mind itself determined to abandon all but this is now at hand. We do not hasten it, in that what you will offer was concealed from Him Who teaches what forgiveness means.

W-pII.255.1-2 - It does not seem to me that I can choose to have but peace today. And yet, my God assures me that His Son is like Himself. Let me this day have faith in Him Who says I am God's Son. And let the peace I choose be mine today <u>bear witness to the truth of what He says</u>. God's Son can have no cares, and must remain forever in the peace of Heaven. In His Name, I give today to finding what my Father wills for me, accepting it as mine, and giving it to all my Father's Sons, along with me.

And so, my Father, would I pass this day with You. Your Son has not forgotten You. The peace You gave him still is in his mind, and it is there I choose to spend today.

W-pII.319.ti-2 - <u>I came for the salvation of the world</u>.

Here is a thought from which all arrogance has been removed, and only truth remains. For arrogance opposes truth. But when there is no arrogance the truth will come immediately, and fill up the space the ego left unoccupied by lies. Only the ego can be limited, and therefore it must seek for aims which are curtailed and limiting. The ego thinks that what one gains, totality must lose. And yet it is the Will of God I learn that what one gains is given unto all.

Father, Your Will is total. And the goal which stems from it shares its totality. What aim but the salvation of the world could You have given me? And what but this could be the Will my Self has shared with You?

Bible Reference - Text

John 18:38 - Pilate saith unto him, What is truth? And when he had said this, he went out again unto the Jews, and saith unto them, I find in him no fault at all.

Course Ref/s - Citation/s

T-07.XI.6 - Out of your natural environment you may well ask, "What is truth?" since truth is the environment by which and for which you were created. You do not know yourself, because you do not know your Creator. You do not know your creations because you do not know your brothers, who created them with you. I have already said that only the whole Sonship is worthy to be co-creator with God, because only the whole Sonship can create like Him. Whenever you heal a brother by recognizing his worth, you are acknowledging his power to create and yours. He cannot have lost what you recognize, and you must have the glory you see in him. He is a co-creator with God with you. Deny his creative power, and you are denying yours and that of God Who created you.

T-17.IV.4 - In a sense, the special relationship was the ego's answer to the creation of the Holy Spirit, who was God's Answer to the separation. For although the ego did not understand what had been created, it was aware of threat. The whole defense system the ego evolved to protect the separation from the Holy Spirit was in response to the gift with which God blessed it, and by His blessing enabled it to be healed. This blessing holds within itself the truth about everything. And the truth is that the Holy Spirit is in close relationship with you, because in Him is your relationship with God restored to you. The relationship with Him has never been broken, because the Holy Spirit has not been separate from anyone since the separation. And through Him have all your holy relationships been carefully preserved, to serve God's purpose for you.

W-pI.107.ti-1 - <u>Truth will correct all errors in my mind.</u>

What can correct illusions but the truth? And what are errors but illusions that remain unrecognized for what they are? Where truth has entered errors disappear. They merely vanish, leaving not a trace by which to be remembered. They are gone because, without belief, they have no life. And so they disappear to nothingness, returning whence they came. From dust to dust they come and go, for only truth remains.

W-pI.107.2-3 - Can you imagine what a state of mind without illusions is? How it would feel? Try to remember when there was a time, -perhaps a minute, maybe even less -when nothing came to interrupt your peace; when you were certain you were loved and safe. Then try to picture what it would be like to have that moment be extended to the end of time and to eternity. Then let the sense of quiet that you felt be multiplied a hundred times, and then be multiplied another hundred more.

And now you have a hint, not more than just the faintest intimation of the state your mind will rest in when the truth has come. Without illusions there could be no fear, no doubt and no attack. <u>When truth has come</u> all pain is over, for there is no room for transitory thoughts and dead ideas to linger in your mind. Truth occupies your mind completely, liberating you from all beliefs in the ephemeral. They have no place because the truth has come, and they are nowhere. They can not be found, for truth is everywhere forever, now.

W-pI.107.7-9 - We do not ask for what we do not have. We merely ask for what belongs to us, that we may recognize it as our own. Today we practice on the happy note of certainty that has been born of <u>truth</u>. The shaky and unsteady footsteps of illusion are not our approach today. We are as certain of success as we are sure we live and hope and breathe and think. We do not doubt we walk with truth today, and count on it to enter into all the exercises that we do this day.

Begin by asking Him Who goes with you upon this undertaking that He be in your awareness as you go with Him. <u>You are not made of flesh and blood and bone, but were created by the self-same Thought which gave the gift of life to Him as well. He is your Brother, and so like to you your Father knows that you are both the same.</u> It is your Self you ask to go with you, and how could He be absent where you are?

<u>Truth</u> will correct all errors in your mind which tell you, you could be apart from Him. You speak to Him today, and make your pledge to let His function be fulfilled through you. To share His function is to share His joy.

His confidence is with you, as you say: Truth will correct all errors in my mind, And I will rest in Him Who is my Self. Then let Him lead you gently to the truth, which will envelop you and give you peace so deep and tranquil that you will return to the familiar world reluctantly.

Bible Reference - Text

John 18:38 - Pilate saith unto him, What is truth? And....
(Continued) - (To read the full text of the above go to page 402.)

Course Ref/s - Citation/s

W-pII.248.1-2 - I have disowned the truth. Now let me be as faithful in disowning falsity. Whatever suffers is not part of me. What grieves is not myself. What is in pain is but illusion in my mind. What dies was never living in reality, and did but mock <u>the truth about myself</u>. Now I disown self- concepts and deceits and lies about the holy Son of God. Now am I ready to accept him back as God created him, and as he is.

Father, my ancient love for You returns, and lets me love Your Son again as well. Father, I am as You created me. Now is Your Love remembered, and my own. Now do I understand that they are one.

W-pII.262.1-2 - Father, You have one Son. And it is he that I would look upon today. He is Your one creation. Why should I perceive a thousand forms in what remains as one? Why should I give this one a thousand names, when only one suffices? For <u>Your Son</u> must bear Your Name, for You created him. Let me not see him as a stranger to his Father, nor as stranger to myself. For he <u>is part of me and I of him, and we are part of You Who are our Source, eternally united in Your Love; eternally the holy Son of God</u>.

We who are one would recognize this day the truth about ourselves. We would come home, and rest in unity. For there is peace, and nowhere else can peace be sought and found.

W-pII.325.ti-2 - All things I think I see reflect ideas.

This is salvation's keynote: What I see reflects a process in my mind, which starts with my idea of what I want. From there, the mind makes up an image of the thing the mind desires, judges valuable, and therefore seeks to find. These images are then projected outward, looked upon, esteemed as real and guarded as one's own. From insane wishes comes an insane world. From judgment comes a world condemned. And from forgiving thoughts a gentle world comes forth, with mercy for the holy Son of God, to offer him a kindly home where he can rest a while before he journeys on, and help his brothers walk ahead with him, and find the way to Heaven and to God.

<u>Our Father, Your ideas reflect the truth, and mine apart from Yours but make up dreams.</u> Let me behold what only Yours reflect, for Yours and Yours alone establish truth.

W-pII.fl.5 - We will not end this year without the gift our Father promised to His holy Son. We are forgiven now. And we are saved from all the wrath we thought belonged to God, and found it was a dream. We are restored to sanity, in which we understand that anger is insane, attack is mad, and vengeance merely foolish fantasy. We have been saved from wrath because we learned we were mistaken. Nothing more than that. And is a father angry at his son because he failed to understand <u>the truth</u>?

M-29.4 - Here again is the paradox often referred to in the course. To say, "Of myself I can do nothing" is to gain all power. And yet it is but a seeming paradox. <u>As God created you, you have all power.</u> The image you made of yourself has none. <u>The Holy Spirit knows the truth about you.</u> The image you made does not. Yet, despite its obvious and complete ignorance, this image assumes it knows all things because you have given that belief to it. Such is your teaching, and teaching of the world that was made to uphold it. But the Teacher Who knows the truth has not forgotten it. His decisions bring benefit to all, being wholly devoid of attack. And therefore incapable of arousing guilt.

Bible Reference - Text

John 19:5 - Then came Jesus forth, wearing the crown of thorns, and the purple robe. And Pilate saith unto them, Behold the man!

Course Ref/s - Citation/s

T-29.V.5 - There is no gift the Father asks of you but that you see in all creation but the shining glory of His gift to you. <u>Behold His Son,</u> His perfect gift, in whom his Father shines forever, and to whom is all creation given as his own. Because he has it is it given you, and where it lies in him behold your peace. The quiet that surrounds you dwells in him, and from this quiet come the happy dreams in which your hands are joined in innocence. These are not hands that grasp in dreams of pain. They hold no sword, for they have left their hold on every vain illusion of the world. And being empty they receive, instead, a brother's hand in which completion lies.

Bible Reference - Text

John 20:17 - Jesus saith unto her, Touch me not; for I am not yet ascended to my Father: but go to my brethren, and say unto them, I ascend unto my Father, and your Father; and to my God, and your God.

Course Ref/s - Citation/s

T-11.VI.1 - It is impossible not to believe what you see, but it is equally impossible to see what you do not believe. Perceptions are built up on the basis of experience, and experience leads to beliefs. It is not until beliefs are fixed that perceptions stabilise. In effect, then, what you believe you do see. That is what I meant when I said, "Blessed are ye who have not seen and still believe," for those who believe in the resurrection will see it. The resurrection is the complete triumph of Christ over the ego, not by attack but by transcendence. For Christ does rise above the ego and all its works, and <u>ascends to the Father</u> and His Kingdom.

T-11.VI.4 - I am your resurrection and your life. You live in me because you live in God. And everyone lives in you, as you live in everyone. Can you, then, perceive unworthiness in a brother and not perceive it in yourself? And can you perceive it in yourself and not perceive it in God? Believe in the resurrection because it has been accomplished, and it has been accomplished in you. This is as true now as it will ever be, for the resurrection is the Will of God, which knows no time and no exceptions. But make no exceptions yourself, or you will not perceive what has been accomplished for you. For we <u>ascend unto the Father</u> together, as it was in the beginning, is now and ever shall be, for such is the nature of God's Son as his Father created him.

T-15.I.14 - How long is an instant? As long as it takes to re-establish perfect sanity, perfect peace and perfect love for everyone, for God and for yourself. As long as it takes to remember immortality, and your immortal creations who share it with you. As long as it takes to exchange hell for Heaven. Long enough to transcend all of the ego's making, and <u>ascend unto your Father</u>.

T-17.IV.16 - As God ascends into His rightful place and you to yours, you will experience again the meaning of relationship and know it to be true. Let us <u>ascend</u> in peace together <u>to the Father</u>, by giving Him ascendance in our minds. We will gain everything by giving Him the power and the glory, and keeping no illusions of where they are. They are in us, through His ascendance. What He has given is His. It shines in every part of Him, as in the whole. The whole reality of your relationship with Him lies in our relationship to one another. The holy instant shines alike on all relationships, for in it they are one. For here is only healing, already complete and perfect. For here is God, and where He is only the perfect and complete can be.

Bible Reference - Text

John 20:19 - Then the same day at evening, being the first day of the week, when the doors were shut where the disciples were assembled for fear of the Jews, came Jesus and stood in the midst, and saith unto them, Peace be unto you.

Course Ref/s - Citation/s

T-11.IV.8 - Blessed is the Son of God whose radiance is of his Father, and whose glory he wills to share as his Father shares it with him. There is no condemnation in the Son, for there is no condemnation in the Father. Sharing the perfect Love of the Father the Son must share what belongs to Him, for otherwise he will not know the Father or the Son. <u>Peace be unto you</u> who rest in God, and in whom the whole Sonship rests.

T-14.V.8 - <u>Peace, then, be unto everyone</u> who becomes a teacher of peace. For peace is the acknowledgement of perfect purity, from which no one is excluded. Within its holy circle is everyone whom God created as His Son. Joy is its unifying attribute, with no one left outside to suffer guilt alone. The power of God draws everyone to its safe embrace of love and union.

Stand quietly within this circle, and attract all tortured minds to join with you in the safety of its peace and holiness. Abide with me within it, as teachers of Atonement, not of guilt.

T-27.V.11 - <u>Peace be to you</u> to whom is healing offered. And you will learn that peace is given you when you accept the healing for yourself. Its total value need not be appraised by you to let you understand that you have benefited from it. What occurred within the instant that love entered in without attack will stay with you forever. Your healing will be one of its effects, as will your brother's. Everywhere you go, will you behold its multiplied effects. Yet all the witnesses that you behold will be far less than all there really are. Infinity cannot be understood by merely counting up its separate parts. God thanks you for your healing, for He knows it is a gift of love unto His Son, and therefore is it given unto Him.

W-pI.124.8 - <u>Peace be to you</u> today. Secure your peace by practicing awareness you are one with your Creator, as He is with you. Sometime today, whenever it seems best, devote a half an hour to the thought that you are one with God. This is our first attempt at an extended period for which we give no rules nor special words to guide your meditation. We will trust God's Voice to speak as He sees fit today, certain He will not fail. Abide with Him this half an hour. He will do the rest.

W-pI.140.5 - <u>Peace be to you</u> who have been cured in God, and not in idle dreams. For cure must come from holiness, and holiness can not be found where sin is cherished. God abides in holy temples. He is barred where sin has entered. Yet there is no place where He is not. And therefore sin can have no home in which to hide from His beneficence. There is no place where holiness is not, and nowhere sin and sickness can abide.

W-pI.200.11 - Today we seek no idols. Peace can not be found in them. The peace of God is ours, and only this will we accept and want. <u>Peace be to us</u> today. For we have found a simple, happy way to leave the world of ambiguity, and to replace our shifting goals and solitary dreams with single purpose and companionship. For peace is union, if it be of God. We seek no further. We are close to home, and draw still nearer every time we say: There is no peace except the peace of God, and I am glad and thankful it is so.

Bible Reference - Text

John 20:25 - The other disciples therefore said unto him, We have seen the Lord. But he said unto them, Except I shall see in his hands the print of the nails, and put my finger into the print of the nails, and thrust my hand into his side, I will not believe.

Course Ref/s - Citation/s

T-24.III.8 - The slaves of specialness will yet be free. Such is the Will of God and of His Son. Would God condemn Himself to hell and to damnation? And do you will that this be done unto your savior? God calls to you from him to join His Will to save you both from hell. <u>Look on the print of nails upon his hands</u> that he holds out for your forgiveness. God asks your mercy on His Son and on Himself. Deny Them not. They ask of you but that your will be done. They seek your love that you may love yourself. Love not your specialness instead of Them. The print of nails is on your hands as well. Forgive your Father it was not His Will that you be crucified.

W-pI.161.11 - Select one brother, symbol of the rest, and ask salvation of him. See him first as clearly as you can, in that same form to which you are accustomed. See his face, his hands and feet, his clothing. Watch him smile, and see familiar gestures which he makes so frequently. Then think of this: What you are seeing now conceals from you the sight of one who can forgive you all your sins; whose sacred hands can take away <u>the nails which pierce</u> your own, and lift the crown of thorns which you have placed upon your bleeding head. Ask this of him, that he may set you free: Give me your blessing, holy Son of God. I would behold you with the eyes of Christ, and see my perfect sinlessness in you.

Bible Reference - Text

John 20:29 - Jesus saith unto him, Thomas, because thou hast seen me, thou hast believed: blessed are they that have not seen, and yet have believed.

Course Ref/s - Citation/s

T-11.VI.1 - It is impossible not to believe what you see, but it is equally impossible to see what you do not believe. Perceptions are built up on the basis of experience, and experience leads to beliefs. It is not until beliefs are fixed that perceptions stabilise. In effect, then, what you believe you do see. That is what I meant when I said, "<u>Blessed are ye who have not seen and still believe</u>," for those who believe in the resurrection will see it. The resurrection is the complete triumph of Christ over the ego, not by attack but by transcendence. For Christ does rise above the ego and all its works, and ascends to the Father and His Kingdom.

T. Acts

The following are references from the book of Acts of the Bible which are cited from A Course in Miracles:

[1:8], [17:27-28], [20:35] and [22:16].

Bible Reference - Text

Acts 1:8 - But ye shall receive power, after that the Holy Ghost is come upon you: and ye shall be witnesses unto me both in Jerusalem, and in all Judaea, and in Samaria, and unto the uttermost part of the earth.

Course Ref/s - Citation/s

T-01.IV.3-4 - Darkness is lack of light as sin is lack of love. It has no unique properties of its own. It is an example of the "scarcity" belief, from which only error can proceed. Truth is always abundant. Those who perceive and acknowledge that they have everything have no needs of any kind. The purpose of the Atonement is to restore everything to you; or rather, to restore it to your awareness. You were given everything when you were created, just as everyone was.

The emptiness engendered by fear must be replaced by forgiveness. That is what the Bible means by "There is no death," and why I could demonstrate that death does not exist. I came to fulfil the law by reinterpreting it. The law itself, if properly understood, offers only protection. It is those who have not yet changed their minds who brought the "hell-fire" concept into it. I assure you that I will witness for anyone who lets me, and to whatever extent he permits it. Your witnessing demonstrates your belief, and thus strengthens it. Those who witness for me are expressing, through their miracles, that they have abandoned the belief in deprivation in favor of the abundance they have learned belongs to them.

C-6.1 - Jesus is the manifestation of the Holy Spirit, Whom he called down upon the earth after he ascended into Heaven, or became completely identified with the Christ, the Son of God as He created Him. The Holy Spirit, being a creation of the one Creator, creating with Him and in His likeness or spirit, is eternal and has never changed. He was "called down upon the earth" in the sense that it was now possible to accept Him and to hear His Voice. His is the Voice for God, and has therefore taken form.

This form is not His reality, which God alone knows along with Christ, His real Son, Who is part of Him.

Bible Reference - Text

Acts 17:27-28 - That they should seek the Lord, if haply they might feel after him, and find him, though he be not far from every one of us: For in him we live, and move, and have our being; as certain also of your own poets have said, For we are also his offspring.

Course Ref/s - Citation/s

T-05.IV.8 - How can you who are so holy suffer? All your past except its beauty is gone, and nothing is left but a blessing. I have saved all your kindnesses and every loving thought you ever had. I have purified them of the errors that hid their light, and kept them for you in their own perfect radiance. They are beyond destruction and beyond guilt. They came from the Holy Spirit within you, and we know what God creates is eternal. You can indeed depart in peace because I have loved you as I loved myself. You go with my blessing and for my blessing. Hold it and share it, that it may always be ours. I place the peace of God in your heart and in your hands, to hold and share. The heart is pure to hold it, and the hands are strong to give it. We cannot lose. My judgment is as strong as the wisdom of <u>God, in Whose Heart and Hands we have our being</u>. His quiet children are His blessed Sons. The Thoughts of God are with you.

T-07.IV.7 - Seek ye first the Kingdom of Heaven, because that is where the laws of God operate truly, and they can operate only truly because they are the laws of truth. But seek this only, because you can find nothing else. There is nothing else. God is All in all in a very literal sense. <u>All being is in Him Who is all Being.</u> You are therefore in Him since your being is His. Healing is a way of forgetting the sense of danger the ego has induced in you, by not recognizing its existence in your brother. This strengthens the Holy Spirit in both of you, because it is a refusal to acknowledge fear. Love needs only this invitation. It comes freely to all the Sonship, being what the Sonship is. By your awakening to it, you are merely forgetting what you are not. This enables you to remember what you are.

T-24.VI.5 - Look on your brother, and behold in him the whole reversal of the laws that seem to rule this world. See in his freedom yours, for such it is. Let not his specialness obscure the truth in him, for not one law of death you bind him to will you escape. And not one sin you see in him but keeps you both in hell. Yet will his perfect sinlessness release you both, for holiness is quite impartial, with one judgment made for all it looks upon. And that is made, not of itself, but through the Voice that speaks for God in everything that <u>lives and shares His Being</u>.

T-31.VIII.12 - And now we say "Amen." For Christ has come to dwell in the abode You set for Him before time was, in calm eternity. The journey closes, ending at the place where it began. No trace of it remains. Not one illusion is accorded faith, and not one spot of darkness still remains to hide the face of Christ from anyone. Thy Will is done, complete and perfectly, and all creation recognizes You, and knows You as the only Source it has. Clear in Your likeness does the light shine forth from everything that <u>lives and moves in You</u>. For we have reached where all of us are one, and we are home, where You would have us be.

W-pI.156.2 - We are not inconsistent in the thoughts that we present in our curriculum. Truth must be true throughout, if it be true. It cannot contradict itself, nor be in parts uncertain and in others sure. You cannot walk the world apart from God, because you could not be without Him. He is what your life is. Where you are He is. There is one life. That life you share with Him. <u>Nothing can be apart from Him and live.</u>

W-pI.163.9 - Our Father, bless our eyes today. We are Your messengers, and we would look upon the glorious reflection of Your Love which shines in everything. <u>We live and move in You alone.</u> We are not separate from Your eternal life. There is no death, for death is not Your Will. And we abide where You have placed us, in the life we share with You and with all living things, to be like You and part of You forever. We accept Your Thoughts as ours, and our will is one with Yours eternally. Amen.

W-pI.197.6-7 - Withdraw the gifts you give, and you will think that what is given you has been withdrawn. But learn to let forgiveness take away the sins you think you see outside yourself, and you can never think the gifts of God are lent but for a little while, before He snatches them away again in death. For death will have no meaning for you then.

And with the end of this belief is fear forever over. Thank your Self for this, for He is grateful only unto God, and He gives thanks for you unto Himself. To everyone who lives will Christ yet come, for <u>everyone must live and move in Him</u>. His Being in His Father is secure, because Their

Will is One. Their gratitude to all They have created has no end, for gratitude remains a part of love.

Bible Reference - Text

Acts 17:27-28 - That they should seek the Lord, if haply ....
(Continued) - (To read the full text of the above go to page 412.)

Course Ref/s - Citation/s

W-pII.222.ti-1 - God is with me. I live and move in Him.

God is with me. He is my Source of life, the life within, the air I breathe, the food by which I am sustained, the water which renews and cleanses me. He is my home, wherein I live and move; the Spirit which directs my actions, offers me Its Thoughts; and guarantees my safety from all pain. He covers me with kindness and with care, and holds in love the Son He shines upon, who also shines on Him. How still is he who knows the truth of what He speaks today!

Bible Reference - Text

Acts 20:35 - I have shewed you all things, how that so labouring ye ought to support the weak, and to remember the words of the Lord Jesus, how he said, It is more blessed to give than to receive.

Course Ref/s - Citation/s

T-01.I.16 - Miracles are teaching devices for demonstrating it is as blessed to give as to receive. They simultaneously increase the strength of the giver and supply strength to the receiver.

T-09.VI.6 - Miracles have no place in eternity, because they are reparative. Yet while you still need healing, your miracles are the only witnesses to your reality that you can recognize. You cannot perform a miracle for yourself, because miracles are a way of giving acceptance and receiving it. In time the giving comes first, though they are simultaneous in eternity, where they cannot be separated. When you have learned they are the same, the need for time is over.

T-19.IV.D.14:6-15:10 - The "enemies" of Christ, the worshippers of sin, know not Whom they attack.

This is your brother, crucified by sin and waiting for release from pain. Would you not offer him forgiveness, when only he can offer it to you? For his redemption he will give you yours, as surely as God created every living thing and loves it. And he will give it truly, for it will be both offered and received. There is no grace of Heaven that you cannot offer to your brother, and receive from your most holy Friend. Let him withhold it not, for by receiving it you offer it to him. And he will receive of you what you received of him. <u>Redemption has been given you to give your brother, and thus receive it.</u> Whom you forgive is free, and what you give you share. Forgive the sins your brother thinks he has committed, and all the guilt you think you see in him.

T-19.IV.D.17 - Give faith to your brother, for faith and hope and mercy are yours to give. Into the hands that give, the gift is given. Look on your brother, and see in him the gift of God you would receive. It is almost Easter, the time of resurrection. Let us give redemption to each other and share in it, that we may rise as one in resurrection, not separate in death. Behold the gift of freedom that I gave the Holy Spirit for you. And be you and your brother free together, as you offer to <u>the Holy Spirit</u> this same gift. <u>And giving it, receive it of Him in return for what you gave.</u>
He leadeth you and me together, that we might meet here in this holy place, and make the same decision.

T-19.IV.D.19:6-20:7 - Heaven is the gift you owe your brother, the debt of gratitude you offer to the Son of God in thanks for what he is, and what his Father created him to be.

Think carefully how you would look upon the giver of this gift, for as you look on him so will the gift itself appear to be. As he is seen as either the giver of guilt or salvation, so will his offering be seen and so received. The crucified give pain because they are in pain. But the redeemed give joy because they have been healed of pain. <u>Everyone gives as he receives, but he must choose what it will be that he receives. And he will recognize his choice by what he gives, and what is given him</u>. Nor is it given anything in hell or Heaven to interfere with his decision.

T-20.II.2 - <u>Gifts are not made through bodies, if they be truly given and received.</u> For bodies can neither offer nor accept; hold out nor take. Only the mind can value, and only the mind decides on what it would receive and give. And every gift it offers depends on what it wants. It will adorn its chosen home most carefully, making it ready to receive the gifts it wants by offering them to those who come unto its chosen home, or those it would attract to it. And there they will exchange their gifts, offering and receiving what their minds judge to be worthy of them.

Bible Reference - Text

Acts 20:35 - I have shewed you all things, how that so....
(Continued) - (To read the full text of the above go to page 414.)

Course Ref/s - Citation/s

T-20.II.3 - <u>Each gift is an evaluation of the receiver and the giver.</u> No one but sees his chosen home as an altar to himself. No one but seeks to draw to it the worshippers of what he placed upon it, making it worthy of their devotion. And each has set a light upon his altar, that they may see what he has placed upon it and take it for their own. Here is the value that you lay upon your brother and on yourself. Here is your gift to both; your judgment on the Son of God for what he is. Forget not that it is your savior to whom the gift is offered. Offer him thorns and you are crucified. Offer him lilies and it is yourself you free.

T-21.VI.9 - You are your brother's savior. He is yours. Reason speaks happily indeed of this. This gracious plan was given love by Love. And what Love plans is like Itself in this: Being united, It would have you learn what you must be. And being one with It, it must be given you to give what It has given, and gives still. Spend but an instant in the glad acceptance of what is given you to give your brother, and learn with him what has been given both of you. <u>To give is no more blessed than to receive.</u> But neither is it less.

T-25.IX.10 - <u>The miracle that you receive, you give.</u> Each one becomes an illustration of the law on which salvation rests; that justice must be done to all, if anyone is to be healed. No one can lose, and everyone must benefit. Each miracle is an example of what justice can accomplish when it is offered to everyone alike. <u>It is received and given equally.</u> It is awareness that <u>giving and receiving are the same.</u> Because it does not make the same unlike, it sees no differences where none exists. And thus it is the same for everyone, because it sees no differences in them. Its offering is universal, and it teaches but one message: What is God's belongs to everyone, and is his due.

T-26.I.3 - The little that the body fences off becomes the self, preserved through sacrifice of all the rest. And all the rest must lose this little part, remaining incomplete to keep its own identity intact. In this perception of yourself the body's loss would be a sacrifice indeed. For sight of bodies becomes the sign that sacrifice is limited, and something still remains for you alone. And for this little to belong to you are limits placed on everything outside, just as they are on everything you think is yours. For <u>giving and receiving are the same</u>. And to accept the limits of a body is to impose these limits on each brother whom you see. For you must see him as you see yourself.

W-pI.105.3 - A major learning goal this course [A course in Miracles] has set is to reverse your view of <u>giving, so you can receive</u>. For giving has become a source of fear, and so you would avoid the only means by which you can receive. Accept God's peace and joy, and you will learn a different way of looking at a gift. God's gifts will never lessen when they are given away. They but increase thereby.

W-pI.105.4 - As Heaven's peace and joy intensify when you accept them as God's gift to you, so does the joy of your Creator grow when you accept His joy and peace as yours. True giving is creation. It extends the limitless to the unlimited, eternity to timelessness, and love unto itself. It adds to all that is complete already, not in simple terms of adding more, for that implies that it was less before. It adds by letting what cannot contain itself fulfil <u>its aim of giving everything it has away, securing it forever for itself</u>.

W-pI.105.5 - Today accept God's peace and joy as yours. Let Him complete Himself as He defines completion. You will understand that what completes Him must complete His Son as well. He cannot give through loss. No more can you. <u>Receive His gift of joy and peace today, and He will thank you for your gift to Him.</u>

W-pI.106.6:4-7:3 - Listen today, and you will hear a Voice Which will resound throughout the world through you. The bringer of all miracles has need that you receive them first, and thus <u>become the joyous giver of what you received</u>.

Thus does salvation start and thus it ends; <u>when everything is yours and everything is given away, it will remain with you forever</u>. And the lesson has been learned. Today we practice giving, not the way you understand it now, but as it is.

Bible Reference - Text

Acts 20:35 - I have shewed you all things, how that so....
(Continued) - (To read the full text of the above go to page 414.)

Course Ref/s - Citation/s

W-pI.122.5-6 - God's plan for your salvation cannot change, nor can it fail. Be thankful it remains exactly as He planned it. Changelessly it stands before you like an open door, with warmth and welcome calling from beyond the doorway, bidding you to enter in and make yourself at home, where you belong.

Here is the answer! Would you stand outside while all of Heaven waits for you within? Forgive and be forgiven. <u>As you give you will receive.</u> There is no plan but this for the salvation of the Son of God. Let us today rejoice that this is so, for here we have an answer, clear and plain, beyond deceit in its simplicity. All the complexities the world has spun of fragile cobwebs disappear before the power and the majesty of this extremely simple statement of the truth.

W-pI.126.6-7 - You do not understand forgiveness. As you see it, it is but a check upon overt attack, without requiring correction in your mind. It cannot give you peace as you perceive it. It is not a means for your release from what you see in someone other than yourself. It has no power to restore your unity with him to your awareness. It is not what God intended it to be for you.

Not having given Him the gift He asks of you, you cannot recognize His gifts, and think He has not given them to you. Yet would He ask you for a gift unless it was for you? Could He be satisfied with empty gestures, and evaluate such petty gifts as worthy of His Son? Salvation is a better gift than this. And true forgiveness, as the means by which it is attained, must heal the mind that gives, for <u>giving is receiving</u>. What remains as unreceived has not been given, but what has been given must have been received.

W-pI.126.8 - Today we try to understand the truth that <u>giver and receiver are the same</u>. You will need help to make this meaningful, because it is so alien to the thoughts to which you are accustomed. But the Help [the Holy Spirit] you need is there. Give Him your faith today, and ask Him that He share your practicing [All that I give is given to myself.] in truth today. And if you only catch a tiny glimpse of the release that lies in the idea we practice for today, this is a day of glory for the world.

W-pI.154.8 - Would you receive the messages of God? For thus do you become His messengers. You are appointed now. And yet you wait to give the messages you have received. And so you do not know that they are yours, and do not recognize them. <u>No one can receive and understand he has received until he gives. For in the giving is his own acceptance of what he received.</u>

W-pI.158.ti-2 - Today I learn <u>to give as I receive</u>.

What has been given you? The knowledge that you are a mind, in Mind and purely mind, sinless forever, wholly unafraid, because you were created out of love. Nor have you left your Source, remaining as you were created. This was given you as knowledge which you cannot lose. It was given as well to every living thing, for by that knowledge only does it live.

You have received all this. No one who walks the world but has received it. It is not this knowledge which you give, for that is what creation gave. All this cannot be learned. What, then, are you to learn to give today? Our lesson yesterday [Into His Presence would I enter now.] evoked a theme found early in the text. Experience cannot be shared directly, in the way that vision can. The revelation that the Father and the Son are one will come in time to every mind. Yet is that time determined by the mind itself, not taught.

W-pI.158.10 - Thus do you learn to <u>give as you receive</u>. And thus Christ's vision looks on you as well. This lesson is not difficult to learn, if you remember in your brother you but see yourself. If he be lost in sin, so must you be, if you see light in him, your sins have been forgiven by yourself. Each brother whom you meet today provides another chance to let Christ's vision shine on you, and offer you the peace of God.

W-pI.159.4 - Christ's vision is the miracle in which all miracles are born. It is their source, remaining with each miracle you give, and yet remaining yours. It is the bond by which <u>the giver and receiver are united</u> in extension here on earth, as they are one in Heaven. Christ beholds no sin in anyone.

And in His sight the sinless are as one. Their holiness was given by His Father and Himself.

Bible Reference - Text

Acts 20:35 - I have shewed you all things, how that so.... (Continued) - (To read the full text of the above go to page 414.)

Course Ref/s - Citation/s

W-pI.159.8 - Christ's vision is the holy ground in which the lilies of forgiveness set their roots. This is their home. They can be brought from here back to the world, but they can never grow in its unnourishing and shallow soil. They need the light and warmth and kindly care Christ's charity provides. They need the love with which He looks on them. And they become His messengers, who <u>give as they received</u>.

W-pII.316.ti-1 - All gifts I give my brothers are my own.

<u>As every gift my brothers give is mine, so every gift I give belongs to me.</u> Each one allows a past mistake to go, and leave no shadow on the holy mind my Father loves. His grace is given me in every gift a brother has received throughout all time, and past all time as well. My treasure house is full, and angels watch its open doors that not one gift is lost, and only more are added. Let me come to where my treasures are, and enter in where I am truly welcome and at home, among the gifts that God has given me.

W-pII.349.ti-1 - Today I let Christ's vision look upon All things for me and judge them not, but give Each one a miracle of love instead.

So would I liberate all things I see, and give to them the freedom that I seek. For thus do I obey the law of love, and give what I would find and make my own. It will be given me, because I have chosen it as the gift I want to give. Father, Your gifts are mine. Each one that I accept gives me a miracle to give. And <u>giving as I would receive</u>, I learn Your healing miracles belong to me.

M-2.5 - When pupil and teacher come together, a teaching-learning situation begins. For the teacher is not really the one who does the teaching. God's Teacher speaks to any two who join together for learning purposes. The relationship is holy because of that purpose, and God has promised to send His Spirit into any holy relationship. In the teaching-learning situation, each one learns that giving and receiving are the same. The demarcations they have drawn between their roles, their minds, their bodies, their needs, their interests, and all the differences they thought separated them from one another, fade and grow dim and disappear. Those who would learn the same course share one interest and one goal. And thus he who was the learner becomes a teacher of God himself, for he has made the one decision that gave his teacher to him. He has seen in another person the same interests as his own.

M-6.2 - Healing will always stand aside when it would be seen as threat. The instant it is welcome it is there. Where healing has been given it will be received. And what is time before the gifts of God? We have referred many times in the text to the storehouse of treasures laid up equally for the giver and the receiver of God's gifts. Not one is lost, for they can but increase. No teacher of God should feel disappointed if he has offered healing and it does not appear to have been received. It is not up to him to judge when his gift should be accepted. Let him be certain it has been received, and trust that it will be accepted when it is recognized as a blessing and not a curse.

P-2.II.8 - What must the teacher do to ensure learning? What must the therapist do to bring healing about? Only one thing; the same requirement salvation asks of everyone. Each one must share one goal with someone else, and in so doing, lose all sense of separate interests. Only by doing this is it possible to transcend the narrow boundaries the ego would impose upon the self. Only by doing this can teacher and pupil, therapist and patient, you and I, accept Atonement and learn to give it as it was received.

Bible Reference - Text

Acts 22:16 - And now why tarriest thou? arise, and be baptized, and wash away thy sins, calling on the name of the Lord.

Course Ref/s - Citation/s

W-pI.98.2 - How happy to be certain! All our doubts we lay aside today, and take our stand with certainty of purpose, and with thanks that doubt is gone and surety has come. We have a mighty purpose to fulfill and have been given everything we need with which to reach the goal. Not one mistake stands in our way. For we have been absolved from errors. <u>All our sins are washed away</u> by realizing they were but mistakes.

U. Romans

The following are the references from the Letter of Paul to the Romans which are cited in the Course:

[2:14-16], [3:28], [6:23], [8:26], [8:28],

[12:19] and [13:1].

.

Bible Reference - Text

Romans 2:14-16 - For when the Gentiles, which have not the law, do by nature the things contained in the law, these, having not the law, are a law unto themselves: Which shew the work of the law written in their hearts, their conscience also bearing witness, and their thoughts the mean while accusing or else excusing one another;) In the day when God shall judge the secrets of men by Jesus Christ according to my gospel.

Course Ref/s - Citation/s

W-pII.14.5 - We are the holy messengers of God who speak for Him, and carrying His Word to everyone whom He has sent to us, we learn that it is written on our hearts. And thus our minds are changed about the aim for which we came, and which we seek to serve. We bring glad tidings to the Son of God, who thought he suffered. Now is he redeemed. And as he sees the gate of Heaven stand open before him, he will enter in and disappear into the Heart of God.

M-26.1 - God indeed can be reached directly, for there is no distance between Him and His Son. His awareness is in everyone's memory, and His Word is written on everyone's heart. Yet this awareness and this memory can arise across the threshold of recognition only where all barriers to truth have been removed. In how many is this the case? Here, then, is the role of God's teachers. They, too, have not attained the necessary understanding as yet, but they have joined with others. This is what sets them apart from the world. And it is this that enables others to leave the world with them. Alone they are nothing. But in their joining is the power of God.

Bible Reference - Text

Romans 3:28 - Therefore we conclude that a man is justified by faith without the deeds of the law.

Course Ref/s - Citation/s

T-17.V.6:5-7:13 - If you believed the Holy Spirit was there to accept the relationship, why would you now not still believe that He is there to purify what He has taken under His guidance? Have faith in your brother in what but seems to be a trying time. The goal is set. And your relationship has sanity as its purpose. For now you find yourself in an insane relationship, recognized as such in the light of its goal.

Now the ego counsels thus; substitute for this another relationship to which your former goal was quite appropriate. You can escape from your distress only by getting rid of your brother. You need not part entirely if you choose not to do so. But you must exclude major areas of fantasy from your brother, to save your sanity. Hear not this now! Have faith in Him Who answered you. He heard. Has He not been very explicit in His answer? You are not now wholly insane. Can you deny that He has given you a most explicit statement? Now He asks for faith a little longer, even in bewilderment. For this will go, and you will see the justification for your faith emerge, to bring you shining conviction. Abandon Him not now, nor your brother. This relationship has been reborn as holy.

T-19.I.9 - To have faith is to heal. It is the sign that you have accepted the Atonement for yourself, and would therefore share it. By faith, you offer the gift of freedom from the past, which you received. You do not use anything your brother has done before to condemn him now. You freely choose to overlook his errors, looking past all barriers between yourself and him, and seeing them as one. And in that one you see your faith is fully justified. There is no justification for faithlessness, but faith is always justified.

T-19.IV.B.10-11 - Faith in the eternal is always justified, for the eternal is forever kind, infinite in its patience and wholly loving. It will accept you wholly, and give you peace. Yet it can unite only with what already is at peace in you, immortal as itself. The body can bring you neither peace nor turmoil; neither joy nor pain. It is a means, and not an end. It has no purpose of itself, but only what is given to it. The body will seem to be whatever is the means for reaching the goal that you assign to it. Only the mind can set a purpose, and only the mind can see the means for its accomplishment, and justify its use. Peace and guilt are both conditions of the mind, to be attained. And these conditions are the home of the emotion that calls them forth, and therefore is compatible with them.

But think you which it is that is compatible with you. Here is your choice, and it is free. But all that lies in it will come with it, and what you think you are can never be apart from it. The body is the great seeming betrayer of faith. In it lies disillusionment and the seeds of faithlessness, but only if you ask of it what it cannot give. Can your mistake be reasonable grounds for depression and disillusionment, and for retaliative attack on what you think has failed you? Use not your error as <u>the justification for your faithlessness</u>. You have not sinned, but you have been mistaken in what is faithful. And the correction of your mistake will give you grounds for faith.

T-20.III.11 - Your gift unto your brother has given me the certainty our union will be soon. <u>Share, then, this faith with me, and know that it is justified.</u> There is no fear in perfect love because it knows no sin, and it must look on others as on itself. Looking with charity within, what can it fear without? The innocent see safety, and the pure in heart see God within His Son, and look unto the Son to lead them to the Father. And where else would they go but where they will to be? You and your brother now will lead the other to the Father as surely as God created His Son holy, and kept him so. In your brother is the light of God's eternal promise of your immortality. See him as sinless, and there can *be* no fear in you.

Bible Reference - Text

Romans 6:23 - For the wages of sin is death; but the gift of God is eternal life through Jesus Christ our Lord.

Course Ref/s - Citation/s

T-10.V.1 - The rituals of the god of sickness are strange and very demanding. Joy is never permitted, for depression is the sign of allegiance to him. Depression means that you have forsworn God. Many are afraid of blasphemy, but they do not understand what it means. They do not realize that to deny God is to deny their own Identity, and in this sense <u>the wages of sin is death</u>. The sense is very literal; denial of life perceives its opposite, as all forms of denial replace what is with what is not. No one can really do this, but that you think you can and believe you have is beyond dispute.

T-19.II.3 - The Son of God can be mistaken; he can deceive himself; he can even turn the power of his mind against himself. But he cannot sin. There is nothing he can do that would really change his reality in any way, nor make him really guilty. That is what sin would do, for such is its purpose. Yet for all the wild insanity inherent in the whole idea of sin, it is impossible. For the wages of sin is death, and how can the immortal die?

T-25.VII.1 - Yet if the Holy Spirit can commute each sentence that you laid upon yourself into a blessing, then it cannot be a sin. Sin is the only thing in all the world that cannot change. It is immutable. And on its changelessness the world depends. The magic of the world can seem to hide the pain of sin from sinners, and deceive with glitter and with guile. Yet each one knows the cost of sin is death. And so it is. For sin is a request for death, a wish to make this world's foundation sure as love, dependable as Heaven, and as strong as God Himself. The world is safe from love to everyone who thinks sin possible. Nor will it change. Yet is it possible what God created not should share the attributes of His creation, when it opposes it in every way?

T-25.VIII.3 - There is a kind of justice in salvation of which the world knows nothing. To the world, justice and vengeance are the same, for sinners see justice only as their punishment, perhaps sustained by someone else, but not escaped. The laws of sin demand a victim. Who it may be makes little difference. But death must be the cost and must be paid. This is not justice, but insanity. Yet how could justice be defined without insanity where love means hate, and death is seen as victory and triumph over eternity and timelessness and life?

Bible Reference - Text

Romans 8:26 - Likewise the Spirit also helpeth our infirmities: for we know not what we should pray for as we ought: but the Spirit itself maketh intercession for us with groanings which cannot be uttered.

Course Ref/s - Citation/s

M-29.6 - Never forget that the Holy Spirit does not depend on your words. He understands the requests of your heart, and answers them. Does this mean that, while attack remains attractive to you, He will respond with evil? Hardly! For God has given Him the power to translate your prayers of the heart into His language. He understands that an attack is a call for help. And He responds with help accordingly. God would be cruel if He let your words replace His Own. A loving father does not let his child harm himself, or choose his own destruction. He may ask for injury, but his father will protect him still. And how much more than this does your Father love His Son?

Bible Reference - Text

Romans 8:28 - And we know that all things work together for good to them that love God, to them who are the called according to his purpose.

Course Ref/s - Citation/s

T-04.V.1 - All things work together for good. There are no exceptions except in the ego's judgment. The ego exerts maximal vigilance about what it permits into awareness, and this is not the way a balanced mind holds together. The ego is thrown further off balance because it keeps its primary motivation from your awareness, and raises control rather than sanity to predominance. The ego has every reason to do this, according to the thought system which gave rise to it and which it serves. Sane judgment would inevitably judge against the ego, and must be obliterated by the ego in the interest of its self-preservation.

T-06.II.10 - The Holy Spirit uses time, but does not believe in it. Coming from God He uses everything for good, but He does not believe in what is not true. Since the Holy Spirit is in your mind, your mind can also believe only what is true. The Holy Spirit can speak only for this, because He speaks for God. He tells you to return your whole mind to God, because it has never left Him. If it has never left Him, you need only perceive it as it is to be returned. The full awareness of the Atonement, then, is the recognition that the separation never occurred. The ego cannot prevail against this because it is an explicit statement that the ego never occurred.

T-26.VIII.6 - The working out of all correction takes no time at all. Yet the acceptance of the working out can seem to take forever. The change of purpose the Holy Spirit brought to your relationship has in it all effects that you will see. They can be looked at now. Why wait till they unfold in time and fear they may not come, although already there? You have been told that <u>everything brings good that comes from God</u>. And yet it seems as if this is not so. Good in disaster's form is difficult to credit in advance. Nor is there really sense in this idea.

W-pII.292.ti – 2 - A happy outcome to all things is sure.

<u>God</u>'s promises make no exceptions. And He <u>guarantees that only joy can be the final outcome found for everything</u>. Yet it is up to us when this is reached; how long we let an alien will appear to be opposing His. And while we think this will is real, we will not find the end He has appointed as the outcome of all problems we perceive, all trials we see, and every situation that we meet. Yet is the ending certain. For God's Will is done in earth and Heaven. We will seek and we will find according to His Will, which guarantees that our will is done.

<u>We thank you, Father, for Your guarantee of only happy outcomes in the end.</u> Help us not interfere, and so delay the happy endings You have promised us for every problem that we can perceive; for every trial we think we still must meet.

Bible Reference - Text

Romans 12:19 - Dearly beloved, avenge not yourselves, but rather give place unto wrath: for it is written, Vengeance is mine; I will repay, saith the Lord.

Course Ref/s - Citation/s

T-03.I.3 - The statement "<u>Vengeance is mine, sayeth the Lord</u>" is a misperception by which one assigns his own "evil" past to God. The "evil" past has nothing to do with God. He did not create it and He does not maintain it. God does not believe in retribution. His Mind does not create that way. He does not hold your "evil" deeds against you. Is it likely that He would hold them against me? Be very sure that you recognize how utterly impossible this assumption is, and how entirely it arises from projection. This kind of error is responsible for a host of related errors, including the belief that God rejected Adam and forced him out of the

Garden of Eden. It is also why you may believe from time to time that I am misdirecting you. I have made every effort to use words that are almost impossible to distort, but it is always possible to twist symbols around if you wish.

T-05.VI.7 - "<u>Vengeance is mine, sayeth the Lord</u>" is easily reinterpreted if you remember that ideas increase only by being shared. The statement emphasizes that vengeance cannot be shared. Give it therefore to the Holy Spirit, Who will undo it in you because it does not belong in your mind, which is part of God.

T-25.VIII.5:3-9 - But justice does He know, and knows it well. For He is wholly fair to everyone. <u>Vengeance is alien to God's Mind</u> because He knows of justice. To be just is to be fair, and not be vengeful. Fairness and vengeance are impossible, for each one contradicts the other and denies that it is real. It is impossible for you to share the Holy Spirit's justice with a mind that can conceive of specialness at all. Yet how could He be just if He condemns a sinner for the crimes he did not do, but thinks he did?

W-pI.170.10 - Where does the totally insane <u>belief in gods of vengeance</u> come from? Love has not confused its attributes with those of fear. Yet must the worshippers of fear perceive their own confusion in fear's "enemy"; its cruelty as now a part of love. And what becomes more fearful than the Heart of Love Itself? The blood appears to be upon His Lips; the fire comes from Him. And He is terrible above all else, cruel beyond conception, striking down all who acknowledge Him to be their God.

S-3.IV.5 - Never forget this; it is you who are God's Son, and as you choose to be to him so are you to yourself, and God to you. Nor will your judgment fail to reach to God, for you will give the role to Him you see in His creation. Do not choose amiss, or you will think that it is you who are creator in His place, and He is then no longer Cause but only an effect. Now healing is impossible, for He is blamed for your deception and your guilt. He Who is Love becomes the source of fear, for only fear can now be justified. <u>Vengeance is His.</u> His great destroyer, death. And sickness, suffering and grievous loss become the lot of everyone on earth, which He abandoned to the devil's care, swearing He will deliver it no more.

Bible Reference - Text

Romans 13:1 - Let every soul be subject unto the higher powers. For there is no power but of God: the powers that be are ordained of God.

U. Romans

Course Ref/s - Citation/s

T-11.V.3 - Let us begin this lesson in "ego dynamics" by understanding that the term itself does not mean anything. It contains the very contradiction in terms that makes it meaningless. "Dynamics" implies the power to do something, and the whole separation fallacy lies in the belief that the ego has the power to do anything. The ego is fearful to you because you believe this. Yet the truth is very simple: <u>All power is of God.</u>

V. 1 Corinthians

The following are the references from the First Letter of Paul to the Corinthians as cited in the Course:

[6:15-17], [6:19], [13:1-13], [14:33],

[15:26], [15:28], and [15:51-54].

Bible Reference - Text

1 Corinthians 6:15-17 - Know ye not that your bodies are the members of Christ? Shall I then take the members of Christ, and make them the members of an harlot? God forbid. What? Know ye not that he which is joined to an harlot is one body? For two, saith he, shall be one flesh. But he that is joined unto the Lord is one spirit.

Course Ref/s - Citation/s

T-08.IX.7 - The Bible enjoins you to be perfect, to heal all errors, to take no thought of the body as separate and to accomplish all things in my name. This is not my name alone, for ours is a shared identification. The Name of God's Son is one, and you are enjoined to do the works of love because we share this Oneness. Our minds are whole because they are one. If you are sick you are withdrawing from me. Yet you cannot withdraw from me alone. You can only withdraw from yourself and me.

Bible Reference - Text

1 Corinthians 6:19 - What? Know ye not that your body is the temple of the Holy Ghost which is in you, which ye have of God, and ye are not your own?

Course Ref/s - Citation/s

T-02.III.1 - The Atonement can only be accepted within you by releasing the inner light. Since the separation, defenses have been used almost entirely to defend against the Atonement, and thus maintain the separation.

This is generally seen as a need to protect the body. The many body fantasies in which minds engage arise from the distorted belief that the body can be used as a means for attaining "atonement." <u>Perceiving the body as a temple</u> is only the first step in correcting this distortion, because it alters only part of it. It does recognize that Atonement in physical terms is impossible. The next step, however, is to realize that a temple is not a structure at all. Its true holiness lies at the inner altar around which the structure is built. The emphasis on beautiful structures is a sign of the fear of Atonement, and an unwillingness to reach the altar itself. The real beauty of the temple cannot be seen with the physical eye. Spiritual sight, on the other hand, cannot see the structure at all because it is perfect vision. It can, however, see the altar with perfect clarity.

T-08.VII.9 - In this world, not even the body is perceived as whole. Its purpose is seen as fragmented into many functions with little or no relationship to each other, so that it appears to be ruled by chaos. Guided by the ego, it is. Guided by the Holy Spirit, it is not. It becomes a means by which the part of the mind you tried to separate from spirit can reach beyond its distortions and return to spirit. <u>The ego's temple thus becomes the temple of the Holy Spirit</u>, where devotion to Him replaces devotion to the ego. In this sense the body does become a temple to God; His Voice abides in it by directing the use to which it is put.

T-20.VI.05 - <u>The Holy Spirit's temple is not a body, but a relationship.</u> The body is an isolated speck of darkness; a hidden secret room, a tiny spot of senseless mystery, a meaningless enclosure carefully protected, yet hiding nothing. Here the unholy relationship escapes reality, and seeks for crumbs to keep itself alive. Here it would drag its brothers, holding them here in its idolatry. Here it is "safe," for here love cannot enter. The Holy Spirit does not build His temples where love can never be. Would He Who sees the face of Christ choose as His home the only place in all the universe where it can not be seen?

T-20.VI.06 - <u>You cannot make the body the Holy Spirit's temple</u>, and it will never be the seat of love. It is the home of the idolater, and of love's condemnation. For here is love made fearful and hope abandoned. Even the idols that are worshipped here are shrouded in mystery, and kept apart from those who worship them. This is the temple dedicated to no relationships and no return. Here is the "mystery" of separation perceived in awe and held in reverence. What God would have not be is here kept "safe" from Him. But what you do not realize is what you fear within your brother, and would not see in him, is what makes God seem fearful to you, and kept unknown.

Bible Reference - Text

1 Corinthians 6:19 - What? Know ye not that your body ....
(Continued)) - (To read the full text of the above go to page 431.)

Course Ref/s - Citation/s

T-20.VI.09 - Idols must disappear, and leave no trace behind their going. The unholy instant of their seeming power is frail as is a snowflake, but without its loveliness. Is this the substitute you want for the eternal blessing of the holy instant and its unlimited beneficence? Is the malevolence of the unholy relationship, so seeming powerful and so bitterly misunderstood and so invested in a false attraction your preference to the holy instant, which offers you peace and understanding? Then <u>lay aside the body and quietly transcend it, rising to welcome what you really want. And from His holy temple,</u> look you not back on what you have awakened from. For no illusions can attract the mind that has transcended them, and left them far behind.

P-2.II.1 - To be a teacher of God, it is not necessary to be religious or even to believe in God to any recognizable extent. It is necessary, however, to teach forgiveness rather than condemnation. Even in this, complete consistency is not required, for one who had achieved that point could teach salvation completely, within an instant and without a word. Yet he who has learned all things does not need a teacher, and the healed have no need for a therapist. <u>Relationships are still the temple of the Holy Spirit,</u> and they will be made perfect in time and restored to eternity.

P-3.III.6 - One rule should always be observed: No one should be turned away because he cannot pay. No one is sent by accident to anyone. <u>Relationships are always purposeful. Whatever their purpose may have been before the Holy Spirit entered them, they are always His potential temple</u>; the resting place of Christ and home of God Himself. Whoever comes has been sent. Perhaps he was sent to give his brother the money he needed. Both will be blessed thereby. Perhaps he was sent to teach the therapist how much he needs forgiveness, and how valueless is money in comparison. Again will both be blessed. Only in terms of cost could one have more. In sharing, everyone must gain a blessing without cost.

Bible Reference - Text

1 Corinthians 13:1-13 - Though I speak with the tongues of men and of angels, and have not charity, I am become as sounding brass, or a tinkling cymbal. And though I have the gift of prophecy, and understand all mysteries, and all knowledge; and though I have all faith, so that I could remove mountains, and have not charity, I am nothing. And though I bestow all my goods to feed the poor, and though I give my body to be burned, and have not charity, it profiteth me nothing.

Charity suffereth long, and is kind; charity envieth not; charity vaunteth not itself, is not puffed up, Doth not behave itself unseemly, seeketh not her own, is not easily provoked, thinketh no evil; Rejoiceth not in iniquity, but rejoiceth in the truth; Beareth all things, believeth all things, hopeth all things, endureth all things.

Charity never faileth: but whether there be prophecies, they shall fail; whether there be tongues, they shall cease; whether there be knowledge, it shall vanish away. For we know in part, and we prophesy in part. But when that which is perfect is come, then that which is in part shall be done away.

When I was a child, I spake as a child, I understood as a child, I thought as a child: but when I became a man, I put away childish things. For now we see through a glass, darkly; but then face to face: now I know in part; but then shall I know even as also I am known. And now abideth faith, hope, charity, these three; but the greatest of these is charity.

Course Ref/s - Citation/s

T-02.V.09 - Healing is an ability that developed after the separation, before which it was unnecessary. Like all aspects of the belief in space and time, it is temporary. However, as long as time persists, healing is needed as a means of protection. This is because healing rests on charity, and <u>charity is a way of perceiving the perfection of another even if you cannot perceive it in yourself</u>. Most of the loftier concepts of which you are capable now are time-dependent. Charity is really a weaker reflection of a much more powerful love- encompassment that is far beyond any form of charity you can conceive of as yet. Charity is essential to right-mindedness in the limited sense in which it can now be attained.

T-02.V.10 - <u>Charity is a way of looking at another as if he had already gone far beyond his actual accomplishments</u> in time. Since his own thinking is faulty he cannot see the Atonement for himself, or he would have no need of charity. The charity that is accorded him is both an acknowledgement that he needs help, and a recognition that he will accept it. Both of these perceptions clearly imply their dependence on time, making it apparent that charity still lies within the limitations of this world. I said before that only revelation transcends time. The miracle, as an expression of charity, can only shorten it. It must be understood, however, that whenever you offer a miracle to another, you are shortening the suffering of both of you. This corrects retroactively as well as progressively.

T-04.IV.1 - If you cannot hear the Voice for God, it is because you do not choose to listen. That you do listen to the voice of your ego is demonstrated by your attitudes, your feelings and your behavior. Yet this is what you want. This is what you are fighting to keep, and what you are vigilant to save. Your mind is filled with schemes to save the face of your ego, and you do not seek the face of Christ. <u>The glass in which the ego seeks to see its face is dark indeed.</u> How can it maintain the trick of its existence except with mirrors? But where you look to find yourself is up to you.

T-04.IV.2 - I have said that you cannot change your mind by changing your behavior, but I have also said, and many times, that you can change your mind. When your mood tells you that you have chosen wrongly, and this is so whenever you are not joyous, then know this need not be.
In every case you have thought wrongly about some brother God created, and are <u>perceiving images your ego makes in a darkened glass</u>. Think honestly what you have thought that God would not have thought, and what you have not thought that God would have you think. Search sincerely for what you have done and left undone accordingly, and then change your mind to think with God's. This may seem hard to do, but it is much easier than trying to think against it. Your mind is one with God's. Denying this and thinking otherwise has held your ego together, but has literally split your mind. As a loving brother I am deeply concerned with your mind, and urge you to follow my example as you look at yourself and at your brother, and see in both the glorious creations of a glorious Father.

V. 1 Corinthians

Bible Reference - Text

1 Corinthians 13:1-13 - Though I speak with the tongues of men.... (Continued) - (To read the full text of the above go to page 434.)

Course Ref/s - Citation/s

T-04.IV.9 - You are a mirror of truth, in which God Himself shines in perfect light. <u>To the ego's dark glass you need but say, "I will not look there because I know these images are not true."</u> Then let the Holy One shine on you in peace, knowing that this and only this must be. His Mind shone on you in your creation and brought your mind into being. His Mind still shines on you and must shine through you. Your ego cannot prevent Him from shining on you, but it can prevent you from letting Him shine through you.

T-19.IV.D.17 - <u>Give faith to your brother, for faith and hope and mercy are yours to give.</u> Into the hands that give, the gift is given. Look on your brother, and see in him the gift of God you would receive. It is almost Easter, the time of resurrection. Let us give redemption to each other and share in it, that we may rise as one in resurrection, not separate in death. Behold the gift of freedom that I gave the Holy Spirit for you. And be you and your brother free together, as you offer to the Holy Spirit this same gift. And giving it, receive it of Him in return for what you gave.
He leadeth you and me together, that we might meet here in this holy place, and make the same decision.

T-29.IX.6 - <u>There is a time when childhood should be passed and gone forever. Seek not to retain the toys of children. Put them all away, for you have need of them no more.</u> The dream of judgment is a children's game, in which the child becomes the father, powerful, but with the little wisdom of a child. What hurts him is destroyed; what helps him, blessed. Except he judges this as does a child, who does not know what hurts and what will heal. And bad things seem to happen, and he is afraid of all the chaos in a world he thinks is governed by the laws he made. Yet is the real world unaffected by the world he thinks is real. Nor have its laws been changed because he does not understand.

T-31.VII.7 - The concept of the self stands like a shield, a silent barricade before the truth, and hides it from your sight. All things you see are images, because you look on them as through a barrier that dims your sight and warps your vision, so that you behold nothing with clarity. The light is kept from everything you see. At most, you glimpse a shadow of what lies beyond. At least, you merely look on darkness, and perceive the terrified imaginings that come from guilty thoughts and concepts born of fear. And what you see is hell, for fear is hell. All that is given you is for release; the sight, the vision and the inner Guide all lead you out of hell with those you love beside you, and the universe with them.

W-pI.159.3 - Christ's vision is a miracle. It comes from far beyond itself, for it reflects eternal love and the rebirth of love which never dies, but has been kept obscure. Christ's vision pictures Heaven, for it sees a world so like to Heaven that what God created perfect can be mirrored there. The darkened glass the world presents can show but twisted images in broken parts. The real world pictures Heaven's innocence.

Bible Reference - Text

1 Corinthians 14:33 - For God is not the author of confusion, but of peace, as in all churches of the saints.

Course Ref/s - Citation/s

T-4.I.9 - God is not the author of fear. You are. You have chosen to create unlike Him, and have therefore made fear for yourself. You are not at peace because you are not fulfilling your function. God gave you a very lofty function that you are not meeting. Your ego has chosen to be afraid instead of meeting it. When you awaken you will not be able to understand this, because it is literally incredible. Do not believe the incredible now. Any attempt to increase its believableness is merely to postpone the inevitable. The word "inevitable" is fearful to the ego, but joyous to the spirit. God is inevitable, and you cannot avoid Him any more than He can avoid you.

Bible Reference - Text

1 Corinthians 15:26 - The last enemy that shall be destroyed is death.

Course Ref/s - Citation/s

M-27.6 - "And the last to be overcome will be death." Of course! Without the idea of death there is no world. All dreams will end with this one. This is salvation's final goal; the end of all illusions. And in death are all illusions born. What can be born of death and still have life? But what is born of God and still can die? The inconsistencies, the compromises and the rituals the world fosters in its vain attempts to cling to death and yet to think love real are mindless magic, ineffectual and meaningless. God is, and in Him all created things must be eternal. Do you not see that otherwise He has an opposite, and fear would be as real as love?

Bible Reference - Text

1 Corinthians 15:28 - And when all things shall be subdued unto him, then shall the Son also himself be subject unto him that put all things under him, that God may be all in all.

Course Ref/s - Citation/s

T-07.IV.7 - Seek ye first the Kingdom of Heaven, because that is where the laws of God operate truly, and they can operate only truly because they are the laws of truth. But seek this only, because you can find nothing else. There is nothing else. God is All in all in a very literal sense. All being is in Him Who is all Being. You are therefore in Him since your being is His. Healing is a way of forgetting the sense of danger the ego has induced in you, by not recognizing its existence in your brother. This strengthens the Holy Spirit in both of you, because it is a refusal to acknowledge fear. Love needs only this invitation. It comes freely to all the Sonship, being what the Sonship is. By your awakening to it, you are merely forgetting what you are not. This enables you to remember what you are.

T-08.IV.1 - If God's Will for you is complete peace and joy, unless you experience only this you must be refusing to acknowledge His Will. His Will does not vacillate, being changeless forever. When you are not at peace it can only be because you do not believe you are in Him. Yet He is All in all. His peace is complete, and you must be included in it. His laws govern you because they govern everything. You cannot exempt yourself from His laws, although you can disobey them. Yet if you do, and only if you do, you will feel lonely and helpless, because you are denying yourself everything.

S-2.II.7 - What would you show your brother? Would you try to reinforce his guilt and thus your own? Forgiveness is the means for your escape. How pitiful it is to make of it the means for further slavery and pain. Within the world of opposites there is a way to use forgiveness for the goal of God, and find the peace He offers you. Take nothing else, or you have sought your death, and prayed for separation from your Self. <u>Christ is for all because He is in all</u>. It is His face forgiveness lets you see. ⁹It is His face in which you see your own.

Bible Reference - Text

1 Corinthians 15:51-54 - Behold, I shew you a mystery; We shall not all sleep, but we shall all be changed, In a moment, in the twinkling of an eye, at the last trump: for the trumpet shall sound, and the dead shall be raised incorruptible, and we shall be changed. For this corruptible must put on incorruption, and this mortal must put on immortality. So when this corruptible shall have put on incorruption, and this mortal shall have put on immortality, then shall be brought to pass the saying that is written, Death is swallowed up in victory.

Course Ref/s - Citation/s

T-2.I.3 - The Garden of Eden, or the pre-separation condition, was a state of mind in which nothing was needed. When Adam listened to the "lies of the serpent," all he heard was untruth. You do not have to continue to believe what is not true unless you choose to do so. All that can literally <u>disappear in the twinkling of an eye</u> because it is merely a misperception. What is seen in dreams seems to be very real. Yet the Bible says that a deep sleep fell upon Adam, and nowhere is there reference to his waking up. The world has not yet experienced any comprehensive reawakening or rebirth. Such a rebirth is impossible as long as you continue to project or miscreate. It still remains within you, however, to extend as God extended His Spirit to you. In reality this is your only choice, because your free will was given you for your joy in creating the perfect.

T-27.II.6 - A miracle can offer nothing less to him than it has given unto you. So does your healing show your mind is healed, and has forgiven what he did not do. And so is he convinced his innocence was never lost, and healed along with you. Thus does the miracle undo all things the world attests can never be undone. And hopelessness and <u>death must disappear before the ancient clarion call</u> of life. This call has power far beyond the weak and miserable cry of death and guilt. The ancient calling of the Father to His Son, and of the Son unto His Own, will yet be the last trumpet that the world will ever hear. Brother, there is no death. And this you learn when you but wish to show your brother that you had no hurt of him. He thinks your blood is on his hands, and so he stands condemned. Yet it is given you to show him, by your healing, that his guilt is but the fabric of a senseless dream.

W-pI.162.2 - Here is the Word [I am as God created me.] by which the Son became his Father's happiness, His Love and His completion. Here creation is proclaimed, and honored as it is. There is no dream these words will not dispel; no thought of sin and no illusion which the dream contains that will not fade away before their might. They are <u>the trumpet of awakening</u> that sounds around the world. <u>The dead awake in answer to its call.</u> And those who live and hear this sound will never look on death.

W. 2 Corinthians

The following three references from the Second Letter of Paul to the Corinthians are cited in the Course:

[6:2], [12:9] and [13:11].

Bible Reference - Text

2 Corinthians 6:2 - For he saith, I have heard thee in a time accepted, and in the day of salvation have I succoured thee: behold, now is the accepted time; behold, now is the day of salvation.

Course Ref/s - Citation/s

T-13.VI.8 - <u>Now is the time of salvation,</u> for now is the release from time. Reach out to all your brothers, and touch them with the touch of Christ. In timeless union with them is your continuity, unbroken because it is wholly shared. God's guiltless Son is only light. There is no darkness in him anywhere, for he is whole. Call all your brothers to witness to his wholeness, as I am calling you to join with me. Each voice has a part in the song of redemption, the hymn of gladness and thanksgiving for the light to the Creator of light. The holy light that shines forth from God's Son is the witness that his light is of his Father.

Bible Reference - Text

2 Corinthians 12:9 - And he said unto me, My grace is sufficient for thee: for my strength is made perfect in weakness. Most gladly therefore will I rather glory in my infirmities, that the power of Christ may rest upon me.

Course Ref/s - Citation/s

T-04.I.11 - The ego has built a shabby and unsheltering home for you, because it cannot build otherwise. Do not try to make this impoverished house stand. <u>Its weakness is your strength.</u> Only God could make a home that is worthy of His creations, who have chosen to leave it empty by their own dispossession. Yet His home will stand forever, and is ready for you when you choose to enter it. Of this you can be wholly certain. God is as incapable of creating the perishable as the ego is of making the eternal.

T-13.XI.7 - Have faith in only this one thing, and it will be sufficient: God wills you be in Heaven, and nothing can keep you from it, or it from you. Your wildest misperceptions, your weird imaginings, your blackest nightmares all mean nothing. They will not prevail against the peace God wills for you. The Holy Spirit will restore your sanity because insanity is not the Will of God. <u>If that suffices Him, it is enough for you.</u> You will not keep what God would have removed, because it breaks communication with you with whom He would communicate. His Voice will be heard.

T-13.XI.9 - You will learn salvation because you will learn how to save. It will not be possible to exempt yourself from what the Holy Spirit wants to teach you. Salvation is as sure as <u>God. His certainty suffices.</u> Learn that even the darkest nightmare that disturbs the mind of God's sleeping Son holds no power over him. He will learn the lesson of awaking.
God watches over him and light surrounds him.

T-15.II.3 - How long can it take to be where God would have you? For you are where you have forever been and will forever be. All that you have, you have forever. The blessed instant reaches out to encompass time, as God extends Himself to encompass you. <u>You who have spent days, hours and even years in chaining your brothers to your ego in an attempt to support it and uphold its weakness, do not perceive the Source of strength. In this holy instant you will unchain all your brothers, and refuse to support either their weakness or your own.</u>

T-15.II.6 - Start now to practice your little part in separating out the holy instant. You will receive very specific instructions as you go along. To learn to separate out this single second, and to experience it as timeless, is to begin to experience yourself as not separate. Fear not that you will not be given help in this. <u>God's Teacher and His lesson will support your strength. It is only your weakness that will depart from you in this practice, for it is the practice of the power of God in you.</u> Use it but for one instant, and you will never deny it again. Who can deny the Presence of what the universe bows to, in appreciation and gladness? Before the recognition of the universe that witnesses to It, your doubts must disappear.

T-16.VII.10 - Remember that you always choose between truth and illusion; between the real Atonement that would heal and the ego's "atonement" that would destroy. <u>The power of God and all His Love, without limit, will support you</u> as you seek only your place in the plan of

Atonement arising from His Love. Be an ally of God and not the ego in seeking how Atonement can come to you. <u>His help suffices</u>, for His Messenger understands how to restore the Kingdom to you, and to place all your investment in salvation in your relationship with Him.

Bible Reference - Text

2 Corinthians 12:9 - And he said unto me, My grace is sufficient for.... (Continued) - (To read the full text of the above go to page 441.)

Course Ref/s - Citation/s

T-31.VIII.01-02 - Temptation has one lesson it would teach, in all its forms, wherever it occurs. It would persuade the holy Son of God he is a body, born in what must die, unable to escape its frailty, and bound by what it orders him to feel. It sets the limits on what he can do; <u>its power is the only strength he has</u>; his grasp cannot exceed its tiny reach. Would you be this, if Christ appeared to you in all His glory, asking you but this:

> Choose once again if you would take your place among the saviors of the world, or would remain in hell, and hold your brothers there.

For He has come, and He is asking this.

How do you make the choice? How easily is this explained! <u>You always choose between your weakness and the strength of Christ in you.</u> And what you choose is what you think is real. Simply by never using weakness to direct your actions, you have given it no power. And the light of Christ in you is given charge of everything you do. <u>For you have brought your weakness unto Him, and He has given you His strength instead.</u>

T-31.VIII.05 - Learn, then, the happy habit of response to all temptation to perceive yourself as weak and miserable with these words, I am as God created me. His Son can suffer nothing. And I am His Son. <u>Thus is Christ's strength invited to prevail, replacing all your weakness with the strength that comes from God</u> and that can never fail. And thus are miracles as natural as fear and agony appeared to be before the choice for holiness was made. For in that choice are false distinctions gone, illusory alternatives laid by, and nothing left to interfere with truth.

W-pI.062.3 - Remember that in every attack you call upon your own weakness, while each time you forgive you call upon the strength of Christ in you. Do you not then begin to understand what forgiveness will do for you? It will remove all sense of weakness, strain and fatigue from your mind. It will take away all fear and guilt and pain. It will restore the invulnerability and power God gave His Son to your awareness.

W-pI.092.3 - It is God's strength in you that is the light in which you see, as it is His Mind with which you think. His strength denies your weakness. It is your weakness that sees through the body's eyes, peering about in darkness to behold the likeness of itself; the small, the weak, the sickly and the dying, those in need, the helpless and afraid, the sad, the poor, the starving and the joyless. These are seen through eyes that cannot see and cannot bless.

W-pI.153.6 - Defenselessness is strength. It testifies to recognition of the Christ in you. Perhaps you will recall the text maintains that choice is always made between Christ's strength and your own weakness, seen apart from Him. Defenselessness can never be attacked, because it recognizes strength so great attack is folly, or a silly game a tired child might play, when he becomes too sleepy to remember what he wants.

W-pI.153.19 - Today our theme is our defenselessness. We clothe ourselves in it, as we prepare to meet the day. We rise up strong in Christ, and let our weakness disappear, as we remember that His strength abides in us. We will remind ourselves that He remains beside us through the day, and never leaves our weakness unsupported by His strength. We call upon His strength each time we feel the threat of our defenses undermine our certainty of purpose. We will pause a moment, as He tells us, "I am here."

W-pII.348.ti-2 - I have no cause for anger or for fear, For You surround me. And in every need That I perceive, Your grace suffices me.
Father, let me remember You are here, and I am not alone. Surrounding me is everlasting Love. I have no cause for anything except the perfect peace and joy I share with You. What need have I for anger or for fear? Surrounding me is perfect safety. Can I be afraid, when Your eternal promise goes with me? Surrounding me is perfect sinlessness. What can I fear, when You created me in holiness as perfect as Your Own?

God's grace suffices us in everything that He would have us do. And only that we choose to be our will as well as His.

Bible Reference - Text

2 Corinthians 12:9 - And he said unto me, My grace is sufficient for....
(Continued) - (To read the full text of the above go to page 441.)

Course Ref/s - Citation/s

M-29.7 - Remember you are His completion and His Love. Remember your weakness is His strength. But do not read this hastily or wrongly. If His strength is in you, what you perceive as your weakness is but illusion. And He has given you the means to prove it so. Ask all things of His Teacher, and all things are given you. Not in the future but immediately; now. God does not wait, for waiting implies time and He is timeless. Forget your foolish images, your sense of frailty and your fear of harm, your dreams of danger and selected "wrongs." God knows but His Son, and as he was created so he is. In confidence I place you in His hands, and I give thanks for you that this is so.

Bible Reference - Text

2 Corinthians 13:11 - Finally, brethren, farewell. Become complete. Be of good comfort, be of one mind, live in peace; and the God of love and peace will be with you.

Course Ref/s - Citation/s

T-02.V.17 - The injunction "Be of one mind" is the statement for revelation-readiness. My request "Do this in remembrance of me" is the appeal for cooperation from miracle workers. The two statements are not in the same order of reality. Only the latter involves an awareness of time, since to remember is to recall the past in the present. Time is under my direction, but timelessness belongs to God. In time we exist for and with each other. In timelessness we coexist with God.

T-03.II.4 - You are afraid of God's Will because you have used your own mind, which He created in the likeness of His Own, to miscreate. The mind can miscreate only when it believes it is not free. An "imprisoned" mind is not free because it is possessed, or held back, by itself. It is therefore limited, and the will is not free to assert itself. To be one is to be of one mind or will. When the Will of the Sonship and the Father are one, their perfect accord is Heaven.

T-06.V.A.3 - I have said that the Holy Spirit is the motivation for miracles. He always tells you that only the mind is real, because only the mind can be shared. The body is separate, and therefore cannot be part of you. To be of one mind is meaningful, but to be one body is meaningless. By the laws of mind, then, the body is meaningless.

T-07.V.10 - You cannot forget the Father because I am with you, and I cannot forget Him. To forget me is to forget yourself and Him Who created you. Our brothers are forgetful. That is why they need your remembrance of me and of Him Who created me. Through this remembrance, you can change their minds about themselves, as I can change yours. Your mind is so powerful a light that you can look into theirs and enlighten them, as I can enlighten yours. I do not want to share my body in communion because this is to share nothing. Would I try to share an illusion with the most holy children of a most holy Father? Yet I do want to share my mind with you because we are of one Mind, and that Mind is ours. See only this Mind everywhere, because only this is everywhere and in everything. It is everything because it encompasses all things within itself. Blessed are you who perceive only this, because you perceive only what is true.

T-10.IV.6 - When you have experienced the protection of God, the making of idols becomes inconceivable. There are no strange images in the Mind of God, and what is not in His Mind cannot be in yours, because you are of one mind and that mind belongs to Him. It is yours because it belongs to Him, for to Him ownership is sharing. And if it is so for Him, it is so for you. His definitions are His laws, for by them He established the universe as what it is. No false gods you attempt to interpose between yourself and your reality affect truth at all. Peace is yours because God created you.

T-10.IV.7 - The miracle is the act of a Son of God who has laid aside all false gods, and calls on his brothers to do likewise. It is an act of faith, because it is the recognition that his brother can do it. It is a call to the Holy Spirit in his mind, a call that is strengthened by joining. Because the miracle worker has heard God's Voice, he strengthens It in a sick brother by weakening his belief in sickness, which he does not share. The power of one mind can shine into another, because all the lamps of God were lit by the same spark. It is everywhere and it is eternal.

X. Galatians

There are two references from the Letter of Paul to the Galatians that are cited in the Course. They are:

[**2:21**] and [**6:7**].

Bible Reference - Text

Galatians 2:21 - I do not frustrate the grace of God: for if righteousness come by the law, then Christ is dead in vain.

Course Ref/s - Citation/s

T-11.VI.7 - You will not find peace until you have removed the nails from the hands of God's Son, and taken the last thorn from his forehead. The Love of God surrounds His Son whom the god of crucifixion condemns. Teach not that I died in vain. Teach rather that I did not die by demonstrating that I live in you. For the undoing of the crucifixion of God's Son is the work of the redemption, in which everyone has a part of equal value. God does not judge His guiltless Son. Having given Himself to him, how could it be otherwise?

Bible Reference - Text

Galatians 6:7 - Be not deceived; God is not mocked: for whatsoever a man soweth, that shall he also reap.

Course Ref/s - Citation/s

T-01.V.4 - Ultimately, every member of the family of God must return. The miracle calls him to return because it blesses and honors him, even though he may be absent in spirit. "God is not mocked" is not a warning but a reassurance. God would be mocked if any of His creations lacked holiness. The creation is whole, and the mark of wholeness is holiness. Miracles are affirmations of Sonship, which is a state of completion and abundance.

T-05.VI.6 - "As ye sow, so shall ye reap" He [the Holy Spirit] interprets to mean what you consider worth cultivating you will cultivate in yourself. Your judgment of what is worthy makes it worthy for you.

T-21.VI.11 - The power you have over the Son of God is not a threat to his reality. It but attests to it. Where could his freedom lie but in himself, if he be free already? And who could bind him but himself, if he deny his freedom? God is not mocked; no more His Son can be imprisoned save by his own desire. And it is by his own desire that he is freed. Such is his strength, and not his weakness. He is at his own mercy. And where he chooses to be merciful, there is he free. But where he chooses to condemn instead, there is he held a prisoner, waiting in chains his pardon on himself to set him free.

Y. Ephesians

The five references from the Letter of Paul to the Ephesians which are cited in the Course are as follows:

[2:8], [2:19], [3:9], [3:19] and [4:26].

Bible Reference - Text

Ephesians 2:8 - For by grace are ye saved through faith; and that not of yourselves: it is the gift of God:

Course Ref/s - Citation/s

T-1.VI.5-6 - All aspects of fear are untrue because they do not exist at the creative level, and therefore do not exist at all. To whatever extent you are willing to submit your beliefs to this test, to that extent are your perceptions corrected. In sorting out the false from the true, the miracle proceeds along these lines:

Perfect love casts out fear.

If fear exists,

Then there is not perfect love.

But:

Only perfect love exists.

If there is fear,

It produces a state that does not exist.

Believe this and you will be free. Only God can establish this solution, and this faith is His gift.

T-19.I.11 - Faith is the gift of God, through Him Whom God has given you. Faithlessness looks upon the Son of God, and judges him unworthy of forgiveness. But through the eyes of faith, the Son of God is seen already forgiven, free of all the guilt he laid upon himself. Faith sees him only now because it looks not to the past to judge him, but would see in him only what it would see in you. It sees not through the body's eyes, nor looks to bodies for its justification. It is the messenger of the new perception, sent forth to gather witnesses unto its coming, and to return their messages to you.

Bible Reference - Text

Ephesians 2:19 - Now therefore ye are no more strangers and foreigners, but fellow citizens with the saints, and of the household of God;

Course Ref/s - Citation/s

C-ep.2 - <u>You are a stranger here.</u> But you belong to Him Who loves you as He loves Himself. Ask but my help to roll the stone away, and it is done according to His Will. We have begun the journey. Long ago the end was written in the stars and set into the Heavens with a shining Ray that held it safe within eternity and through all time as well. And holds it still; unchanged, unchanging and unchangeable.

Bible Reference - Text

Ephesians 3:9 - And to make all men see what is the fellowship of the mystery, which from the beginning of the world hath been hid in God, who created all things by Jesus Christ:

Course Ref/s - Citation/s

T-08.II.7 - When I said, "All power and glory are yours because the Kingdom is His," this is what I meant. The Will of God is without limit, and all power and glory lie within it. It is boundless in strength and in love and in peace. It has no boundaries because its extension is unlimited, and it encompasses all things because it <u>created all things. By creating all things</u>, it made them part of itself. You are the Will of God because that is how you were created. Because your Creator creates only like Himself, you are like Him. You are part of Him Who is all power and glory, and are therefore as unlimited as He is.

T-30.V.1 - The real world is the state of mind in which the only purpose of the world is seen to be forgiveness. Fear is not its goal, for the escape from guilt becomes its aim. The value of forgiveness is perceived and takes the place of idols, which are sought no longer, for their "gifts" are not held dear. No rules are idly set, and no demands are made of anyone or anything to twist and fit into the dream of fear. Instead, there is a wish to understand all things created as they really are. And it is recognized that all things must be first forgiven, and then understood.

W-pI.038.3 - If you are holy, so is everything God created. You are holy because all things He created are holy. And all things He created are holy because you are. In today's exercises, we will apply the power of your holiness to all problems, difficulties or suffering in any form that you happen to think of, in yourself or in someone else. We will make no distinctions because there are no distinctions.

W-pI.096.9-10 - Begin with saying this:
Salvation comes from my one Self. Its Thoughts are mine to use.
Then seek Its Thoughts, and claim them as your own. These are your own real thoughts you have denied, and let your mind go wandering in a world of dreams, to find illusions in their place. Here are your thoughts, the only ones you have. Salvation is among them; find it there.
If you succeed, the thoughts that come to you will tell you, you are saved, and that your mind has found the function that it sought to lose. Your Self will welcome it and give it peace. Restored in strength, it will again flow out from spirit to the spirit in all things created by the Spirit as Itself. Your mind will bless all things. Confusion done, you are restored, for you have found your Self.

W-pI.167.6 - The mind can think it sleeps, but that is all. It cannot change what is its waking state. It cannot make a body, nor abide within a body. What is alien to the mind does not exist, because it has no source. For mind creates all things that are, and cannot give them attributes it lacks, nor change its own eternal, mindful state. It cannot make the physical. What seems to die is but the sign of mind asleep.

M-27.6 - "And the last to be overcome will be death." Of course! Without the idea of death there is no world. All dreams will end with this one. This is salvation's final goal; the end of all illusions. And in death are all illusions born. What can be born of death and still have life? But what is born of God and still can die? The inconsistencies, the compromises and the rituals the world fosters in its vain attempts to cling to death and yet to think love real are mindless magic, ineffectual and meaningless. <u>God is, and in Him all created things</u> must be eternal. Do you not see that otherwise He has an opposite, and fear would be as real as love?

Bible Reference - Text

Ephesians 3:19 - And to know the love of Christ, which passeth knowledge, that ye might be filled with all the fulness of God.

Course Ref/s - Citation/s

T-07.IX.2 - Spirit knows that the awareness of all its brothers is included in its own, as it is included in God. <u>The power of the whole Sonship and of its Creator is therefore spirit's own fullness</u>, rendering its creations equally whole and equal in perfection. The ego cannot prevail against a totality that includes God, and any totality must include God. Everything He created is given all His power, because it is part of Him and shares His Being with Him. Creating is the opposite of loss, as blessing is the opposite of sacrifice. Being must be extended. That is how it retains the knowledge of itself. Spirit yearns to share its being as its Creator did. Created by sharing, its will is to create. It does not wish to contain God, but wills to extend His Being.

T-11.IV.6 - Christ is at God's altar, waiting to welcome His Son. But come wholly without condemnation, for otherwise you will believe that the door is barred and you cannot enter. The door is not barred, and it is impossible that you cannot enter the place where God would have you be. But love yourself with <u>the Love of Christ,</u> for so does your Father love you. You can refuse to enter, but you cannot bar the door that Christ holds open. Come unto me who holds it open for you, for while I live it cannot be shut, and I live forever. God is my life and yours, and nothing is denied by God to His Son.

Bible Reference - Text

Ephesians 4:26 - Be ye angry, and sin not: let not the sun go down upon your wrath:.

Course Ref/s - Citation/s

T-pr.HIC.1:8-13 - Helen, the one who received the material, describes herself:

Psychologist, educator, conservative in theory and atheistic in belief. I was working in a prestigious and highly academic setting. And then something happened that triggered a chain of events I could never have predicted. The head of my department unexpectedly announced that he was tired of the angry and aggressive feelings our attitudes reflected, and concluded that "there must be another way." As if on cue, I agreed to help him find it. Apparently this Course is the other way.

T-12.III.3 - Whenever you become angry with a brother, for whatever reason, you are believing that the ego is to be saved, and to be saved by attack. If he attacks, you are agreeing with this belief; and if you attack, you are reinforcing it. Remember that those who attack are poor. Their poverty asks for gifts, not for further impoverishment. You who could help them are surely acting destructively if you accept their poverty as yours. If you had not invested as they had, it would never occur to you to overlook their need.

T-29.IV.4 - When you are angry, is it not because someone has failed to fill the function you allotted him? And does not this become the "reason" your attack is justified? The dreams you think you like are those in which the functions you have given have been filled; the needs which you ascribe to you are met. It does not matter if they be fulfilled or merely wanted. It is the idea that they exist from which the fears arise. Dreams are not wanted more or less. They are desired or not. And each one represents some function that you have assigned; some goal which an event, or body, or a thing should represent, and should achieve for you. If it succeeds you think you like the dream. If it should fail you think the dream is sad. But whether it succeeds or fails is not its core, but just the flimsy covering.

T-31.V.2-4 - A concept of the self is made by you. It bears no likeness to yourself at all. It is an idol, made to take the place of your reality as Son of God. The concept of the self the world would teach is not the thing that it appears to be. For it is made to serve two purposes, but one of which the mind can recognize. The first presents the face of innocence, the aspect acted on. It is this face that smiles and charms and even seems to love. It searches for companions and it looks, at times with pity, on the suffering, and sometimes offers solace. It believes that it is good within an evil world.

This aspect can grow <u>angry</u>, for the world is wicked and unable to provide the love and shelter innocence deserves. And so this face is often wet with tears at the injustices the world accords to those who would be generous and good. This aspect never makes the first attack. But every day a hundred little things make small assaults upon its innocence, provoking it to irritation, and at last to open insult and abuse.

The face of innocence the concept of the self so proudly wears can tolerate attack in self-defense, for is it not a well-known fact the world deals harshly with defenseless innocence? No one who makes a picture of himself omits this face, for he has need of it. The other side he does not want to see. Yet it is here the learning of the world has set its sights, for it is here the world's "reality" is set, to see to it the idol lasts.

W-pI.072.5-7 - If God is a body, what must His plan for salvation be? What could it be but death? In trying to present Himself as the Author of life and not of death, He is a liar and a deceiver, full of false promises and offering illusions in place of truth. The body's apparent reality makes this view of God quite convincing. In fact, if the body were real, it would be difficult indeed to escape this conclusion. And every grievance that you hold insists that the body is real. It overlooks entirely what your brother is. It reinforces your belief that he is a body, and condemns him for it. And it asserts that his salvation must be death, projecting this attack onto God, and holding Him responsible for it.

To this carefully prepared arena, where <u>angry</u> animals seek for prey and mercy cannot enter, the ego comes to save you. God made you a body. Very well. Let us accept this and be glad. As a body, do not let yourself be deprived of what the body offers. Take the little you can get. God gave you nothing. The body is your only savior. It is the death of God and your salvation.

This is the universal belief of the world you see. Some hate the body, and try to hurt and humiliate it. Others love the body, and try to glorify and exalt it. But while the body stands at the center of your concept of yourself, you are attacking God's plan for salvation, and holding your grievances against Him and His creation, that you may not hear the Voice of truth and welcome It as Friend. Your chosen savior takes His place instead. It is your friend; He is your enemy.

Bible Reference - Text

Ephesians 4:26 - Be ye angry, and sin not: let not the sun go down upon your wrath: (Continued).

Course Ref/s - Citation/s

W-pI.093.11:1-4 - If a situation arises that seems to be disturbing, quickly dispel the illusion of fear by repeating these thoughts again. Should you be tempted to become angry with someone, tell him silently:
Light and joy and peace abide in you.
Your sinlessness is guaranteed by God.

W-pI.121.3 - The unforgiving mind is torn with doubt, confused about itself and all it sees; afraid and angry, weak and blustering, afraid to go ahead, afraid to stay, afraid to waken or to go to sleep, afraid of every sound, yet more afraid of stillness; terrified of darkness, yet more terrified at the approach of light. What can the unforgiving mind perceive but its damnation? What can it behold except the proof that all its sins are real?

W-pI.192.9 - Therefore, hold no one prisoner. Release instead of bind, for thus are you made free. The way is simple. Every time you feel a stab of anger, realize you hold a sword above your head. And it will fall or be averted as you choose to be condemned or free. Thus does each one who seems to tempt you to be angry represent your savior from the prison house of death. And so you owe him thanks instead of pain.

M-17.4 - Perhaps it will be helpful to remember that no one can be angry at a fact. It is always an interpretation that gives rise to negative emotions, regardless of their seeming justification by what appears as facts. Regardless, too, of the intensity of the anger that is aroused. It may be merely slight irritation, perhaps too mild to be even clearly recognized. Or it may also take the form of intense rage, accompanied by thoughts of violence, fantasised or apparently acted out. It does not matter. All of these reactions are the same. They obscure the truth, and this can never be a matter of degree. Either truth is apparent, or it is not. It cannot be partially recognized. Who is unaware of truth must look upon illusions.

Z. Philippians

The following are the three references from the Letter of Paul to the Philippians that are cited in the Course:

[**2:2**], [**2:5**] and [**4:7**].

Bible Reference - Text

Philippians 2:2 - Fulfil ye my joy, that ye be likeminded, having the same love, being of one accord, of one mind.

Course Ref/s - Citation/s

T-23.IV.7 - See no one from the battleground, for there you look on him from nowhere. You have no reference point from where to look, where meaning can be given what you see. For only bodies could attack and murder, and if this is your purpose, then you must be one with them. Only a purpose unifies, and those who share a purpose have a mind as one. The body has no purpose of itself, and must be solitary. From below, it cannot be surmounted. From above, the limits it exerts on those in battle still are gone, and not perceived. The body stands between the Father and the Heaven He created for His Son because it has no purpose.

Bible Reference - Text

Philippians 2:5 - Let this mind be in you, which was also in Christ Jesus:

Course Ref/s - Citation/s

T-05.I.2-3 - Let us start our process of reawakening with just a few simple concepts:

> Thoughts increase by being given away.
> The more who believe in them the stronger they become.
> Everything is an idea.
> How, then, can giving and losing be associated?

This is the invitation to the Holy Spirit. I have said already that I can reach up and bring the Holy Spirit down to you, but I can bring Him to you only at your own invitation. The Holy Spirit is in your right mind, as He was in mine. The Bible says, "<u>May the mind be in you that was also in Christ Jesus</u>," and uses this as a blessing. It is the blessing of miracle-mindedness. It asks that you may think as I thought, joining with me in Christ thinking.

T-05.IV.4 - I heard one Voice because I understood that I could not atone for myself alone. Listening to one Voice implies the decision to share It in order to hear It yourself. <u>The Mind that was in me</u> is still irresistibly drawn to every mind created by God, because God's Wholeness is the Wholeness of His Son. You cannot be hurt, and do not want to show your brother anything except your wholeness. Show him that he cannot hurt you and hold nothing against him, or you hold it against yourself. This is the meaning of "turning the other cheek."

T-05.IV.5 - Teaching is done in many ways, above all by example. Teaching should be healing, because it is the sharing of ideas and the recognition that to share ideas is to strengthen them. I cannot forget my need to teach what I have learned, which arose in me because I learned it. I call upon you to teach what you have learned, because by so doing you can depend on it. Make it dependable in my name because my name is the Name of God's Son. What I learned I give you freely, and <u>the Mind that was in me</u> rejoices as you choose to hear it.

T-05.VI.3 - Remember the Kingdom always, and remember that you who are part of the Kingdom cannot be lost. <u>The Mind that was in me</u> is in you, for God creates with perfect fairness. Let the Holy Spirit remind you always of His fairness, and let me teach you how to share it with your brothers. How else can the chance to claim it for yourself be given you? The two voices speak for different interpretations of the same thing simultaneously; or almost simultaneously, for the ego always speaks first. Alternate interpretations were unnecessary until the first one was made.

Bible Reference - Text

Philippians 4:7 - And the peace of God, which passeth all understanding, shall keep your hearts and minds through Christ Jesus.

Course Ref/s - Citation/s

T-02.II.1:7-14 - If you are afraid, you will inevitably value wrongly, and by endowing all thoughts with equal power will inevitably destroy peace. That is why the Bible speaks of "<u>the peace of God which passeth understanding</u>." This peace is totally incapable of being shaken by errors of any kind. It denies the ability of anything not of God to affect you. This is the proper use of denial. It is not used to hide anything, but to correct error. It brings all error into the light, and since error and darkness are the same, it corrects error automatically.

T-13.VII.8 - <u>The peace of God passeth your understanding</u> only in the past. Yet here it is, and you can understand it now. God loves His Son forever, and His Son returns his Father's Love forever. The real world is the way that leads you to remembrance of the one thing that is wholly true and wholly yours. For all else you have lent yourself in time, and it will fade. But this one thing is always yours, being the gift of God unto His Son. Your one reality was given you, and by it God created you as one with Him.

AA. Colossians

The two verses from the Letter of Paul to the Colossians that are cited in the Course are as follows:

[**1:16**] and [**2:12**].

Bible Reference - Text

Colossians 1:16 - For by him were all things created, that are in heaven, and that are in earth, visible and invisible, whether they be thrones, or dominions, or principalities, or powers: all things were created by him, and for him:

Course Ref/s - Citation/s

M-29.8 - And now in all your doings be you blessed. God turns to you for help to save the world. Teacher of God, His thanks He offers you, And all the world stands silent in the grace You bring from Him. You are the Son He loves, And it is given you to be the means Through which His Voice is heard around the world, To close all things of time; to end the sight Of <u>all things visible</u>; and to undo All things that change. Through you is ushered in A world unseen, unheard, yet truly there. Holy are you, and in your light the world Reflects your holiness, for you are not Alone and friendless. I give thanks for you, And join your efforts on behalf of God, Knowing they are on my behalf as well, And for all those who walk to God with me.

Bible Reference - Text

Colossians 2:12 - Buried with him in baptism, wherein also ye are risen with him through the faith of the operation of God, who hath raised him from the dead.

Course Ref/s - Citation/s

T-13.V.11 - The Holy Spirit is the light in which Christ stands revealed. And all who would behold Him can see Him, for they have asked for light. Nor will they see Him alone, for He is no more alone than they are.

Because they saw the Son, they have risen in Him to the Father. And all this will they understand, because they looked within and saw beyond the darkness the Christ in them, and recognized Him. In the sanity of His vision they looked upon themselves with love, seeing themselves as the Holy Spirit sees them. And with this vision of the truth in them came all the beauty of the world to shine upon them.

BB. 1 Thessalonians

The three references from the First Letter of Paul to the Thessalonians that are cited in the Course are:

[2:19], [5:5] and [5:17].

Bible Reference - Text

1 Thessalonians 2:19 - For what is our hope, or joy, or crown of rejoicing? Are not even ye in the presence of our Lord Jesus Christ at his coming?

Course Ref/s - Citation/s

T-04.IV.10 - The First Coming of Christ is merely another name for the creation, for Christ is the Son of God. The Second Coming of Christ means nothing more than the end of the ego's rule and the healing of the mind. I was created like you in the First, and I have called you to join me in the Second. I am in charge of the Second Coming, and my judgment, which is used only for protection, cannot be wrong because it never attacks. Yours may be so distorted that you believe I was mistaken in choosing you. I assure you this is a mistake of your ego. Do not mistake it for humility. Your ego is trying to convince you that it is real and I am not, because if I am real, I am no more real than you are. That knowledge, and I assure you that it is knowledge, means that Christ has come into your mind and healed it.

T-09.IV.09 - The ego literally lives on borrowed time, and its days are numbered. Do not fear the Last Judgment, but welcome it and do not wait, for the ego's time is "borrowed" from your eternity. This is the Second Coming that was made for you as the First was created. The Second Coming is merely the return of sense. Can this possibly be fearful?

T-09.IV.11 - The impossible can happen only in fantasy. When you search for reality in fantasies you will not find it. The symbols of fantasy are of the ego, and of these you will find many. But do not look for meaning in them. They have no more meaning than the fantasies into which they are woven. Fairy tales can be pleasant or fearful, but no one calls them true. Children may believe them, and so, for a while, the tales are true for them. Yet when reality dawns, the fantasies are gone. Reality has not gone in the meanwhile. The Second Coming is the awareness of reality, not its return.

W-pII.09.1 - Christ's Second Coming, which is sure as God, is merely the correction of mistakes, and the return of sanity. It is a part of the condition that restores the never lost, and re-establishes what is forever and forever true. It is the invitation to God's Word to take illusion's place; the willingness to let forgiveness rest upon all things without exception and without reserve.

W-pII.09.3-5 - The Second Coming ends the lessons that the Holy Spirit teaches, making way for the Last Judgment, in which learning ends in one last summary that will extend beyond itself, and reaches up to God.
The Second Coming is the time in which all minds are given to the hands of Christ, to be returned to spirit in the name of true creation and the Will of God.

The Second Coming is the one event in time which time itself can not affect. For every one who ever came to die, or yet will come or who is present now, is equally released from what he made. In this equality is Christ restored as one Identity, in which the Sons of God acknowledge that they all are one. And God the Father smiles upon His Son, His one creation and His only joy.

Pray that the Second Coming will be soon, but do not rest with that.
It needs your eyes and ears and hands and feet. It needs your voice.
And most of all it needs your willingness. Let us rejoice that we can do God's Will, and join together in its holy light. Behold, the Son of God is one in us, and we can reach our Father's Love through Him.

W-pII.10.1 - Christ's Second Coming gives the Son of God this gift: to hear the Voice for God proclaim that what is false is false, and what is true has never changed. And this the judgment is in which perception ends.
At first you see a world that has accepted this as true, projected from a now corrected mind. And with this holy sight, perception gives a silent blessing and then disappears, its goal accomplished and its mission done.

Bible Reference - Text

1 Thessalonians 5:5 - Ye are all the children of light, and the children of the day: we are not of the night, nor of darkness.

Course Ref/s - Citation/s

T-11.III.6 - <u>The children of light cannot abide in darkness</u>, for darkness is not in them. Do not be deceived by the dark comforters, and never let them enter the mind of God's Son, for they have no place in His temple. When you are tempted to deny Him remember that there are no other gods to place before Him, and accept His Will for you in peace. For you cannot accept it otherwise.

Bible Reference - Text

1 Thessalonians 5:17 - Pray without ceasing.

Course Ref/s - Citation/s

S-1.II.2- These forms of prayer, or asking-out-of-need, always involve feelings of weakness and inadequacy, and could never be made by a Son of God who knows Who he is. No one, then, who is sure of his Identity could pray in these forms. Yet it is also true that no one who is uncertain of his Identity can avoid praying in this way. And prayer is as continual as life. <u>Everyone prays without ceasing.</u> Ask and you have received, for you have established what it is you want.

CC. 1 Timothy

The only reference from the First Letter of Paul to Timothy that is cited in the Course is [6:10].

Bible Reference - Text

1 Timothy 6:10 - For the love of money is the root of all evil: which while some coveted after, they have erred from the faith, and pierced themselves through with many sorrows.

Course Ref/s - Citation/s

T-03.VI.7-8 - I have spoken of different symptoms, and at that level there is almost endless variation. There is, however, only one cause for all of them: the authority problem. This is "the root of all evil." Every symptom the ego makes involves a contradiction in terms, because the mind is split between the ego and the Holy Spirit, so that whatever the ego makes is incomplete and contradictory. This untenable position is the result of the authority problem which, because it accepts the one inconceivable thought as its premise, can produce only ideas that are inconceivable.

The issue of authority is really a question of authorship. When you have an authority problem, it is always because you believe you are the author of yourself and project your delusion onto others. You then perceive the situation as one in which others are literally fighting you for your authorship. This is the fundamental error of all those who believe they have usurped the power of God. This belief is very frightening to them, but hardly troubles God. He is, however, eager to undo it, not to punish His children, but only because He knows that it makes them unhappy. God's creations are given their true Authorship, but you prefer to be anonymous when you choose to separate yourself from your Author. Being uncertain of your true Authorship, you believe that your creation was anonymous. This leaves you in a position where it sounds meaningful to believe that you created yourself. The dispute over authorship has left such uncertainty in your mind that it may even doubt whether you really exist at all.

T-11.III.1 - When you are weary, remember you have hurt yourself. Your Comforter will rest you, but you cannot. You do not know how, for if you did you could never have grown weary. Unless you hurt yourself you could never suffer in any way, for that is not God's Will for His Son. Pain is not of Him, for He knows no attack and His peace surrounds you silently. God is very quiet, for there is no conflict in Him. <u>Conflict is the root of all evil</u>, for being blind it does not see whom it attacks. Yet it always attacks the Son of God, and the Son of God is you.

P-3.III.1 - No one can pay for therapy, for healing is of God and He asks for nothing. It is, however, part of His plan that everything in this world be used by the Holy Spirit to help in carrying out the plan. Even an advanced therapist has some earthly needs while he is here. Should he need money it will be given him, not in payment, but to help him better serve the plan. <u>Money is not evil.</u> It is nothing. But no one here can live with no illusions, for he must yet strive to have the last illusion be accepted by everyone everywhere. He has a mighty part in this one purpose, for which he came. He stays here but for this. And while he stays he will be given what he needs to stay.

DD. Hebrews

The Letter to the Hebrews has three references that are cited in the Course. They are:

[**8:10-11**], [**13:5**] and [**13:8**].

Bible Reference - Text

Hebrews 8:10-11 - For this is the covenant that I will make with the house of Israel after those days, saith the Lord; I will put my laws into their mind, and write them in their hearts: and I will be to them a God, and they shall be to me a people: And they shall not teach every man his neighbour, and every man his brother, saying, Know the Lord: for all shall know me, from the least to the greatest.

Course Ref/s - Citation/s

W-pII.14.5 - We are the holy messengers of God who speak for Him, and carrying His Word to everyone whom He has sent to us, we learn that it is written on our hearts. And thus our minds are changed about the aim for which we came, and which we seek to serve. We bring glad tidings to the Son of God, who thought he suffered. Now is he redeemed. And as he sees the gate of Heaven stand open before him, he will enter in and disappear into the Heart of God.

M-26.1 - God indeed can be reached directly, for there is no distance between Him and His Son. His awareness is in everyone's memory, and His Word is written on everyone's heart. Yet this awareness and this memory can arise across the threshold of recognition only where all barriers to truth have been removed. In how many is this the case? Here, then, is the role of God's teachers. They, too, have not attained the necessary understanding as yet, but they have joined with others. This is what sets them apart from the world. And it is this that enables others to leave the world with them. Alone they are nothing. But in their joining is the power of God.

Bible Reference - Text

Hebrews 13:5 - Let your conversation be without covetousness; and be content with such things as ye have: for he hath said, I will never leave thee, nor forsake thee.

Course Ref/s - Citation/s

T-04.III.7 - It has never really entered your mind to give up every idea you ever had that opposes knowledge. You retain thousands of little scraps of fear that prevent the Holy One from entering. Light cannot penetrate through the walls you make to block it, and it is forever unwilling to destroy what you have made. No one can see through a wall, but I can step around it. Watch your mind for the scraps of fear, or you will be unable to ask me to do so. I can help you only as our Father created us. I will love you and honor you and maintain complete respect for what you have made, but I will not uphold it unless it is true. <u>I will never forsake you</u> any more than God will, but I must wait as long as you choose to forsake yourself. Because I wait in love and not in impatience, you will surely ask me truly. I will come in response to a single unequivocal call.

T-05.IV.6 - The Holy Spirit atones in all of us by undoing, and thus lifts the burden you have placed in your mind. By following Him you are led back to God where you belong, and how can you find the way except by taking your brother with you? My part in the Atonement is not complete until you join it and give it away. As you teach so shall you learn. <u>I will never leave you or forsake you</u>, because to forsake you would be to forsake myself and God Who created me. You forsake yourself and God if you forsake any of your brothers. You must learn to see them as they are, and understand they belong to God as you do. How could you treat your brother better than by rendering unto God the things that are God's?

Bible Reference - Text

Hebrews 13:8 - Jesus Christ the same yesterday, and to day, and for ever.

Course Ref/s - Citation/s

T-11.VI.4 - I am your resurrection and your life. You live in me because you live in God. And everyone lives in you, as you live in everyone. Can you, then, perceive unworthiness in a brother and not perceive it in yourself? And can you perceive it in yourself and not perceive it in God? Believe in the resurrection because it has been accomplished, and it has been accomplished in you. This is as true now as it will ever be, for the resurrection is the Will of God, which knows no time and no exceptions. But make no exceptions yourself, or you will not perceive what has been accomplished for you. For we ascend unto the Father together, as it was in the beginning, is now and ever shall be, for such is the nature of God's Son as his Father created him.

T-26.I.7 - Yet every instant can you be reborn, and given life again.
His [Your brother's] holiness gives life to you, who cannot die because his sinlessness is known to God; and can no more be sacrificed by you than can the light in you be blotted out because he sees it not. You who would make a sacrifice of life, and make your eyes and ears bear witness to the death of God and of His holy Son, think not that you have power to make of Them what God willed not They be. In Heaven, God's Son is not imprisoned in a body, nor is sacrificed in solitude to sin. And as he is in Heaven, so must he be eternally and everywhere. He is the same forever. Born again each instant, untouched by time, and far beyond the reach of any sacrifice of life or death. For neither did he make, and only one was given him by One Who knows His gifts can never suffer sacrifice and loss.

T-29.VI.2 - Swear not to die, you holy Son of God! You make a bargain that you cannot keep. The Son of Life cannot be killed. He is immortal as his Father. What he is cannot be changed. He is the only thing in all the universe that must be one. What seems eternal all will have an end.
The stars will disappear, and night and day will be no more. All things that come and go, the tides, the seasons and the lives of men; all things that change with time and bloom and fade will not return. Where time has set an end is not where the eternal is. God's Son can never change by what men made of him. He will be as he was and as he is, for time appointed not his destiny, nor set the hour of his birth and death. Forgiveness will not change him. Yet time waits upon forgiveness that the things of time may disappear because they have no use.

W-pI.167.12 - We share one life because we have one Source, a Source from which perfection comes to us, remaining always in the holy minds which He created perfect. As we were, so are we now and will forever be. A sleeping mind must waken, as it sees its own perfection mirroring the Lord of Life so perfectly it fades into what is reflected there. And now it is no more a mere reflection. It becomes the thing reflected, and the light which makes reflection possible. No vision now is needed. For the wakened mind is one that knows its Source, its Self, its Holiness.

EE. 1 Peter

There is only one reference from the First Letter from Peter that is cited in the Course; it is verse [5:6-7].

Bible Reference - Text

1 Peter 5:6-7 - Humble yourselves therefore under the mighty hand of God, that he may exalt you in due time: Casting all your care upon him; for he careth for you.

Course Ref/s - Citation/s

T-05.VII.1 - Do you really believe you can make a voice that can drown out God's? Do you really believe you can devise a thought system that can separate you from Him? Do you really believe you can plan for your safety and joy better than He can? You need be neither careful nor careless; you need merely <u>cast your cares upon Him because He careth for you</u>. You are His care because He loves you. His Voice reminds you always that all hope is yours because of His care. You cannot choose to escape His care because that is not His Will, but you can choose to accept His care and use the infinite power of His care for all those He created by it.

FF. 1 John

The following are the references from the First Letter of John that are cited in the Course:

[1:5-7], [2:18], [3:1-2], [4:2];

[4:8], [4:18] and [4:20-21].

Bible Reference - Text

1 John 1:5-7 - This then is the message which we have heard of him, and declare unto you, that God is light, and in him is no darkness at all. If we say that we have fellowship with him, and walk in darkness, we lie, and do not the truth: But if we walk in the light, as he is in the light, we have fellowship one with another, and the blood of Jesus Christ his Son cleanseth us from all sin.

Course Ref/s - Citation/s

T-02.VII.5:1-5 - Nothing and everything cannot coexist. To believe in one is to deny the other. Fear is really nothing and love is everything. <u>Whenever light enters darkness, the darkness is abolished.</u> What you believe is true for you.

T-03.I.7 - The Atonement itself radiates nothing but truth. It therefore epitomizes harmlessness and sheds only blessing. It could not do this if it arose from anything but perfect innocence. Innocence is wisdom because it is unaware of evil, and evil does not exist. It is, however, perfectly aware of everything that is true. The resurrection demonstrated that nothing can destroy truth. Good can withstand any form of evil, as <u>light abolishes forms of darkness</u>. The Atonement is therefore the perfect lesson. It is the final demonstration that all the other lessons I taught are true. If you can accept this one generalization now, there will be no need to learn from many smaller lessons. You are released from all errors if you believe this.

T-13.VI.8 - Now is the time of salvation, for now is the release from time. Reach out to all your brothers, and touch them with the touch of Christ. In timeless union with them is your continuity, unbroken because it is wholly shared. <u>God's guiltless Son is only light. There is no darkness in him anywhere</u>, for he is whole. Call all your brothers to witness to his wholeness, as I am calling you to join with me. Each voice has a part in the song of redemption, the hymn of gladness and thanksgiving for the light to the Creator of light. The holy light that shines forth from God's Son is the witness that his light is of his Father.

T-14.II.4 - Like you, the Holy Spirit did not make truth. Like God, He knows it to be true. <u>He brings the light of truth into the darkness</u>, and lets it shine on you. And as it shines your brothers see it, and realizing that this light is not what you have made, they see in you more than you see. They will be happy learners of the lesson this light brings to them, because it teaches them release from nothing and from all the works of nothing. The heavy chains that seem to bind them to despair they do not see as nothing, until you bring the light to them. And then they see the chains have disappeared, and so they must have been nothing. And you will see it with them. Because you taught them gladness and release, they will become your teachers in release and gladness.

T-14.II.7 - The happy learner meets the conditions of learning here, as he meets the conditions of knowledge in the Kingdom. All this lies in the Holy Spirit's plan to free you from the past, and open up the way to freedom for you. For truth is true. What else could ever be, or ever was? This simple lesson holds the key to the dark door that you believe is locked forever. You made this door of nothing, and behind it is nothing. <u>The key is only the light</u> that shines away the shapes and forms and fears of nothing. <u>Accept this key to freedom from the hands of Christ Who gives it to you, that you may join Him in the holy task of bringing light.</u> For, like your brothers, you do not realize the light has come and freed you from the sleep of darkness.

T-14.III.6 - No penalty is ever asked of God's Son except by himself and of himself. Every chance given him to heal is another opportunity to <u>replace darkness with light</u> and fear with love. If he refuses it he binds himself to darkness, because he did not choose to free his brother and enter light with him. By giving power to nothing, he throws away the joyous opportunity to learn that nothing has no power. And by not dispelling darkness, he became afraid of darkness and of light. The joy of learning that darkness has no power over the Son of God is the happy lesson the Holy Spirit teaches, and would have you teach with Him. It is His joy to teach it, as it will be yours.

Bible Reference - Text

1 John 2:18 - Little children, it is the last time: and as ye have heard that antichrist shall come, even now are there many antichrists; whereby we know that it is the last time.

Course Ref/s - Citation/s

T-20.I.14 - We said you can begin a happy day with the determination not to make decisions by yourself. This seems to be a real decision in itself. And yet, you cannot make decisions by yourself. The only question really is with what you choose to make them. That is really all. The first rule, then, is not coercion, but a simple statement of a simple fact. You will not make decisions by yourself whatever you decide. For they are made with idols or with God. And you ask help of anti-Christ or Christ, and which you choose will join with you and tell you what to do.

T-29.VIII.ti-2 - The Anti-Christ

What is an idol? Do you think you know? For idols are unrecognized as such, and never seen for what they really are. That is the only power that they have. Their purpose is obscure, and they are feared and worshipped, both, because you do not know what they are for, and why they have been made. An idol is an image of your brother that you would value more than what he is. Idols are made that he may be replaced, no matter what their form. And it is this that never is perceived and recognized. Be it a body or a thing, a place, a situation or a circumstance, an object owned or wanted, or a right demanded or achieved, it is the same.

Let not their form deceive you. Idols are but substitutes for your reality. In some way, you believe they will complete your little self, for safety in a world perceived as dangerous, with forces massed against your confidence and peace of mind. They have the power to supply your lacks, and add the value that you do not have. No one believes in idols who has not enslaved himself to littleness and loss. And thus must seek beyond his little self for strength to raise his head, and stand apart from all the misery the world reflects. This is the penalty for looking not within for certainty and quiet calm that liberates you from the world, and lets you stand apart, in quiet and in peace.

T-29.VIII.3-4 - An idol is a false impression, or a false belief; some form of anti-Christ, that constitutes a gap between the Christ and what you see. An idol is a wish, made tangible and given form, and thus perceived as real and seen outside the mind. Yet it is still a thought, and cannot leave the mind that is its source. Nor is its form apart from the idea it represents. All forms of Anti-Christ oppose the Christ. And fall before His face like a dark veil that seems to shut you off from Him, alone in darkness. Yet the light is there. A cloud does not put out the sun. No more a veil can banish what it seems to separate, nor darken by one whit the light itself.

This world of idols is a veil across the face of Christ, because its purpose is to separate your brother from yourself. A dark and fearful purpose, yet a thought without the power to change one blade of grass from something living to a sign of death. Its form is nowhere, for its source abides within your mind where God abideth not. Where is this place where what is everywhere has been excluded and been kept apart? What hand could be held up to block God's way? Whose voice could make demand He enter not? The "more-than-everything" is not a thing to make you tremble and to quail in fear. Christ's enemy is nowhere. He can take no form in which he ever will be real.

T-29.VIII.6 - An idol is established by belief, and when it is withdrawn the idol "dies." This is the Anti-Christ; the strange idea there is a power past omnipotence, a place beyond the infinite, a time transcending the eternal. Here the world of idols has been set by the idea this power and place and time are given form, and shape the world where the impossible has happened. Here the deathless come to die, the all-encompassing to suffer loss, the timeless to be made the slaves of time. Here does the changeless change; the peace of God, forever given to all living things, give way to chaos. And the Son of God, as perfect, sinless and as loving as his Father, come to hate a little while; to suffer pain and finally to die.

W-pI.137.6 - Yet think not healing is unworthy of your function here. For anti-Christ becomes more powerful than Christ to those who dream the world is real. The body seems to be more solid and more stable than the mind. And love becomes a dream, while fear remains the one reality that can be seen and justified and fully understood.

Bible Reference - Text

1 John 3:1-2 - Behold, what manner of love the Father hath bestowed upon us, that we should be called the sons of God: therefore the world knoweth us not, because it knew him not. Beloved, now are we the sons of God, and it doth not yet appear what we shall be: but we know that, when he shall appear, we shall be like him; for we shall see him as he is.

Course Ref/s - Citation/s

T-03.II.5 - Nothing can prevail against a Son of God who commends his Spirit into the Hands of his Father. By doing this the mind awakens from its sleep and remembers its Creator. All sense of separation disappears. The Son of God is part of the Holy Trinity, but the Trinity Itself is one. There is no confusion within Its Levels, because They are of one Mind and one Will. This single purpose creates perfect integration and establishes the peace of God. Yet this vision can be perceived only by the truly innocent. Because their hearts are pure, the innocent defend true perception instead of defending themselves against it. Understanding the lesson of the Atonement they are without the wish to attack, and therefore they see truly. This is what the Bible means when it says, "<u>When he shall appear (or be perceived) we shall be like him, for we shall see him as he is.</u>"

T-30.VIII.5 - Because reality is changeless is a miracle already there to heal all things that change, and offer them to you to see in happy form, devoid of fear. It will be given you to look upon your brother thus. But not while you would have it otherwise in some respects. For this but means you would not have him healed and whole. The Christ in him is perfect. Is it this that you would look upon? Then let there be no dreams about him that you would prefer to seeing this. And you will see the Christ in him because you let Him come to you. <u>And when He has appeared to you, you will be certain you are like Him</u>, for He is the changeless in your brother and in you.

Bible Reference - Text

1 John 4:2 - Hereby know ye the Spirit of God: Every spirit that confesseth that Jesus Christ is come in the flesh is of God:

Course Ref/s - Citation/s

C-5.2 - <u>The name of Jesus is the name of one who was a man but saw the face of Christ</u> in all his brothers and remembered God. So he became identified with Christ, a man no longer, but at one with God. The man was an illusion, for he seemed to be a separate being, walking by himself, within a body that appeared to hold his self from Self, as all illusions do. Yet who can save unless he sees illusions and then identifies them as what they are? Jesus remains a Savior because he saw the false without accepting it as true. And Christ needed his form that He might appear to men and save them from their own illusions.

Bible Reference - Text

1 John 4:8 - He that loveth not knoweth not God; for God is love.

Course Ref/s - Citation/s

T-09.I.9 - Ultimately everyone must remember the Will of God, because ultimately everyone must recognize himself. This recognition is the recognition that his will and God's are one. In the presence of truth, there are no unbelievers and no sacrifices. In the security of reality, fear is totally meaningless. To deny what is can only seem to be fearful. Fear cannot be real without a cause, and God is the only Cause. God is Love and you do want Him. This is your will. Ask for this and you will be answered, because you will be asking only for what belongs to you.

T-18.I.7 - When you seem to see some twisted form of the original error rising to frighten you, say only, "God is not fear, but Love," and it will disappear. The truth will save you. It has not left you, to go out into the mad world and so depart from you. Inward is sanity; insanity is outside you. You but believe it is the other way; that truth is outside, and error and guilt within. Your little, senseless substitutions, touched with insanity and swirling lightly off on a mad course like feathers dancing insanely in the wind, have no substance. They fuse and merge and separate, in shifting and totally meaningless patterns that need not be judged at all. To judge them individually is pointless. Their tiny differences in form are no real differences at all. None of them matters. That they have in common and nothing else. Yet what else is necessary to make them all the same?

T-29.I.8 - The body, innocent of goals, is your excuse for variable goals you hold, and force the body to maintain. You do not fear its weakness, but its lack of strength or weakness. Would you know that nothing stands between you and your brother? Would you know there is no gap behind which you can hide? There is a shock that comes to those who learn their savior is their enemy no more. There is a wariness that is aroused by learning that the body is not real. And there are overtones of seeming fear around the happy message, "God is Love."

T-31.I.10 - The fear of God results as surely from the lesson that His Son is guilty as God's Love must be remembered when he learns his innocence. For hate must father fear, and look upon its father as itself. How wrong are you who fail to hear the call that echoes past each seeming call to death, that sings behind each murderous attack and pleads that love restore the dying world. You do not understand Who calls to you beyond each form of hate; each call to war. Yet you will recognize Him as you give Him answer in the language that He calls. He will appear when you have answered Him, and you will know in Him that God is Love.

W-pI.099.4-5 - What joins the separated mind and thoughts with Mind and Thought which are forever one? What plan could hold the truth inviolate, yet recognize the need illusions bring, and offer means by which they are undone without attack and with no touch of pain? What but a Thought of God could be this plan, by which the never done is overlooked, and sins forgotten which were never real?

The Holy Spirit holds this plan of God exactly as it was received of Him within the Mind of God and in your own. It is apart from time in that its Source is timeless. Yet it operates in time, because of your belief that time is real. Unshaken does the Holy Spirit look on what you see; on sin and pain and death, on grief and separation and on loss. Yet does He know one thing must still be true; God is still Love, and this is not His Will.

W-pI.099.11 - There is a special message for today which has the power to remove all forms of doubt and fear forever from your mind. If you are tempted to believe them true, remember that appearances can not withstand the truth these mighty words contain:

Salvation is my only function here.

God still is Love, and this is not His Will.

W-pI.103.ti-1 - God, being Love, is also happiness.

Happiness is an attribute of love. It cannot be apart from it. Nor can it be experienced where love is not. Love has no limits, being everywhere. And therefore joy is everywhere as well. Yet can the mind deny that this is so, believing there are gaps in love where sin can enter, bringing pain instead of joy. This strange belief would limit happiness by redefining love as limited, and introducing opposition in what has no limit and no opposite.

Bible Reference - Text

1 John 4:8 -   He that loveth not knoweth not God; for God is love. (Continued)

Course Ref/s - Citation/s

W-pI.127.03 - Love cannot judge. As it is one itself, it looks on all as one. Its meaning lies in oneness. And it must elude the mind that thinks of it as partial or in part. There is no love but God's, and all of love is His. There is no other principle that rules where love is not. Love is a law without an opposite. Its wholeness is the power holding everything as one, the link between the Father and the Son which holds Them both forever as the same.

W-pI.127.11-12 - The world in infancy is newly born. And we will watch it grow in health and strength, to shed its blessing upon all who come to learn to cast aside the world they thought was made in hate to be love's enemy. Now are they all made free, along with us. Now are they all our brothers in God's Love.

We will remember them throughout the day, because we cannot leave a part of us outside our love if we would know our Self. At least three times an hour think of one who makes the journey with you, and who came to learn what you must learn. And as he comes to mind, give him this message from your Self: I bless you, brother, with the Love of God, which I would share with you. For I would learn the joyous lesson that there is no love but God's and yours and mine and everyone's.

W-pI.rV.04 - This is the thought which should precede the thoughts that we review. Each one but clarifies some aspect of this thought, or helps it be more meaningful, more personal and true, and more descriptive of the holy Self we share and now prepare to know again: God is but Love, and therefore so am I. This Self alone knows love. This Self alone is perfectly consistent in Its thoughts; knows Its Creator, understands Itself, is perfect in Its knowledge and Its love, and never changes from Its constant state of union with Its Father and Itself.

W-pI.rV.10 - Let this review become a time in which we share a new experience for you, yet one as old as time and older still. Hallowed your

Name. Your glory undefiled forever. And your wholeness now complete, as God established it. You are His Son, completing His extension in your own. We practice but an ancient truth we knew before illusion seemed to claim the world. And we remind the world that it is free of all illusions every time we say: <u>God is but Love,</u> and therefore so am I.

S-3.IV.5 - Never forget this; it is you who are God's Son, and as you choose to be to him so are you to yourself, and God to you. Nor will your judgment fail to reach to God, for you will give the role to Him you see in His creation. Do not choose amiss, or you will think that it is you who are creator in His place, and He is then no longer Cause but only an effect. Now healing is impossible, for He is blamed for your deception and your guilt. <u>He Who is Love</u> becomes the source of fear, for only fear can now be justified. Vengeance is His. His great destroyer, death. And sickness, suffering and grievous loss become the lot of everyone on earth, which He abandoned to the devil's care, swearing He will deliver it no more.

Bible Reference - Text

1 John 4:18 - There is no fear in love; but perfect love casteth out fear: because fear hath torment. He that feareth is not made perfect in love.

Course Ref/s - Citation/s

T-1.VI.5-6 - All aspects of fear are untrue because they do not exist at the creative level, and therefore do not exist at all. To whatever extent you are willing to submit your beliefs to this test, to that extent are your perceptions corrected. In sorting out the false from the true, the miracle proceeds along these lines:

<u>Perfect love casts out fear.</u>

<u>If fear exists,</u>

<u>Then there is not perfect love.</u>

<u> But:</u>

<u>Only perfect love exists.</u>

<u>If there is fear,</u>

<u>It produces a state that does not exist.</u>

Believe this and you will be free. Only God can establish this solution, and this faith is His gift.

T-12.II.8 - <u>There is no fear in perfect love.</u> We will but be making perfect to you what is already perfect in you. You do not fear the unknown but the known. You will not fail in your mission because I [Jesus] did not fail in mine. Give me but a little trust in the name of the complete trust I have in you, and we will easily accomplish the goal of perfection together.
For perfection is, and cannot be denied. To deny the denial of perfection is not so difficult as to deny truth, and what we can accomplish together will be believed when you see it as accomplished.

T-13.X.10 - Release from guilt as you would be released. There is no other way to look within and see the light of love, shining as steadily and as surely as God Himself has always loved His Son. And as His Son loves Him. <u>There is no fear in love</u>, for love is guiltless. You who have always loved your Father can have no fear, for any reason, to look within and see your holiness. You cannot be as you believed you were. Your guilt is without reason because it is not in the Mind of God, where you are.
And this is reason, which the Holy Spirit would restore to you. He would remove only illusions. All else He would have you see. And in Christ's vision He would show you the perfect purity that is forever within God's Son.

T-14.III.6 - No penalty is ever asked of God's Son except by himself and of himself. Every chance given him to heal is another opportunity to replace darkness with light and <u>fear with love</u>. If he refuses it he binds himself to darkness, because he did not choose to free his brother and enter light with him. By giving power to nothing, he throws away the joyous opportunity to learn that nothing has no power. And by not dispelling darkness, he became afraid of darkness and of light. The joy of learning that darkness has no power over the Son of God is the happy lesson the Holy Spirit teaches, and would have you teach with Him. It is His joy to teach it, as it will be yours.

T-15.V.4 - Because of guilt, all special relationships have elements of fear in them. This is why they shift and change so frequently. They are not based on changeless love alone. And <u>love, where fear has entered</u>, cannot be depended on because it <u>is not perfect</u>. In His function as interpreter of what you made, the Holy Spirit uses special relationships, which you have chosen to support the ego, as learning experiences that point to truth. Under His teaching, every relationship becomes a lesson in love.

Bible Reference - Text

1 John 4:18 - There is no fear in love; but perfect love....
(Continued) - (To read the full text of the above go to page 480.)

Course Ref/s - Citation/s

T-18.I.7- When you seem to see some twisted form of the original error rising to frighten you, say only, "<u>God is not fear, but Love,</u>" and it will disappear. The truth will save you. It has not left you, to go out into the mad world and so depart from you. Inward is sanity; insanity is outside you. You but believe it is the other way; that truth is outside, and error and guilt within. Your little, senseless substitutions, touched with insanity and swirling lightly off on a mad course like feathers dancing insanely in the wind, have no substance. They fuse and merge and separate, in shifting and totally meaningless patterns that need not be judged at all. To judge them individually is pointless. Their tiny differences in form are no real differences at all. None of them matters. That they have in common and nothing else. Yet what else is necessary to make them all the same?

T-20.II.8 - Your chosen home is on the other side, beyond the veil. It has been carefully prepared for you, and it is ready to receive you now. You will not see it with the body's eyes. Yet all you need you have. Your home has called to you since time began, nor have you ever failed entirely to hear. You heard, but knew not how to look, nor where. And now you know. In you the knowledge lies, ready to be unveiled and freed from all the terror that kept it hidden. <u>There is no fear in love.</u> The song of Easter is the glad refrain the Son of God was never crucified. Let us lift up our eyes together, not in fear but faith. And there will be no fear in us, for in our vision will be no illusions; only a pathway to the open door of Heaven, the home we share in quietness and where we live in gentleness and peace, as one together.

T-20.III.11 - Your gift unto your brother has given me the certainty our union will be soon. Share, then, this faith with me, and know that it is justified. <u>There is no fear in perfect love</u> because it knows no sin, and it must look on others as on itself. Looking with charity within, what can it fear without? The innocent see safety, and the pure in heart see God within His Son, and look unto the Son to lead them to the Father. And where else would they go but where they will to be? You and your brother now will lead the other to the Father as surely as God created His Son holy, and kept him so. In your brother is the light of God's eternal promise of your immortality. See him as sinless, and there can *be* no fear in you.

T-28.V.1:6-2:7 - God is the Alternate to dreams of fear. Who shares in them can never share in Him. But who withdraws his mind from sharing them is sharing Him. There is no other choice. Except you share it, nothing can exist. And you exist because God shared His Will with you, that His creation might create.

It is the sharing of the evil dreams of hate and malice, bitterness and death, of sin and suffering and pain and loss, that makes them real. Unshared, they are perceived as meaningless. The fear is gone from them because you did not give them your support. <u>Where fear has gone there love must come,</u> because there are but these alternatives. Where one appears, the other disappears. And which you share becomes the only one you have. You have the one that you accept, because it is the only one you wish to have.

W-pI.103.1:1-2:5 - Happiness is an attribute of love. It cannot be apart from it. Nor can it be experienced where love is not. Love has no limits, being everywhere. And therefore joy is everywhere as well. Yet can the mind deny that this is so, believing there are gaps in love where sin can enter, bringing pain instead of joy. This strange belief would limit happiness by redefining love as limited, and introducing opposition in what has no limit and no opposite.

Fear is associated then with love, and its results become the heritage of minds that think what they have made is real. These images, with no reality in truth, bear witness to the fear of God, forgetting being Love, He must be joy. This basic error we will try again to bring to truth today, and teach ourselves: <u>God, being Love, is also happiness. To fear Him is to be afraid of joy.</u>

M-25.4 - Nothing that is genuine is used to deceive. The Holy Spirit is incapable of deception, and He can use only genuine abilities. What is used for magic is useless to Him. But what He uses cannot be used for magic. There is, however, a particular appeal in unusual abilities that can be curiously tempting. Here are strengths which the Holy Spirit wants and needs. Yet the ego sees in these same strengths an opportunity to glorify itself. Strengths turned to weakness are tragedy indeed. Yet what is not given to the Holy Spirit must be given to weakness, for <u>what is withheld from love is given to fear</u>, and will be fearful in consequence.

Bible Reference - Text

1 John 4:18 - There is no fear in love; but perfect love....
(Continued) - (To read the full text of the above go to page 480.)

Course Ref/s - Citation/s

S-3.III.6 - God's Voice [the Holy Spirit] alone can tell you how to heal. Listen, and you will never fail to bring His kindly remedy to those He sends to you, to let Him heal them, and to bless all those who serve with Him in healing's name. The body's healing will occur because its cause has gone. And now without a cause, it cannot come again in different form. Nor will death any more be feared because it has been understood. <u>There is no fear in one who has been truly healed, for love has entered now where idols used to stand, and fear has given way at last to God.</u>

S-3.IV.2 - As witness to forgiveness, aid to prayer, and the effect of mercy truly taught, healing is blessing. And the world responds in quickened chorus through the voice of prayer. Forgiveness shines its merciful reprieve upon each blade of grass and feathered wing and all the living things upon the earth. <u>Fear has no haven here, for love has come</u> in all its holy oneness. Time remains only to let the last embrace of prayer rest on the earth an instant, as the world is shined away. This instant is the goal of all true healers, whom the Christ has taught to see His likeness and to teach like Him.

Bible Reference - Text

1 John 4:20-21 - If a man say, I love God, and hateth his brother, he is a liar: for he that loveth not his brother whom he hath seen, how can he love God whom he hath not seen? And this commandment have we from him, That he who loveth God love his brother also.

Course Ref/s - Citation/s

W-pII.246.ti-1 - <u>**To love my Father is to love His Son.**</u>

Let me not think that I can find the way to God, if I have hatred in my heart. Let me not try to hurt God's Son, and think that I can know his Father or my Self. Let me not fail to recognize myself, and still believe that my awareness can contain my Father, or my mind conceive of all the love my Father has for me, and all the love which I return to Him.

GG. Revelation

There are eight references from this book of the Bible which are cited in the Course. They are as follows:

[1:8], [2:28], [5:12], [12:7-9],

[20:11-15], [21:1], [21:4] and [21:6].

Bible Reference - Text

Revelation 1:8 - I am Alpha and Omega, the beginning and the ending, saith the Lord, which is, and which was, and which is to come, the Almighty.

Course Ref/s - Citation/s

T-07.I.7 - God does not take steps, because His accomplishments are not gradual. He does not teach, because His creations are changeless. He does nothing last, because He created first and for always. It must be understood that the word "first" as applied to Him is not a time concept. He is first in the sense that He is the First in the Holy Trinity Itself. He is the Prime Creator, because He created His co-creators. Because He did, time applies neither to Him nor to what He created. <u>The "last step" that God will take was therefore true in the beginning, is true now, and will be true forever.</u> What is timeless is always there, because its being is eternally changeless. It does not change by increase, because it was forever created to increase. If you perceive it as not increasing you do not know what it is. You also do not know Who created it. God does not reveal this to you because it was never hidden. His light was never obscured, because it is His Will to share it. How can what is fully shared be withheld and then revealed?

Bible Reference - Text

Revelation 2:28 - And I will give him the morning star.

Course Ref/s - Citation/s

C-ep.5 - Let us go out and meet the newborn world, knowing that Christ has been reborn in it, and that the holiness of this rebirth will last forever. We had lost our way but He has found it for us. Let us go and bid Him welcome Who returns to us to celebrate salvation and the end of all we thought we made. The morning star of this new day looks on a different world where God is welcomed and His Son with Him. We who complete Him offer thanks to Him, as He gives thanks to us. The Son is still, and in the quiet God has given him enters his home and is at peace at last.

Bible Reference - Text

Revelation 5:12 - Saying with a loud voice, Worthy is the Lamb that was slain to receive power, and riches, and wisdom, and strength, and honour, and glory, and blessing.

Course Ref/s - Citation/s

T-14.VII.7- Joining with Him in seeing is the way in which you learn to share with Him the interpretation of perception that leads to knowledge. You cannot see alone. Sharing perception with Him Whom God has given you teaches you how to recognize what you see. It is the recognition that nothing you see means anything alone. Seeing with Him will show you that all meaning, including yours, comes not from double vision, but from the gentle fusing of everything into one meaning, one emotion and one purpose. God has one purpose which He shares with you. The single vision which the Holy Spirit offers you will bring this oneness to your mind with clarity and brightness so intense you could not wish, for all the world, not to accept what God would have you have. Behold your will, accepting it as His, with all His Love as yours. All honor to you through Him, and through Him unto God.

T-15.III.6 - The Holy Spirit can hold your magnitude, clean of all littleness, clearly and in perfect safety in your mind, untouched by every little gift the world of littleness would offer you. But for this, you cannot side against Him in what He wills for you. Decide for God through Him. For littleness, and the belief that you can be content with littleness, are decisions you make about yourself. The power and the glory that lie in you from God are for all who, like you, perceive themselves as little, and believe that littleness can be blown up into a sense of magnitude that can content them. Neither give littleness, nor accept it. All honor is due the host of God. Your littleness deceives you, but your magnitude is of Him Who dwells in you, and in Whom you dwell. Touch no one, then, with littleness in the Name of Christ, eternal Host unto His Father.

Bible Reference - Text

Revelation 12:7-9 - And there was war in heaven: Michael and his angels fought against the dragon; and the dragon fought and his angels, And prevailed not; neither was their place found any more in heaven. And the great dragon was cast out, that old serpent, called the Devil, and Satan, which deceiveth the whole world: he was cast out into the earth, and his angels were cast out with him.

Course Ref/s - Citation/s

T-03.VII.2:4-8 - The "devil" is a frightening concept because he seems to be extremely powerful and extremely active. He is perceived as a force in combat with God, battling Him for possession of His creations. The devil deceives by lies, and builds kingdoms in which everything is in direct opposition to God. Yet he attracts men rather than repels them, and they are willing to "sell" him their souls in return for gifts of no real worth. This makes absolutely no sense.

T-03.VII.5 - The mind can make the belief in separation very real and very fearful, and this belief is the "devil." It is powerful, active, destructive and clearly in opposition to God, because it literally denies His Fatherhood. Look at your life and see what the devil has made. But realize that this making will surely dissolve in the light of truth, because its foundation is a lie. Your creation by God is the only Foundation that cannot be shaken, because the light is in it. Your starting point is truth, and you must return to your Beginning. Much has been seen since then, but nothing has really happened. Your Self is still in peace, even though your mind is in conflict. You have not yet gone back far enough, and that is why you become so fearful. As you approach the Beginning, you feel the fear of the destruction of your thought system upon you as if it were the fear of death. There is no death, but there is a belief in death.

T-21.V.8 - Faith and perception and belief can be misplaced, and serve the great deceiver's needs as well as truth. But reason has no place at all in madness, nor can it be adjusted to fit its end. Faith and belief are strong in madness, guiding perception toward what the mind has valued. But reason enters not at all in this. For the perception would fall away at once, if reason were applied. There is no reason in insanity, for it depends entirely on reason's absence. The ego never uses it, because it does not realize that it exists. The partially insane have access to it, and only they have need of it. Knowledge does not depend on it, and madness keeps it out.

Bible Reference - Text

Revelation 20:11-15 - And I saw a great white throne, and him that sat on it, from whose face the earth and the heaven fled away; and there was found no place for them. And I saw the dead, small and great, stand before God; and the books were opened: and another book was opened, which is the book of life: and the dead were judged out of those things which were written in the books, according to their works. And the sea gave up the dead which were in it; and death and hell delivered up the dead which were in them: and they were judged every man according to their works.
And death and hell were cast into the lake of fire. This is the second death. And whosoever was not found written in the book of life was cast into the lake of fire.

Course Ref/s - Citation/s

W-pII.10.2 - The final judgment on the world contains no condemnation. For it sees the world as totally forgiven, without sin and wholly purposeless. Without a cause, and now without a function in Christ's sight, it merely slips away to nothingness. There it was born, and there it ends as well. And all the figures in the dream in which the world began go with it. Bodies now are useless, and will therefore fade away, because the Son of God is limitless.

W-pII.10.3 - You who believed that God's Last Judgment would condemn the world to hell along with you, accept this holy truth: God's Judgment is the gift of the Correction He bestowed on all your errors, freeing you from them, and all effects they ever seemed to have. To fear God's saving grace is but to fear complete release from suffering, return to peace, security and happiness, and union with your own Identity.

W-pII.10.4 - God's Final Judgment is as merciful as every step in His appointed plan to bless His Son, and call him to return to the eternal peace

He shares with him. Be not afraid of love. For it alone can heal all sorrow, wipe away all tears, and gently waken from his dream of pain the Son whom God acknowledges as His. Be not afraid of this. Salvation asks you give it welcome. And the world awaits your glad acceptance, which will set it free.

W-pII.10.5 - This is God's Final Judgment: "You are still My holy Son, forever innocent, forever loving and forever loved, as limitless as your Creator, and completely changeless and forever pure. Therefore awaken and return to Me. I am Your Father and you are My Son."

Bible Reference - Text

Revelation 21:1 - And I saw a new heaven and a new earth: for the first heaven and the first earth were passed away; and there was no more sea.

Course Ref/s - Citation/s

T-11.VII.1:1-5 - The world as you perceive it cannot have been created by the Father, for the world is not as you see it. God created only the eternal, and everything you see is perishable. Therefore, there must be another world that you do not see. The Bible speaks of a new Heaven and a new earth, yet this cannot be literally true, for the eternal are not re-created. To perceive anew is merely to perceive again, implying that before, or in the interval between, you were not perceiving at all.

T-11.VII.4 - The perception of goodness is not knowledge, but the denial of the opposite of goodness enables you to recognize a condition in which opposites do not exist. And this is the condition of knowledge. Without this awareness you have not met its conditions, and until you do you will not know it is yours already. You have made many ideas that you have placed between yourself and your Creator, and these beliefs are the world as you perceive it. Truth is not absent here, but it is obscure. You do not know the difference between what you have made and what God created, and so you do not know the difference between what you have made and what you have created. To believe that you can perceive the real world is to believe that you can know yourself. You can know God because it is His Will to be known. The real world is all that the Holy Spirit has saved for you out of what you have made, and to perceive only this is salvation, because it is the recognition that reality is only what is true.

T-13.V.10 - You have but two emotions, and one you made and one was given you. Each is a way of seeing, and different worlds arise from their different sights. See through the vision that is given you, for through Christ's vision He beholds Himself. And seeing what He is, He knows His Father. Beyond your darkest dreams He sees God's guiltless Son within you, shining in perfect radiance that is undimmed by your dreams. And this you will see as you look with Him, for His vision is His gift of love to you, given Him of the Father for you.

T-13.VI.11 - There is a light that this world cannot give. Yet you can give it, as it was given you. And as you give it, it shines forth to call you from the world and follow it. For this light will attract you as nothing in this world can do. And you will lay aside the world and find another. This other world is bright with love which you have given it. And here will everything remind you of your Father and His holy Son. Light is unlimited, and spreads across this world in quiet joy. All those you brought with you will shine on you, and you will shine on them in gratitude because they brought you here. Your light will join with theirs in power so compelling, that it will draw the others out of darkness as you look on them.

T-13.VII.01 - Sit quietly and look upon the world you see, and tell yourself: "The real world is not like this. It has no buildings and there are no streets where people walk alone and separate. There are no stores where people buy an endless list of things they do not need. It is not lit with artificial light, and night comes not upon it. There is no day that brightens and grows dim. There is no loss. Nothing is there but shines, and shines forever."

T-13.VII.02 - The world you see must be denied, for sight of it is costing you a different kind of vision. You cannot see both worlds, for each of them involves a different kind of seeing, and depends on what you cherish. The sight of one is possible because you have denied the other. Both are not true, yet either one will seem as real to you as the amount to which you hold it dear. And yet their power is not the same, because their real attraction to you is unequal.

T-13.VII.03 - You do not really want the world you see, for it has disappointed you since time began. The homes you built have never sheltered you. The roads you made have led you nowhere, and no city that you built has withstood the crumbling assault of time. Nothing you made but has the mark of death upon it. Hold it not dear, for it is old and tired and ready to return to dust even as you made it. This aching world has not the power to touch the living world at all. You could not give it that, and so although you turn in sadness from it, you cannot find in it the road that leads away from it into <u>another world</u>.

Bible Reference - Text

Revelation 21:1 - And I saw a new heaven and a new earth: for.... (Continued) - (To read the full text of the above go to page 490.)

Course Ref/s - Citation/s

T-13.VII.04 - Yet <u>the real world</u> has the power to touch you even here, because you love it. And what you call with love will come to you. Love always answers, being unable to deny a call for help, or not to hear the cries of pain that rise to it from every part of this <u>strange world you made</u> but do not want. All that you need to give this world away in glad exchange for what you did not make is willingness to learn the one you made is false.

T-13.VII.05 - You have been <u>wrong about the world</u> because you have misjudged yourself. From such a twisted reference point, what could you see? All seeing starts with the perceiver, who judges what is true and what is false. And what he judges false he does not see. You who would judge reality cannot see it, for whenever judgment enters reality has slipped away. The out of mind is out of sight, because what is denied is there but is not recognized. Christ is still there, although you know Him not. His Being does not depend upon your recognition. He lives within you in the quiet present, and waits for you to leave the past behind and enter into <u>the world He holds out to you in love</u>.

T-13.VII.06 - No one in <u>this distracted world</u> but has seen some glimpses of <u>the other world</u> about him. Yet while he still lays value on his own, he will deny the vision of the other, maintaining that he loves what he loves not, and following not the road that love points out. Love leads so gladly! As you follow Him, you will rejoice that you have found His company, and learned of Him the joyful journey home. You wait but for yourself. To give this sad world over and exchange your errors for the peace of God is but your will. And Christ will always offer you the Will of God, in recognition that you share it with Him.

T-13.VII.07 - It is God's Will that nothing touch His Son except Himself, and nothing else comes nigh unto him. He is as safe from pain as God Himself, Who watches over him in everything. <u>The world about him shines with love</u> because God placed him in Himself where pain is not, and love surrounds him without end or flaw. Disturbance of his peace can never be. In perfect sanity he looks on love, for it is all about him and within him. He must deny <u>the world of pain</u> the instant he perceives the arms of love around him. And from this point of safety he looks quietly about him and recognizes that the world is one with him.

T-13.VII.08 - The peace of God passeth your understanding only in the past. Yet here it is, and you can understand it now. God loves His Son forever, and His Son returns his Father's Love forever. <u>The real world</u> is the way that leads you to remembrance of the one thing that is wholly true and wholly yours. For all else you have lent yourself in time, and it will fade. But this one thing is always yours, being the gift of God unto His Son. Your one reality was given you, and by it God created you as one with Him.

T-13.VII.09 - You will first dream of peace, and then awaken to it. Your first exchange of what you made for what you want is the exchange of nightmares for the happy dreams of love. In these lie your true perceptions, for the Holy Spirit corrects <u>the world of dreams</u>, where all perception is. Knowledge needs no correction. Yet the dreams of love lead unto knowledge. In them you see nothing fearful, and because of this they are the welcome that you offer knowledge. Love waits on welcome, not on time, and <u>the real world</u> is but your welcome of what always was. Therefore the call of joy is in it, and your glad response is your awakening to what you have not lost.

T-13.VII.10 - Praise, then, the Father for the perfect sanity of His most holy Son. Your Father knoweth that you have need of nothing. In Heaven this is so, for what could you need in eternity? <u>In your world you do need things. It is a world of scarcity</u> in which you find yourself because you are lacking. Yet can you find yourself in such a world? Without the Holy Spirit the answer would be no. Yet because of Him the answer is a joyous yes! As Mediator between the <u>two worlds,</u> He knows what you have need of and what will not hurt you. Ownership is a dangerous concept if it is left to you. The ego wants to have things for salvation, for possession is its law. Possession for its own sake is the ego's fundamental creed, a basic cornerstone in the churches it builds to itself. And at its altar it demands you lay all of the things it bids you get, leaving you no joy in them.

Bible Reference - Text

Revelation 21:1 - And I saw a new heaven and a new earth: for.... (Continued) - (To read the full text of the above go to page 490.)

Course Ref/s - Citation/s

T-30.V.1 - <u>The real world</u> is the state of mind in which the only purpose of the world is seen to be forgiveness. Fear is not its goal, for the escape from guilt becomes its aim. The value of forgiveness is perceived and takes the place of idols, which are sought no longer, for their "gifts" are not held dear. No rules are idly set, and no demands are made of anyone or anything to twist and fit into the dream of fear. Instead, there is a wish to understand all things created as they really are. And it is recognized that all things must be first forgiven, and then understood.

T-30.V.7 - When brothers join in purpose in <u>the world of fear</u>, they stand already at the edge of <u>the real world</u>. Perhaps they still look back, and think they see an idol that they want. Yet has their path been surely set away from idols toward reality. For when they joined their hands it was Christ's hand they took, and they will look on Him Whose hand they hold. The face of Christ is looked upon before the Father is remembered. For He must be unremembered till His Son has reached beyond forgiveness to the Love of God. Yet is the Love of Christ accepted first. And then will come the knowledge They are one.

C-ep.5 - Let us go out and meet the <u>newborn world</u>, knowing that Christ has been reborn in it, and that the holiness of this rebirth will last forever. We had lost our way but He has found it for us. Let us go and bid Him welcome Who returns to us to celebrate salvation and the end of all we thought we made. The morning star of this new day looks on a different world where God is welcomed and His Son with Him. We who complete Him offer thanks to Him, as He gives thanks to us. The Son is still, and in the quiet God has given him enters his home and is at peace at last.

Bible Reference - Text

Revelation 21:4 - And God shall wipe away all tears from their eyes; and there shall be no more death, neither sorrow, nor crying, neither shall there be any more pain: for the former things are passed away.

Course Ref/s - Citation/s

T-01.IV.4 - The emptiness engendered by fear must be replaced by forgiveness. That is what the Bible means by "There is no death," and why I [Jesus] could demonstrate that death does not exist. I came to fulfill the law by reinterpreting it. The law itself, if properly understood, offers only protection. It is those who have not yet changed their minds who brought the "hell-fire" concept into it. I assure you that I will witness for anyone who lets me, and to whatever extent he permits it. Your witnessing demonstrates your belief, and thus strengthens it. Those who witness for me are expressing, through their miracles, that they have abandoned the belief in deprivation in favor of the abundance they have learned belongs to them.

T-03.VII.5 - The mind can make the belief in separation very real and very fearful, and this belief is the "devil." It is powerful, active, destructive and clearly in opposition to God, because it literally denies His Fatherhood. Look at your life and see what the devil has made. But realize that this making will surely dissolve in the light of truth, because its foundation is a lie. Your creation by God is the only Foundation that cannot be shaken, because the light is in it. Your starting point is truth, and you must return to your Beginning. Much has been seen since then, but nothing has really happened. Your Self is still in peace, even though your mind is in conflict. You have not yet gone back far enough, and that is why you become so fearful. As you approach the Beginning, you feel the fear of the destruction of your thought system upon you as if it were the fear of death. There is no death, but there is a belief in death.

T-06.V.A.1 - When your body and your ego and your dreams are gone, you will know that you will last forever. Perhaps you think this is accomplished through death, but nothing is accomplished through death, because death is nothing. Everything is accomplished through life, and life is of the mind and in the mind. The body neither lives nor dies, because it cannot contain you who are life. If we share the same mind, you can overcome death because I [Jesus] did. Death is an attempt to resolve conflict by not deciding at all. Like any other impossible solution the ego attempts, it will not work.

T-27.II.6 - A miracle can offer nothing less to him than it has given unto you. So does your healing show your mind is healed, and has forgiven what he did not do. And so is he convinced his innocence was never lost, and healed along with you. Thus does the miracle undo all things the world attests can never be undone. And hopelessness and death must disappear before the ancient clarion call of life. This call has power far beyond the weak and miserable cry of death and guilt. The ancient calling of the Father to His Son, and of the Son unto His Own, will yet be the last trumpet that the world will ever hear. Brother, <u>there is no death</u>. And this you learn when you but wish to show your brother that you had no hurt of him. He thinks your blood is on his hands, and so he stands condemned. Yet it is given you to show him, by your healing, that his guilt is but the fabric of a senseless dream.

T-27.VII.14 - Accept the dream He gave instead of yours. It is not difficult to change a dream when once the dreamer has been recognized. Rest in the Holy Spirit, and allow His gentle dreams to take the place of those you dreamed in terror and in fear of death. He brings forgiving dreams, in which the choice is not who is the murderer and who shall be the victim. In the dreams He brings there is no murder and <u>there is no death</u>. The dream of guilt is fading from your sight, although your eyes are closed. A smile has come to lighten up your sleeping face. The sleep is peaceful now, for these are happy dreams.

T-29.VI.4 - Change is the greatest gift God gave to all that you would make eternal, to ensure that only Heaven would not pass away. You were not born to die. You cannot change, because your function has been fixed by God. All other goals are set in time and change that time might be preserved, excepting one. Forgiveness does not aim at keeping time, but at its ending, when it has no use. Its purpose ended, it is gone. And where it once held seeming sway is now restored the function God established for His Son in full awareness. Time can set no end to its fulfilment nor its changelessness. <u>There is no death</u> because the living share the function their Creator gave to them. Life's function cannot be to die. It must be life's extension, that it be as one forever and forever, without end.

T-29.VII.9:6-10:7 - The fear of God is but the fear of loss of idols. It is not the fear of loss of your reality. But you have made of your reality an idol, which you must protect against the light of truth. And all the world becomes the means by which this idol can be saved. Salvation thus appears to threaten life and offer death.

It is not so. Salvation seeks to prove <u>there is no death,</u> and only life exists. The sacrifice of death is nothing lost. An idol cannot take the place of God. Let Him remind you of His Love for you, and do not seek to drown His Voice in chants of deep despair to idols of yourself. Seek not outside your Father for your hope. For hope of happiness is not despair.

Bible Reference - Text

Revelation 21:4 - And God shall wipe away all tears from their.... (Continued) - (To read the full text of the above go to page 495.)

Course Ref/s - Citation/s

W-pI.163.ti-1 - <u>There is no death.</u> The Son of God is free.

Death is a thought that takes on many forms, often unrecognized. It may appear as sadness, fear, anxiety or doubt; as anger, faithlessness and lack of trust; concern for bodies, envy, and all forms in which the wish to be as you are not may come to tempt you. All such thoughts are but reflections of the worshipping of death as savior and as giver of release.

W-pI.163.8 - Death's worshippers may be afraid. And yet, can thoughts like these be fearful? If they saw that it is only this which they believe, they would be instantly released. And you will show them this today. <u>There is no death,</u> and we renounce it now in every form, for their salvation and our own as well. God made not death. Whatever form it takes must therefore be illusion. This the stand we take today. And it is given us to look past death, and see the life beyond.

W-pI.163.9 - Our Father, bless our eyes today. We are Your messengers, and we would look upon the glorious reflection of Your Love which shines in everything. We live and move in You alone. We are not separate from Your eternal life. <u>There is no death,</u> for death is not Your Will. And we abide where You have placed us, in the life we share with You and with all living things, to be like You and part of You forever. We accept Your Thoughts as ours, and our will is one with Yours eternally. Amen.

W-pI.167.1 - There are not different kinds of life, for life is like the truth. It does not have degrees. It is the one condition in which all that God created share. Like all His Thoughts, it has no opposite. There is no death because what God created shares His Life. There is no death because an opposite to God does not exist. <u>There is no death</u> because the Father and the Son are one.

M-17.9 - Madness but seems terrible. In truth it has no power to make anything. Like the magic which becomes its servant, it neither attacks nor protects. To see it and to recognize its thought system is to look on nothing. Can nothing give rise to anger? Hardly so. Remember, then, teacher of God, that anger recognizes a reality that is not there; yet is the anger certain witness that you do believe in it as fact. Now is escape impossible, until you see you have responded to your own interpretation, which you have projected on an outside world. Let this grim sword be taken from you now. <u>There is no death.</u> This sword does not exist. The fear of God is causeless. But His Love is Cause of everything beyond all fear, and thus forever real and always true.

C-5.6 - Is he God's only Helper? No, indeed. For Christ takes many forms with different names until their oneness can be recognized. But Jesus is for you the bearer of Christ's single message of the Love of God. You need no other. It is possible to read his words and benefit from them without accepting him into your life. Yet he would help you yet a little more if you will share your pains and joys with him, and leave them both to find the peace of God. Yet still it is his lesson most of all that he would have you learn, and it is this: <u>There is no death</u> because the Son of God is like his Father. Nothing you can do can change Eternal Love. Forget your dreams of sin and guilt, and come with me instead to share the resurrection of God's Son. And bring with you all those whom He has sent to you to care for as I care for you.

Bible Reference - Text

Revelation 21:6 - And he said unto me, It is done. I am Alpha and Omega, the beginning and the end. I will give unto him that is athirst of the fountain of the water of life freely.

Course Ref/s - Citation/s

T-03.III.6 - Right perception is necessary before God can communicate directly to His altars, which He established in His Sons. There He can communicate His certainty, and His knowledge will bring peace without question. God is not a stranger to His Sons, and His Sons are not strangers to each other. Knowledge preceded both perception and time, and will ultimately replace them. That is the real meaning of "<u>Alpha and Omega, the beginning and the end</u>" and "Before Abraham was I am." Perception can and must be stabilised, but knowledge is stable. "Fear God and keep His commandments" becomes "Know God and accept His certainty."

T-11.I.2 - To be alone is to be separated from infinity, but how can this be if infinity has no end? No one can be beyond the limitless, because what has no limits must be everywhere. <u>There are no beginnings and no endings in God</u>, Whose universe is Himself. Can you exclude yourself from the universe, or from God Who is the universe? I and my Father are one with you, for you are part of Us. Do you really believe that part of God can be missing or lost to Him?

T-11.I.5 - The laws of the universe do not permit contradiction. What holds for God holds for you. If you believe you are absent from God, you will believe that He is absent from you. Infinity is meaningless without you, and you are meaningless without God. <u>There is no end to God and His Son</u>, for we are the universe. God is not incomplete, and He is not childless. Because He did not will to be alone, He created a Son like Himself. Do not deny Him His Son, for your unwillingness to accept His Fatherhood has denied you yours. See His creations as His Son, for yours were created in honor of Him. The universe of love does not stop because you do not see it, nor have your closed eyes lost the ability to see. Look upon the glory of His creation, and you will learn what God has kept for you.

T-11.VI.9 - You will awaken to your own call, for the Call to awake is within you. If I live in you, you are awake. Yet you must see the works I do through you, or you will not perceive that I have done them unto you. Do not set limits on what you believe I can do through you, or you will not accept what I can do for you. Yet <u>it is done</u> already, and unless you give all that you have received you will not know that your Redeemer liveth, and that you have awakened with him. Redemption is recognized only by sharing it.

T-12.II.6 - You still want what God wills, and no nightmare can defeat a child of God in his purpose. For your purpose was given you by God, and you must accomplish it because it is His Will. Awake and remember your purpose, for it is your will to do so. <u>What has been accomplished for you</u> must be yours. Do not let your hatred stand in the way of love, for nothing can withstand the Love of Christ for His Father, or His Father's Love for Him.

Bible Reference - Text

Revelation 21:6 - And he said unto me, It is done. I am Alpha ....
(Continued) - (To read the full text of the above go to page 598.)

Course Ref/s - Citation/s

T-14.IV.1 - When you accept a brother's guiltlessness you will see the Atonement in him. For by proclaiming it in him you make it yours, and you will see what you sought. You will not see the symbol of your brother's guiltlessness shining within him while you still believe it is not there. His guiltlessness is your Atonement. Grant it to him, and you will see the truth of what you have acknowledged. Yet truth is offered first to be received, even as God gave it first to His Son. The first in time means nothing, but the First in eternity is God the Father, Who is both First and One. Beyond the First there is no other, for there is no order, no second or third, and nothing but the First.

III. Epilogue

In the Introduction I mentioned that the book, <u>A Course in Miracles</u> was written through a process called "inner dictation" from the "Voice" whom the Scribe believed to be that of Jesus Christ. This, of course, is an incredible and controversial idea and I put it to the readers to decide on the basis of the content of the book by reading it. In this Epilogue though, I would like to put my views in the controversy. Personally, I believe that the "inner dictation" can happen. This is because I had an aunt who could allow her body to be taken over by the spirit of those who passed away and become the means or "medium" of communicating to those left behind. I have seen this happen and saw the complete transformation of my aunt into the personality of the spirit who took over.

This phenomenon, as strange and seldom as it is, does happen and has been reported to happen to some individuals in some parts of the world. The "inner dictation" that happened to <u>A Course in Miracles</u> though is not as dramatic as what happened whenever my aunt become a "medium". It just involved the calm and conscious willingness on the part of the Scribe to hear the "Voice" and write down what was heard in that instant. The reason cited by the Voice in the use of this process is as follows:

"The world situation is worsening to an alarming degree. People all over the world are being called on to help, and are making their individual contributions as part of an overall prearranged plan. Part of the plan is taking down *A Course in Miracles*, and I am fulfilling my part in the agreement, as you will fulfil yours. You will be using abilities you developed long ago, and which you are not really ready to use again. Because of the acute urgency, however, the usual slow, evolutionary process is being by-passed in what might best be described as a "celestial speed-up."

On the question of content, or whether the materials dictated really came from Jesus Christ, I again believe that this is so. The overall message of the Course is love and forgiveness which is the same message that is conveyed in the New Testament. There might be some disagreements or differences on some subject matters but then again these could be attributed to the fact that the teachings of Jesus are as novel and difficult to comprehend before as it is now. It takes a high level of spiritual maturity to be able to readily comprehend those teachings, let alone write them down or convey them to others. Jesus in the Course has noted this difficulty among his disciples when He said in T-6.I.15:2-3 "If the Apostles had not felt guilty, they never could have quoted me as saying, "I come not to bring peace but a sword." This is clearly the opposite of everything I taught."

Again these differences, from my perspective, should not serve as a hindrance or barrier in reading the Course. These differences are thoroughly explained in the Course in the light of the thought system that it is advocating. The Course has a wealth of knowledge and inspirations which could contribute to one's spiritual development and it will be a pity if they are missed based solely on the differences emphasized in one's evaluation. Finally, Jesus in John 14:15-17 has promised us the Holy Spirit to be our Helper and Guide in everything that we think, say and do. The Holy Spirit therefore is available to everyone. All that is required is the little willingness to consult Him and letting Him be part of one's decision-making. Consult the Holy Spirit thus in your evaluation of the Course as in every decision that you have to make in your daily life. He is our Teacher here and now as promised by the greatest Teacher of them all, Jesus Christ.

Footnotes

[1] A Course in Miracles, third edition, Foundation for Inner Peace, p. vii-viii.

[2] Skutch, Robert. Journey Without Distance, Foundation for Inner Peace, pp. 60 & 134-5.

[3] Ibid, p. 134.

[4] Wapnick, Kenneth. Love Does Not Condemn, 2nd ed., Foundation for A Course in Miracles, p. 4

[5] Skutch, Robert. Journey Without Distance, Foundation for Inner Peace, pp. 60.

Index of Biblical References

Book	Verse/s	Page
1 Corinthians	6:15-17	432
1 Corinthians	6:19	432
1 Corinthians	13:1-13	435
1 Corinthians	14:33	438
1 Corinthians	15:26	438
1 Corinthians	15:28	439
1 Corinthians	15:51-54	440
1 John	1:5-7	473
1 John	2:18	475
1 John	3:1-2	476
1 John	4:2	477
1 John	4:8	478
1 John	4:18	481
1 John	4:20-21	485
1 Kings	19:12-13	59
1 Peter	5:6-7	472
1 Thessalonians	2:19	463
1 Thessalonians	5:5	464
1 Thessalonians	5:17	465
1 Timothy	6:10	466
2 Corinthians	6:2	442
2 Corinthians	12:9	442
2 Corinthians	13:11	446
Acts	1:8	412
Acts	17:27-28	413
Acts	20:35	415
Acts	22:16	422
Colossians	1:16	461
Colossians	2:12	461
Deuteronomy	5:26	55
Deuteronomy	31:6	57
Deuteronomy	33:27	57
Ecclesiastes	12:13	83
Ephesians	2:8	450
Ephesians	2:19	451
Ephesians	3:9	451
Ephesians	3:19	453

Book	Verse/s	Page
Ephesians	4:26	454
Exodus	3:5	42
Exodus	3:13-14	44
Exodus	20:3	45
Exodus	20:4-5	48
Exodus	20:16	49
Exodus	26:33	50
Ezekiel	2:1	94
Galatians	2:21	448
Galatians	6:7	448
Genesis	1:1	5
Genesis	1:3	5
Genesis	1:26	8
Genesis	1:28	12
Genesis	1:31	22
Genesis	2:7	23
Genesis	2:15-17	24
Genesis	2:21	25
Genesis	3:1-7	27
Genesis	3:8-9	29
Genesis	3:23-24	30
Genesis	4:9	31
Genesis	7:9	32
Genesis	19:23-26	32
Genesis	25:31-33	34
Genesis	28:16-17	35
Hebrews	8:10-11	468
Hebrews	13:5	469
Hebrews	13:8	469
Hosea	6:6	97
Isaiah	1:18	84
Isaiah	9:6	84
Isaiah	11:6	85
Isaiah	25:8	86
Isaiah	26:19	87
Isaiah	37:10	88
Isaiah	40:3	89

Index of Biblical References

Book	Verse/s	Page
Isaiah	45:21	90
Isaiah	51:3	90
Isaiah	60:1-2	91
Isaiah	64:4	91
Jeremiah	31:3	93
Job	2:9	61
Job	19:5	61
John	1:1-5	328
John	1:7-8	332
John	1:14	333
John	1:29-34	334
John	3:3	335
John	3:6	340
John	3:16	340
John	3:35	341
John	3:36	342
John	4:10	342
John	5:30	343
John	6:19-20	345
John	6:68-69	347
John	7:24	348
John	8:12	348
John	8:16	351
John	8:31-32	352
John	8:51	356
John	8:58	356
John	10:30	357
John	11:1-4	360
John	11:11	361
John	11:25	361
John	11:43-44	362
John	12:12-15	363
John	12:46	365
John	14:1	366
John	14:2-3	366
John	14:5-6	369
John	14:7-9	372
John	14:13-14	373
John	14:16	375
John	14:18	378
John	14:26	380
John	14:27	386
John	14:28	388
John	15:2	389
John	15:11	391
John	15:12-15	393
John	15:18	396
John	15:19	397
John	16:12	398
John	16:16	398
John	16:32-33	399
John	17:16-17	400
John	18:36	400
John	18:37	401
John	18:38	403
John	19:5	407
John	20:17	407
John	20:19	408
John	20:25	410
John	20:29	411
Joshua	6:20	58
Leviticus	19:18	52
Luke	1:19	267
Luke	1:28	269
Luke	1:31-33	270
Luke	1:76-79	270
Luke	2:7	271
Luke	2:12	273
Luke	2:14	273
Luke	2:29-31	274
Luke	5:18-25	275
Luke	6:36	276
Luke	6:48	276
Luke	8:13	277
Luke	9:49-50	277
Luke	9:62	278

Index of Biblical References 506

Book	Verse/s	Page
Luke	14:16-23	278
Luke	15:7	279
Luke	15:11-32	280
Luke	16:8	285
Luke	17:5-6	285
Luke	17:21	286
Luke	19:1-10	289
Luke	22:19	305
Luke	22:34	307
Luke	22:39-46	307
Luke	22:48	308
Luke	23:33	309
Luke	23:34	314
Luke	23:39-43	317
Luke	23:46	318
Luke	24:1-7	319
Luke	24:13-16	327
Mark	5:9	263
Mark	8:17-18	263
Mark	10:9	264
Mark	10:51-52	266
Matthew	1:23	99
Matthew	2:1-2	101
Matthew	3:16-17	101
Matthew	4:1-11	105
Matthew	4:18-19	106
Matthew	5:3-11	107
Matthew	5:5	109
Matthew	5:8	110
Matthew	5:12	111
Matthew	5:14	112
Matthew	5:16	119
Matthew	5:17	120
Matthew	5:29	120
Matthew	5:39	121
Matthew	5:41	122
Matthew	5:43-45	123
Matthew	5:48	124
Matthew	6:7-8	126
Matthew	6:9-13	127
Matthew	6:14-15	140
Matthew	6:19-21	141
Matthew	6:24	144
Matthew	6:25	145
Matthew	6:31-32	146
Matthew	6:33	147
Matthew	7:1-2	148
Matthew	7:3-5	155
Matthew	7:7-8	156
Matthew	7:9-11	189
Matthew	7:12	190
Matthew	7:15-16	191
Matthew	7:21	192
Matthew	7:24-27	193
Matthew	8:21-22	195
Matthew	8:26	196
Matthew	9:2	196
Matthew	9:6	199
Matthew	9:20-22	200
Matthew	10:8	201
Matthew	10:19-20	202
Matthew	10:34	202
Matthew	11:3-5	202
Matthew	11:15	203
Matthew	11:21-22	204
Matthew	11:25	209
Matthew	11:27	210
Matthew	11:28	211
Matthew	11:29	212
Matthew	11:30	213
Matthew	12:24-25	214
Matthew	12:30	214
Matthew	13:12	215
Matthew	13:44-46	216
Matthew	16:18	217
Matthew	16:19	221

Index of Biblical References

Book	Verse/s	Page
Matthew	16:26	227
Matthew	16:27	228
Matthew	17:1-2	229
Matthew	17:20	229
Matthew	18:3	231
Matthew	18:11	232
Matthew	18:19-20	232
Matthew	19:6	235
Matthew	19:14	238
Matthew	19:18-21	239
Matthew	19:24-26	240
Matthew	20:16	242
Matthew	20:18-19	244
Matthew	20:28	244
Matthew	21:22	245
Matthew	22:19-21	246
Matthew	22:29	247
Matthew	24:35	248
Matthew	25:35	249
Matthew	25:40	250
Matthew	25:44-45	250
Matthew	26:14-15	251
Matthew	26:24	251
Matthew	26:26-29	252
Matthew	26:63-65	253
Matthew	27:29	254
Matthew	28:2	256
Matthew	28: 18	256
Matthew	28:19-20	259
Numbers	25:25-26	54
Philippians	2:2	458
Philippians	2:5	458
Philippians	4:7	459
Proverbs	10:2	81

Book	Verse/s	Page
Proverbs	23:7	81
Psalms	8:4	63
Psalms	8:4	63
Psalms	23:1-3	66
Psalms	23:4	66
Psalms	23:6	67
Psalms	37:20	68
Psalms	40:8	68
Psalms	46:1	69
Psalms	46:7	69
Psalms	46:10	70
Psalms	62:1-2	77
Psalms	121:1	78
Psalms	89:46	78
Psalms	139:5	79
Psalms	149:6	79
Psalms	150:1-6	80
Revelation	1:8	487
Revelation	2:28	487
Revelation	5:12	488
Revelation	12:7-9	489
Revelation	20:11-15	490
Revelation	21:1	491
Revelation	21:4	496
Revelation	21:6	499
Romans	2:14-16	424
Romans	3:28	425
Romans	6:23	426
Romans	8:26	427
Romans	8:28	428
Romans	12:19	429
Romans	13:1	431

About the Author

The Author or more precisely the Compiler is an IT professional who was forced to reflect upon his life because of an unresolved and on-going heart problem. He sought early retirement for a change in lifestyle in the hope that it might help cure his illness and at the same time embarked on a search for something that is more meaningful and rewarding in life. His search led him and ended to a book *A Course in Miracles*. As a regular Bible reader, the *Course* gave the Author a better understanding of the Holy Book especially that of the New Testament and at a deeper level a better understanding and appreciation of the purpose and meaning of life. He continues to study the *Course* and practises its teachings. His book Biblical Citations from A Course in Miracles is an offshoot of his study and his desire to make the path of other students of life much easier and certain. Specifically he wants to share his book to all the Christian readers who are longing for a fresh or new perspective about the Bible and to all open-minded readers searching for something meaningful and purposeful in life.

www.ingramcontent.com/pod-product-compliance
Lightning Source LLC
Chambersburg PA
CBHW070417010526
44118CB00014B/1790